EDUCATION
and the
LEGAL SYSTEM

A Guide to Understanding the Law

EDUCATION
and the
LEGAL SYSTEM

A Guide to Understanding the Law

Susan D. Looney

Upper Saddle River, New Jersey
Columbus, Ohio

Library of Congress Cataloging-in-Publication Data

Looney, Susan D.
   Education and the legal system: a guide to understanding the law /
Susan D. Looney—1st ed.
      p. cm.
Includes bibliographical references and index.
   ISBN 0-13-091550-5
   1. Educational law and legislation—United States.   I. Title.
   KF4118.L66 2004
   344.73'07—dc21

                                                    2003014111

Vice President and Executive Publisher: Jeffery W. Johnston
Executive Editor: Debra A. Stollenwerk
Editorial Assistant: Mary Morrill
Production Editor: Kris Robinson-Roach
Production Coordination: *The GTS Companies*/York, PA Campus
Design Coordinator: Diane C. Lorenzo
Cover Designer: Rod Harris
Production Manager: Susan Hannahs
Director of Marketing: Ann Castel Davis
Marketing Manager: Darcy Betts Prybella
Marketing Coordinator: Tyra Poole

This book was set in New Caledonia by *The GTS Companies*/York, PA Campus. It was printed and bound by R.R. Donnelley & Sons Company. The cover was printed by R.R. Donnelley & Sons Company.

Pearson Education Ltd.
Pearson Education Singapore Pte. Ltd.
Pearson Education Canada, Ltd.
Pearson Education—Japan

Pearson Education Australia Pty. Limited
Pearson Education North Asia Ltd.
Pearson Educación de Mexico, S.A. de C.V.
Pearson Education Malaysia Pte. Ltd.

10 9 8 7 6 5 4 3 2 1
ISBN: 0-13-091550-5

To my husband, whose support and friendship have been a continual inspiration.

Preface

EDUCATIONAL leaders in the 21st century will continue to face a myriad of legal issues that affect their daily decisions. *Education and the Legal System: A Guide to Understanding the Law* provides a comprehensive yet easy to understand coverage of the laws that most often shape policies and procedures in educational institutions. In the past, public schools were typically immune from litigation. But the law has substantially changed over the past 30 years, especially with the new rules that now govern individuals with disabilities and sexual harassment in the workplace. Additionally, unprecedented violence in today's schools may change the current laws protecting students' rights to speech and privacy. Hence, it is critical that administrators understand the laws that both expand and restrict their rights and responsibilities.

This book was designed to teach students and future educational leaders about education law through the use of legal principles, case analysis, and a discussion of legal principles and how administrators can practice preventive law. For many readers, this book will be their first exposure to the law; thus, it was written to be student-friendly. At the same time, it exposes students to landmark cases as well as up-to-date court decisions, reviews important legal issues that are of concern to most school officials, and ultimately assists administrators in making decisions. The book will not make the reader a lawyer, nor is it intended to replace legal counsel. Rather, readers will gain the skills they need to recognize legal issues when they occur and practice preventive law to the extent possible. Understanding the law can help educators and their institutions avoid being involved in litigation.

Every attempt has been made to include the most prevalent and most up-to-date legal issues currently affecting public education. Every chapter includes pertinent cases, boxed sections called "Best Practices," and discussion questions and student activities—all with the goal of engaging students in active learning. Additionally, because most cases are extremely long and difficult to read, an explanation of how to "brief" a case is included. This prompts students to think about the legal principles they must follow and grasp the concept that the law is not black and white but gray.

Below are brief descriptions of special sections that appear throughout this book:

• **Best Practices**   In each chapter of the book, after critical points of law are reviewed, are easy-to-reference boxes called "Best Practices" that are important to administrators. They apply real-life tips and give helpful hints to avoid being involved in litigation.

• **Discussion Questions and Activities**   Two additional features in this book are the end-of-chapter discussion questions and the chapter activities titled "Deepening Your Understanding." Many education law textbooks include no opportunity for class discussion or homework assignments. This book gives students an opportunity to both broaden their knowledge of the law by relating it various scenarios and engage in active learning activities.

• **Resources for Administrators**   At the end of the text is a comprehensive appendix titled "Resources for Administrators." This is a thorough list of federal statutes that commonly affects those involved in public education. It allows the student reader to reference some of the most important statutes affecting education quickly.

• **Glossary of Legal Terms**   Finally, the glossary helps readers learn legal terminology, so students do not have to invest in a law dictionary to understand professional legal jargon.

It is my hope that this book will help students gain an understanding of the law and assist administrators in providing a safe learning environment where fairness is common, laws are followed, and educators can do what they love—teach with the intent of producing the leaders of our future.

Acknowledgments

I WOULD like to thank the following reviewers, who provided valuable comments and suggestions:

Morris L. Anderson, *Wayne State College;* Gary D. Brooks, *University of Texas at El Paso;* Stacey Edmonson, *Sam Houston State University;* Margaret Grogan, *University of Virginia;* Robbe Lynn Henderson, *California State University—Dominguez Hills;* Michael Jacobs, *University of Northern Colorado;* Lori Kim, *California State University, Los Angeles;* Karen B. Lieuallen, *Marian College;* Louise L. Mackay, *East Tennessee State University;* Glen C. Newman, *California Baptist University;* JoAnne Newcombe, *Bridgewater State College;* and Laurence Parker, *University of Illinois at Urbana-Champaign*

Brief Contents

Contents

3   RELIGION IN SCHOOLS   53

4   STUDENTS WITH DISABILITIES   85

7 TEACHERS' RIGHTS   173

8 PARENTS' RIGHTS   205

9   Equal Coverage Under the Law   233

10   Employment and Tenure   261

1

THE AMERICAN JUDICIAL SYSTEM

INTRODUCTION

Educational leaders of the 21st century must be aware of the laws that affect them daily. They must recognize how the law changes as well as have a basic comprehension of the U.S. Constitution, federal and state statutes, regulations, and school board policies. This chapter reviews the workings of the court systems, steps involved in filing a lawsuit, and alternative dispute resolution measures. Although not designed to make the student a lawyer, the chapter considers legal research and the steps involved in learning how to "brief" the cases.

IMPORTANCE OF UNDERSTANDING THE LAW

In today's litigious society, educators must have a solid understanding of the laws that affect them and their institutions. Every day educators make decisions, many of which may have significant legal implications. Often, however, they are not aware of the law or are fearful of the legal system. Although the law is not something to fear, many educators are frightened and intimidated by the legal system because they do not understand it. The reasons for this apprehension are numerous.

First, the law is an evolving entity; it is continually changing. Additionally, most education-based undergraduate programs rarely cover the topic of law. Most new graduates entering the classroom simply learn on the job. Second, once on the job, educators receive little or no training concerning the laws that pertain to education, even though they affect both teachers and administrators in their personal and professional lives. While some individuals may receive a short seminar on sexual harassment during an in-service day, overall there is little legal training for educators. Third, school law is broad. The laws that govern education run the gamut of what every lawyer studies during years of law school. For example, within the educational system a lawsuit may be brought due to a school official's negligence or intentional act (tort law), bargaining issues or unfair contract negotiations (contract law), student and teacher rights concerning freedom of expression or sex discrimination (constitutional law). And this list just mentions a few of the many sorts of legal issues that may arise. Because education law is so vast, this book focuses on the areas most relevant to professionals in the educational system.

Educators often underestimate the importance of the laws and the procedures that set forth the guidelines that public institutions must follow. Unfortunately, the number of lawsuits filed against school districts has increased dramatically, to the point that legal action has become a regular occurrence that affects the entire educational system. Hence, the importance of the law should never be trivialized, nor should educators assume that litigation "will never happen to me."

Understanding the law is critical, and this book will help you accomplish that goal. It is not, however, intended to replace the advice of a licensed attorney. Rather, it will give educators the opportunity to understand the legal system so that they may incorporate best practices to prevent lawsuits. Anyone who has ever been involved in a lawsuit will probably agree that litigation is expensive. Even if successful, the process of being deposed, taking time off from work, and possibly having to take the stand in a jury trial is time-consuming and emotional. If you know and understand your legal rights and responsibilities, the law can be a source of guidance and protection. The greater your understanding of the law, the easier it is to take steps to avoid a lawsuit altogether rather than react once a lawsuit has commenced.

CHANGES IN SOCIETY AND THE LAW

AT ONE time, the words *litigation* and *education* were rarely spoken in the same sentence. But during the past 50 years, the number of lawsuits involving schools has dramatically increased. Compared with citizens of other countries, those in the United States are apt to enter quickly into costly litigation to recover large settlements from institutions with financially deep pockets instead of solving problems through compromise. In education the movement to use the law to resolve disputes and conflicts began slowly but has since grown into a major concern for administrators.

By the late 1900s, the law in education underwent a dramatic change. With the civil rights movement of the 1960s, U.S. society as a whole began to move from a nation of conformance to one that recognized the rights of individuals. The issues of equal opportunity and due process brought many cases involving education to the attention of the U.S. Supreme Court. At one time education was immune from many types of lawsuits; but by the end of the 1960s, it was clear that the public school system had become increasingly susceptible to litigation.

As society focused on individual freedoms such as dress, speech, and personal lifestyle choices, the civil rights movement emerged, as did the number of lawsuits against public schools. In reviewing the history of the connection between the law and education, the rights of students and faculty have been paramount. Some argue, however, that in today's changing environment and in the aftermath of occurrences such as the Columbine school shootings and the September 11 terrorist attacks, the pendulum may begin to swing back and a different review begin to emerge. Only time will tell. Hence, administrators and future administrators have an important reason to be aware of the laws that may affect their daily decisions.

THE U.S. CONSTITUTION

THE THREE branches of government created by the Constitution are all unique in their capacities yet fulfill the important role of ensuring that no one branch becomes too powerful. This is accomplished through a system of checks and balances. Of the three branches, the legislative branch has the power, through Congress, to make the laws. The executive branch, through the president, has the power to enforce the laws; and the judicial branch, through the courts, has the power to interpret the laws.

The Constitution sets forth the complete framework in which the government functions and is commonly referred to as "the law of the land." Although the United States has a two-tier court system, federal law is superior to any state law. This is set forth under the supremacy clause of the Constitution. There have been cases in which the state court has disagreed with the decision of the Supreme Court. Regardless of the disagreement, however, the state law is deemed unconstitutional if it does not follow federal guidelines. This is illustrated in the following case.

Cooper v. Aaron
Supreme Court of the United States, 1958
358 U.S. 1

Opinion written by Justice Warren.

As this case reaches us it raises questions of the highest importance to the maintenance of our federal system of government. It necessarily involves a claim by the Governor and Legislature of a State that there is no duty on state officials to obey federal court orders resting on this Court's considered interpretation of the United States Constitution. Specifically it involves actions by the Governor and Legislature of Arkansas upon the premise that they are not bound by our holding in *Brown* v. *Board of Education*. That holding was that the Fourteenth Amendment forbids States to use their governmental powers to bar children on racial grounds from attending schools where there is state participation through any arrangement, management, funds or property. We are urged to uphold a suspension of the Little Rock School Board's plan to do away with segregated public schools in Little Rock until state laws and efforts to upset and nullify our holding in *Brown* v. *Board of Education* have been further challenged and tested in the courts. We reject these contentions. . . .

The following are the facts and circumstances so far as necessary to show how the legal questions are presented.

On May 17, 1954, this Court decided that enforced racial segregation in the public schools of a State is a denial of the equal protection of the laws enjoined by the Fourteenth Amendment. The Court postponed, pending further argument, formulation of a decree to effectuate this decision. That decree was rendered May 31, 1955. In the formulation of that decree the Court recognized that good faith compliance with the principles declared in *Brown* might in some situations "call for elimination of a variety of obstacles in making the transition to school systems operated in accordance with the constitutional principles set forth in our May 17, 1954, decision." The Court went on to state: "Courts of equity may properly take into account the public interest in the elimination of such obstacles in a systematic and effective manner. But it should go without saying that the vitality of these constitutional principles cannot be allowed to yield simply because of disagreement with them.

"While giving weight to these public and private considerations, the courts will require that the defendants make a prompt and reasonable start toward full compliance with our May 17, 1954, ruling. Once such a start has been made, the courts may find that additional time is necessary to carry out the ruling in an effective manner. The burden rests upon the defendants to establish that such time is necessary in the public interest and is consistent with good faith compliance at the earliest practicable date. To that end, the courts may consider problems related to administration, arising from the physical condition of the school plant, the school transportation system, personnel, revision of school districts and attendance areas into compact units to achieve a system of determining admission to the public schools on a nonracial basis, and revision of local laws and regulations which may be necessary in solving the foregoing problems."

Under such circumstances, the District Courts were directed to require "a prompt and reasonable start toward full compliance," and to take such action as was necessary to bring about the end of racial segregation in the public schools "with all deliberate speed." Of course, in many locations, obedience to the duty of desegregation would require the immediate general admission of Negro children, otherwise qualified as students for their appropriate classes, at particular schools. On the other hand, a District Court, after analysis of the relevant factors (which, of course, excludes hostility to racial desegregation), might conclude that justification existed for not requiring the present nonsegregated admission of all qualified Negro children. In such circumstances, however, the courts should scrutinize the program of the school authorities to make sure that they had developed arrangements pointed toward the earliest practicable completion of desegregation, and had taken appropriate steps to put their program into effective operation. It was made plain that delay in any guise in order to deny the constitutional rights of Negro children could not be countenanced, and that only a prompt start, diligently and earnestly pursued, to eliminate racial segregation from the public schools could constitute good faith compliance. State authorities were thus duty bound to devote every effort toward initiating desegregation and bringing about the elimination of racial discrimination in the public school system.

On May 20, 1954, three days after the first *Brown* opinion, the Little Rock District School Board adopted, and on May 23, 1954, made public, a statement of policy entitled "Supreme Court Decision—Segregation in Public Schools." In this statement the Board recognized that "It is our responsibility to comply with Federal Constitutional Requirements and we intend to do so when the Supreme Court of the United States outlines the method to be followed."

Thereafter the Board undertook studies of the administrative problems confronting the transition to a desegregated public school system at Little Rock. It instructed the Superintendent of Schools to prepare a plan for desegregation, and approved such a plan on May 24, 1955, seven days before the second *Brown* opinion. The plan provided for desegregation at the senior high school level (grades 10 through 12) as the first stage. Desegregation at the junior high and elementary levels was to follow. It was contemplated that desegregation at the high school level would commence in the fall of 1957, and the expectation was that complete desegregation of the school system would be accomplished by 1963. Following the adoption of this plan, the Superintendent of Schools discussed it with a large number of citizen groups in the city. As a result of these discussions, the Board reached the conclusion that "a large majority of the residents" of Little Rock were of "the belief . . . that the Plan, although objectionable in principle," from the point of view of those supporting segregated schools, "was still the best for the interests of all pupils in the District."

Upon challenge by a group of Negro plaintiffs desiring more rapid completion of the desegregation process, the District Court upheld the School Board's plan. The Court of Appeals affirmed. Review of that judgment was not sought here.

While the School Board was thus going forward with its preparation for desegregating the Little Rock school system, other state authorities, in contrast, were actively pursuing a program designed to perpetuate in Arkansas the system of racial segregation which this Court had held violated the Fourteenth Amendment. First came, in November 1956, an amendment to the State Constitution flatly commanding the Arkansas General Assembly to oppose "in every Constitutional manner the Un-constitutional desegregation decisions of May 17, 1954 and May 31, 1955 of the United States Supreme Court." Pursuant to this state constitutional command, a law relieving school children from compulsory attendance at racially mixed schools, and a law establishing a State Sovereignty Commission Act, were enacted by the General Assembly in February 1957.

The School Board and the Superintendent of Schools nevertheless continued with preparations to carry out the first stage of the desegregation program. Nine Negro children were scheduled for admission in September 1957 to Central High School, which has more than two thousand students. Various administrative measures, designed to assure the smooth transition of this first stage of desegregation, were undertaken.

On September 2, 1957, the day before these Negro students were to enter Central High, the school authorities were met with drastic opposing action on the part of the Governor of Arkansas who dispatched units of the Arkansas National Guard to the Central High School grounds and placed the school "off limits" to colored students. As found by the District Court in subsequent proceedings, the Governor's action had not been requested by the school authorities, and was entirely unheralded. The findings were these: "Up to this time [September 2], no crowds had gathered about Central High School and no acts of violence or threats of violence in connection with the carrying out of the plan had occurred. Nevertheless, out of an abundance of caution, the school authorities had frequently conferred with the Mayor and Chief of Police of Little Rock about taking appropriate steps by the Little Rock police to prevent any possible disturbances or acts of violence in connection with the attendance of the 9 colored students at Central High School. The Mayor considered that the Little Rock police force could adequately cope with any incidents which might arise at the opening of school. The Mayor, the Chief of Police, and the school authorities made no request to the Governor or any representative of his for State assistance in maintaining peace and order at Central High School. Neither the Governor nor any other official of the State government consulted with the Little Rock authorities about whether the Little Rock police were prepared to cope with any incidents which might arise at the school, about any need for State assistance in maintaining peace and order, or about stationing the Arkansas National Guard at Central High School."

The Board's petition for postponement in this proceeding states: "The effect of that action [of the Governor] was to harden the core of opposition to the Plan and cause many persons who theretofore had reluctantly accepted the Plan to believe there was some power in the State of Arkansas which, when exerted, could nullify the Federal law and permit disobedience of the decree of this [District] Court, and from that date hostility to the Plan was increased and criticism of the officials of the [School] District has become more bitter and unrestrained." The Governor's action caused the School Board to request the Negro students on September 2 not to attend the high school "until the legal dilemma was solved." The next day, September 3, 1957, the Board petitioned the District Court for instructions, and the court, after a hearing, found that the Board's request of the Negro students to stay away from the high school had been made because of the stationing of the military guards by the state authorities. The court determined that this was not a reason for departing from the approved plan, and ordered the School Board and Superintendent to proceed with it.

On the morning of the next day, September 4, 1957, the Negro children attempted to enter the high school but, as the District Court later found, units of the Arkansas National Guard "acting pursuant to the Governor's order, stood shoulder to shoulder at the school grounds and thereby forcibly prevented the 9 Negro students . . . from entering," as they continued to do every school day during the following three weeks.

That same day, September 4, 1957, the United States Attorney for the Eastern District of Arkansas was requested by the District Court to begin an immediate investigation in order to fix responsibility for the interference with the orderly implementation of the District Court's direction to carry out the desegregation program. Three days later, September 7, the District Court denied a petition of the School Board and the Superintendent of Schools for an order temporarily suspending continuance of the program.

Upon completion of the United States Attorney's investigation, he and the Attorney General of the United States, at the District Court's request, entered the proceedings and filed a petition on behalf of the United States, as *amicus curiae*, to enjoin the Governor of

Arkansas and officers of the Arkansas National Guard from further attempts to prevent obedience to the court's order. After hearings on the petition, the District Court found that the School Board's plan had been obstructed by the Governor through the use of National Guard troops, and granted a preliminary injunction on September 20, 1957, enjoining the Governor and the officers of the Guard from preventing the attendance of Negro children at Central High School, and from otherwise obstructing or interfering with the orders of the court in connection with the plan. The National Guard was then withdrawn from the school.

The next school day was Monday, September 23, 1957. The Negro children entered the high school that morning under the protection of the Little Rock Police Department and members of the Arkansas State Police. But the officers caused the children to be removed from the school during the morning because they had difficulty controlling a large and demonstrating crowd which had gathered at the high school. On September 25, however, the President of the United States dispatched federal troops to Central High School and admission of the Negro students to the school was thereby effected. Regular army troops continued at the high school until November 27, 1957. They were then replaced by federalized National Guardsmen who remained throughout the balance of the school year. Eight of the Negro students remained in attendance at the school throughout the school year.

We come now to the aspect of the proceedings presently before us. On February 20, 1958, the School Board and the Superintendent of Schools filed a petition in the District Court seeking a postponement of their program for desegregation. Their position in essence was that because of extreme public hostility, which they stated had been engendered largely by the official attitudes and actions of the Governor and the Legislature, the maintenance of a sound educational program at Central High School, with the Negro students in attendance, would be impossible. The Board therefore proposed that the Negro students already admitted to the school be withdrawn and sent to segregated schools, and that all further steps to carry out the Board's desegregation program be postponed for a period later suggested by the Board to be two and one-half years.

After a hearing the District Court granted the relief requested by the Board. Among other things the court found that the past year at Central High School had been attended by conditions of "chaos, bedlam and turmoil"; that there were "repeated incidents of more or less serious violence directed against the Negro students and their property"; that there was "tension and unrest among the school administrators, the classroom teachers, the pupils, and the latters' parents, which inevitably had an adverse effect upon the educational program"; that a school official was threatened with violence; that a "serious financial burden" had been cast on the School District; that the education of the students had suffered "and under existing conditions will continue to suffer"; that the Board would continue to need "military assistance or its equivalent"; that the local police department would not be able "to detail enough men to afford the necessary protection"; and that the situation was "intolerable." . . .

In affirming the judgment of the Court of Appeals which reversed the District Court we have accepted without reservation the position of the School Board, the Superintendent of Schools, and their counsel that they displayed entire good faith in the conduct of these proceedings and in dealing with the unfortunate and distressing sequence of events which has been outlined. We likewise have accepted the findings of the District Court as to the conditions at Central High School during the 1957–1958 school year, and also the findings that the educational progress of all the students, white and colored, of that school has suffered and will continue to suffer if the conditions which prevailed last year are permitted to continue.

The significance of these findings, however, is to be considered in light of the fact, indisputably revealed by the record before us, that the conditions they depict are directly traceable to the actions of legislators and executive officials of the State of Arkansas, taken in their official capacities, which reflect their own determination to resist this Court's decision in the *Brown* case and which have brought about violent resistance to that decision in Arkansas. In its petition for certiorari filed in this Court, the School Board itself describes the situation in this language: "The legislative, executive, and judicial departments of the state government opposed the desegregation of Little Rock schools by enacting laws, calling out troops, making statements villifying federal law and federal courts, and failing to utilize state law enforcement agencies and judicial processes to maintain public peace."

One may well sympathize with the position of the Board in the face of the frustrating conditions which have confronted it, but, regardless of the Board's good faith, the actions of the other state agencies responsible for those conditions compel us to reject the Board's legal position. Had Central High School been under the direct management of the State itself, it could hardly be suggested that those immediately in charge of the school should be heard to assert their own good faith as a legal excuse for delay in implementing the constitutional rights of these respondents, when vindication of those rights was rendered difficult or impossible by the actions of other state officials. The situation here is in no different posture because the members of the School Board and the Superintendent of Schools are local officials; from the point of view of the Fourteenth Amendment, they stand in this litigation as the agents of the State.

The constitutional rights of respondents are not to be sacrificed or yielded to the violence and disorder which have followed upon the actions of the Governor and Legislature. As this Court said some 41 years ago in a unanimous opinion in a case involving another aspect of racial segregation: "It is urged that this proposed segregation will promote the public peace by preventing race conflicts. Desirable as this is, and important as is the preservation of the public peace, this aim cannot be accomplished by laws or ordinances which deny rights created or protected by the Federal Constitution." Thus law and order are not here to be preserved by depriving the Negro children of their constitutional rights. The record before us clearly establishes that the growth of the Board's difficulties to a magnitude beyond its unaided power to control is the product of state action. Those difficulties, as counsel for the Board forthrightly conceded on the oral argument in this Court, can also be brought under control by state action.

The controlling legal principles are plain. The command of the Fourteenth Amendment is that no "State" shall deny to any person within its jurisdiction the equal protection of the laws. "A State acts by its legislative, its executive, or its judicial authorities. It can act in no other way. The constitutional provision, therefore, must mean that no agency of the State, or of the officers or agents by whom its powers are exerted, shall deny to any person within its jurisdiction the equal protection of the laws. Whoever, by virtue of public position under a State government, . . . denies or takes away the equal protection of the laws, violates the constitutional inhibition; and as he acts in the name and for the State, and is clothed with the State's power, his act is that of the State. This must be so, or the constitutional prohibition has no meaning." Thus the prohibitions of the Fourteenth Amendment extend to all action of the State denying equal protection of the laws; whatever the agency of the State taking the action. In short, the constitutional rights of children not to be discriminated against in school admission on grounds of race or color declared by this Court in the *Brown* case can neither be nullified openly and directly by state legislators or state executive or judicial officers, nor nullified indirectly by them through evasive schemes for segregation whether attempted "ingeniously or ingenuously."

What has been said, in the light of the facts developed, is enough to dispose of the case. However, we should answer the premise of the actions of the Governor and Legislature that they are not bound by our holding in the *Brown* case. It is necessary only to recall some basic constitutional propositions which are settled doctrine.

Article VI of the Constitution makes the Constitution the "supreme Law of the Land." In 1803, Chief Justice Marshall, speaking for a unanimous Court, referring to the Constitution as "the fundamental and paramount law of the nation," declared in the notable case of *Marbury* v. *Madison*, that "It is emphatically the province and duty of the judicial department to say what the law is." This decision declared the basic principle that the federal judiciary is supreme in the exposition of the law of the Constitution, and that principle has ever since been respected by this Court and the Country as a permanent and indispensable feature of our constitutional system. It follows that the interpretation of the Fourteenth Amendment enunciated by this Court in the *Brown* case is the supreme law of the land, and Art. VI of the Constitution makes it of binding effect on the States "any Thing in the Constitution or Laws of any State to the Contrary notwithstanding." Every state legislator and executive and judicial officer is solemnly committed by oath taken pursuant to Art. VI, cl. 3, "to support this Constitution." Chief Justice Taney, speaking for a unanimous Court in 1859, said that this requirement reflected the framers' "anxiety to preserve it [the Constitution] in full force, in all its powers, and to guard against resistance to or evasion of its authority, on the part of a State. . . . "

No state legislator or executive or judicial officer can war against the Constitution without violating his undertaking to support it. Chief Justice Marshall spoke for a unanimous Court in saying that: "If the legislatures of the several states may, at will, annul the judgments of the courts of the United States, and destroy the rights acquired under those judgments, the constitution itself becomes a solemn mockery. . . . " A Governor who asserts a power to nullify a federal court order is similarly restrained. If he had such power, said Chief Justice Hughes, in 1932, also for a unanimous Court, "it is manifest that the fiat of a state Governor, and not the Constitution of the United States, would be the supreme law of the land; that the restrictions of the Federal Constitution upon the exercise of state power would be but impotent phrases. . . . "

It is, of course, quite true that the responsibility for public education is primarily the concern of the States, but it is equally true that such responsibilities, like all other state activity, must be exercised consistently with federal constitutional requirements as they apply to state action. The Constitution created a government dedicated to equal justice under law. The Fourteenth Amendment embodied and emphasized that ideal. State support of segregated schools through any arrangement, management, funds, or property cannot be squared with the Amendment's command that no State shall deny to any person within its jurisdiction the equal protection of the laws. The right of a student not to be segregated on racial grounds in schools so maintained is indeed so fundamental and pervasive that it is embraced in the concept of due process of law. The basic decision in *Brown* was unanimously reached by this Court only after the case had been briefed and twice argued and the issues had been given the most serious consideration. Since the first *Brown* opinion three new Justices have come to the Court. They are at one with the Justices still on the Court who participated in that basic decision as to its correctness, and that decision is now unanimously reaffirmed. The principles announced in that decision and the obedience of the States to them, according to the command of the Constitution, are indispensable for the protection of the freedoms guaranteed by our fundamental charter for all of us. Our constitutional ideal of equal justice under law is thus made a living truth.

The U.S. Constitution does not specifically mention education. As the courts have interpreted, powers not directly granted to the federal government are deemed to be controlled by the states. Additionally, implied through the Tenth Amendment, the courts repeatedly confirm that control over education should be performed through the states. The Tenth Amendment reads: "The powers not delegated to the United States by the Constitution, nor prohibited by it to the States, are reserved to the States respectively, or to the people. The powers not delegated to the United States by the Constitution, nor prohibited by it to the States, are reserved to the States respectively, or to the people." Education, therefore, is specifically addressed by state constitutions. The states, through legislative powers, make the laws that control the education systems in each of the 50 states. While items such as curriculum and the hiring of teachers are performed at the state level, there is little doubt that the federal government controls education through the budgetary process. If a public school does not abide by federal statutes or follow the Constitution, the federal government can withhold funding.

While states control education through legislation, administration is performed at the local level, generally through the local school board. The extent of control, however, depends on the state. Some states give considerable control to local school boards. Other states keep tight control over school boards and the individuals who serve on them. Such decisions are determined by state legislatures.

State legislatures set minimum standards, establish graduation requirements, and determine some curricular design and course content. School boards also can set minimum standards as long as they meet the state's standard and have the power to create curriculum and advance program development.

THE FEDERAL LEGAL SYSTEM

THE UNITED States has two judicial systems: federal and state. Altogether there are 50 state courts and one federal system. Can an individual choose one court over another? Who decides where a case will be heard? In some cases, a party has no choice; in others a party may bring its claim to either system.

If the issue revolves around a state claim, the case must be heard in state court. It is common to hear someone say, "I'll take this case all the way to the Supreme Court." But if the issue deals only with a state law or regulation, the case may end up only in the state's Supreme Court, not in the U.S. Supreme Court. So if a student is injured on the playground and the parents bring a claim of negligence, what court will hear their claim? If there are no other issues involved, this case will never be heard by the U.S. Supreme Court because there is no federal question to be answered, only a state claim of negligence.

Article III of the U.S. Constitution gives federal courts the power to hear only limited types of cases. In other words, not every legal issue is a "federal issue." For a case to be brought in federal court, it must meet one of the following criteria:

1. A federal question of law must be reviewed. For example, a student is strip-searched by a principal in school. Although this case may be brought to state court, it revolves around the student's right to privacy. Because the Fourth Amendment will be applied, the case can be brought to federal court since it is a constitutional issue.
2. The court must be fair to parties from different states. If a case arises between individuals from two different states and the matter of controversy concerns more than $75,000, diversity of citizenship exists; and the case can be brought to federal court. This is based on the concept of fairness. For example, if a teacher from Arizona is involved in a car accident in Nevada with an individual who resides in California, and the damages being requested are greater than $75,000, the case may be brought to federal court. Because state laws differ, a hearing in federal court offers parties a fair option. The parties, however, may agree to have the case heard in the other person's state; hence, a state claim can still be made.
3. The government is a party to the claim. For example, if the state of California were a defendant in a claim, the case, for reasons of fairness, can be heard in federal court instead of a California state court.

Most cases involving education use the state system. Nevertheless, some of the most important decisions affecting education today have arisen in the federal system. For example, the landmark case *Brown v. Board of Education* addressed the constitutional issue of equal protection under the Fourteenth Amendment.[1] *Tinker v. Des Moines* was decided in the federal courts because the issue concerned the First Amendment rights of a student in school.[2]

---

[1] *Brown v. Board of Education,* 347 U.S. 483 (1954)
[2] *Tinker v. Des Moines,* 393 U.S. 503 (1969)

U.S. Supreme Court: final court of appeals;
cases heard by discretion only
↑
Circuit courts: federal courts of appeal
↑
U.S. district courts: federal trial courts
↑
Specialty courts:
Bankruptcy court
Court of military appeals
U.S. claims court
U.S. court of international trade
Tax court

FIGURE 1.1 *Structure of the federal court system*

The federal system is composed of three levels: district courts, circuit courts, and the U.S. Supreme Court (see Figure 1.1). At the trial level are federal district courts. Every state has at least one district court, with heavily populated states having several. At the time of publication there are 95 federal district courts. In the district courts, also known as the courts of original jurisdiction, typically a jury hears evidence and a judge applies the law.

If a party is dissatisfied with the outcome at the district court level, it may appeal to one of the 13 circuit courts, also known as the intermediate appellate courts, or courts of appeal. These appellate courts are organized into circuit courts and are based on a party's geographical location. As Figure 1.2 illustrates, there are 11 circuit courts for the states, one court for the District of Columbia, and one for federal judicial districts such as the court of international trade and the court of claims.

To many people's surprise, when a case is appealed to the circuit court level, there is not another trial, nor is there a jury. Rather, a panel of circuit court judges, typically three, review a summary of the case and determine only whether the judge in the lower court made an error of law. For example, the lower-court judge may have allowed inadmissible evidence to be heard against an objection or may have given the jury incorrect instructions about the standard of law jurors must apply to find in favor of a party. The facts themselves are not reheard, nor does a jury form to redecide the outcome of the case. It is common to refer to the jury as the "finder of fact," while the judge is the "finder of law." Hence, the only issue reviewed is whether there was an error of law made by the judge in the lower court.

The final court of appeals is the U.S. Supreme Court, which is the highest federal court in the country. The decisions rendered by the U.S. Supreme Court are commonly referred to as the law of the land, meaning that all lower courts, both federal and state, must abide by its decisions. Many people believe they have a right to take their case to

District of Columbia:	District of Columbia
First:	Maine, Massachusetts, New Hampshire, Puerto Rico, Rhode Island
Second:	Connecticut, New York, Vermont
Third:	Delaware, New Jersey, Pennsylvania, Virgin Islands
Fourth:	Maryland, North Carolina, South Carolina, Virginia, West Virginia
Fifth:	District of the Canal Zone, Louisiana, Mississippi, Texas
Sixth:	Kentucky, Michigan, Ohio, Tennessee
Seventh:	Illinois, Indiana, Wisconsin
Eighth:	Arkansas, Iowa, Minnesota, Missouri, Nebraska, North Dakota, South Dakota
Ninth:	Alaska, Arizona, California, Idaho, Montana, Nevada, Oregon, Washington, Guam, Hawaii
Tenth:	Colorado, Kansas, New Mexico, Oklahoma, Utah, Wyoming
Eleventh:	Alabama, Florida, Georgia
Federal:	All federal judicial districts

FIGURE 1.2 *The thirteen federal circuit courts and their geographical areas*

the Supreme Court. However, the U.S. Supreme Court is not obligated to hear any case; rather, the members of the Supreme Court decide whether or not they will review a case. In legal terms, cases reach the Court by means of *writ of certiorari*. Under this method, an unsuccessful litigant in a lower court can set forth reasons explaining why the case should be granted a writ. A case is accepted for review only if four justices vote to grant a writ of certiorari. Acceptance for review under this "rule of four" indicates that at least four of the nine members of the U.S. Supreme Court consider the case to have sufficient merit to be considered by the entire court. If the Supreme Court denies a writ of certiorari, the decision made at the lower court will stand undisturbed.

The nine justices of the U.S. Supreme Court are appointed by the president of the United States, approved by the Senate, and serve for life unless removed for committing a crime. Except on rare occasions when one justice excludes him or herself, agreement among five of the nine justices forms a majority opinion. Justices who disagree may file a dissenting opinion. In fact, some dissenting opinions have been more compassionate, more compelling, and much longer than the majority opinion. Nevertheless, dissenting opinions do not have the force of law and are not used to make legal arguments. In other cases, justices will agree with the outcome but disagree with the rationale. In this situation it is common practice that a justice will file a concurring opinion explaining the reasons they felt the case was decided.

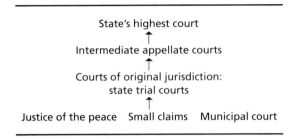

FIGURE 1.3   *Typical state court structure*

THE STATE LEGAL SYSTEM

THERE are 50 state courts, each having some form of appellate hierarchy. Because each state has the power to create its own system, the states may vary in their court structures. Most state systems have a court of original jurisdiction (commonly called the superior court), which is the trial court. All states have at least one appellate court, but more commonly there are two levels of appeals available. Depending on the state, the court structure may vary. Hence, it is important to understand the system in your state. For example, the New York state structure is very different from New Jersey's, even though the states are close in location. Figure 1.3 illustrates a typical state court structure.

STEPS IN FILING A LAWSUIT

A LAWSUIT involves numerous steps. Because most cases that deal with education are civil claims, the following is a sample of the various steps involved in bringing or defending a lawsuit. Typically, the first step is filing the complaint. The plaintiff (the person who brings the claim) meets with a lawyer to explain the facts or files the paperwork themselves. The complaint sets forth the basis of the facts, the legal issue, and the damages being requested. Attorneys must follow the laws of civil procedures and, within this, must ensure that the statute of limitations has not run out on the claim. Depending on what the plaintiff is claiming, timing may be of great importance.

Once the complaint is created, it is delivered through the service of process to the defendant. After the complaint is served, the defendant typically has 20 days to file an answer. The answer states that the defendant admits to the claim, denies the claim, or does not have enough information to adequately respond. In answering the claim, the defendant at this time may file a counterclaim or a cross claim.

A counterclaim states that the defendant is now filing a claim against the original plaintiff because of a wrong done to him or her.

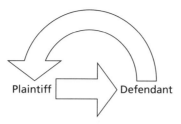

Plaintiff sues defendant, but with a counterclaim the defendant is now suing the plaintiff.

In some claims, one defendant is listed in the complaint but suggests that if he is sued, then a second defendant should be sued as well.

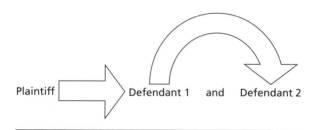

The plaintiff sues defendant 1, but defendant 1 then files a cross claim against defendant 2.

All of these initial filings are called pleadings. Once the initial pleadings have been filed with the proper court, the discovery stage begins. The goal of discovery is to gather information pertaining to the case. This usually includes interviewing witnesses and examining papers, records, or photos. With the goal of obtaining all the evidence pertaining to the case, discovery may take a long time to gather and typically includes depositions and interrogatories. A deposition is sworn testimony, answered under oath, that occurs outside the courtroom. A court stenographer transcribes all statements, and each party is permitted to question the witness. The testimony stated during the deposition may be used at trial by either party.

An interrogatory is also sworn testimony but is much less time-consuming and involves responding to written questions. The rules of civil procedures set forth how many questions are permitted. The discovery process can be long and tedious. There have been cases in which discovery of all witnesses and document reproduction took years to gather. For the individuals involved, the process takes time away from work and can be stressful.

While only a few cases actually make it to trial, a case may still go through all these stages, yet still settle on the courthouse steps. It has been estimated that 95 percent of all cases filed are settled out of court. However, in those 5 percent that do continue forward to the trial stage, a jury of six to twelve people may decide the case.

ETHICS AND THE LAW

WHAT one person considers ethical may be unethical to another. Ethics are a standard of conduct but may vary from person to person based on many factors, including personal views. As an administrator and an educational leader, you must act in an ethical manner and ensure that members of your organization adhere to a code of conduct. There are many ways to accomplish this, including the process of ensuring that facilities are safe, that staff and faculty are properly trained, and that the schools continually promote student success and institutional effectiveness.

Ethically, it is the duty of the administration to be competent and knowledgeable about certain subjects, including awareness of changing legislation and regulations that affect education. Ignoring changing laws and legislation can result in litigation and also greatly affect a school district's public funding. Additionally, educational leaders must communicate operational procedures to all involved in education, including the board, faculty, staff, parents, and constituents of the community. Educational leaders cannot close their eyes to the legal problems that may affect their organization, nor can they ignore the possibility of litigation. It would be unethical for an administrator to take the stand that litigation cannot happen to his or her institution. Unfortunately, with millions of lawsuits filed every year, the odds of being involved in a lawsuit are more likely than not.

Taking an active role in safety, security, training, financial management, and technology will ultimately save the school time, money, and resources. Being aware of changing laws, statutes, and regulations and making appropriate changes and plans based on such laws are key roles for educators.

Another ethical issue that educators commonly face is the decision to settle a pending lawsuit or fight the case in court. Sometimes the issue is not about who is right or wrong but whether it is economical to go to court. Litigation is expensive and time-consuming. In a cost-benefit analysis, is it less expensive to settle a claim out of court, even though the institution did nothing wrong? Or should every case be fought in court? These are challenging decisions and ones that administrators, school districts, and their insurance representatives must consider. For many educational institutions, it is more cost-efficient to settle a small claim to avoid the expenses of attorneys, time spent away from work, as well as possible publicity. On the other hand, many institutions, like many businesses, do not want to set a precedent for settling cases out of court. Rather, they fight each case as it occurs.

STANDARDS OF PROOF: CIVIL CASES VERSUS CRIMINAL CASES

IN THE American court system, there are two types of cases: civil and criminal. Civil law deals with wrongs against individuals, while criminal law deals with wrongs against society. In analyzing civil law, an important distinction is the party that brings forward the complaint or lawsuit. In civil law, an individual brings the claim against another individual. In criminal law, the government brings charges. In civil law, an individual is wronged or injured by another. In criminal law, a statute or a law is broken. Under civil law, the damages being requested are monetary or will make up for the injury or loss. In criminal law, the individual who is found guilty is punished through incarceration, fines, or another penalty. But the most important difference between the two types of law is the burden of proof required.

Under the civil structure, the burden is a "preponderance of the evidence." In other words, the evidence presented must tip the scales of justice to at least 51 percent. The wrong has to be more likely than not to have occurred. Under the criminal structure, because the punishment is much more severe, the burden of proof is "beyond a reasonable doubt." After comparing all the evidence, the jury must believe beyond all possible doubt that the defendant deserves to be acquitted. A familiar example deals with the two different verdicts against O. J. Simpson, who was tried for murdering his wife. To understand the distinction between the two cases, it is critical to recognize that they were two separate cases brought forward under two different types of law. In the first trial, the state prosecutor brought forward the charges, and the jury was instructed to determine whether the state's evidence proved that Simpson was guilty beyond a reasonable doubt. Because the charge was murder, this was a criminal case. Therefore, the standard of proof was "beyond a reasonable doubt." The jury, however, could not determine by that standard that Simpson had committed the crime and thus acquitted him.

Later a second trial occurred. In this case, the claim was wrongful death, which is a civil charge. The parents of Ron Goldman and Nicole Simpson brought forward the charges, not the state prosecutor. The burden of proof was an important factor in the case. In civil cases, the standard of proof for wrongful death is the much lower standard of "preponderance of the evidence." Additionally, since the case was in civil court, different procedural rules applied. For example, one cannot go to jail if found responsible. There are no constitutional protections such as pleading the Fifth. Hence, the jury in the second case determined that there was more evidence than not that O. J. Simpson was responsible for the deaths of Nicole Simpson and Ron Goldman.

While there are hundreds of thousands of civil cases filed in the United States annually, most do not end up at trial. Rather, most are settled in advance or through alternative dispute resolution (ADR). Two of the most common forms of ADR are mediation and arbitration. In mediation both parties sit down with an agreed upon third person who helps negotiate an agreement that both parties find acceptable. Arbitration is more formalized and instead of negotiating the outcome, the arbitrator is responsible for making a fair decision.

Legal Research

THE CONCEPT of legal research can seem overwhelming. Traditionally, to perform legal research, one had to find the local law library and sort through volumes of casebooks. Typically, such a task would take hours, if not days. Fortunately, legal research has kept stride with technology, and today there are numerous ways to perform legal research using the Internet. It is still important, however, to understand where the cases are printed in hard copy. The federal system has five different reporters for filing cases. For example, a decision from the U.S. Supreme Court can be found in the *U.S. Reporter* (U.S.); the *Supreme Court Reporter* (S.Ct.); *U.S. Supreme Court Reports, Lawyers Edition* (L.Ed.); or the *U.S. Law Week* (U.S.L. Week). Circuit court decisions can be located in the *Federal Reporter* (F.2d). Decisions from the district courts will be filed in the *Federal Supplement* (F. Supp.). In many instances, a case will be filed in more than one place. Because there are official and unofficial reporters, it is common to find cases printed in numerous publications, yet contain the same information.

In addition to the various federal court reports, each state has its own official reporter. There is also the *National Reporter,* which publishes all state appellate court cases. Figure 1.4 illustrates the geographical areas that each reporter covers.

In addition to researching case law through reporters, students can find legal definitions in *Black's Law Dictionary, Merriam Webster's Dictionary of Law,* and *Oran's Dictionary of the Law.* A more detailed description of terms and concepts can be found in

Atlantic Reporter (A.2d):	Connecticut, Delaware, Maine, New Hampshire, New Jersey, Pennsylvania, Rhode Island, Vermont, District of Columbia courts of appeal
North Eastern Reporter (N.E.2d):	Illinois, Indiana, Massachusetts, New York, Ohio
North Western Reporter (N.W.2d):	Iowa, Michigan, Minnesota, Nebraska, North Dakota, South Dakota, Wisconsin
Pacific Reporter (P.2d):	Arizona, California, Colorado, Hawaii, Idaho, Kansas, Montana, Nevada, New Mexico, Oklahoma, Oregon, Utah, Washington, Wyoming
South Eastern Reporter (S.E.2d):	Georgia, North Carolina, South Carolina, Virginia, West Virginia
South Western Reporter (S.W.2d):	Arkansas, Kentucky, Missouri, Tennessee, Texas
Southern Reporter (So.2d):	Alabama, Florida, Louisiana, Mississippi
California Reporter (Cal.Rptr.2d)	
New York Supplement (N.Y.2d)	

FIGURE 1.4 *Areas covered by West's* National Reporter *system*

one of the two legal encyclopedias: *Corpus Juris Secundum* and *American Jurisprudence*. For clarification and explanations of laws and terminology, these dictionaries and encyclopedias can be extremely helpful in allowing the reader to understand terms and theories common in the legal profession.

Every local courthouse should have these reporters, codes, encyclopedias, and dictionaries as well as an abundance of other material that can be used for legal research. It is also becoming very common to search the Internet and use legal data bases such as WESTLAW or LEXIS/NEXIS. Additionally, each state has its own website, which generally includes important sources of law such as statutes, cases, and regulations.

HOW TO PREPARE A BRIEF

NO MATTER how research is performed, the most important part is to comprehend the history of the law and how it relates to other fact patterns as well as have a clear understanding of the court's rationale for its decision. Unfortunately, accomplishing this goal is not always an easy task when faced with a 20-page case written in legalese. In many instances, interpreting court cases can be a long and difficult process. An easy way to condense the material and determine the law is to prepare a case brief. A brief is a one- to two-page synopsis of the important points of a case. This gives the reader the opportunity to pull out the critical factors relating to the case and then clarify the key issues by transferring the information into his or her own words.

A brief typically consists of five major categories: the facts, procedural posture, the issue, analysis of the case, and the holding (see Figure 1.5).

The first step is to read through the case to gain a general understanding of the facts. In some cases the facts can become very cumbersome. In the brief, however, they should simply be summarized.

The second step is to determine the procedural posture—The question of how the case got to this point. In other words, how did the lower courts hold?

The third step is to determine the legal issue. The issue is the legal question that the court is answering. Usually, the issue can be summarized in one or two questions.

The fourth step, and probably the most important, is the analysis. This step requires a thorough investigation of why the court has made its decision. This step is critical because it interprets the law as it applies to various fact patterns.

Facts: A *brief* summary of the facts.
Procedural Posture: How did the case get here? In other words, how did the lower courts rule?
Issue: What legal question is the court answering?
Analysis: What did this court say and (more important) why did they say it?
Holding: Either the lower court decision is "affirmed" or "reversed."

FIGURE 1.5 *How to prepare a brief*

The last step is the holding of the court. The holding is the decision the court has made in the case. Typically, the decision is to affirm the lower court's decision or to reverse it.

SUMMARY

The law is constantly evolving and it is the duty of the educational administrator to be aware of such changes. In the past, educators did not have to be concerned with lawsuits; it was a rare occurrence that a public school would be involved in litigation. However, society has changed as have the courts' decisions over the last few decades and increased the rights of both students and faculty. With these changes comes an increase in the number of lawsuits filed each year against public schools. Through the addition of numerous federal statutes and changing laws, educators can no longer be unfamiliar with the law, nor can they assume that they will never be named a defendant in a lawsuit. Hence, administrators must take proactive steps to avoid litigation to the extent possible.

In understanding the field of education law and being proactive, an administrator should have a basic understanding of the federal and state legal structure, the steps involved in a lawsuit, and the knowledge of how to research points of law. Additionally, administrators need to be aware of changes in the law that may directly affect their institutions.

While educational administrators cannot spend the majority of their day researching the law, at a minimum, it is important that they know the difference between the standards of proof between a civil and criminal lawsuit, as well as the economic and ethical dilemmas that they may encounter when confronted with questions of law.

DISCUSSION QUESTIONS

1. Describe the responsibilities of the three branches of government. Which branch has the most influence on education?
2. Define preventive law and give examples of how a public school administrator may practice preventive law.
3. Does the U.S. Constitution mention education? How does the Constitution influence education?
4. What factors are considered when choosing to file a lawsuit?
5. Does every case have the opportunity to be heard by the U.S. Supreme Court? Why or why not?
6. What steps are taken in filing a lawsuit? Should any other issues be analyzed before filing a lawsuit?
7. List in order from lowest to highest the court system in your state. Also list in order from lowest to highest the federal court system. How do you decide which court system to use to bring a claim?

8. Compare and contrast the difference between civil and criminal cases.
9. In which court system would a teacher bring a breach of contract claim after being wrongfully discharged from her position because she is pregnant? Why?
10. What is the common structure of a brief? What benefit is there to briefing educational law cases?

DEEPENING YOUR UNDERSTANDING

1. Research an educational journal and find a recent article pertaining to litigation in education. (Hint: A good source of information is *www.edweek.org;* for higher education issues, visit *www.chronicle.com.*) Once you find an article, discuss whether such an issue would have arisen 10 years ago? 20 years ago? In small groups, discuss your responses. Then review what social factors may have contributed to such cases.
2. Brief the *Cooper v. Aaron* case using the recommended format. Attempt to focus on the rationale section and explain the decision in your own words.

2

Torts and School Liability

Introduction

School districts are increasingly concerned about potential legal liability due to the acts of administrators, faculty, and staff. Based on the legal doctrine of respondeat superior, employers are responsible for acts of their employees in the scope of their employment. Hence, schools are responsible for the intentional and negligent acts of their employees.

The laws of torts deals with civil, not criminal, wrongs against individuals. Torts can be categorized into intentional and nonintentional. Intentional torts require an intentional act, while nonintentional or negligent acts simply fall below a reasonable standard. While school districts still claim governmental immunity, courts are moving toward requiring schools, and their employees, to be held responsible for their actions.

Tort is defined as a civil wrong resulting from a breach of duty and is based on the theory that one should be compensated for the wrongful intentional or negligent acts of another. Based on legal theories outside of criminal law, the law allows injured parties to be monetarily compensated for their injuries.

Respondeat Superior

RESPONDEAT *superior* is a Latin term meaning the "master is responsible for the servant." Today it is taken to mean that employers are responsible for acts of employees while they are within the scope of their employment. Laws pertaining to this issue fall generally under agency law and are important for schools because actions of administrators, faculty, and staff can make the district financially responsible for negligent or willful acts they commit while performing their job. This transfer of responsibility is called vicarious liability. In most lawsuits, the injured party will attempt to claim that the employee was within the scope of his or her employment when the injury occurred. If this is proven to be true, both employer and employee will be responsible for damages. In most cases, however, the employee is limited in what damages he or she can pay toward the final judgment. Consequently, school districts bear the financial burden of paying for damages when employees are negligent. Additionally, for those seeking damages, the school district appears to have "deep pockets" as well as liability insurance that will pay off judgments or large settlements.

While the employer is responsible for acts of the employee, this only applies when the employee is acting within the scope of his or her employment, not outside of assigned duties. For example, in Louisiana, a high school football coach was riding his bicycle to school to review films of past games. Traveling quickly on the wrong side of the street, he hit a pedestrian who was attempting to cross the street. The pedestrian suffered numerous injuries, including a broken pelvis. Due to complications, the injured man later died. His widow sued the school on the basis of vicarious liability. According to the court,

> an employer's vicarious liability for acts not its own extends only to the employee's tortuous conduct that is within the course and scope of the employment. Generally speaking, an employee going to and/or from work is not considered as acting within course and scope of his employment to such an extent as to render his employer liable to third persons for employee's negligent acts. The rationale of this principle is that an employee usually does not begin work until he reaches his employer's premises. Therefore, unless the employee has a duty to perform a service or task en route, the employee's commute to and from work is usually considered outside the course and scope of employment.[1]

While a school district may not always be responsible for negligent acts of their employees, clearly, it is important to take all possible preventive steps to ensure that faculty and staff are properly trained in an attempt to be proactive and avoid litigation to the greatest extent possible.

INTENTIONAL TORTS

INTENTIONAL torts, as the name indicates, require a deliberate act toward another individual. For school districts, the most common type of intentional torts include civil assault and battery; false imprisonment; intentional infliction of emotional distress; and defamation, which consists of libel and slander. A more common nonintentional tort occurs in cases of negligence.

---

[1] *Fasullo v. Finley*, 782 So.2d 76 (2001)

Among intentional torts, assault and battery are commonly associated; but one can claim assault without battery, and vice versa. Assault occurs when someone is placed in apprehension of immediate harm. According to a Minnesota court, "Mere words or threats do not constitute an assault, unless accompanied by an offer of physical violence."[2] "The display of force must be such as to cause plaintiff reasonable apprehension of immediate bodily harm."[3] Battery is the physical attack itself. An easy way to distinguish the two is that assault is the mental attack and battery is the physical.

Assault and battery claims against a school generally occur when a teacher or an administrator inflicts excessive corporal punishment on a student. While corporal punishment is legal in a number of states, if the punishment is extreme or intentionally malicious, a civil claim may arise (see Chapter 5).

Sansone v. Bechtel
Supreme Court of Connecticut, 1980
429 A.2d 820

Opinion by Justice Parskey.

The single issue raised by this appeal is whether a public school teacher who inflicts excessive corporal punishment upon a pupil is immunized from liability. The trial court's resolution of this issue against the teacher generated this appeal.

The defendant is a music teacher at the Jared Eliot School in Clinton. The plaintiff, Kenneth Sansone, twelve years of age, was a student in the defendant's class. One day Kenneth and three other boys were misbehaving in class by interposing improvised sounds in a song which the class was supposed to sing in unison. Before this event Kenneth had never been a disciplinary problem in the defendant's class. At the disruption the defendant did not caution Kenneth or speak to him about his conduct but instead grabbed him by the arm and projected him from his chair into a movable chalk board. He then took Kenneth into the corridor where he grabbed the boy's arm and swung him against a wall. Kenneth was neither engaging in any tumultuous behavior nor threatening the defendant or any other person. He was not struggling nor did he offer any physical resistance to the defendant's forceful discipline. As a result of the defendant's conduct Kenneth sustained a displaced fracture of the clavicle. In his complaint the plaintiff charged the defendant, with causing personal injuries as a result of excessive punishment.

I. The defendant claims the immunity of a public officer in the performance of discretionary duties. He asserts that such persons are not subject to liability for common-law negligence and that the plaintiff's complaint is based solely on such negligence. He concedes, as he must, that teachers have been held liable, under a complaint for assault and battery, for

---

[2]*Johnson v. Sampson*, 208 N.W. 814, 815 (1926)

[3]*Dahlin v. Fraser*, 288 N.W. 851, 852 (1939)

inflicting excessive punishment on a pupil; but contends that since the plaintiff chose to bring an action in common-law negligence he either recovers on that ground or else he cannot recover at all.

The defendant cites no direct authority for the proposition that, in Connecticut, teachers enjoy the immunity conferred upon public officers. We have stated that "[a] teacher is not an officer in the ordinary sense of the word." Rather, teachers are employees of the board of education.

Although not entitled to assert the governmental immunity that extends to public officers, teachers are accorded certain legal protection in their administration of discipline. A teacher is a surrogate parent to his pupils. This relationship imposes upon him a duty to maintain discipline in his classroom. In discharging this duty the teacher is authorized to use reasonable means to compel a disobedient pupil to comply with his orders; including the use of corporal punishment. In evaluating the necessity and extent of punishment considerable allowance should be made to the teacher to protect him in the exercise of his discretion. He will, therefore, not be held liable unless the punishment inflicted is clearly excessive. The power to punish, however, does not include punishment which is disproportionate to the offense, unnecessarily degrading or likely to cause serious or permanent harm. Furthermore, whether a particular punishment exceeds the ambit of the teacher's disciplinary authority ordinarily presents a pure question of fact for the trier.

The complaint as particularized charged the defendant with a negligent assault and battery. We have long adhered to the rule that "an unintentional trespass to the person, or assault and battery, if it be the direct and immediate consequence of a force exerted by the defendant wantonly, or imposed without the exercise by him of due care, would make him liable for resulting injury." This principle has been applied to the case of an unintended injury incident to disciplinary action taken by a teacher. It is also applicable to the facts of the present case.

Even if we view the finding as supporting an intentional rather than a negligent injury, the judgment can still be supported. There is nothing in the record before us to suggest that the defendant objected to the evidence of excessive corporal punishment. If the defendant believed that the evidence would support an intentional but not a negligent act, then it was incumbent upon him to object to it insofar as it tended to prove conduct not alleged in the complaint. His failure to do so constituted a waiver of any variance between the pleadings and the proof.

II. Finally, we consider whether the defendant is immune from liability under the provisions of General Statutes § 4-165.

This statute is part of chapter 53 which covers claims against the state. "The manifest legislative intent expressed by chapter 53 is that an employee is immune where and because the state may be sued, and that the state may be sued in instances where a private person would be liable." Under § 4-141 a "state employee" is defined to include every person employed in any office, position or post in the state government. A school teacher does not come within this definition. Although a town board of education is an agent of the state when carrying out the interests of the state, its members are not state but town officers.

Similarly, teachers as employees of a town board of education are also not employed in the state government. There is nothing in the language of chapter 53 or in its legislative history to suggest that the state was to assume financial responsibility for the conduct of teachers and members of local boards of education. Giving chapter 53 the strict construction which any statute in derogation of the principle of sovereignty must be given; we hold that this chapter in general and § 4-165 in particular do not apply to teachers in local school systems.

There is no error.

In this opinion the other judges concurred.

To maintain discipline, administrators and teachers must have disciplinary rules in place. There have been cases, however, in which the wrongful implementation of such rules crossed over into a claim for assault and battery. For example, a teacher was held liable for the tortious act of battery after he took an unruly student into an empty classroom and shook him severely and punched him in the stomach.[4]

Other intentional torts which too often occur in education are intentional infliction of emotional distress, false imprisonment, and defamation. Intentional infliction of emotional distress occurs only when the injured party can prove that the act was outrageous and unconscionable. As the Arkansas Supreme Court defined, "we can and do now recognize that one who by extreme and outrageous conduct willfully or wantonly causes severe emotional distress to another is subject to liability for such emotional distress and for bodily harm, resulting from the distress. . . . We mean conduct that is so outrageous in character, and so extreme in degree, as to go beyond all possible bonds of decency, and to be regarded as atrocious, and utterly intolerable in a civilized society."[5] To avoid opening the floodgates of litigation, courts generally do not allow such claims. But in cases in which a teacher specifically intended to mentally harm a child, such claims will stand.

While not a common concern for school districts, there have been claims brought by students for the intentional tort of false imprisonment. "False imprisonment is the unlawful restraint of an individual's personal liberty or freedom of locomotion."[6] To maintain discipline within the school, administrators and faculty are legally permitted under *in loco parentis* to reasonably and temporarily detain students. According to a Minnesota court, to have a claim for false imprisonment, a three-pronged test must be met: "(1) words or acts intended to confine, (2) actual confinement, and (3) awareness by the plaintiff that he is confined."[7]

NEGLIGENCE

WHILE intentional tort claims do arise in public education, the most common type of torts affecting schools is negligence. Through the doctrine of respondeat superior, if a teacher is negligent, the school district may be liable. Such liability is of major concern because negligence can occur not from a particular act but from not acting in accordance

---

[4]*Thomas v. Bedford,* 389 So. 2d 405 (1980)

[5]*M.B.M. Co. v. Counce,* 596 S.W.2d 681 (1980)

[6]*Stowers v. Wolodzko,* 386 Mich. 119 (1971)

[7]*Blaz v. Molin Concrete Prods.,* 244 N.W.2d 277 (1976)

with a certain standard of care. There are two primary reasons for school districts to pay special attention to avoid negligence claims. One is that such acts are not intentional but occur when an individual fails to act in a reasonable manner. The second is that the monetary damages awarded to child defendants are generally quite large. To be held negligent, four things must be proven: duty, breach, proximate cause, and damages.

Duty

Under common law, there is a no-duty rule. This doctrine has a few exceptions, but generally an individual has no duty to assist another who is in peril. General exceptions to the no-duty doctrine occur when there is a special relationship. For example, a parent has a special duty to protect his or her child; and under in loco parentis, a special relationship exists between the teacher and the student. This relationship sets forth a duty for the teacher to protect and warn the student of any known dangers, which is typically performed through proper supervision while the child is on school property.

"A duty may be defined as an obligation recognized by law to conform to a particular standard of conduct toward another."[8] "The standard of care for school teachers and administrators is that of a reasonable person in such a position acting under similar circumstances. Reasonable care includes protecting against unreasonable risk of injury from dangerous or hazardous objects in the school buildings and on the grounds."[9] For example, consider a student who is injured after slipping on a wet floor at school. In this case, the school had knowledge of the water problem and did not take steps to prevent such an incident, consequently breaching its duty to protect the students.

The special duty between the school and the students requires that teachers and staff adequately supervise students and protect them from reasonable, foreseeable injury. In determining whether one has breached a duty to protect, courts implement a two-part test.

First, was reasonable care exercised? Reasonable care is based on the ideal of a reasonable person. In determining how this factitious person would act, the court asks what a reasonable person with the same qualifications and education would do in the same situation.

Some courts have suggested that, because teachers are specially trained to deal with students, they are expected to act at a high level of responsibility. Factors such as the age of the children being supervised, the students' special needs, and the dangerousness of the activities that were being performed at the time of the accident are also weighed when determining what is reasonable.

Second, was the injury foreseeable? In determining whether the standard of reasonable care is upheld, courts analyze the foreseeability of the incident. Of course, as one court pointed out, "After the event, hindsight makes every occurrence foreseeable, but whether the law imposes a duty does not depend upon foreseeability alone. The likelihood of injury,

---

[8]*St. Hill,* 542 So. 2d 502 (1987)
[9]*Capers v. Orleans School Board,* 365 So. 2d 23, 24 (1978)

the magnitude of the burden of guarding against it and the consequences of placing that burden upon the defendant, must also be taken into account."[10]

Does this mean students must have constant supervision? According to the courts, "constant supervision of all students is not possible, nor is it required, for educators to discharge their duty to provide adequate supervision."[11] In carrying out the duty to supervise, school officials and teachers must use the degree of care "that a person of ordinary prudence, charged with the duties involved, would exercise under the same circumstances."[12]

In New York, a student was injured when struck in the eye with a pencil that a classmate had thrown across the room. The teacher was temporarily absent from the room at the time of the incident. In its holding, the court reviewed both the number of similar incidents that had occurred as well as the common danger that a pencil could cause and concluded that such an incident had never previously occurred, nor would one determine that a pencil was an inherently dangerous object. Finally, the court determined that such an incident could have occurred regardless of the location of the teacher and "that this is one of those events which could occur equally as well in the presence of the teacher as during her absence."[13]

> It is well established that a school board, through its agents and teachers, is responsible for reasonable supervision over students. However, this duty to supervise does not make the board the insurer of the safety of the children. Furthermore, constant supervision of all students is not possible nor required for educators to discharge their duty to provide adequate supervision. Before liability can be imposed upon a school board, there must be proof of negligence in providing supervision and also proof of a causal connection between the lack of supervision and the accident. Further, the unreasonable risk of injury must be foreseeable, constructively or actually known, and preventable, if the requisite degree of supervision had been exercised. Said differently, educators are required to exercise only that supervision and discipline expected of a reasonably prudent person under the circumstances at hand. Obviously then, the failure to take every precaution against all foreseeable risk of injury does not necessarily constitute negligence. It is well established that the fact that each student is not personally supervised every moment of each school day does not constitute fault on the part of the school board or its employees.[14]

Based on the court decisions, the reasonable care standard does not necessarily mean that a teacher must give constant supervision and every incident where a child is injured is not always foreseeable. Consequently every accident does not necessarily mean a teacher was negligent.

---

[10]*Lance v. Senior*, 224 N.E.2d 231 (1967)

[11]*Collins v. Bossier Parish School Board*, 480 So. 2d 846 (1985)

[12]Ibid.

[13]*Ohman v. Board of Education of the City of New York*, 300 N.Y. 306 (1949)

[14]*Bell v. Ayio*, 731 So. 2d 893 at 899 (1998)

Lawes v. Board of Education of the City of New York
Court of Appeals of New York, 1965
213 N.E.2d 667

Opinion by Justice Bergan.

Plaintiff Nuvia Alicia Lawes, a pupil at Public School No. 144 in Brooklyn, was struck by a snowball thrown by a fellow pupil while she was on her way from her home to her classroom after lunch on February 17, 1960. Plaintiff, then 11 years old, suffered a serious eye injury. A judgment for $45,000 has been rendered against the Board of Education and affirmed by a divided Appellate Division.

The snowball was thrown on school property in a yard between the street and school entrance, but this was not during a recreation period. Children were then on the property on their way into the school after having been home to lunch. The school had made a rule against snowball throwing and plaintiff's teacher had warned her pupils not to throw snowballs.

If a school is to become liable to one pupil for a snowball thrown at him by a fellow pupil, the rule governing such responsibility should be laid down clearly and be precise enough to be generally understood in the schools.

No one grows up in this climate without throwing snowballs and being hit by them. If snow is on the ground as children come to school, it would require intensive policing, almost child by child, to take all snowball throwing out of play. It is unreasonable to demand or expect such perfection in supervision from ordinary teachers or ordinary school management; and a fair test of reasonable care does not demand it.

The classic New York statement of the measure of school care for children is laid out in Judge Loughran's noted opinion in *Hoose v. Drumm:* "Teachers have watched over the play of their pupils time out of mind. At recess periods, not less than in the classroom, a teacher owes it to his charges to exercise such care of them as a parent of ordinary prudence would observe in comparable circumstances."

A parent of ordinary prudence would not invariably stop his children from making and throwing snowballs. Indeed, he might encourage it. He would stop dangerous throwing, if he learned hard frozen snow or ice had come into play, or the pelting of one child by several others, but ordinary snowball throwing would not necessarily be stopped.

A reasonable measure of a school's responsibility for snowball throwing is to control or prevent it during recreation periods according to its best judgment of conditions, and to take energetic steps to intervene at other times if dangerous play comes to its notice while children are within its area of responsibility.

The facts in the present case do not spell out any notice of special danger. There is no proof whatever in the record that teachers had notice of any other snowball throwing on the day plaintiff was hit. Proof that a snowball was thrown on the previous day is very thin and, even if fully credited, would not give fair notice of the kind of continued danger which should have been prevented by the active intervention of teachers.

A fellow pupil and friend of plaintiff testified that she was struck by a snowball on February 16 and that she reported this to a teacher. She did not testify that she reported that she was injured. She said: "I told her I got hit. Somebody hit me with a snowball."

The teacher denied having been told this and the Education Department records marked for identification, which the trial court refused to receive, show that this pupil reported in writing that she had been struck by a snowball, not before, but some five weeks after, plaintiff's injury.

No requirement on this kind of a record is imposed on teachers to enforce the rule against snowballs by standing outside in the cold to watch to see that children do not violate the rule as they come into the school. And it is an undue burden on the school to impose a liability because teachers did not stand outside for active intervention in the circumstances shown by this record.

A school is not liable for every thoughtless or careless act by which one pupil may injure another. Nor is liability invariably to fall on it because a school rule has been violated and an injury has been caused by another pupil.

It is not easy to find a decided case either in New York or other jurisdictions where a school has been cast in liability for a snowball thrown by one pupil at another, and no authority sustaining such a liability is cited by respondents. In its result the judgment in this case imposes a greatly enlarged risk of liability on a school without showing notice of a particular danger at a particular time. A long line of decisions should cause us to proceed warily toward such an enlarged area of liability.

The order should be reversed and the complaint dismissed, without costs.

Breach

School districts are not liable for every incident that occurs at their institution. When a teacher does not protect a student from foreseeable harm or fails to act in a reasonable manner, then there is a breach of duty. For example, in a 1975 case, a school was required to pay $37,100 in damages when a third-grade student was hit on the nose with a bat by an older student. The incident occurred during recess, when both students were playing baseball. There were two teachers on duty, but neither was in the immediate proximity at the time of the incident. Against school policy, the younger student was playing baseball, even though only students from the fourth grade and higher were permitted to play baseball during recess. In analyzing the facts, the court reviewed whether the school breached its duty. In determining this, the question is asked, did the school exercise reasonable care? Applying the reasonable person standard, the court also asks the question, was it for seeable that such an incident could occur if children of such age were left unsupervised? Due to the fact that the school did not follow its own policy, the court found in favor of the plaintiff, stating that the school failed to act in a reasonable manner.

As discussed, teachers are not required to provide constant supervision. There are cases, however, that suggest that the more dangerous the activity, the more supervision is required. Hence, it is reasonable to expect that such activities like shop class, field trips, and sporting events, would require a higher level of supervision.

Roberts v. Robertson County Board of Education
Court of Appeals of Tennessee, 1985
692 S.W.2d 863

Opinion by Justice Koch.

Wallace Glenn Roberts, Jr. suffered a serious head injury on December 17, 1976, during a vocational agriculture class at Greenbrier High School when a fellow student, William Edward Yount, asked him for assistance in using a power driven drill press. He filed this action on October 22, 1980, in the Circuit Court for Robertson County pursuant to Tenn. Code Ann. § 29-20-101 et seq. [the "Tennessee Governmental Tort Liability Act"] against the Robertson County Board of Education as well as the county school superintendent, the principal of Greenbrier High School, and his vocational agriculture teacher, Billy Ross Ballard. . . .

I.   The Facts.

Wallace Glenn Roberts, Jr. was a fourteen year old freshman at the Greenbrier High School in 1976. He elected to enroll in the school's Vocational Agriculture I class that was taught by Billy Ross Ballard. Mr. Ballard had taught this class at Greenbrier High School since 1960. There were twenty-three students enrolled in this class when it began in the middle of August, 1976. The class met one hour each day during the school week.

According to the rules of the State Board of Education, Vocational Agriculture I is one of two basic courses which students must take in the ninth grade in order to be eligible to enroll in more specialized areas. It is intended to acquaint the students with basic farm techniques. In the words of Mr. Ballard, it was intended to train students in any general area of shop dealing with anything that he is going to come in contact with the rest of his life—I guess you would say around the home, around the farm, around the shop.

This course was taught in a separate modular building in back of the old Greenbrier High School. This building contained a classroom outfitted with tables and chairs, a tool room, two restrooms, Mr. Ballard's office, and an L-shaped shop area. There were a number of entrances to the shop area from the interior rooms and one primary outside entrance separated from the shop area by a hallway running between the tool room, the classroom, and the two restrooms.

Mr. Ballard testified that he taught this course in 1976 in much the same way he had taught it in past years. He did not rely upon a written lesson plan but generally relied upon his memory and his "philosophy on learning the students." In this regard, Mr. Ballard testified that I just go historically day to day. After so many years, it just sort of falls in. And there are some old lesson books there, maybe ten, twelve years old. Every once in a while you will thumb through and pick up where you left off.

The teachers of vocational agriculture will conduct courses in the broad field of agriculture under the direction of local education officials and under the technical supervision of the Division of Vocational Education. They shall be responsible for classroom instruction, laboratory, shop, and other educational experiences required as a part of the instructional program. The teacher shall be responsible for planning, developing, and supervising and/or coordinating the supervised work experiences of the students throughout the year.

Mr. Ballard also testified that in addition to these general safety rules, there were a number of specific safety rules with regard to the operation of the drill press that he reviewed with his students when he demonstrated the use of each piece of equipment. A number of these operational rules were also included in a sign posted on the wall near the drill press which contained a list of eight safety precautions.

Mr. Ballard and his students also testified that certain students were given more latitude to work with machinery than others. Mr. Ballard stated that this was based on each student's ability and responsibility demonstrated in the way that he used each piece of equipment. While these students were not exempted completely from complying with Mr. Ballard's safety rules, they had more latitude to use the machinery without Mr. Ballard's direct supervision. While Mr. Ballard was generally complimentary of Yount's work, the record is not clear concerning whether Yount was considered one of these better students.

The class in which Roberts and Yount were students received its group instruction in the use of the drill press in late October or early November, 1976. This instruction included a demonstration wherein Mr. Ballard showed students how to drill holes in metal and how to carve letters in wood using a short router bit. Mr. Ballard could not state whether either Roberts or Yount viewed this demonstration and did not testify to any steps he took to make sure that each student attended the demonstration or understood the basic techniques he was teaching. Yount testified, in fact, that he was not directly involved in Mr. Ballard's demonstration of the drill press because he was using the welding equipment at the time in another area of the shop. There is no evidence in this record that this demonstration of the drill press or any other instruction included warnings to the students of the dangers attendant to more complicated uses of the drill press or instructions concerning how students should help each other use the drill press.

On December 17, 1976, the last school day before the Christmas vacation, Yount desired to use the drill press to drill a hole through a fourteen inch, cylindrical piece of wood he was fashioning into a lamp base he intended to give as a Christmas present. Mr. Yount had only seen the drill press used to drill holes in metal and to carve names in wood. The work he wanted to do was not one of the basic uses of the drill press that had been covered in Mr. Ballard's demonstration conducted a month earlier. Yount had never received instruction concerning the use of the drill press to drill holes in larger pieces of wood. Likewise, he had never tried to do this before and had never seen anyone else try to use the drill press in this way. Mr. Ballard testified that this use required a more elaborate setup and that it could be dangerous if the drill press was not set up properly.

Yount talked to Mr. Ballard about what he wanted to do. Mr. Ballard understood from this conversation that Yount was eager to do this work that day because he wanted to take the lamp base home. This job could not be done using the drill bits that the students were accustomed to using. It required a much longer drill bit that Mr. Ballard kept in his desk drawer in his office. Even though the students were not making full use of the shop that day, Mr. Ballard took this special drill bit from his desk drawer and gave it to Yount. While there is some disagreement concerning Mr. Ballard's instructions at this point, Mr. Ballard testified that he instructed Yount to wait before he started to use the drill bit because he wanted to be present to supervise the student's work. Yount went into the shop and set up the drill press as best he knew how. He then waited for Mr. Ballard.

Mr. Ballard was not in the shop area at that time, nor did he follow Yount into the shop. He was in another part of the building. He had promised to give his students free soft drinks that day, and at the time Yount was ready to work on his lamp base, Mr. Ballard was near the outside entrance to the shop building where he was moving the soft drink machine into the classroom area. The drill press could not be seen from where Mr. Ballard was located near the outside door.

Yount waited for approximately ten minutes for Mr. Ballard to return to the shop. There were other students using shop machinery during this time. When Mr. Ballard did not come in, Yount asked his classmate, Roberts, to assist him in drilling a hole in the lamp base. Roberts had been helping another classmate use a hand saw, and this was the first time he was aware that Yount desired to use the drill press. He was not aware that Yount had talked with Mr. Ballard about this job and thus, was not aware of any instructions that Mr. Ballard might have given Yount. He was just helping a friend. Roberts had never been instructed or warned concerning the danger of what Yount was doing or the manner in which people could be injured when using a longer drill bit. At Yount's request to hold the piece of wood while the hole was drilled, Roberts knelt down next to the drill press and held the piece of wood firmly in both hands. His face was approximately ten to twelve inches away from the drill itself. Yount turned on the drill, and in an instant, the long drill bit deflected at an angle of approximately forty-five degrees striking Roberts on the right temple. The drill bit caused a long cut and skull fracture from Roberts' right temple to behind his right ear. He fell back immediately from the machine, and other students came to his aid and carried him to Mr. Ballard's office. Mr. Ballard did not know what had happened until one of the students came to get him. Mr. Ballard and the school principal then transported Roberts to the hospital.

The neurosurgeon who treated Roberts testified that he made an excellent recovery, although he stated that Roberts would have some minor permanent problems due to the weakness in his skull caused by the fracture. The scarring from the wound is not visible because it is above Roberts' hairline. The neurosurgeon's opinion was that this injury resulted in a five percent disability to the body as a whole.

Mr. Ballard testified later that Yount had not set up the drill press properly because he had not reduced the drill bit's speed and had not properly clamped the cylindrical piece of wood in place before he started. Mr. Ballard stated that the drill press would have been properly adjusted had he been supervising Yount and that this accident would not have happened had he been in the shop when Yount was working on his lamp base.

II. The Negligence of the School Officials.

Roberts alleged in his complaint that his injury was the result of the negligence of his vocational agriculture teacher, the local school administrators, and the county school board. As in all negligence actions, he must prove in order to recover that the defendants had a legally recognized duty to him, that this duty was breached, and that this action or failure to act was the proximate cause of his injury. . . .

The trial court in this case determined that Mr. Ballard had a duty "to properly supervise and properly instruct" his students. While we agree with this generalized determination as far as it goes, we find it necessary to define this duty more precisely and to describe carefully the scope of the teacher's standard of care.

Teachers and local school districts are not expected to be insurers of the safety of students while they are at school. Nor are teachers expected in every instance to supervise all the activities of all students at all times. However, most courts having occasion to consider cases involving injuries to students while in shop class have determined that teachers, and through them their local school systems, are required to exercise such care as ordinarily reasonable and prudent persons would exercise under the same or similar circumstances. Thus, the Louisiana Court of Appeal has held: The standard of care for school teachers and administrators is that of a reasonable person in such a position acting under similar circumstances.

The Tennessee Supreme Court has adopted the reasonable person standard in other cases involving the safety of students. In a case where a high school student was injured when she fell on the steps of a school bus, the Tennessee Supreme Court held the school system to the standard of "reasonable and ordinary care under the circumstances." However, our courts have also recognized that this standard of care can be related directly to the nature of the persons to whom the duty is owed and the circumstances giving rise to the duty. The Tennessee Supreme Court has recognized, for example, that an adult's standard of care to children should be tempered by the recognition of children's youthful impulsiveness and inexperience. Likewise, this Court has recognized that a person who deals with inherently dangerous instrumentalities has a duty to exercise caution commensurate with the dangers involved. Thus, with regard to the duty of care owed by school bus drivers to students placed in their charge, the Tennessee Supreme Court held: Reasonable and ordinary care under the circumstances, when one of the circumstances is that the care of a child of tender years is entrusted to the school bus driver, requires that the driver exercise special care proportionate to the age of the child and its ability, or lack of ability, to care for itself.

Based upon these precedents, we find that a high school vocational teacher has the duty to take those precautions that any ordinarily reasonable and prudent person would take to protect his shop students from the unreasonable risk of injury. The extent of these precautions must be determined with reference to the age and inexperience of the students involved, their less than mature judgment with regard to their conduct, and the inherently dangerous nature of the power driven equipment available for their use in the shop. In order to discharge this duty, it is incumbent upon a teacher, at a minimum, to instruct his students in the safe and proper use of the equipment, to warn the students of known dangers, and to supervise the students to the extent necessary for the enforcement of adequate rules of shop safety.

Once the trial court has determined that the defendant was under a duty to protect the plaintiff against the event that did, in fact, occur, then it must be proven that the defendant's actions or failure to act constituted a breach of this duty. This second element of proof in a negligence case usually requires a factual determination that can only be made upon the unique facts of each case.

The final element of proof in a negligence action is the issue of causation. This is the ultimate question. A defendant in a negligence action cannot be found liable unless it has been determined that his conduct was the proximate cause of the plaintiff's injuries. While the proximate cause concept has been described in many ways, the Tennessee Supreme Court has described proximate causation as that act or omission which immediately causes or fails to prevent the injury; an act or omission occurring or concurring with another which, if it had not happened, the injury would not have been inflicted. A defendant's conduct will be regarded as the proximate cause of the plaintiff's injury if it was the "procuring," "efficient," or "predominant" cause of the injury. As long as the defendant's conduct is a substantial factor causing the injury, it need not be the sole cause or even the last act prior to the injury.

However, there can be more than one proximate cause for an injury. Thus, this Court has recognized that the rule is well established in this State that if an injury occurs from two causes, both due to the negligence of different persons, but together constituting an efficient cause, all persons whose acts contribute to the injury are liable therefore, and the negligence of one does not excuse the negligence of the other.

Thus, the Tennessee Supreme Court has held that a person injured by the concurrent negligent acts of two parties can recover from either or both parties.

Foreseeability is also an essential element of the proof of proximate causation. If the injury giving rise to the action could not have been reasonably foreseen or anticipated, then there is no proximate cause. However, this foreseeability requirement is not so strict as to require that a defendant must foresee the exact manner in which an injury takes place. The requirement is met as long as it has been determined that the defendant could foresee, or through the exercise of reasonable diligence should have foreseen, the general manner in which the injury occurred.

With specific reference to the conduct of teachers, we do not impose upon them the duty to anticipate or foresee the hundreds of unexpected student acts that occur daily in our public schools. However, like other courts, we have no hesitation in holding a teacher or local school system to the duty of safeguarding students while at school from reasonably foreseeable dangerous conditions including the dangerous acts of fellow students.

Based upon our de novo review of this record, we conclude that the evidence supports a finding that Mr. Ballard was negligent and that his failure to furnish adequate instruction and supervision to his vocational agriculture students was the proximate cause of Roberts' injuries. There are four separate aspects of Mr. Ballard's conduct that support this conclusion. First, Mr. Ballard had a practice of permitting inexperienced freshman students to remain in the shop area unsupervised in the presence of fully operational power driven equipment which, if used improperly, could cause serious injury. Second, there is no proof that Mr. Ballard ever instructed his students in the proper techniques for assisting others in operating shop machinery. Third, there is no proof that Mr. Ballard ever gave his students any instruction concerning the ways a drill press could cause injury if it was not used properly. While there is proof that Mr. Ballard demonstrated two of the many ways that a drill press could be used, neither Mr. Ballard nor any of his students testified that any instruction was given concerning the other ways that a drill press, if improperly used, could cause injury. Fourth, Mr. Ballard gave Yount a drill bit knowing that he had never used the drill bit before and that he was eager to use it during that class period.

The evidence supports a conclusion that Mr. Ballard was aware that Yount did not know how to use the longer drill bit properly when he gave it to him and that Mr. Ballard knew that this drill bit could be dangerous if used improperly. Apart from his conceded general recognition that fourteen year old boys have a characteristic impatience and curiosity, Mr. Ballard also had direct knowledge that Yount intended to use the special drill bit at that time because this was his last opportunity to do so before Christmas vacation. Rather than keeping the drill bit and telling Yount that he would come into the shop area to supervise his work, Mr. Ballard gave Yount the instrument that caused Roberts' injury. Providing the drill bit to Yount, knowing at the time that the shop equipment was fully operable, that other students were working in the shop area without supervision, and that Yount was eager to use the drill bit constitutes a breach of Mr. Ballard's duty to supervise his students properly and provides a sufficient basis for a judgment in Roberts' favor. . . .

The issue of damages remains. The record contains evidence that Roberts' family sustained approximately $4,225 in medical bills as a result of this injury. Further, Roberts himself was hospitalized for ten days and experienced moderate pain for some time thereafter. His surgical treatment required that his head be shaved, and thus, for some time after the accident, he was subjected to the ridicule and teasing of his peers. This embarrassment to a fourteen year old boy can be as painful as the injury itself. His treating physician also determined that this injury has caused a permanent weakening of his skull in the area of the injury. While placing no limitation on Roberts' activities, his doctor determined that this injury has resulted in a five percent disability to the body as a whole. Based upon this testimony, we find that an award of $25,000 in damages is warranted.

For the reasons stated herein, the judgment of the trial court is reversed and the case is remanded with directions that a judgment in the amount of $25,000 be entered in favor of Wallace Glenn Roberts, Jr. and against Billy R. Ballard and the Robertson County Board of Education.

The costs of this cause are taxed against the Robertson County Board of Education.

Proximate Cause

The third element required to claim a cause of action of negligence is proximate cause, also commonly known as the "but for" test. This element of negligence requires that there be a connection or a nexus between the breach and the injury. In other words, would the same result occur if a person did not breach his or her duty to protect? Is there a causal connection in the following case? Between classes, when teachers are monitoring the halls, a sixth grader is pushed into a hallway wall. At the time of the incident, no teacher could see the students. The student strikes her head and, due to the injury, suffers seizures for several years. In a lawsuit filed by her parents, she claims negligence on part of the school. Based on the quickness of the incident and the fact that the teachers were on duty, the court held that "School boards are required to exercise and maintain only the supervision that is expected of a reasonable person under the circumstances of the particular case."[15] Hence, the school was not found liable.

In another case involving the issue of proximate cause, two female high school students were brutally raped by four male students. The female students were unaware that band practice had been canceled for the day and were unable to contact their parents to receive a ride home. According to the facts, both the school bus and school officials had left the premises. Consequently, the girls accepted a ride from four male students, who drove them to a field and raped them. In recognizing the duty the school owes its students, the court noted: "School Boards owe a duty of reasonable competent supervision commensurate with the student's age and the circumstances of the case. Such a duty applies when a student is on campus during regular school hours, when waiting on the school grounds for a school bus, and when participating in after-hour, school-sanctioned activities."[16] In its holding, the court found that, even with full supervision, such an incident could not have been prevented. In the words of the court, "the school has no control or authority over that which happens off of school grounds. . . . more probably than not, supervision would have yielded the same result; thus, supervision was irrelevant to the ultimate harm suffered."[17]

Field trips also require heightened supervision by teachers. In a recent case before a Louisiana appeals court, a school was found to have "constructive notice" of a dangerous swing that struck a kindergarten student and permanently disabled the child. The park was located on an acre and a half and possessed more than 100 pieces of playground equipment. The court described the park setting as a "virtual children's wonderland."[18] Unfortunately, while at the park, the six-year-old student was struck by a 60-pound, two-person metal swing and severely injured.

On the day of the incident, there were 3 teachers and 11 parents supervising 78 children while at the park. Before the visit, the children had been told to avoid certain areas of the park and to play only on certain pieces of playground equipment. The teachers reviewed safety instructions and told the children "not to play on the swings." Nevertheless, a student was injured. According to the court, "due to the park's size and the number of pieces of equipment, the school should have delegated adults to watch areas

[15]*Jackson v. Madison Parish School Board*, 779 So.2d 59 (2001)

[16]*Frederick v. Vermillion Parish School Board*, 772 So.2d 208 (2000)

[17]Ibid., at 212

[18]*Glandker v. Rapids Parish School Board*, 610 So.2d 1020, at 1031 (1992)

Best Practices

- Inform faculty members of their duty to protect students. Ensure that they understand their legal obligation to protect students.

- Ensure that school grounds are safe.

- Set forth a policy that covers reasonable teacher actions in certain situations. For example, teachers should heighten supervision during sporting activities or field trips.

- Define faculty and staff obligations to foresee danger and protect students from possible injury.

- Require faculty and staff members to notify proper school officials about any accidents that occur on campus.

- Implement a training program that makes faculty and staff members aware of civil law litigation. For example, review case law and illustrate situations in which schools have been held responsible for students' injuries.

of the park and ensure that there was adequate supervision."[19] Hence, but for the school breaching its duty, the child would not have been injured.

Damages

In the final element of negligence, the plaintiff incurs damages or some form of injury. So if a student falls on school property, was there negligence? Working through the elements of negligence, we first ask, Is there a duty? Because the incident occurred on school property, there was a duty to protect, if the incident occurred during school hours. Second, we ask, Was there a breach of duty? Why did the student slip? Would a reasonably prudent teacher have prevented or foreseen the incident? Third, we ask, Is there a nexus between the breach and the fall? Finally, we ask, Was the student injured? If the answer to the first three questions is yes but no to the final question, there has been no negligence. For a valid tort claim, all four elements must be met.

DEFENSES AGAINST NEGLIGENCE

IF A SCHOOL is found negligent, it will not necessarily have to pay monetary damages. In its defense, a school district may claim that, while it was somewhat responsible for the injury, it was not completely the district's fault. In claiming such defense, a school may argue that the injured party contributed to his or her own injury. Additional defenses include assumption of risk, which suggests that the plaintiff knew there was a possibility of harm and accepted that risk. Lastly, a school district may claim that it is protected from such claims based on governmental immunity.

---

[19]Ibid., at 1033

Contributory and Comparative Negligence

When a school district is found negligent, its typical defense is to claim that, while the school may have been negligent, the plaintiff contributed, at least in part, to his or her own injuries. Depending on the state, two defenses can be claimed; contributory or comparative negligence.

First, contributory negligence. Under this doctrine of law, the school claims that the student "contributed" to his or her own injuries and therefore the school should not be held responsible. This rule is considered severe based on the outcome that if the plaintiff is found to be just slightly responsible for his or her own injuries, then he or she recovers zero damages. This "all or nothing" rule is viewed in some courts as very harsh; for if the student is even 1% responsible while the school is 99% responsible, the student is still barred from any recovery and hence will receive nothing in monetary damages.

For example, in *Aronson v. Horace Mann–Barnard School,* a student was found contributorily negligent for her own injuries while practicing for a swim meet.[20] According to the facts, the plaintiff was a high school senior who was an experienced swimmer and was familiar with the pool depth. While practicing a dive from the shallow end of the pool, however, the student was injured when she hit the bottom, injuring her head. The evidence indicated that the student was negligent and that her own actions were the reason for her injuries. Based on that fact, the case was dismissed.

Due to the severity of contributory negligence, some states have moved to a more equitable structure known as comparative negligence. In states that have adopted this doctrine, liability is proportioned based on percentage of responsibility. In other words, monetary damages are determined based on the parties' responsibilities. For example, if a student were filing a negligence claim for $100,000 and the school was found to be 70% responsible, the school would pay only $70,000 in damages. If the state followed a contributory negligence doctrine, the same student would receive no money because he or she was 30% responsible for the injuries.

Assumption of Risk

In some cases, especially in sports-related injures, the defendant will argue in his or her defense that the student knew of the risk yet still participated in the activity. This doctrine is known as assumption of risk. But not every student who engages in a dangerous activity may understand the consequences. Therefore, in many courts, age is a factor when determining assumption of risk.

---

[20]224 A.D.2d 249 (1996)

Berman v. Philadelphia Board of Education
Superior Court of Pennsylvania, 1983
456 A.2d 545

Opinion by Justice Hester.

In April, 1976, Brad Berman was an eleven year old, fifth grade student, attending Sharswood Elementary School in Philadelphia. In response to a flyer distributed to each classroom announcing an after-school floor hockey league, Brad enrolled in the program and was assigned to play for the Capitals, one of the eight league teams. All games were played in the school's gymnasium.

Daniel Caputo, a physical education instructor at Sharswood, began the program during the 1974–75 school year. He instructed the student players, at the beginning of each season, that slapshots, raising hockey sticks above the waist, checking and foul language were prohibited. During the 1975–76 school year, which included the date of April 21, 1976 at issue here, the students were equipped with hockey sticks composed of wooden shafts and plastic blades; however, no helmets, face masks, mouth guards, shin guards or gloves were provided.

On April 21, 1976, Brad Berman was facing an opposing player moving toward goal. The opposing player made a backhanded shot and his follow through motion caused the stick blade to strike Brad's mouth. Three maxillary and two mandibular teeth were severed resulting in severe pain and extensive dental treatment.

As a result of the injuries, Brad Berman, a minor, by his parents and natural guardians, Leonard and Sheila Berman, and Leonard and Sheila Berman in their own individual capacities, filed a Complaint in Trespass against appellant, the Philadelphia Board of Education, in the Court of Common Pleas of Philadelphia County. A non-jury trial was conducted on December 12, 1980; however, a verdict was not then returned because the lower court reopened the case for the purpose of admitting life expectancy tables on Brad's life. On April 14, 1981, a verdict was finally entered for Brad Berman in the amount of $83,190.00 and for Leonard and Sheila Berman in the amount of $1,810.00. The appellant's exceptions and amended exceptions to the order of April 14, 1981 were denied, and an Order for Judgment in favor of the appellees in the amounts stated above was entered on August 4, 1981. This appeal followed.

It is the appellant's first contention that there was insufficient evidence to support a finding of negligence. The expert testimony of Cosmo R. Castaldi, a pediatric dentist, and member of the Safety and Protective Equipment Committee of the Amateur Hockey Association of the United States, testified on cross examination that no regulation existed in April, 1976, requiring any kind of mouth guards for participants of amateur ice or floor hockey; consequently, the appellant reasons, no standard of care was established upon which a finding of negligence could stand. Without a regulation to the contrary, Daniel Caputo, as the appellant's agent, was not required to furnish mouth guards. His general instructions, officiating games and calling penalties were sufficient actions to satisfy any applicable standard of care. We disagree with this reasoning and hold that the record supports a finding of negligence.

In *Rutter v. Northeastern Beaver County School District*, the plaintiff was a sixteen year old student member of the Riverside High School football squad. During a summer session of "jungle football," supervised and conducted by two Riverside coaches, the plaintiff was struck in the right eye by the outstretched hand of a teammate playing for the opposing side. A detached retina and blindness resulted. The particular style of football was especially dangerous in that it was played without any protective equipment whatsoever. At the close of plaintiff's case, the defendant's motion for a compulsory nonsuit was granted. The Pennsylvania Superior Court affirmed the lower court's denial of the plaintiff's motion to strike the nonsuit; the Supreme Court granted allocatur and reversed.

Among other issues, the Supreme Court in *Rutter*, considered whether there was enough evidence of negligence to present a jury question of the School District's liability. In concluding affirmatively, the *Rutter* court was led by the following facts: "jungle football" involved tackling and body blocking without equipment; it was organized, supervised and participated in by the coaches; and, the students played with intensity in an effort to impress the coaches. We recognize, of course, that our procedural review is somewhat different than that of the *Rutter* court. We are not reviewing the propriety of a lower court's granting of a compulsory nonsuit; rather, we concern ourselves with whether the evidence was sufficient to sustain the nonjury verdict. This distinction is inconsequential; as in *Rutter*, supra, we are determining whether there is enough evidence of negligence to perceive reasonable men disagreeing on the issue of liability.

In review of a lower court verdict, it is not the appellate court's function to substitute its judgment for that of the fact-finder so long as some credible evidence supports the verdict. All evidence must be interpreted in favor of the verdict winner below.

In light of these guidelines and our perusal of the record, we find enough evidence supporting a determination of negligence. Daniel Caputo was familiar with the safety and protective equipment available for ice or floor hockey. He was also aware that mouth injuries were recurring consequences of playing the sport. In fact, he appreciated the inherent risks enough to request on two or three separate occasions during the program's first year (1975–76) that the appellant purchase safety equipment for the students. The Philadelphia Board of Education, however, turned a deaf ear to these continual requests; no helmets, shin guards, gloves, face masks or mouth guards were provided for the students until 1977.

The standard of care was not diminished by Dr. Castaldi's admission that no rules or regulations for the adornment of mouth guards were imposed on floor hockey in 1976. The absence of a mouth guard mandate does not necessarily excuse the appellant's failure to impose similar rules itself. A duty of care is imposed upon a board of education for the safety and welfare of students under conditions such as those before us. Having found sufficient evidence to support a breach of that duty of care, we must defer to the lower court's judgment.

Appellant's second contention is that the appellee, Brad Berman, assumed the risk of incurring his injury and was contributory negligent; therefore, an affirmative defense precludes any finding of liability. When considering the tortuous acts of minors, we are led by a different set of guidelines and criteria. A determination of the negligence of a minor defendant begins with the application of three presumptions: (1) minors under the age of seven years are conclusively presumed incapable of negligence; (2) minors over the age of fourteen years are presumptively capable of negligence; (3) minors between the ages of seven and fourteen years are presumed incapable of negligence; however, such presumption is rebuttable and grows weaker as the fourteenth year grows closer. Although these presumptions were initially applied only to minor *defendant*, later decisional law found them applicable to a determination of contributory negligence also. The *Dunn* court opined that "utilization of the presumptions solely [with respect to a minor defendant, to] which their application is long recognized and soundly established, would result in holding a child less responsible for his acts when he is a plaintiff than when he is a defendant." In accordance with *Dunn*, we find the effects of immaturity to be equally applicable to a minor plaintiff and minor defendant; consequently, the presumptions of negligence espoused in *Kuhns*, can assist a minor whether he is pursuing or defending a negligence cause of action.

Appellee, Brad Berman, being eleven years of age at the time five of his teeth were severed, is presumed incapable of contributory negligence. Whether this presumption was rebutted engages a review of his conduct in light of the behavior of a child of similar age, intelligence and experience. Under cross-examination, Brad testified that he had played in "a numerous amount" of hockey games prior to the accident. It is not known whether his hockey experience extends to other leagues or years previous to the accident; accordingly, we conclude only that his experience with playing hockey was gathered entirely from those games played earlier in the season at Sharswood Elementary School. Furthermore, we find no evidence in the record that portrays Brad as a young boy possessed of superior intelligence thereby giving him exceptional perceptions of the risks and dangers of hockey. Neither his experience nor intelligence was so outstanding, then, to rebut the presumption against a finding of negligence. It should be noted further that Daniel Caputo testified to the nonoccurrence of any other injuries during the 1975–76 hockey campaign; therefore, Brad was unable to witness any serious injury by which we could charge him with knowing the risks involved. Without support in the record to the contrary, we must defer to the lower court's judgment that the presumption rendering Brad Berman incapable of contributory negligence was not rebutted by the appellant.

When judging the negligence or contributory negligence of parties less than majority age, an objective standard is applied. The standard applied to a minor who allegedly assumes the risk of incurring injury, however, is a subjective one, concerning only what a *particular* minor plaintiff knows, sees, hears, comprehends and appreciates. Through the application of different tests, a plaintiff may be deemed to not have assumed the risk, yet a finding of contributory negligence for the same behavior is possible. For this reason, assumption of the risk and contributory negligence remain separately applied defenses.

Unlike the theory of contributory negligence, we are not predisposed to apply the *Kuhn* presumptions to minors alleged to have assumed the risk of injuries; we find such presumptions to be incongruous to a defense theory whose success depends upon a purely subjective analysis. Without the aid of the *Kuhn* presumptions, we review Brad Berman's actions in light only of his own particular human characteristics. If by reason of his tender age and lack of intelligence, experience and information, Brad did not appreciate the dangers of floor hockey, assumption of risk is not a viable defense. The trial judge obviously reached that conclusion; absent some overwhelming evidence to the contrary, we will not deem this determination to be an abuse of discretion. . . . Judgment affirmed.

Governmental Immunity

Traditionally, school districts were immune from tort litigation. The theory was based on the idea that public schools were funded with taxpayers' dollars; hence, private individuals who were suing a school would ultimately be suing themselves. Additionally, because public schools were viewed as an arm of the state, they were protected under governmental immunity. But "with the greatest frequency, it is erroneously stated by American judges, text writers and commentators that, by the common law of England, school districts were not liable for negligence because of sovereign immunity, notwithstanding the fact that there were no free public schools in England before 1870, and there, schools have always been vicariously liable for negligence."[21]

Purzycki v. Town of Fairfield
Supreme Court of Connecticut, 1998
708 A. 2d 937

Opinion by Justice Borden.

The sole issue in this certified appeal is whether the plaintiffs failed to prove that the plaintiff Jason Purzycki (child) was subject to imminent harm, so as to come within an applicable exception to the doctrine of governmental immunity for discretionary acts performed by municipal employees. The named plaintiff, Gary Purzycki, filed this action as parent and next friend of the child, and on his own behalf for his medical expenses, against the defendants for injuries that the child had sustained when he was tripped by another student in a school hallway and suffered facial lacerations. The plaintiffs appeal from the judgment of the Appellate Court affirming the judgment of the trial court, which granted the defendants' motion to set aside the jury verdict for the plaintiffs. The plaintiffs claim that there was sufficient evidence for the jury to have found that the imminent harm exception to governmental immunity applied. The defendants contend that the plaintiffs failed to produce sufficient evidence to prove that governmental immunity did not apply. We agree with the plaintiffs and, accordingly, we reverse the judgment of the Appellate Court.

The Appellate Court decision sets forth the procedural history, and the facts that the jury reasonably could have found. "The [child] was an eight year old second grade student at the Roger Sherman School in Fairfield. School rules required that teachers escort students to an

---

[21]*Sherwood v. Moxee School District No. 90*, 363 P.2d 138, at 141 (1961)

all-purpose room, which served as a cafeteria during lunchtime. While eating lunch, the students were supervised by two adults. After eating lunch, the students were dismissed on a table by table basis to go to the playground for recess. To get to the playground from the lunchroom, the students proceeded down a hallway. The hallway was not monitored, but teachers in the classrooms abutting the hallway were instructed to keep their doors open in order to hear or see any activity in the hallway. This process was in accordance with the policies, rules and regulations promulgated by school officials.

"On June 13, 1989, at approximately 12:30 p.m., [the child], along with the rest of his class, was escorted to lunch by a teacher. After being dismissed for recess, [he] proceeded to his locker, where he removed his coat and hat. He then ran down the hallway, and, as he neared the exit door, another student extended his leg and tripped him. [The child] fell, head first, through the wire mesh window of the exit door and sustained injuries.

"The relevant procedural history is as follows. The plaintiffs filed a personal injury action against the defendants, sounding in negligence and nuisance. The defendants alleged as a special defense that they were shielded from liability pursuant to the doctrine of qualified governmental immunity. After a trial, the jury rendered a verdict in favor of the plaintiffs. In answers to special interrogatories, the jury stated that the defendants were 60 percent negligent, the [child] was 40 percent negligent and the defendants' negligence subjected [him] to imminent harm. The defendants moved to set aside the jury verdict, asserting that the plaintiffs failed to prove their claim that the imminent harm exception to the qualified governmental immunity doctrine applied to this case. The trial court granted the defendants' motion and rendered judgment notwithstanding the verdict."

The Appellate Court was divided, with the majority deciding that the jury reasonably could not have concluded that the lack of supervision, standing alone, subjected the child to imminent harm as required for liability under the doctrine of qualified governmental immunity. It concluded that the case was analogous to *Evon v. Andrews*. The majority determined that it was "[a] combination of the lack of supervision, [the child's] own conduct and the conduct of another student [which] caused the injuries," and as a result could "not rise to the level of imminence necessary to overcome the defendants' immunity."

The dissent concluded, however, that the facts of the present case were more analogous to *Burns v. Board of Education*. More specifically, because the question of the existence of imminent harm is a factual issue, and because there was sufficient evidence for the jury to have concluded that the lack of supervision subjected the child to a risk of imminent harm, the dissent concluded that the trial court should have rendered judgment in accordance with the jury verdict. Upon the plaintiffs' application, we granted certification to appeal limited to the following issue: "Was the trial court correct in setting aside the verdict on the ground that the plaintiffs failed to prove that the plaintiff child was subject to imminent harm, an exception to a municipal employee's immunity from liability when performing discretionary acts?"

I.   The plaintiffs claim that the trial court improperly set aside the jury verdict in their favor. The plaintiffs contend that the jury correctly found that the imminent harm–identifiable person exclusion to the doctrine of governmental immunity was applicable to this case. Specifically, they argue that "the danger of the . . . child's unsupervised use of the school hallways during recess was of an imminent nature as it was limited to the one-half hour lunch recess of the second grade lunch period for each day the child was compelled by statute to be on school premises." Further, the plaintiffs emphasize, as Judge Heiman noted in his dissent, that "'the principal of the elementary school admitted that if elementary schoolchildren are not supervised, they tend to run and engage in horseplay that often results in injuries.'" We agree with the plaintiffs.

"The trial court's function in setting aside a verdict and this court's role in reviewing that action are well settled. . . . The trial court should not set a verdict aside where there was some evidence upon which the jury could reasonably have based its verdict, but should not refuse to set it aside where the manifest injustice of the verdict is so plain and palpable as clearly to denote that some mistake was made by the jury in the application of legal principles. . . . Ultimately, the decision to set aside a verdict entails the exercise of a broad legal discretion. . . . Limiting that discretion, however, is the litigants' constitutional right to have issues of fact determined by a jury where there is room for a reasonable difference of opinion among fair-minded jurors. . . . Because, in setting aside the verdict, the trial court has deprived the party in whose favor the verdict was rendered of [the] constitutional right to have factual issues resolved by the jury, we must examine the evidential basis of the verdict itself to determine whether the trial court abused its discretion. . . . In so doing, we must consider the evidence, including reasonable inferences which may be drawn therefrom, in the light most favorable to the parties who were successful at trial. . . . "

"Although municipalities are generally immune from liability in tort, municipal employees historically were personally liable for their own tortuous conduct. The doctrine of governmental immunity has provided some exceptions to the general rule of tort liability for municipal employees. [A] municipal employee . . . has a qualified immunity in the performance of a governmental duty, but he may be liable if he misperforms a ministerial act, as opposed to a discretionary act." "The ultimate determination of whether qualified immunity applies is ordinarily a question of law for the court . . . [unless] there are unresolved factual issues material to the applicability of the defense . . . [where] resolution of those factual issues is properly left to the jury."

The plaintiffs concede that any duty owed by the defendants to the child was discretionary, not ministerial in nature. Therefore, in order to prevail, the plaintiffs' claim must fall within one of the recognized exceptions to qualified immunity for discretionary acts. "Our cases recognize three such exceptions: first, where the circumstances make it apparent to the public officer that his or her failure to act would be likely to subject an identifiable person to imminent harm . . . second, where a statute specifically provides for a cause of action against a municipality or municipal official for failure to enforce certain laws . . . and third, where the alleged acts involve malice, wantonness or intent to injure, rather than negligence."

The only exception to the qualified immunity of a municipal employee for discretionary acts that is relevant to the present case is the exception permitting a tort action in circumstances of likely imminent harm to an identifiable person. "We have construed this exception to apply not only to identifiable individuals but also to narrowly defined identified classes of foreseeable victims." Moreover, we have established specifically that schoolchildren who are statutorily compelled to attend school, during school hours on school days, can be an identifiable class of victims. Therefore, we must inquire whether there was sufficient evidence for a jury to have found that imminent harm existed under these circumstances.

In *Burns*, a schoolchild slipped and fell due to icy conditions on a main accessway of the school campus, during school hours. In that case, "the danger was limited to the duration of the temporary icy condition in this particularly 'treacherous' area of the campus . . . [and] the potential for harm from a fall on ice was significant and foreseeable." We concluded that governmental immunity was not a defense because a "[schoolchild] was one of a class of foreseeable victims to whom the superintendent owed a duty of protection in relation to the maintenance and safety of the school grounds. . . . "

Finally, the risk of harm was significant and foreseeable, as shown by the principal's testimony "that if elementary schoolchildren are not supervised, they tend to run and engage in horseplay that often results in injuries." Thus, we follow *Burns* and, under the facts of the present case, conclude that there was sufficient evidence from which the jury reasonably could have found a foreseeably dangerous condition that was limited in duration and geographical scope.

The defendants and the amici curiae claim that the risk of harm presented here was more similar to *Evon* because there was evidence that this type of harm had not previously occurred during the twenty-two year time period in which the same level of supervision had occurred. The defendants also point out that the hallway itself harbored no dangers or defects. We disagree. There was no evidence from which the jury could have inferred that no such injuries had occurred. Moreover, although the absence of prior similar incidents may induce a jury to find an absence of liability, it does not foreclose a finding of liability, as a matter of law, for the first incident that occurs.

Furthermore, as noted previously, the imminent harm was limited to a one-half hour period each day when the second grade students were dismissed to traverse an unsupervised hallway, when school administrators were aware that unsupervised children are more likely to run and engage in horseplay leading to injuries. Therefore, because the school administrators here had reason to foresee the danger that could occur on a daily basis, the harm in the present case was not as remote a possibility as was the harm in *Evon*.

II.   The defendants also offer four alternate grounds for affirming the Appellate Court's judgment, namely, that: (1) the doctrine of sovereign immunity would bar the plaintiffs' claim; (2) the jury reasonably could not have found that the defendants' negligence was an actual or proximate cause of the child's injuries; (3) there was insufficient evidence for the jury to have found a duty to supervise or a breach of such a duty; and (4) the defendants stood in loco parentis to the child and are thereby granted immunity. We do not find any of these alternate grounds persuasive.

A.   First, the defendants proffer the doctrine of sovereign immunity as a basis for affirming the judgment of the Appellate Court. The defendants argue that local boards of education are agents of the state when performing educational functions. They follow this assertion with the proposition that the state, unless it consents to be sued, enjoys sovereign immunity from suit, and that such immunity has been extended to agents of the state acting on its behalf and is not subject to the governmental immunity exceptions.

B.   Although these statements of the law are accurate, our jurisprudence has created a dichotomy in which local boards of education are agents of the state for some purposes and agents of the municipality for others. To determine whether the doctrine of sovereign immunity applies to a local school board, we look to whether the "action would operate to control or interfere with the activities of the state. . . . " The duty to supervise students is performed for the benefit of the municipality. Therefore, sovereign immunity is not implicated in the present case. . . .

C.   Next, the defendants claim that judgment should be affirmed because there was insufficient evidence to establish any basis upon which the jury could find the existence of a duty to supervise or a breach of such a duty. In support of this claim, the defendants argue, "Connecticut case law has never recognized, a specific duty to supervise students." *Heigl* does not, however, support the defendants' claim. In that case we declared: "Neither the General Statutes nor our decisional law has ever stated that a board of education has a specific duty to supervise high school students." The child in the present case was a second grade student and not a high school student. In *Heigl*, we further stated that, if such a duty existed, actions taken pursuant to such a duty are discretionary. On the basis of our conclusion that the plaintiffs have adequately proven the imminent harm to an identifiable person exception to governmental immunity for discretionary acts, this alternate theory also must fail.

D.   Finally, the defendants argue that the judgment of the Appellate Court should be affirmed because the defendants stood in loco parentis to the child and are thereby immune from liability for negligence. They state that a teacher in a public school stands in loco parentis toward a pupil, and that the parental immunity doctrine bars an unemancipated minor from bringing an action against his or her parents for injuries sustained by the negligence of the parents. Completing the syllogism, they argue that the tort liability of school officials for negligence must also fall within parental immunity. We are not persuaded.

"The purpose of the doctrine [of parental immunity] is to preserve the integrity and unity of the family and to avoid unnecessarily injecting 'the machinery of the state' into the day-to-day exercise of parental discretion. . . . There are few things more disruptive of familial harmony than a legal action by an unemancipated minor child against a parent." These concerns are not present here where an unemancipated minor and his parent are bringing an action against a school principal and a school board. Therefore, we decline to utilize this alternate ground as a basis for affirming the decision of the Appellate Court.

The judgment of the Appellate Court is reversed and the case is remanded to that court with direction to reverse the judgment of the trial court and to remand the case to that court with direction to render judgment for the plaintiffs in accordance with the jury verdict.

Waivers

It is common practice among public schools to ensure that parents sign a consent form or a waiver before their child participates in a field trip or sport related activity. Many individuals assume that waivers prohibit them from bringing a lawsuit. Such an assumption is incorrect. The majority of court rulings involving waivers generally find they are void and do not protect the school from negligence claims.

In *Wagenblast v. Odessa School District,* the court discussed the legality of a school district's requirement that parents or guardians sign a preprinted release form before their children participated in any school-related activity.[22] The form released the school from "liability resulting from any ordinary negligence that may arise in connection with the school district's interscholastic activities programs."[23] A group of parents claimed that such waivers were void against public policy, and the court agreed.

In its analysis the court held that the school had a duty to reasonably protect the students and hence could not waive such responsibility. "A school district owes a duty to its students to employ ordinary care and to anticipate reasonably foreseeable dangers so as to take precautions for protecting the children in its custody from such dangers. This duty extends to students engaged in interscholastic sports. As a natural incident to the relationship of a student athlete and his or her coach, the student athlete is usually placed under the coach's considerable degree of control. The student is thus subject to the risk that the school district or its agent will breach this duty of care."[24]

The importance of waivers, then, is to make parents aware of any risks, but they do not bar recovery by the parents. Nor does a waiver reduce the school's duty to protect students from foreseeable danger. Such a release form would be not only void but also against public policy.

MONETARY DAMAGES

IN CRIMINAL cases, the penalty can be imprisonment or fines. Under civil law, the losing defendant compensates the plaintiff for losses, generally through monetary reward. There are various types of monetary damages that can be awarded to the injured defendant. The usual forms are compensatory, nominal, and punitive.

The most common monetary damages are compensatory. Compensatory damages are awarded to compensate parties for their injuries. Typical compensatory damages include medical expenses. Nominal damages are small in nature and symbolic in reality. In this type of case, the injury may have been minor; hence, the court gives only a nominal amount in damages. Lastly, punitive damages are awarded when the court intends to punish the individual for his or her negligence. Typically, this is done when the jury wants to make an example of the defendant. Punitive damages are also granted in cases in which the act was outrageous or extreme.

---

[22]*Wagenblast v. Odessa School District,* 758 P.2d 968 (1988)
[23]Ibid., at 969
[24]Ibid., at 973

Summary

The law of torts is broad and is one of the most common areas of litigation within education law. Based on the theory of *respondeat superior*, the employer or educational institution is responsible for the acts of their employees while they are acting within the scope of their employment. Therefore, administrators are responsible for the acts of their faculty and staff while they are at work. Based on this theory, the idea of training faculty and staff on these issues is critical.

The two most common areas of tort law within education are intentional torts and negligence. Intentional torts must have the element of intent. On the other hand, for a claim of negligence to arise, there is no need to have the element of intent; rather one can be negligent by not acting as a reasonable prudent person. Such high standards requires educators be aware of such standards and act in such a manner. If an educator falls below this standard and the four elements of negligence are present (duty, breach, proximate cause, and damages), a claim for negligence may cost the school greatly.

There are defenses to negligent acts such as contributory, comparative negligence, as well as the assumption of risk. In the past, a common defense was governmental immunity, but such defense is becoming less effective based on the view that the school should be responsible for the acts of its employees. Lastly, since tort law falls under a civil claim, the injured plaintiff is typically seeking monetary damages as recovery which can range from compensatory to punitive, depending on the factual circumstances.

Discussion Questions

1. Define *respondeat superior* and explain how it applies to school districts.
2. Do the laws of agency and vicarious liability seem fair to the employer? Why do most lawsuits include both the employee and the employer?
3. Compare intentional torts to negligence.
4. Describe civil assault and battery. What is required to have a claim for each? Must they always occur simultaneously? Give examples of how they may occur in an educational environment.
5. Describe the four elements of negligence.
6. While the teacher of a third-grade class was temporarily out of the classroom, a student was injured when another student threw a ruler across the room. The student was hit in the face with the ruler, sustaining an injury requiring five stitches. The injured student's family sued the school district, claiming it failed to maintain a safe classroom environment. Discuss.
7. Describe a reasonable person. Does the definition change depending on the circumstances?
8. Discuss the various defenses a school district may claim in a negligence case. Give examples of when each would be appropriate to use as a legal defense.

9. Why do some states apply comparative negligence versus contributory negligence? What is the law in your state?
10. Describe the types of monetary damages an injured party may recover.

DEEPENING YOUR UNDERSTANDING

1. Teachers have a duty to properly supervise students. But is a teacher required to watch a student at all times? Research *Cirielo v. City of Milwaukee*, 150 N.W. 2d 460, and *Woodsmall v. Mount Diablo Unified School District*, 188 Cal. App. 2d 262, and compare and contrast the court decisions. Determine how long a teacher may be absent from the classroom without being negligent.
2. In small-group collaborations, list two situations in which a teacher would not be liable for leaving a classroom unattended.

3

RELIGION IN SCHOOLS

INTRODUCTION

Religion in schools is one of the most controversial issues in American educa-
tion. According to the First Amendment of the U.S. Constitution, "Congress
shall make no law respecting an establishment of religion or prohibiting the
free exercise thereof." In other words, the First Amendment does not prohibit
religion but states that the government will neither require nor prohibit any
individual from following his or her own religious belief. Because public
schools are viewed as arms of the state, they are required to remain neutral
about religion. Nevertheless, while our laws mandate a wall between church
and state, both the public and the courts continually dispute the height of
that wall.

PRAYER IN SCHOOLS

IN 1962, the issue of whether to allow prayer in school reached the Supreme Court in the
case of *Engel v. Vitale*.[1] In *Engel*, "the parents of ten students brought a claim in a New
York State Court insisting that use of prayer in the public schools was contrary to the beliefs, religions, or religious practices of both themselves and their children."[2] The prayer,
which each class read aloud in unison in the presence of a teacher at the beginning of

---

[1]370 U.S. 421, 82 S.Ct. 1261, 8 L.Ed.2d 601 (1962)
[2]Ibid., at 423

each school day, was "Almighty God, we acknowledge our dependence upon Thee, and we beg Thy blessings upon us, our parents, our teachers and our Country."[3]

Interpreting the intent of the First Amendment and holding that the school's requirement of a daily prayer was unconstitutional, the court stated:

> It has been argued that to apply the Constitution in such a way as to prohibit state laws respecting an establishment of religious services in public schools is to indicate hostility toward religion or toward prayer. Nothing, of course, could be more wrong. The history of man is inseparable from the history of religion. And perhaps it is not too much to say that since the beginning of that history many people have devoutly believed that "More things are wrought by prayer than this world dreams of." It was doubtless largely due to men who believed this that there grew up a sentiment that caused men to leave the cross-currents of officially established state religions and religious persecution in Europe and come to this country filled with the hope that they could find a place in which they could pray when they pleased to the God of their faith in the language they chose. And there were men of this same faith in the power of prayer who led the fight for adoption of our Constitution and also for our Bill of Rights with the very guarantees of religious freedom that forbid the sort of governmental activity which New York has attempted here. These men knew that the First Amendment, which tried to put an end to governmental control of religion and of prayer, was not written to destroy either. They knew rather that it was written to quiet well-justified fears which nearly all of them felt arising out of an awareness that governments of the past had shackled men's tongues to make them speak only the religious thoughts that government wanted them to speak and to pray only to the God that government wanted them to pray to. It is neither sacrilegious nor antireligious to say that each separate government in this country should stay out of the business of writing or sanctioning official prayers and leave that purely religious function to the people themselves and to those the people choose to look to for religious guidance.[4]

The following year, the Supreme Court analyzed two cases at once concerning whether or not the establishment clause of the First Amendment was violated when a Pennsylvania school required the reading, without comment, of the Bible and the Lord's Prayer at the opening of each school day. In its holding, the Court held that such prayer did violate the establishment clause and stated:

> The Amendment's purpose was not to strike merely at the official establishment of a single sect, creed or religion, outlawing only a formal relation such as had prevailed in England and some of the colonies. Necessarily it was to uproot all such relationships. But the object was broader than separating church and state in this narrow

---

[3]Ibid., at 422
[4]Ibid., at 434–435

sense. It was to create a complete and permanent separation of the spheres of religious activity and civil authority by comprehensively forbidding every form of public aid or support for religion.

Over the years, the Supreme Court has made it clear that school-initiated prayer is unconstitutional. But when these cases were first decided, many individuals within the community severely criticized the Court for its decision. In an attempt to work around the law, many schools have implemented school prayer and a moment of silence, as illustrated in *Wallace v. Jaffree.*[5]

Wallace v. Jaffree
Supreme Court of the United States, 1985
472 U.S. 38

Justice Stevens delivered the opinion.

At an early stage of this litigation, the constitutionality of three Alabama statutes was questioned: (1) § 16-1-20, enacted in 1978, which authorized a 1-minute period of silence in all public schools "for meditation"; (2) § 16-1-20.1, enacted in 1981, which authorized a period of silence "for meditation or voluntary prayer"; and (3) § 16-1-20.2, enacted in 1982, which authorized teachers to lead "willing students" in a prescribed prayer to "Almighty God . . . the Creator and Supreme Judge of the world."

At the preliminary-injunction stage of this case, the District Court distinguished § 16-1-20 from the other two statutes. It then held that there was "nothing wrong" with § 16-1-20, but that §§ 16-1-20.1 and 16-1-20.2 were both invalid because the sole purpose of both was "an effort on the part of the State of Alabama to encourage a religious activity." After the trial on the merits, the District Court did not change its interpretation of these two statutes, but held that they were constitutional because, in its opinion, Alabama has the power to establish a state religion if it chooses to do so.

The Court of Appeals agreed with the District Court's initial interpretation of the purpose of both § 16-1-20.1 and § 16-1-20.2, and held them both unconstitutional. We have already affirmed the Court of Appeals' holding with respect to § 16-1-20.2. Moreover, appellees have not questioned the holding that § 16-1-20 is valid. Thus, the narrow question for decision is whether § 16-1-20.1, which authorizes a period of silence for "meditation or voluntary prayer," is a law respecting the establishment of religion within the meaning of the First Amendment.

I

Appellee Ishmael Jaffree is a resident of Mobile County, Alabama. On May 28, 1982, he filed a complaint on behalf of three of his minor children; two of them were second-grade

---

[5]472 U.S. 38 (1985)

students and the third was then in kindergarten. The complaint named members of the Mobile County School Board, various school officials, and the minor plaintiffs' three teachers as defendants. The complaint alleged that the appellees brought the action "seeking principally a declaratory judgment and an injunction restraining the Defendants and each of them from maintaining or allowing the maintenance of regular religious prayer services or other forms of religious observances in the Mobile County Public Schools in violation of the First Amendment as made applicable to states by the Fourteenth Amendment to the United States Constitution." The complaint further alleged that two of the children had been subjected to various acts of religious indoctrination "from the beginning of the school year in September, 1981"; that the defendant teachers had "on a daily basis" led their classes in saying certain prayers in unison; that the minor children were exposed to ostracism from their peer group class members if they did not participate; and that Ishmael Jaffree had repeatedly but unsuccessfully requested that the devotional services be stopped. The original complaint made no reference to any Alabama statute. . . .

In November 1982, the District Court held a 4-day trial on the merits. The evidence related primarily to the 1981–1982 academic year—the year after the enactment of § 16-1-20.1 and prior to the enactment of § 16-1-20.2. The District Court found that during that academic year each of the minor plaintiffs' teachers had led classes in prayer activities, even after being informed of appellees' objections to these activities.[6] In its lengthy conclusions of law, the District Court reviewed a number of opinions of this Court interpreting the Establishment Clause of the First Amendment, and then embarked on a fresh examination of the question whether the First Amendment imposes any barrier to the establishment of an official religion by the State of Alabama. After reviewing at length what it perceived to be newly discovered historical evidence, the District Court concluded that "the establishment

---

[6]The District Court wrote: "Defendant Boyd, as early as September 16, 1981, led her class at E. R. Dickson in singing the following phrase:

'God is great, God is good,
'Let us thank him for our food,
'bow our heads we all are fed,
'Give us Lord our daily bread.
'Amen!'

The recitation of this phrase continued on a daily basis throughout the 1981–82 school year.

Defendant Pixie Alexander has led her class at Craighead in reciting the following phrase:

'God is great, God is good,
'Let us thank him for our food.'

'Further, defendant Pixie Alexander had her class recite the following, which is known as the Lord's Prayer:

'Our Father, which are in heaven, hallowed be Thy name. Thy kingdom come. Thy will be done on earth as it is in heaven. Give us this day our daily bread and forgive us our debts as we forgive our debtors. And lead us not into temptation but deliver us from evil for thine is the kingdom and the power and the glory forever. Amen.'

The recitation of these phrases continued on a daily basis throughout the 1981–82 school year.

Ms. Green admitted that she frequently leads her class in singing the following song: 'For health and strength and daily food, we praise Thy name, Oh Lord.' This activity continued throughout the school year, despite the fact that Ms. Green had knowledge that plaintiff did not want his child exposed to the above-mentioned song" (*Jaffree v. Board of School Commissioners of Mobile County*, 554 F.Supp., at 1107–1108).

clause of the first amendment to the United States Constitution does not prohibit the state from establishing a religion." In a separate opinion, the District Court dismissed appellees' challenge to the three Alabama statutes because of a failure to state any claim for which relief could be granted. The court's dismissal of this challenge was also based on its conclusion that the Establishment Clause did not bar the States from establishing a religion. . . .

II

Our unanimous affirmance of the Court of Appeals' judgment concerning § 16-1-20.2 makes it unnecessary to comment at length on the District Court's remarkable conclusion that the Federal Constitution imposes no obstacle to Alabama's establishment of a state religion. Before analyzing the precise issue that is presented to us, it is nevertheless appropriate to recall how firmly embedded in our constitutional jurisprudence is the proposition that the several States have no greater power to restrain the individual freedoms protected by the First Amendment than does the Congress of the United States.

As is plain from its text, the First Amendment was adopted to curtail the power of Congress to interfere with the individual's freedom to believe, to worship, and to express himself in accordance with the dictates of his own conscience. Until the Fourteenth Amendment was added to the Constitution, the First Amendment's restraints on the exercise of federal power simply did not apply to the States. But when the Constitution was amended to prohibit any State from depriving any person of liberty without due process of law, that Amendment imposed the same substantive limitations on the States' power to legislate that the First Amendment had always imposed on the Congress' power. This Court has confirmed and endorsed this elementary proposition of law time and time again. . . .

Just as the right to speak and the right to refrain from speaking are complementary components of a broader concept of individual freedom of mind, so also the individual's freedom to choose his own creed is the counterpart of his right to refrain from accepting the creed established by the majority. At one time it was thought that this right merely proscribed the preference of one Christian sect over another, but would not require equal respect for the conscience of the infidel, the atheist, or the adherent of a non-Christian faith such as Islam or Judaism. But when the underlying principle has been examined in the crucible of litigation, the Court has unambiguously concluded that the individual freedom of conscience protected by the First Amendment embraces the right to select any religious faith or none at all. This conclusion derives support not only from the interest in respecting the individual's freedom of conscience, but also from the conviction that religious beliefs worthy of respect are the product of free and voluntary choice by the faithful, and from recognition of the fact that the political interest in forestalling intolerance extends beyond intolerance among Christian sects—or even intolerance among "religions"—to encompass intolerance of the disbeliever and the uncertain. As Justice Jackson eloquently stated in *West Virginia Board of Education v. Barnette*:

> *If there is any fixed star in our constitutional constellation, it is that no official, high or petty, can prescribe what shall be orthodox in politics, nationalism, religion, or other matters of opinion or force citizens to confess by word or act their faith therein.*

The State of Alabama, no less than the Congress of the United States, must respect that basic truth.

III

When the Court has been called upon to construe the breadth of the Establishment Clause, it has examined the criteria developed over a period of many years. Thus, in *Lemon v. Kurtzman,* we wrote:

> *Every analysis in this area must begin with consideration of the cumulative criteria developed by the Court over many years. Three such tests may be gleaned from our cases. First, the statute must have a secular legislative purpose; second, its principal or primary effect must be one that neither advances nor inhibits religion; finally, the statute must not foster "an excessive government entanglement with religion."*

It is the first of these three criteria that is most plainly implicated by this case. As the District Court correctly recognized, no consideration of the second or third criteria is necessary if a statute does not have a clearly secular purpose. For even though a statute that is motivated in part by a religious purpose may satisfy the first criterion, the First Amendment requires that a statute must be invalidated if it is entirely motivated by a purpose to advance religion.

In applying the purpose test, it is appropriate to ask "whether government's actual purpose is to endorse or disapprove of religion." In this case, the answer to that question is dispositive. For the record not only provides us with an unambiguous affirmative answer, but it also reveals that the enactment of § 16-1-20.1 was not motivated by any clearly secular purpose—indeed, the statute had no secular purpose.

IV

The sponsor of the bill that became § 16-1-20.1, Senator Donald Holmes, inserted into the legislative record—apparently without dissent—a statement indicating that the legislation was an "effort to return voluntary prayer" to the public schools. Later Senator Holmes confirmed this purpose before the District Court. In response to the question whether he had any purpose for the legislation other than returning voluntary prayer to public schools, he stated: "No, I did not have no other purpose in mind." The State did not present evidence of any secular purpose.

The unrebutted evidence of legislative intent contained in the legislative record and in the testimony of the sponsor of § 16-1-20.1 is confirmed by a consideration of the relationship between this statute and the two other measures that were considered in this case. The District Court found that the 1981 statute and its 1982 sequel had a common, nonsecular purpose. The wholly religious character of the later enactment is plainly evident from its text. When the differences between § 16-1-20.1 and its 1978 predecessor, § 16-1-20, are examined, it is equally clear that the 1981 statute has the same wholly religious character.

There are only three textual differences between § 16-1-20.1 and § 16-1-20: (1) the earlier statute applies only to grades one through six, whereas § 16-1-20.1 applies to all grades;

(2) the earlier statute uses the word "shall" whereas § 16-1-20.1 uses the word "may"; (3) the earlier statute refers only to "meditation" whereas § 16-1-20.1 refers to "meditation or voluntary prayer." The first difference is of no relevance in this litigation because the minor appellees were in kindergarten or second grade during the 1981–1982 academic year. The second difference would also have no impact on this litigation because the mandatory language of § 16-1-20 continued to apply to grades one through six. Thus, the only significant textual difference is the addition of the words "or voluntary prayer."

The legislative intent to return prayer to the public schools is, of course, quite different from merely protecting every student's right to engage in voluntary prayer during an appropriate moment of silence during the schoolday. The 1978 statute already protected that right, containing nothing that prevented any student from engaging in voluntary prayer during a silent minute of meditation. Appellants have not identified any secular purpose that was not fully served by § 16-1-20 before the enactment of § 16-1-20.1. Thus, only two conclusions are consistent with the text of § 16-1-20.1: (1) the statute was enacted to convey a message of state endorsement and promotion of prayer; or (2) the statute was enacted for no purpose. No one suggests that the statute was nothing but a meaningless or irrational act.

We must, therefore, conclude that the Alabama Legislature intended to change existing law and that it was motivated by the same purpose that the Governor's answer to the second amended complaint expressly admitted; that the statement inserted in the legislative history revealed; and that Senator Holmes' testimony frankly described. The legislature enacted § 16-1-20.1, despite the existence of § 16-1-20 for the sole purpose of expressing the State's endorsement of prayer activities for one minute at the beginning of each schoolday. The addition of "or voluntary prayer" indicates that the State intended to characterize prayer as a favored practice. Such an endorsement is not consistent with the established principle that the government must pursue a course of complete neutrality toward religion. . . .

Keeping in mind, as we must, "both the fundamental place held by the Establishment Clause in our constitutional scheme and the myriad, subtle ways in which Establishment Clause values can be eroded," we conclude that § 16-1-20.1 violates the First Amendment. The judgment of the Court of Appeals is affirmed.

Concur by: Justice Powell and Justice O'Connor.

A more recent case involved parents who brought suit against a New York school district for implementing the Bedford Program, which allegedly involves "the promotion of Satanism and occultism, pagan religions and a New Age Spirituality."[7] This included encouraging students to make worry dolls or purchase them from the school store, celebrating Earth Day by inscribing tombstones with the names of extinct birds and animals, as well as meditating and learning yoga. The Court determined that such acts were unconstitutional and set forth an injunction to stop all school sponsorship of the earth, remove all worry dolls and religious symbols from the school, and discontinue all references to God.

---

[7] *Altman v. Bedford Central School District*, 45 F. Supp. 2d 368 (1999)

THE LEMON TEST

IN ITS 1972 decision in the *Lemon v. Kurtzman* case, the Supreme Court set forth a three-part establishment clause test.[8] The test, now commonly referred to as the "Lemon test," is used by the courts to determine whether or not a government policy is unconstitutional.

Lemon v. Kurtzman, while controversial, set forth a standard test by which to analyze a violation of the establishment clause. According to the analysis, government action is permitted if it (1) reflects a clearly secular purpose, (2) has a primary effect that neither advances nor inhibits religion, and (3) avoids excessive government entanglement with religion. If any one of the three parts of the test is not met, the government action will be in violation of the establishment clause.

Today, the Lemon test is frequently debated and criticized.[9] Nevertheless, the five-to-four decision made in *Lemon v. Kurtzman* has not been overturned and hence is still the law.

PRAYER AT GRADUATION

PRAYER at graduation has been common practice at many public schools across the country. But is prayer at graduation ever allowed? If so, when? Such questions have been answered by numerous state courts, however, the landmark case of *Lee v. Weisman* decided by the Supreme Court clarified that school-initiated prayer was unconstitutional. The *Lee v. Weisman* case arose when a middle school principal invited members of the clergy to give an invocation at the school's graduation ceremony. In its holding, the Court stated:

> There can be "no doubt" that the "invocation of God's blessings" delivered at Nathan Bishop Middle School "is a religious activity." In the words of Engel, the rabbi's prayer "is a solemn avowal of divine faith and supplication for the blessings of the Almighty. The nature of such a prayer has always been religious." The question then is whether the government has "placed its official stamp of approval" on the prayer. As the Court ably demonstrates, when the government "composes official prayers," selects the member of the clergy to deliver the prayer, has the prayer delivered at a public school event that is planned, supervised, and given by school officials, and pressures students to attend and participate in the prayer, there can be no doubt that the government is advancing and promoting religion. As our prior decisions teach us, it is this that the Constitution prohibits.

The holding in *Lee v. Weisman* was clear about the constitutionality of school-initiated prayer at graduation. The case did not, however, respond to the issue of whether or not

---

[8]403 U.S. 602 (1971)
[9]See *Lee v. Weisman*, 505 U.S. 577, 644–645 (1992) (Scalia J., jointed by Thomas, J., dissenting)

student-initiated prayer at graduation was permitted, nor did it address whether or not the establishment clause would be violated if students included prayers in their graduation speeches. In many cases today, decisions on whether to allow prayer at graduation are based on who organizes and initiates the prayer. However, school-sponsored prayer is strictly prohibited.

PRAYER AT SPORTING EVENTS

ANOTHER common practice has been players' group prayer before various school sporting events. Until recently, schools continued this practice under the assumption that it was constitutional as long as the prayer was not led or organized by school officials. In 2000, the Supreme Court reviewed the issue of student-led prayer at home football games and clarified some issues that have been unanswered in the past.

Santa Fe Independent School District v. Jane Doe
Supreme Court of the United States, 2000
530 U.S. 290

Opinion by Justice Stevens.

Prior to 1995, the Santa Fe High School student who occupied the school's elective office of student council chaplain delivered a prayer over the public address system before each varsity football game for the entire season. This practice, along with others, was challenged in District Court as a violation of the Establishment Clause of the First Amendment. While these proceedings were pending in the District Court, the school district adopted a different policy that permits, but does not require, prayer initiated and led by a student at all home games. The District Court entered an order modifying that policy to permit only nonsectarian, nonproselytizing prayer. The Court of Appeals held that, even as modified by the District Court, the football prayer policy was invalid. We granted the school district's petition for certiorari to review that holding.

I

The Santa Fe Independent School District (District) is a political subdivision of the State of Texas, responsible for the education of more than 4,000 students in a small community in the southern part of the State. The District includes the Santa Fe High School, two primary schools, an intermediate school and the junior high school. Respondents are two sets of current or former students and their respective mothers. One family is Mormon and the other is Catholic. The District Court permitted respondents (Does) to litigate anonymously to protect them from intimidation or harassment.

Respondents commenced this action in April 1995 and moved for a temporary restraining order to prevent the District from violating the Establishment Clause at the imminent graduation exercises. In their complaint the Does alleged that the District had engaged in several proselytizing practices, such as promoting attendance at a Baptist revival meeting, encouraging membership in religious clubs, chastising children who held minority religious beliefs, and distributing Gideon Bibles on school premises. They also alleged that the District allowed students to read Christian invocations and benedictions from the stage at graduation ceremonies, and to deliver overtly Christian prayers over the public address system at home football games.[10]

On May 10, 1995, the District Court entered an interim order addressing a number of different issues. With respect to the impending graduation, the order provided that "nondenominational prayer" consisting of "an invocation and/or benediction" could be presented by a senior student or students selected by members of the graduating class. The text of the prayer was to be determined by the students, without scrutiny or preapproval by school officials. References to particular religious figures "such as Mohammed, Jesus, Buddha, or the like" would be permitted "as long as the general thrust of the prayer is non-proselytizing."

In response to that portion of the order, the District adopted a series of policies over several months dealing with prayer at school functions. The policies enacted in May and July for graduation ceremonies provided the format for the August and October policies for football games. The May policy provided: "The board has chosen to permit the graduating senior class, with the advice and counsel of the senior class principal or designee, to elect by secret ballot to choose whether an invocation and benediction shall be part of the graduation exercise. If so chosen the class shall elect by secret ballot, from a list of student volunteers, students to deliver nonsectarian, nonproselytizing invocations and benedictions for the purpose of solemnizing their graduation ceremonies."

The parties stipulated that after this policy was adopted, "the senior class held an election to determine whether to have an invocation and benediction at the commencement [and that the] class voted, by secret ballot, to include prayer at the high school graduation." In a second vote the class elected two seniors to deliver the invocation and benediction.[11]

In July, the District enacted another policy eliminating the requirement that invocations and benedictions be "nonsectarian and nonproselytising," but also providing that if the

---

[10]At the 1994 graduation ceremony the senior class president delivered this invocation: "Please bow your heads. 'Dear heavenly Father, thank you for allowing us to gather here safely tonight. We thank you for the wonderful year you have allowed us to spend together as students of Santa Fe. We thank you for our teachers who have devoted many hours to each of us. Thank you, Lord, for our parents and may each one receive the special blessing. We pray also for a blessing and guidance as each student moves forward in the future. Lord, bless this ceremony and give us all a safe journey home. In Jesus' name we pray.'"

[11]The student giving the invocation thanked the Lord for keeping the class safe through 12 years of school and for gracing students' lives with two special people and closed with "Lord, we ask that You keep Your hand upon us during this ceremony and to help us keep You in our hearts through the rest of our lives. In God's name we pray. Amen." The student benediction was similar in content and closed with "Lord, we ask for Your protection as we depart to our next destination and watch over us as we go our separate ways. Grant each of us a safe trip and keep us secure throughout the night. In Your name we pray. Amen."

District were to be enjoined from enforcing that policy, the May policy would automatically become effective.

The August policy, which was titled "Prayer at Football Games," was similar to the July policy for graduations. It also authorized two student elections, the first to determine whether "invocations" should be delivered, and the second to select the spokesperson to deliver them. Like the July policy, it contained two parts, an initial statement that omitted any requirement that the content of the invocation be "nonsectarian and nonproselytising," and a fallback provision that automatically added that limitation if the preferred policy should be enjoined. On August 31, 1995, according to the parties' stipulation, "the district's high school students voted to determine whether a student would deliver prayer at varsity football games . . . . The students chose to allow a student to say a prayer at football games." A week later, in a separate election, they selected a student "to deliver the prayer at varsity football games." . . .

The District Court did enter an order precluding enforcement of the first, open-ended policy. Relying on our decision in *Lee v. Weisman,* it held that the school's "action must not 'coerce anyone to support or participate in' a religious exercise." Applying that test, it concluded that the graduation prayers appealed "to distinctively Christian beliefs," and that delivering a prayer "over the school's public address system prior to each football and baseball game coerces student participation in religious events." Both parties appealed, the District contending that the enjoined portion of the October policy was permissible and the Does contending that both alternatives violated the Establishment Clause. The Court of Appeals majority agreed with the Does. . . .

We granted the District's petition for certiorari, limited to the following question: "Whether petitioner's policy permitting student-led, student-initiated prayer at football games violates the Establishment Clause." We conclude, as did the Court of Appeals, that it does.

II

The first Clause in the First Amendment to the Federal Constitution provides that "Congress shall make no law respecting an establishment of religion, or prohibiting the free exercise thereof." The Fourteenth Amendment imposes those substantive limitations on the legislative power of the States and their political subdivisions. In *Lee v. Weisman,* we held that a prayer delivered by a rabbi at a middle school graduation ceremony violated that Clause. Although this case involves student prayer at a different type of school function, our analysis is properly guided by the principles that we endorsed in *Lee*.

As we held in that case: "The principle that government may accommodate the free exercise of religion does not supersede the fundamental limitations imposed by the Establishment Clause. It is beyond dispute that, at a minimum, the Constitution guarantees that government may not coerce anyone to support or participate in religion or its exercise, or otherwise act in a way which 'establishes a [state] religion or religious faith, or tends to do so.'"

In this case the District first argues that this principle is inapplicable to its October policy because the messages are private student speech, not public speech. It reminds us that "there is a crucial difference between government speech endorsing religion, which the Establishment Clause forbids, and private speech endorsing religion, which the Free Speech and Free Exercise Clauses protect." We certainly agree with that distinction, but we are not persuaded that the pregame invocations should be regarded as "private speech."

These invocations are authorized by a government policy and take place on government property at government-sponsored school-related events. Of course, not every message delivered under such circumstances is the government's own. We have held, for example, that an individual's contribution to a government-created forum was not government speech. . . . [I]t is clear that the pregame ceremony is not the type of forum discussed in those cases. The Santa Fe school officials simply do not "evince either 'by policy or by practice,' any intent to open the [pregame ceremony] to 'indiscriminate use,' . . . by the student body generally." Rather, the school allows only one student, the same student for the entire season, to give the invocation. The statement or invocation, moreover, is subject to particular regulations that confine the content and topic of the student's message. . . .

In this case, as we found in *Lee,* the "degree of school involvement" makes it clear that the pregame prayers bear "the imprint of the State and thus put school-age children who objected in an untenable position."

The District has attempted to disentangle itself from the religious messages by developing the two-step student election process. The text of the October policy, however, exposes the extent of the school's entanglement. The elections take place at all only because the school "board has chosen to permit students to deliver a brief invocation and/or message." The elections thus "shall" be conducted "by the high school student council" and "upon advice and direction of the high school principal." The decision whether to deliver a message is first made by majority vote of the entire student body, followed by a choice of the speaker in a separate, similar majority election. Even though the particular words used by the speaker are not determined by those votes, the policy mandates that the "statement or invocation" be "consistent with the goals and purposes of this policy," which are "to solemnize the event, to promote good sportsmanship and student safety, and to establish the appropriate environment for the competition."

In addition to involving the school in the selection of the speaker, the policy, by its terms, invites and encourages religious messages. The policy itself states that the purpose of the message is "to solemnize the event." A religious message is the most obvious method of solemnizing an event. Moreover, the requirements that the message "promote good citizenship" and "establish the appropriate environment for competition" further narrow the types of message deemed appropriate, suggesting that a solemn, yet nonreligious, message, such as commentary on United States foreign policy, would be prohibited. Indeed, the only type of message that is expressly endorsed in the text is an "invocation"—a term that primarily describes an appeal for divine assistance. In fact, as used in the past at Santa Fe High School, an "invocation" has always entailed a focused religious message. Thus, the expressed purposes of the policy encourage the selection of a religious message, and that is precisely how the students understand the policy. The results of the elections described in the parties' stipulation make it clear that the students understood that the central question before them was whether prayer should be a part of the pregame ceremony. We recognize the important role that public worship plays in many communities, as well as the sincere desire to include public prayer as a part of various occasions so as to mark those occasions' significance. But such religious activity in public schools, as elsewhere, must comport with the First Amendment.

The actual or perceived endorsement of the message, moreover, is established by factors beyond just the text of the policy. Once the student speaker is selected and the message composed, the invocation is then delivered to a large audience assembled as part of a regularly scheduled, school-sponsored function conducted on school property. The message is broadcast over the school's public address system, which remains subject to the control of school officials. It is fair to assume that the pregame ceremony is clothed in the traditional indicia of school sporting events, which generally include not just the team, but also cheerleaders and band members dressed in uniforms sporting the school name and mascot. The school's name is likely written in large print across the field and on banners and flags. The crowd will certainly include many who display the school colors and insignia on their school T-shirts, jackets, or hats and who may also be waving signs displaying the school name. It is in a setting such as this that "the board has chosen to permit" the elected student to rise and give the "statement or invocation."

In this context the members of the listening audience must perceive the pregame message as a public expression of the views of the majority of the student body delivered with the approval of the school administration. In cases involving state participation in a religious activity, one of the relevant questions is "whether an objective observer, acquainted with the text, legislative history, and implementation of the statute, would perceive it as a state endorsement of prayer in public schools."

Regardless of the listener's support for, or objection to, the message, an objective Santa Fe High School student will unquestionably perceive the inevitable pregame prayer as stamped with her school's seal of approval.

The text and history of this policy, moreover, reinforce our objective student's perception that the prayer is, in actuality, encouraged by the school. When a governmental entity professes a secular purpose for an arguably religious policy, the government's characterization is, of course, entitled to some deference. But it is nonetheless the duty of the courts to "distinguish a sham secular purpose from a sincere one."

. . . Furthermore, regardless of whether one considers a sporting event an appropriate occasion for solemnity, the use of an invocation to foster such solemnity is impermissible when, in actuality, it constitutes prayer sponsored by the school. And it is unclear what type of message would be both appropriately "solemnizing" under the District's policy and yet non-religious.

Most striking to us is the evolution of the current policy from the long-sanctioned office of "Student Chaplain" to the candidly titled "Prayer at Football Games" regulation. This history indicates that the District intended to preserve the practice of prayer before football games. The conclusion that the District viewed the October policy simply as a continuation of the previous policies is dramatically illustrated by the fact that the school did not conduct a new election, pursuant to the current policy, to replace the results of the previous election, which occurred under the former policy. Given these observations, and in light of the school's history of regular delivery of a student-led prayer at athletic events, it is reasonable to infer that the specific purpose of the policy was to preserve a popular "state-sponsored religious practice."

School sponsorship of a religious message is impermissible because it sends the ancillary message to members of the audience who are nonadherants "that they are outsiders, not full members of the political community, and an accompanying message to adherants that they are insiders, favored members of the political community." The delivery of such a message—over the school's public address system, by a speaker representing the student body, under the supervision of school faculty, and pursuant to a school policy that explicitly and implicitly encourages public prayer—is not properly characterized as "private" speech.

III

The District next argues that its football policy is distinguishable from the graduation prayer in *Lee* because it does not coerce students to participate in religious observances. Its argument has two parts: first, that there is no impermissible government coercion because the pregame messages are the product of student choices; and second, that there is really no coercion at all because attendance at an extracurricular event, unlike a graduation ceremony, is voluntary. . . .

One of the purposes served by the Establishment Clause is to remove debate over this kind of issue from governmental supervision or control. We explained in *Lee* that the "preservation and transmission of religious beliefs and worship is a responsibility and a choice committed to the private sphere." The two student elections authorized by the policy, coupled with the debates that presumably must precede each, impermissibly invade that private sphere. The election mechanism, when considered in light of the history in which the policy in question evolved, reflects a device the District put in place that determines whether religious messages will be delivered at home football games. The mechanism encourages divisiveness along religious lines in a public school setting, a result at odds with the Establishment Clause. Although it is true that the ultimate choice of student speaker is "attributable to the students."

The District further argues that attendance at the commencement ceremonies at issue in *Lee* "differs dramatically" from attendance at high school football games, which it contends "are of no more than passing interest to many students" and are "decidedly extracurricular," thus dissipating any coercion. Attendance at a high school football game, unlike showing up for class, is certainly not required in order to receive a diploma. Moreover, we may assume that the District is correct in arguing that the informal pressure to attend an athletic event is not as strong as a senior's desire to attend her own graduation ceremony.

There are some students, however, such as cheerleaders, members of the band, and, of course, the team members themselves, for whom seasonal commitments mandate their attendance, sometimes for class credit. The District also minimizes the importance to many students of attending and participating in extracurricular activities as part of a complete educational experience. To assert that high school students do not feel immense social pressure, or have a truly genuine desire, to be involved in the extracurricular event that is American high school football is "formalistic in the extreme." We stressed in *Lee* the obvious observation that "adolescents are often susceptible to pressure from their peers towards conformity, and that the influence is strongest in matters of social convention." High school home football games are traditional gatherings of a school community; they bring together students and faculty as well as friends and family from years present and past to root for a common cause. Undoubtedly, the games are not important to some students, and they voluntarily choose not to attend. For many others, however, the choice between whether to attend these games or to risk facing a personally offensive religious ritual is in no practical sense an easy one. The Constitution, moreover, demands that the school may not force this difficult choice upon these students for "it is a tenet of the First Amendment that the State cannot require one of its citizens to forfeit his or her rights and benefits as the price of resisting conformance to state-sponsored religious practice."

Even if we regard every high school student's decision to attend a home football game as purely voluntary, we are nevertheless persuaded that the delivery of a pregame prayer has the improper effect of coercing those present to participate in an act of religious worship. For "the government may no more use social pressure to enforce orthodoxy than it may use more direct means." As in *Lee*, "what to most believers may seem nothing more than a reasonable request that the nonbeliever respect their religious practices, in a school context may appear to the nonbeliever or dissenter to be an attempt to employ the machinery of the State to enforce a religious orthodoxy." The constitutional command will not permit the District "to exact religious conformity from a student as the price" of joining her classmates at a varsity football game.

The Religion Clauses of the First Amendment prevent the government from making any law respecting the establishment of religion or prohibiting the free exercise thereof. By no means do these commands impose a prohibition on all religious activity in our public schools. Indeed, the common purpose of the Religion Clauses "is to secure religious liberty." Thus, nothing in the Constitution as interpreted by this Court prohibits any public school student from voluntarily praying at any time before, during, or after the schoolday. But the religious liberty protected by the Constitution is abridged when the State affirmatively sponsors the particular religious practice of prayer. . . .

The judgment of the Court of Appeals is, accordingly, affirmed. It is so ordered.

Dissent by Justice Rehnquist, with whom Justice Scalia and Justice Thomas join, dissenting.

Best Practices

- Because each state law varies on the issue of student-led prayer at graduation, know the decisions of both your state and federal district courts on this issue.

- Consult your school attorney before permitting student-sponsored or student-initiated prayer at graduation because the laws change constantly and vary from state to state.

Religious Displays and Holiday Celebrations

DURING the school year, teachers and students commonly celebrate many holidays. Pictures of Santa Claus, the Easter Bunny, and Halloween witches hang on the walls of public schools throughout the year. Most holidays, however, are based on religious celebration; hence, school administrators must ensure that teachers and staff are careful not to promote or enhance a certain religion in the process of celebrating these events. As the Eighth Circuit Court of Appeals has illustrated, guidelines should be clear about how public schools can observe various holidays without violating the establishment clause.

Florey v. Sioux Falls School District
U.S. Court of Appeals, Eighth Circuit, 1980
619 F.2d 1311

Opinion by Circuit Judge Heaney.

I

In response to complaints that public school Christmas assemblies in 1977 and prior years constituted religious exercises, the School Board of Sioux Falls, South Dakota, set up a citizens' committee to study the relationship between church and state as applied to school functions. The committee's deliberations, which lasted for several months, culminated in the formulation of a policy statement and set of rules outlining the bounds of permissible school activity. After a public hearing, the School Board adopted the policy statement and rules recommended by the committee.

The appellants brought suit for declaratory and injunctive relief, alleging that the policy statement and the rules adopted by the School Board violate the Establishment and Free Exercise Clauses of the First Amendment to the United States Constitution. The district court reviewed the practices of the Sioux Falls School District and found that the 1977 Christmas program that was the subject of the initial complaints "exceeded the boundaries of what is constitutionally permissible under the Establishment Clause." The court also found, however, that programs similar to the 1977 Christmas program would not be permitted under the new School Board guidelines and concluded that the new rules, if properly administered and narrowly construed, would not run afoul of the First Amendment. . . .

II

The close relationship between religion and American history and culture has frequently been recognized by the Supreme Court of the United States. Nevertheless, the First Amendment to the Constitution explicitly prescribes the relationship between religion and government: "Congress shall make no law respecting an establishment of religion, or prohibiting the free exercise thereof. . . . " This apparently straightforward prohibition can rarely be applied to a given situation with ease, however. As the Supreme Court has noted, "total separation (between church and state) is not possible in an absolute sense." As a result, the Court has developed a three-part test for determining when certain governmental activity falls within the constitutional boundaries: First, the (activity) must have a secular purpose; second, its principal or primary effect must be one that neither advances nor inhibits religion, . . . finally, the (activity) must not foster "an excessive governmental entanglement with religion."

A. Purpose.

The appellants' contention that the School Board's adoption of the policy and rules was motivated by religious considerations is unsupportable. The record shows that the citizens' committee was formed and the rules drawn up in response to complaints that Christmas observances in some of the schools in the district contained religious exercises. The motivation behind the rules, therefore, was simply to ensure that no religious exercise was a part of officially sanctioned school activities. This conclusion is supported by the opening words of the policy statement: "It is accepted that no religious belief or non-belief should be promoted by the school district or its employees, and none should be disparaged." The statement goes on to affirmatively declare the purpose behind the rules: The Sioux Falls School District recognizes that one of its educational goals is to advance the students' knowledge and appreciation of the role that our religious heritage has played in the social, cultural and historical development of civilization.

The express language of the rules also leads to the conclusion that they were not promulgated with the intent to serve a religious purpose. Rule 1 limits observation of holidays to those that have both a religious and a secular basis. Solely religious holidays may not be observed. Rule 3 provides that music, art, literature and drama having a religious theme or basis may be included in the school curriculum only if "presented in a prudent and objective manner and as a traditional part of the cultural and religious heritage of the particular holiday." Similarly, Rule 4 permits the use of religious symbols only as "a teaching aid or resource" and only if "such symbols are displayed as an example of the cultural and religious heritage of the holiday and are temporary in nature." We view the thrust of these rules to be the advancement of the students' knowledge of society's cultural and religious heritage, as well as the provision of an opportunity for students to perform a full range of music, poetry and drama that is likely to be of interest to the students and their audience.

This purpose is quite different from the express and implied intent of the states of New York, Pennsylvania and Maryland in the Supreme Court "School Prayer Cases." First, we emphasize the different character of the activities involved in those cases. The challenged law in *Engel v. Vitale* provided for the recitation of a state-authored prayer at the start of each school day. The Supreme Court had no difficulty characterizing this practice as a religious activity: There can, of course, be no doubt that New York's program of daily classroom invocation of God's blessings as prescribed in the Regents' prayer is a religious activity. It is a solemn avowal of divine faith and supplication for the blessings of the Almighty. The nature of such a prayer has always been religious.

Since prayer, by its very nature, is undeniably a religious exercise, the conclusion is inescapable that the advancement of religious goals was the purpose sought by the school officials in *Engel*. Indeed, the state officials published the prayer in a document entitled "Statement on Moral and Spiritual Training in the Schools." There can be little doubt that their intent was to promote "spiritual" ends.

Similarly, in *Abington School Dist. v. Schempp,* the Supreme Court emphasized the "pervading religious character of the ceremony" involving daily Bible reading in the schools. Again, when a state intentionally sets up a system that by its essential nature serves a religious function, one can only conclude that the advancement of religion is the desired goal. As explained more fully in the next section of this opinion, however, the programs permitted under the Sioux Falls rules are not unquestionably religious in nature. Thus, we are not required to infer that the Sioux Falls School Board intended to advance religion.

Moreover, in the Supreme Court prayer cases, compulsory religious exercises were imposed on all schools by state law. The Sioux Falls rules, by contrast, do not require the individual schools to have holiday activities; they merely permit the inclusion of certain programs in the curriculum in the event that classroom teachers feel that such programs would enhance their overall instructional plan. The rules are an attempt to delineate the scope of permissible activity within the district, not to mandate a statewide program of religious inculcation.

The appellants argue that the "legislative" history of Rule 1 compels the conclusion that the rule was designed to advance religion. The basis for this argument is a proposed amendment to Rule 1 introduced before both the citizens' committee and the School Board. The proposed amendment would have added to Rule 1 the following words: "Such observances shall be limited to secular aspects of these holidays." The amendment was defeated by both the citizens' committee and the School Board. The School Board rejected the proposal, appellants assert in their brief, "because it wanted to allow schools to observe the religious basis of holidays." This, they maintain, is an unconstitutional purpose.

We do not agree that the rejection of the proposed amendment renders the School Board rules constitutionally infirm. First, the record is devoid of evidence indicating the reasons the proposal was rejected. A number of possibilities suggest themselves, including the ambiguity of the proposed addition. The appellants' assertion that the rejection was due to the School Board's desire "to observe the religious basis of holidays" is thus unsupported. Furthermore, even if the appellants' contention were correct, the Constitution does not necessarily forbid the use of materials that have a "religious basis." Government involvement in an activity of unquestionably religious origin does not contravene the Establishment Clause if its "present purpose and effect" is secular. Thus, although the rules permit the schools to observe holidays that have both a secular and a religious basis, we need not conclude that the School Board acted with unconstitutional motives. To the contrary, we agree with the district court's finding that the School Board did not adopt the policy statement and rules for the purpose of advancing or inhibiting religion.

B.   Effect.

The appellants contend that, notwithstanding the actual intent of the School Board, the "principal or primary effect" of the rules is to either advance or inhibit religion. We cannot agree. The First Amendment does not forbid all mention of religion in public schools; it is the advancement or inhibition of religion that is prohibited. Hence, the study of religion is not forbidden "when presented objectively as part of a secular program of education." We view the term "study" to include more than mere classroom instruction; public performance may be a legitimate part of secular study. This does not mean, of course, that religious ceremonies can be performed in the public schools under the guise of "study." It does mean, however, that when the primary purpose served by a given school activity is secular, that activity is not made unconstitutional by the inclusion of some religious content. As the district court noted in its discussion of Rule 3, "(t)o allow students only to study and not to perform (religious art, literature and music when) such works have developed an independent secular and artistic significance would give students a truncated view of our culture."

The appellants assert, however, that something more than secular study is authorized by the Sioux Falls rules. They point to Rule 1, which states that holidays that have a religious and secular basis may be "observed" in the public schools. "Observation," they maintain, necessarily connotes religious ceremony or exercise and the rule thus has the impermissible effect of advancing religion.

A review of the policy statement and rules as a whole leads us to conclude that the appellants' emphasis of the word "observe" is misplaced and their interpretation of it incorrect. First, as noted in section II.A. of this opinion, the rules must be read together with the policy statement of the School Board. That statement makes it clear that religion is to be neither promoted nor disparaged in the Sioux Falls schools. Consequently, any ambiguity in the meaning of the word "observed" must be resolved in favor of promoting that policy. Moreover, the only evidence presented on the definition of the word "observed" was the testimony of the School Superintendent, Dr. John Harris. Dr. Harris explained that "observed" means "that programs with content relating to both the secular and religious basis of (the holiday) could be performed, could be presented in the school." As noted earlier, we view performance or presentation to be a legitimate and important part of "study" in the public schools. Thus, the use of the word "observe" does not mean that the rules have the effect of advancing religion so long as the religious content of the programs is "presented objectively as part of a secular program of education."

To determine whether religion is advanced or inhibited by the rules, then, we must look to see if a genuine "secular program of education" is furthered by the rules. It is unquestioned that public school students may be taught about the customs and cultural heritage of the United States and other countries. This is the principal effect of the rules. They allow the presentation of material that, although of religious origin, has taken on an independent meaning.

The district court expressly found that much of the art, literature and music associated with traditional holidays, particularly Christmas, has "acquired a significance which is no longer confined to the religious sphere of life. It has become integrated into our national culture and heritage." Furthermore, the rules guarantee that all material used has secular or cultural significance: Only holidays with both religious and secular bases may be observed; music, art, literature and drama may be included in the curriculum only if presented in a prudent and objective manner and only as a part of the cultural and religious heritage of the holiday; and religious symbols may be used only as a teaching aid or resource and only if they are displayed as a part of the cultural and religious heritage of the holiday and are temporary in nature. Since all programs and materials authorized by the rules must deal with the secular or cultural basis or heritage of the holidays and since the materials must be presented in a prudent and objective manner and symbols used as a teaching aid, the advancement of a "secular program of education," and not of religion, is the primary effect of the rules.

The appellants argue that, despite the secular benefits, inclusion of material with a religious theme, basis or heritage invalidates the rules. In support of this assertion, the appellants point out that several of appellants' witnesses, all of them ordained clergymen, testified that the singing of Christmas carols would have some religious effect on them. But the appellants misread the test laid down by the Supreme Court. As noted, *Lemon v. Kurtzman* permits a given activity if "its principal or primary effect (is) one that neither advances nor inhibits religion." It would be literally impossible to develop a public school curriculum that did not in some way affect the religious or nonreligious sensibilities of some of the students or their parents. School administrators should, of course, be sensitive to the religious beliefs or disbeliefs of their constituents and should attempt to avoid conflict, but they need not and should not sacrifice the quality of the students' education. They need only ensure that the primary effect of the school's policy is secular. The district court's finding that they have done this by the challenged rules is not clearly erroneous.

The distinction between an activity that primarily advances religion and one that falls within permissible constitutional limits may be illustrated by comparing the 1977 kindergarten Christmas program found by the district court to be an impermissible religious activity and the programs authorized by the new School Board guidelines. The 1977 program at one of the elementary schools contained a segment that, in the words of the district court, "was replete with religious content including a responsive discourse between the teacher and the class entitled, 'The Beginners Christmas Quiz.'" The "Quiz" read as follows:

Teacher: Of whom did heavenly angels sing, and news about His birthday bring?
Class: Jesus.
Teacher: Now, can you name the little town where the Baby Jesus was found?
Class: Bethlehem.
Teacher: Where had they made a little bed for Christ, the blessed Saviour's head?
Class: In a manger in a cattle stall.
Teacher: What is the day we celebrate as birthday of this One so great?
Class: Christmas.

This "Quiz" and other similar activities constituted, the district court found, "a predominately religious activity" which exceeded constitutional bounds. We agree with this characterization and with the district court's observation that similar programs would be prohibited by the new rules. The administration of religious training is properly in the domain of the family and church. The First Amendment prohibits public schools from serving that function.

C. Entanglement.

The appellants contend that the new guidelines in Sioux Falls unconstitutionally "foster 'an excessive government entanglement with religion.'" All the Supreme Court cases cited by the appellants in support of the "entanglement" test deal with governmental aid to sectarian institutions, not with the permissible scope of activity in the public schools. In a "parochaid" case, the court is presented with a situation in which the state is involving itself with a concededly religious activity or institution. The real danger is the potential for state repression of such institutions. In the present case, by contrast, the school district is called upon to determine whether a given activity is religious. This type of decision inheres in every curriculum choice and would be faced by school administrators and teachers even if the rules did not exist. Indeed, the rules are guidelines designed to aid in the decision making process. Rather than entangling the schools in religion, the rules provide the means to ensure that the district steers clear of religious exercises. We think the district court was correct in finding that the new rules do not unconstitutionally entangle the Sioux Falls school district in religion or religious institutions.

III

The appellants also contend that implementation of the policy and rules of the Sioux Falls School Board should be enjoined because the rules violate the Free Exercise Clause of the First Amendment. This contention does not withstand scrutiny.

The public schools are not required to delete from the curriculum all materials that may offend any religious sensibility. As Mr. Justice Jackson noted in *McCollum v. Board of Education*, "Authorities list 256 separate and substantial religious bodies to exist in the continental United States. Each of them has as good a right as this plaintiff to demand that the courts compel the schools to sift out of their teaching everything inconsistent with its doctrines. If we are to eliminate everything that is objectionable to any of these warring sects or inconsistent with any of their doctrines, we will leave public education in shreds."

These inevitable conflicts with the individual beliefs of some students or their parents, in the absence of an Establishment Clause violation, do not necessarily require the prohibition of a school activity. On the other hand, forcing any person to participate in an activity that offends his religious or nonreligious beliefs will generally contravene the Free Exercise Clause, even without an Establishment Clause violation. In this case, however, the Sioux Falls School Board recognized that problem and expressly provided that students may be excused from activities authorized by the rules if they so choose.

IV

We recognize that this opinion affirming the district court will not resolve for all times, places or circumstances the question of when Christmas carols, or other music or drama having religious themes, can be sung or performed by students in elementary and secondary public schools without offending the First Amendment. The constitutionality of any particular school activity conducted pursuant to the rules, in association with any particular holiday, cannot be determined unless and until there is a specific challenge, supported by evidence, to the school district's implementation of the rules. We simply hold, on the basis of the record before us, that the policy and rules adopted by the Sioux Falls Board of Education, when read in the light of the district court's holding that segments of the 1977 Christmas program at one of the elementary schools were impermissible, are not violative of the First Amendment.

For the foregoing reasons, the judgment of the district court is affirmed.

Dissent by Circuit Judge McMillain.

Religious displays within a public school are strictly prohibited. In *Stone v. Graham*, the Supreme Court of the United States overturned the lower decision and determined that 16-by-20-inch posters of the Ten Commandments that hung on the walls of every classroom in the Commonwealth of Kentucky, were clearly unconstitutional.[12] According to the Court, "if the posted copies of the Ten Commandments are to have any effect at all, it will be to induce the schoolchildren to read, meditate upon, perhaps to venerate and obey, the Commandments. However desirable this might be as a matter of private devotion, it is not a permissible state objective under the Establishment Clause."[13]

While religious displays are unconstitutional, schools are permitted to display seasonal decorations that are secular in nature and have no religious meaning. Due to the mixed decisions within the courts, it is critical that a school have clear, set policies about what is permitted under the law. This issue arises frequently, especially in December. It is important to remember that not all individuals celebrate the same holiday. The basic idea is to remain neutral, neither enhancing nor prohibiting religion.

EQUAL ACCESS ACT

MANY public schools allow outside organizations to use their facilities during noninstructional time. Such acts create strong relationships within the community. But what are the legal implications of allowing religious groups to use the facilities? In taking the question one step further, are there legal issues if a public school permits a religious student group to use the facilities? Because the First Amendment clearly indicates a wall between church and state, there has been much litigation about allowing or denying such groups to use school facilities.

In an attempt to respond to these issues, Congress created and passed the Equal Access Act in 1984. The act reads in part: "It shall be deemed unlawful for any public secondary school which receives Federal financial assistance and which has a limited open forum to deny equal access or a fair opportunity to, or discriminate against, any students

---

[12] 449 U.S. 39 (1980)
[13] Ibid., at 43

who wish to conduct a meeting within that limited open forum on the basis of the religious, political, philosophical, or their content of the speech at such meetings."[14]

The Equal Access Act only affects public secondary schools and schools that have a limited open forum. According to the act, a school has a limited open forum "whenever such school grants an offering to or opportunity for one or more noncurriculum related student groups to meet on school premises during noninstructional hours." But what is noninstructional time? Does that include lunchtime or only times when school is not in session?

In *Ceniceros v. Board of Trustees of San Diego Unified School District*, the Ninth Circuit held that a student-initiated religious club must be permitted to use the school facilities during lunch.[15] Because the school had created an open forum, the court determined that lunch was noninstructional time and that consequently the student group must be permitted to use the facilities.

The issue of allowing religious groups to function in public secondary schools has created much litigation. One recent case discussing this controversy is *Good News Club v. Milford Central School.*

Good News Club v. Milford Central School
Supreme Court of the United States, 2001
533 U.S. 98

Justice Thomas delivered the opinion of the Court.

This case presents two questions. The first question is whether Milford Central School violated the free speech rights of the Good News Club when it excluded the Club from meeting after hours at the school. The second question is whether any such violation is justified by Milford's concern that permitting the Club's activities would violate the Establishment Clause. We conclude that Milford's restriction violates the Club's free speech rights and that no Establishment Clause concern justifies that violation.

I

The State of New York authorizes local school boards to adopt regulations governing the use of their school facilities. In particular, N.Y. Educ. Law § 414 enumerates several purposes for which local boards may open their schools to public use. In 1992, respondent Milford Central School (Milford) enacted a community use policy adopting seven of § 414's purposes for which its building could be used after school. Two of the stated purposes are relevant here. First, district residents may use the school for "instruction in any branch of education, learning or the arts." Second, the school is available for "social, civic and recreational meetings and entertainment events, and other uses pertaining to the welfare of the community, provided that such uses shall be nonexclusive and shall be opened to the general public."

---

[14]Equal Access Act, 20 U.S.C.S. § 4071–74
[15]66 F.3d 1535 (9th Cir. 1995)

Stephen and Darleen Fournier reside within Milford's district and therefore are eligible to use the school's facilities as long as their proposed use is approved by the school. Together they are sponsors of the local Good News Club, a private Christian organization for children ages 6 to 12. Pursuant to Milford's policy, in September 1996 the Fourniers submitted a request to Dr. Robert McGruder, interim superintendent of the district, in which they sought permission to hold the Club's weekly afterschool meetings in the school cafeteria. The next month, McGruder formally denied the Fourniers' request on the ground that the proposed use—to have "a fun time of singing songs, hearing a Bible lesson and memorizing scripture," ibid.—was "the equivalent of religious worship." According to McGruder, the community use policy, which prohibits use "by any individual or organization for religious purposes," foreclosed the Club's activities.

In response to a letter submitted by the Club's counsel, Milford's attorney requested information to clarify the nature of the Club's activities. The Club sent a set of materials used or distributed at the meetings and the following description of its meeting: "The Club opens its session with Ms. Fournier taking attendance. As she calls a child's name, if the child recites a Bible verse the child receives a treat. After attendance, the Club sings songs. Next Club members engage in games that involve learning Bible verses. Ms. Fournier then relates a Bible story and explains how it applies to Club members' lives. The Club closes with prayer. Finally, Ms. Fournier distributes treats and the Bible verses for memorization."

McGruder and Milford's attorney reviewed the materials and concluded that "the kinds of activities proposed to be engaged in by the Good News Club were not a discussion of secular subjects such as child rearing, development of character and development of morals from a religious perspective, but were in fact the equivalent of religious instruction itself." In February 1997, the Milford Board of Education adopted a resolution rejecting the Club's request to use Milford's facilities "for the purpose of conducting religious instruction and Bible study."

In March 1997, petitioners, the Good News Club, Ms. Fournier, and her daughter Andrea Fournier (collectively, the Club), filed an action under 42 U.S.C. § 1983 against Milford in the United States District Court for the Northern District of New York. The Club alleged that Milford's denial of its application violated its free speech rights under the First and Fourteenth Amendments, its right to equal protection under the Fourteenth Amendment, and its right to religious freedom under the Religious Freedom Restoration Act of 1993.

The Club moved for a preliminary injunction to prevent the school from enforcing its religious exclusion policy against the Club and thereby to permit the Club's use of the school facilities. On April 14, 1997, the District Court granted the injunction. The Club then held its weekly afterschool meetings from April 1997 until June 1998 in a high school resource and middle school special education room.

In August 1998, the District Court vacated the preliminary injunction and granted Milford's motion for summary judgment. The court found that the Club's "subject matter is decidedly religious in nature, and not merely a discussion of secular matters from a religious perspective that is otherwise permitted under [Milford's] use policies." Because the school had not permitted other groups that provided religious instruction to use its limited public forum, the court held that the school could deny access to the Club without engaging in unconstitutional viewpoint discrimination. The court also rejected the Club's equal protection claim.

The Club appealed, and a divided panel of the United States Court of Appeals for the Second Circuit affirmed. First, the court rejected the Club's contention that Milford's restriction against allowing religious instruction in its facilities is unreasonable. Second, it held that, because the subject matter of the Club's activities is "quintessentially religious," and the activities "fall outside the bounds of pure 'moral and character development,'" Milford's policy of excluding the Club's meetings was constitutional subject discrimination, not unconstitutional viewpoint discrimination. Judge Jacobs filed a dissenting opinion in which he concluded that the school's restriction did constitute viewpoint discrimination under *Lamb's Chapel v. Center Moriches Union Free School District.*

There is a conflict among the Courts of Appeals on the question whether speech can be excluded from a limited public forum on the basis of the religious nature of the speech. We granted certiorari to resolve this conflict.

II

The standards that we apply to determine whether a State has unconstitutionally excluded a private speaker from use of a public forum depend on the nature of the forum. If the forum is a traditional or open public forum, the State's restrictions on speech are subject to stricter scrutiny than are restrictions in a limited public forum. We have previously declined to decide whether a school district's opening of its facilities pursuant to N.Y. Educ. Law § 414 creates a limited or a traditional public forum. Because the parties have agreed that Milford created a limited public forum when it opened its facilities in 1992, we need not resolve the issue here. Instead, we simply will assume that Milford operates a limited public forum.

When the State establishes a limited public forum, the State is not required to and does not allow persons to engage in every type of speech. The State may be justified "in reserving [its forum] for certain groups or for the discussion of certain topics." The State's power to restrict speech, however, is not without limits. The restriction must not discriminate against speech on the basis of viewpoint, and the restriction must be "reasonable in light of the purpose served by the forum."

III

Applying this test, we first address whether the exclusion constituted viewpoint discrimination. We are guided in our analysis by two of our prior opinions, *Lamb's Chapel* and *Rosenberger.* In *Lamb's Chapel,* we held that a school district violated the Free Speech Clause of the First Amendment when it excluded a private group from presenting films at the school based solely on the films' discussions of family values from a religious perspective. Likewise, in *Rosenberger,* we held that a university's refusal to fund a student publication because the publication addressed issues from a religious perspective violated the Free Speech Clause. Concluding that Milford's exclusion of the Good News Club based on its religious nature is indistinguishable from the exclusions in these cases, we hold that the exclusion constitutes viewpoint discrimination. Because the restriction is viewpoint discriminatory, we need not decide whether it is unreasonable in light of the purposes served by the forum.

Milford has opened its limited public forum to activities that serve a variety of purposes, including events "pertaining to the welfare of the community." Milford interprets its policy to permit discussions of subjects such as child rearing, and of "the development of character and morals from a religious perspective." For example, this policy would allow someone to use Aesop's Fables to teach children moral values. Additionally, a group could sponsor a debate on whether there should be a constitutional amendment to permit prayer in public schools, and the Boy Scouts could meet "to influence a boy's character, development and spiritual growth." In short, any group that "promotes the moral and character development of children" is eligible to use the school building.

Just as there is no question that teaching morals and character development to children is a permissible purpose under Milford's policy, it is clear that the Club teaches morals and character development to children. For example, no one disputes that the Club instructs children to overcome feelings of jealousy, to treat others well regardless of how they treat the children, and to be obedient, even if it does so in a nonsecular way. Nonetheless, because Milford found the Club's activities to be religious in nature—"the equivalent of religious instruction itself,"—it excluded the Club from use of its facilities.

Applying *Lamb's Chapel,* we find it quite clear that Milford engaged in viewpoint discrimination when it excluded the Club from the afterschool forum. In *Lamb's Chapel,* the local New York school district similarly had adopted § 414's "social, civic or recreational use" category as a permitted use in its limited public forum. The district also prohibited use "by any group for religious purposes." Citing this prohibition, the school district excluded a church that wanted to present films teaching family values from a Christian perspective. The court held that, because the films "no doubt dealt with a subject otherwise permissible" under the rule, the teaching of family values, the district's exclusion of the church was unconstitutional viewpoint discrimination.

Like the church in *Lamb's Chapel,* the Club seeks to address a subject otherwise permitted under the rule, the teaching of morals and character, from a religious standpoint. Certainly, one could have characterized the film presentations in *Lamb's Chapel* as a religious use. And one easily could conclude that the films' purpose to instruct that "society's slide toward humanism . . . can only be counterbalanced by a loving home where Christian values are instilled from an early age" was "quintessentially religious." The only apparent difference between the activity of Lamb's Chapel and the activities of the Good News Club is that the Club chooses to teach moral lessons from a Christian perspective through live storytelling and prayer, whereas Lamb's Chapel taught lessons through films. This distinction is inconsequential. Both modes of speech use a religious viewpoint. Thus, the exclusion of the Good News Club's activities, like the exclusion of Lamb's Chapel's films, constitutes unconstitutional viewpoint discrimination.

Our opinion in *Rosenberger* also is dispositive. In *Rosenberger,* a student organization at the University of Virginia was denied funding for printing expenses because its publication, Wide Awake, offered a Christian viewpoint. Just as the Club emphasizes the role of Christianity in students' morals and character, Wide Awake "challenged Christians to live, in word and deed, according to the faith they proclaim and . . . encouraged students to consider what a personal relationship with Jesus Christ means." Because the university "selected for disfavored treatment those student journalistic efforts with religious editorial viewpoints," we held that the denial of funding was unconstitutional. Although in *Rosenberger* there was no prohibition on religion as a subject matter, our holding did not rely on this factor. Instead, we concluded simply that the university's denial of funding to print Wide Awake was viewpoint discrimination, just as the school district's refusal to allow Lamb's Chapel to show its films was viewpoint discrimination. Given the obvious religious content of Wide Awake, we cannot say that the Club's activities are any more "religious" or deserve any less First Amendment protection than did the publication of Wide Awake in *Rosenberger*.

Despite our holdings in *Lamb's Chapel* and *Rosenberger*, the Court of Appeals, like Milford, believed that its characterization of the Club's activities as religious in nature warranted treating the Club's activities as different in kind from the other activities permitted by the school. The "Christian viewpoint" is unique, according to the court, because it contains an "additional layer" that other kinds of viewpoints do not. That is, the Club "is focused on teaching children how to cultivate their relationship with God through Jesus Christ," which it characterized as "quintessentially religious." With these observations, the court concluded that, because the Club's activities "fall outside the bounds of pure 'moral and character development,'" the exclusion did not constitute viewpoint discrimination.

We disagree that something that is "quintessentially religious" or "decidedly religious in nature" cannot also be characterized properly as the teaching of morals and character development from a particular viewpoint. . . . What matters for purposes of the Free Speech Clause is that we can see no logical difference in kind between the invocation of Christianity by the Club and the invocation of teamwork, loyalty, or patriotism by other associations to provide a foundation for their lessons. It is apparent that the unstated principle of the Court of Appeals' reasoning is its conclusion that any time religious instruction and prayer are used to discuss morals and character, the discussion is simply not a "pure" discussion of those issues. According to the Court of Appeals, reliance on Christian principles taints moral and character instruction in a way that other foundations for thought or viewpoints do not. We, however, have never reached such a conclusion. Instead, we reaffirm our holdings in *Lamb's Chapel* and *Rosenberger* that speech discussing otherwise permissible subjects cannot be excluded from a limited public forum on the ground that the subject is discussed from a religious viewpoint. Thus, we conclude that Milford's exclusion of the Club from use of the school, pursuant to its community use policy, constitutes impermissible viewpoint discrimination.

IV

Milford argues that, even if its restriction constitutes viewpoint discrimination, its interest in not violating the Establishment Clause outweighs the Club's interest in gaining equal access to the school's facilities. In other words, according to Milford, its restriction was required to avoid violating the Establishment Clause. We disagree.

We have said that a state interest in avoiding an Establishment Clause violation "may be characterized as compelling," and therefore may justify content-based discrimination.

However, it is not clear whether a State's interest in avoiding an Establishment Clause violation would justify viewpoint discrimination. We need not, however, confront the issue in this case, because we conclude that the school has no valid Establishment Clause interest.

We rejected Establishment Clause defenses similar to Milford's in two previous free speech cases, *Lamb's Chapel* and *Widmar*. In particular, in *Lamb's Chapel,* we explained that "the showing of the film series would not have been during school hours, would not have been sponsored by the school, and would have been open to the public, not just to church members." Accordingly, we found that "there would have been no realistic danger that the community would think that the District was endorsing religion or any particular creed." Likewise, in *Widmar*, where the university's forum was already available to other groups, this Court concluded that there was no Establishment Clause problem.

The Establishment Clause defense fares no better in this case. As in *Lamb's Chapel,* the Club's meetings were held after school hours, not sponsored by the school, and open to any student who obtained parental consent, not just to Club members. As in *Widmar*, Milford made its forum available to other organizations. The Club's activities are materially indistinguishable from those in *Lamb's Chapel* and *Widmar*. Thus, Milford's reliance on the Establishment Clause is unavailing.

Milford attempts to distinguish *Lamb's Chapel* and *Widmar* by emphasizing that Milford's policy involves elementary school children. According to Milford, children will perceive that the school is endorsing the Club and will feel coercive pressure to participate, because the Club's activities take place on school grounds, even though they occur during nonschool hours. This argument is unpersuasive.

First, we have held that "a significant factor in upholding governmental programs in the face of Establishment Clause attack is their neutrality towards religion." . . . Milford's implication that granting access to the Club would do damage to the neutrality principle defies logic. For the "guarantee of neutrality is respected, not offended, when the government, following neutral criteria and evenhanded policies, extends benefits to recipients whose ideologies and viewpoints, including religious ones, are broad and diverse." The Good News Club seeks nothing more than to be treated neutrally and given access to speak about the same topics as are other groups. Because allowing the Club to speak on school grounds would ensure neutrality, not threaten it, Milford faces an uphill battle in arguing that the Establishment Clause compels it to exclude the Good News Club.

Second, to the extent we consider whether the community would feel coercive pressure to engage in the Club's activities, the relevant community would be the parents, not the elementary school children. It is the parents who choose whether their children will attend the Good News Club meetings. Because the children cannot attend without their parents' permission, they cannot be coerced into engaging in the Good News Club's religious activities. Milford does not suggest that the parents of elementary school children would be confused about whether the school was endorsing religion. Nor do we believe that such an argument could be reasonably advanced.

Third, whatever significance we may have assigned in the Establishment Clause context to the suggestion that elementary school children are more impressionable than adults, . . . we have never extended our Establishment Clause jurisprudence to foreclose private religious conduct during nonschool hours merely because it takes place on school premises where elementary school children may be present.

None of the cases discussed by Milford persuades us that our Establishment Clause jurisprudence has gone this far. For example, Milford cites *Lee v. Weisman* for the proposition that "there are heightened concerns with protecting freedom of conscience from subtle coercive pressure in the elementary and secondary public schools." In *Lee,* however, we concluded that attendance at the graduation exercise was obligatory. We did not place independent significance on the fact that the graduation exercise might take place on school premises. Here, where the school facilities are being used for a nonschool function and there is no government sponsorship of the Club's activities, *Lee* is inapposite.

Equally unsupportive is *Edwards v. Aguillard,* in which we held that a Louisiana law that proscribed the teaching of evolution as part of the public school curriculum, unless accompanied by a lesson on creationism, violated the Establishment Clause. In *Edwards,* we mentioned that students are susceptible to pressure in the classroom, particularly given their possible reliance on teachers as role models. But we did not discuss this concern in our application of the law to the facts. Moreover, we did note that mandatory attendance requirements meant that State advancement of religion in a school would be particularly harshly felt by impressionable students. But we did not suggest that, when the school was not actually advancing religion, the impressionability of students would be relevant to the Establishment Clause issue. Even if *Edwards* had articulated the principle Milford believes it did, the facts in *Edwards* are simply too remote from those here to give the principle any weight. *Edwards* involved the content of the curriculum taught by state teachers during the schoolday to children required to attend. Obviously, when individuals who are not schoolteachers are giving lessons after school to children permitted to attend only with parental consent, the concerns expressed in *Edwards* are not present.

Fourth, even if we were to consider the possible misperceptions by schoolchildren in deciding whether Milford's permitting the Club's activities would violate the Establishment Clause, the facts of this case simply do not support Milford's conclusion. There is no evidence that young children are permitted to loiter outside classrooms after the schoolday has ended. Surely even young children are aware of events for which their parents must sign permission forms. The meetings were held in a combined high school resource room and middle school special education room, not in an elementary school classroom. The instructors are not schoolteachers. And the children in the group are not all the same age as in the normal classroom setting; their ages range from 6 to 12. In sum, these circumstances simply do not support the theory that small children would perceive endorsement here.

Finally, even if we were to inquire into the minds of schoolchildren in this case, we cannot say the danger that children would misperceive the endorsement of religion is any greater than the danger that they would perceive a hostility toward the religious viewpoint if the Club were excluded from the public forum. This concern is particularly acute given the reality that Milford's building is not used only for elementary school children. Students, from kindergarten through the 12th grade, all attend school in the same building. There may be as many, if not more, upperclassmen than elementary school children who occupy the school after hours. For that matter, members of the public writ large are permitted in the school after hours pursuant to the community use policy. Any bystander could conceivably be aware of the school's use policy and its exclusion of the Good News Club, and could suffer as much from viewpoint discrimination as elementary school children could suffer from perceived endorsement. . . .

We cannot operate, as Milford would have us do, under the assumption that any risk that small children would perceive endorsement should counsel in favor of excluding the Club's religious activity. We decline to employ Establishment Clause jurisprudence using a modified heckler's veto, in which a group's religious activity can be proscribed on the basis of what the youngest members of the audience might misperceive. . . . There are countervailing constitutional concerns related to rights of other individuals in the community. In this case, those countervailing concerns are the free speech rights of the Club and its members. And, we have already found that those rights have been violated, not merely perceived to have been violated, by the school's actions toward the Club.

We are not convinced that there is any significance in this case to the possibility that elementary school children may witness the Good News Club's activities on school premises, and therefore we can find no reason to depart from our holdings in *Lamb's Chapel* and *Widmar.* Accordingly, we conclude that permitting the Club to meet on the school's premises would not have violated the Establishment Clause.

V

When Milford denied the Good News Club access to the school's limited public forum on the ground that the Club was religious in nature, it discriminated against the Club because of its religious viewpoint in violation of the Free Speech Clause of the First Amendment. Because Milford has not raised a valid Establishment Clause claim, we do not address the question whether such a claim could excuse Milford's viewpoint discrimination.

The judgment of the Court of Appeals is reversed, and the case is remanded for further proceedings consistent with this opinion.

It is so ordered.

In the six-to-three Supreme Court decision, the majority of the Court held that the religious club must be permitted to use the school's facilities. As with other cases dealing with the Equal Access Act and schools, the institution at hand was a secondary public school. It was categorized as an open forum because it had permitted other community groups, such as the 4-H Club and the Boys Scouts of America, to use its facilities. Because the school had allowed after-school access to others, the Supreme Court found that denying access to the children's Bible club was in fact a violation of the club's First Amendment right to free speech. On the other hand, schools that do not create an open forum or allow any groups to use the facilities may deny access to religious clubs or organizations without violating the Establishment Clause.

> **Best Practices**
>
> - If a secondary public school opens its doors to one organization, it is categorized as a public forum and must allow others the same opportunity to use the facilities.
>
> - Do not refuse community members access to the facilities based on personal opinion or disagreement with what the group may represent. It is critical that today's educators understand the implications of the Equal Access Act.
>
> - Faculty and staff members may be present during the meetings but may not participate if the meetings are religious in nature.
>
> - Do not set policy defining instructional time to avoid allowing religious groups to use the school's facilities.

Summary

In analyzing American history and the creation of the U.S. Constitution, escaping we see that religious persecution played a major role in the nation's formation. Consequently, the First Amendment, which was written in 1791, reads: "Congress shall make no law respecting an establishment of religion, or prohibiting the free exercise of thereof." While not always thought of as a part of the government, public schools are arms of the state, hence they must abide by the Constitution and play a neutral role when it comes to religion.

There is still great debate about permitting religion in public school, as well as arguing what is constitutional and what is a violation of the First Amendment. As stated in *Everson v. Board of Education,* "This policy of our Federal Constitution has never been wholly pleasing to most religious groups. They all are quick to invoke its protections; they all are irked when they feel its restraints."[16]

Additional issues concerning religion in schools grow especially since the violence in schools over the last decade has increased. What is religious and what is secular are areas of debate that are expected to continue in the future. With the Supreme Court deciding on cases such as *Good News* and the creation of the Equal Access Act, this is an area that administrators must pay special attention to and make sure they are acting within the scope of the law.

Discussion Questions

1. Must public schools completely exclude religion? Can students pray in school? Can teachers pray in school? Justify your response.
2. Do you believe the founders of the Constitution intended the establishment clause to be interpreted as absolute neutrality between church and state? Discuss.

---

[16]330 U.S. 1, at 27 (1947)

3. Can prayer be permitted at graduation if the student body selects the clergy and provides direction for the invocation? Discuss cases to support your response.
4. Discuss the elements of the Lemon test.
5. What are the options for parents who feel religion should be taught within the school system?
6. What has been your school system's policy regarding prayer at graduation or other school-sponsored activities?
7. The establishment clause requires separation of church and state. The Equal Access Act states that everyone must have equal access during noninstructional time. How do the courts balance these two issues?
8. Can the board of a public school agree to allow religious pictures or symbols to be hung in hallways or classrooms? Why or why not? Discuss.
9. Define the difference between an open forum and a closed forum. Explain the law under each situation.
10. The parents of five public school students objected to the school district's use of the devil as the football team mascot. The students and their parents filed a lawsuit against the school district in U.S. district court, claiming that the use of the mascot violated the establishment clause of the First Amendment, based on their belief that the mascot was satanic. Discuss whether the parents have a legitimate claim and why.

DEEPENING YOUR UNDERSTANDING

1. Under the Equal Access Act schools must allow students to use facilities during non-instructional time. For safety reasons, however, schools have a duty to supervise the students. Does this create a conflict?
2. Research the decision in *Board of Education of Westside Community School v. Mergens*, 496 U.S. 226 (1990). After reading the Equal Access Act (found in the appendix) and the *Mergens* case, define noninstructional time.

4

STUDENTS WITH DISABILITIES

INTRODUCTION

Before the early 1970s, millions of disabled children were intentionally excluded from the public school system and hence were not receiving an education. Unfortunately, a common misconception was that children with disabilities did not belong in the regular public school system because they were different. Students with disabilities, even subtle ones, were excluded from being with other children and denied an education. In some cases families would institutionalize a child if the disability was severe. But as the civil rights movement evolved, so did the movement for the rights of students with disabilities.

HISTORY OF STUDENTS WITH DISABILITIES

BROWN v. Board of Education,[1] mandated racial desegregation in schools, yet was also a catalyst for parents with children who were being excluded from a public education due to their disability. Using the holding in *Brown* that all children deserve an equal education numerous cases were brought forward.

The most significant to the public education system were *Pennsylvania Association for Retarded Children (PARC) v. the Pennsylvania Commonwealth* and *Mills v. Board of Education.*[2]

The *PARC* court held that mentally retarded students between the ages of 6 and 21, must be provided with a free public education. Additionally, the court noted

---

[1]347 U.S. 483
[2]334 F. Supp. 1257 (E.D. Pa. 1971); 348 F. Supp. 866 (D.D.C. 1972)

that children with disabilities should be mainstreamed into regular classrooms when possible.

Less than a year later, the *Mills* case was decided. The court in *Mills* also held for the plaintiffs, but expanded the decision to all school-age children with disabilities, not just those between the ages of 6 and 21. Additionally, the court held that students must be offered alternative educational services if the public school could not meet the child's needs.

INDIVIDUALS WITH DISABILITIES EDUCATION ACT

AFTER THE *PARC* and *Mills* cases were decided, Congress began looking into the issue of disabled students who were not being properly educated within the public school system. In fact, congressional findings for the Education for All Handicapped Children Act determined that there were 8 million disabled children in the United States. Of that number, more than half did not receive appropriate educational services. As a result, Congress created one of the first federal laws protecting the rights of disabled children, the Education for All Handicapped Children Act (EAHCA) of 1975.

Since the first federal law was passed, numerous amendments have been enacted. Currently, the law protecting disabled students is known as the Individuals with Disabilities Education Act (IDEA), 20 USCS § 1401. But when is a student categorized as disabled? According to IDEA, a child with a disability is defined as follows:

> (A) In general. The term "child with a disability" means a child—
> (i) with mental retardation, hearing impairments (including deafness), speech or language impairments, visual impairments (including blindness), serious emotional disturbance (hereinafter referred to as "emotional disturbance"), orthopedic impairments, autism, traumatic brain injury, other health impairments, or specific learning disabilities; and
> (ii) who, by reason thereof, needs special education and related services.

To receive federal funding under IDEA, local school districts must have a plan that indicates how they will comply with IDEA as well as distribute funding throughout the district. In addition, each state must demonstrate that it maintains a policy that assures that all children with disabilities have access to related services and a free public education.

FREE APPROPRIATE PUBLIC EDUCATION

ONE OF the key elements of IDEA is that students are allowed the opportunity to have a free appropriate public education. But what if a student cannot benefit from such an education? Does IDEA pertain to all students or only those who can substantially benefit from an education? The landmark case that answers this question is *Timothy W. v. Rochester School District.*

Timothy W. v. Rochester School District
U.S. Court of Appeals for the First Circuit, 1989
875 F.2d 954

Opinion written by Justice Bownes.

Plaintiff-appellant Timothy W. appeals an order of the district court which held that under the Education for All Handicapped Children Act [EAHCA], a handicapped child is not eligible for special education if he cannot benefit from that education, and that Timothy W., a severely retarded and multiply handicapped child was not eligible under that standard. We reverse.

Timothy W. was born two months prematurely on December 8, 1975 with severe respiratory problems, and shortly thereafter experienced an intracranial hemorrhage, subdural effusions, seizures, hydrocephalus, and meningitis. As a result, Timothy is multiply handicapped and profoundly mentally retarded. He suffers from complex developmental disabilities, spastic quadriplegia, cerebral palsy, seizure disorder and cortical blindness. His mother attempted to obtain appropriate services for him, and while he did receive some services from the Rochester Child Development Center, he did not receive any educational program from the Rochester School District when he became of school age. . . .

On July 15, 1988, the district court rendered its opinion entitled "Order on Motion for Judgment on the Pleadings or in the Alternative, Summary Judgment." . . . The court made rulings of law and findings of fact. It first ruled that "under EAHCA, an initial determination as to the child's ability to benefit from special education, must be made in order for a handicapped child to qualify for education under the Act." After noting that the New Hampshire statute (RSA 186-C) was intended to implement the EAHCA, the court held: "Under New Hampshire law, an initial decision must be made concerning the ability of a handicapped child to benefit from special education before an entitlement to the education can exist." The court then reviewed the materials, reports and testimony and found that "Timothy W. is not capable of benefiting from special education. . . . As a result, the defendant [school district] is not obligated to provide special education under either EAHCA [the federal statute] or RSA 186-C [the New Hampshire statute]." Timothy W. has appealed this order. . . .

The primary issue is whether the district court erred in its rulings of law. Since we find that it did, we do not review its findings of fact.

The Education for All Handicapped Children Act, [hereinafter the Act], 20 U.S.C. §§ 1400 et seq., was enacted in 1975 to ensure that handicapped children receive an education which is appropriate to their unique needs. In assessing the plain meaning of the Act, we first look to its title: The Education for All Handicapped Children Act. The Congressional Findings section of the Act states that there were eight million handicapped children, that more than half of them did not receive appropriate educational services, and that one million were excluded entirely from the public school system. Given these grim statistics, Congress concluded that "State and local educational agencies have a responsibility to provide education for all handicapped children. . . . " In directly addressing the educability of handicapped children, Congress found that "developments in the training of teachers and in diagnostic and instructional procedures and methods have advanced to the point that, given appropriate funding, State and local educational agencies can and will provide effective special education and related services to meet the needs of handicapped children." The Act's stated purpose was "to assure that all handicapped children have available to them . . . a free appropriate public education which emphasizes special education and related services designed to meet their unique needs, . . . [and] to assist states and localities to provide for the education of all handicapped children. . . . "

[The] Act further requires a state to: establish priorities for providing a free appropriate public education to all handicapped children, . . . first with respect to handicapped children who are not receiving an education, and second with respect to handicapped children, within each disability, with the most severe handicaps who are receiving an inadequate education. . . . Thus, not only are severely handicapped children not excluded from the Act, but the most severely handicapped are actually given priority under the Act.

The language of the Act could not be more unequivocal. The statute is permeated with the words "all handicapped children" whenever it refers to the target population. It never speaks of any exceptions for severely handicapped children. Indeed, as indicated, the Act gives priority to the most severely handicapped. Nor is there any language whatsoever which requires as a prerequisite to being covered by the Act, that a handicapped child must demonstrate that he or she will "benefit" from the educational program. Rather, the Act speaks of the state's responsibility to design a special education and related services program that will meet the unique "needs" of all handicapped children. The language of the Act in its entirety makes clear that a "zero-reject" policy is at the core of the Act, and that no child, regardless of the severity of his or her handicap, is to ever again be subjected to the deplorable state of affairs which existed at the time of the Act's passage, in which millions of handicapped children received inadequate education or none at all. In summary, the Act mandates an appropriate public education for all handicapped children, regardless of the level of achievement that such children might attain.

Given that the Act's language mandates that all handicapped children are entitled to a free appropriate education, we must next inquire if Timothy W. is a handicapped child, and if he is, what constitutes an appropriate education to meet his unique needs.

(1) Handicapped Children:

The implementing regulations define handicapped children as "being mentally retarded, hard of hearing, deaf, speech impaired, visually handicapped, seriously emotionally disturbed, orthopedically impaired, other health impaired, deaf-blind, multi-handicapped, or as having specific learning disabilities, who because of those impairments need special education and related services."

There is no question that Timothy W. fits within the Act's definition of a handicapped child: he is multiply handicapped and profoundly mentally retarded. He has been described as suffering from severe spasticity, cerebral palsy, brain damage, joint contractures, cortical blindness, is not ambulatory, and is quadriplegic.

(2) Appropriate Public Education:

The Act and the implementing regulations define a "free appropriate public education" to mean "special education and related services which are provided at public expense . . . [and] are provided in conformity with an individualized education program."

"Special education" means "specially designed instruction, at no cost to the parent, to meet the unique needs of a handicapped child, including classroom instruction, instruction in physical education, home instruction, and instruction in hospitals and institutions." It is of significance that the Act explicitly provides for education of children who are so severely handicapped as to require hospitalization or institutionalization. Timothy W.'s handicaps do not require such extreme measures, as he can be educated at home. The Act goes on to define "physical education" as the "development of: physical and motor fitness; fundamental motor skills and patterns . . . [and] includes special physical education, adapted physical education, movement education, and motor development." Thus, the Act's concept of special education is broad, encompassing not only traditional cognitive skills, but basic functional skills as well.

"Related services" means "transportation and such developmental, corrective, and other supportive services as are required to assist a handicapped child to benefit from special education, and includes speech pathology and audiology, psychological services, physical and occupational therapy, recreation. . . . " "Physical therapy" means "services provided by a qualified physical therapist." "Occupational therapy" includes "improving, developing or restoring functions impaired or lost through illness, injury, or deprivation; improving ability to perform tasks for independent functioning. . . . " Furthermore, the "comment" to these implementing regulations notes that "the list of related services is not exhaustive and may include other developmental, corrective, or supportive services . . . if they are required to assist a handicapped child to benefit from special education."

An "individualized education program" is a written plan developed by the local educational agency in conjunction with the parents and teacher, which provides "specially designed instruction to meet the unique needs" of the handicapped child. . . .

The record shows that Timothy W. is a severely handicapped and profoundly retarded child in need of special education and related services. Much of the expert testimony was to the effect that he is aware of his surrounding environment, makes or attempts to make purposeful movements, responds to tactile stimulation, responds to his mother's voice and touch, recognizes familiar voices, responds to noises, and parts his lips when spoon fed. The record contains testimony that Timothy W.'s needs include sensory stimulation, physical therapy, improved head control, socialization, consistency in responding to sound sources, and partial participation in eating. The educational consultants who drafted Timothy's individualized education program recommended that Timothy's special education program should include goals and objectives in the areas of motor control, communication, socialization, daily living skills, and recreation. The special education and related services that have been recommended to meet Timothy W.'s needs fit well within the statutory and regulatory definitions of the Act.

We conclude that the Act's language dictates the holding that Timothy W. is a handicapped child who is in need of special education and related services because of his handicaps. He must, therefore, according to the Act, be provided with such an educational program. There is nothing in the Act's language which even remotely supports the district court's conclusion that "under [the Act], an initial determination as to a child's ability to benefit from special education, must be made in order for a handicapped child to qualify for education under the Act." The language of the Act is directly to the contrary: a school district has a duty to provide an educational program for every handicapped child in the district, regardless of the severity of the handicap.

An examination of the legislative history reveals that Congress intended the Act to provide a public education for all handicapped children, without exception; that the most severely handicapped were in fact to be given priority attention; and that an educational benefit was neither guaranteed nor required as a prerequisite for a child to receive such education. These factors were central, and were repeated over and over again, in the more than three years of congressional hearings and debates, which culminated in passage of the 1975 Act. . . .

Not only did Congress intend that all handicapped children be educated, it expressly indicated its intent that the most severely handicapped be given priority. This resolve was reiterated over and over again in the floor debates and congressional reports, as well as in the final legislation.

In mandating a public education for all handicapped children, Congress explicitly faced the issue of the possibility of the non-educability of the most severely handicapped. The Senate Report stated, "The Committee recognizes that in many instances the process of providing special education and related services to handicapped children is not guaranteed to produce any particular outcome." The report continued: "The Committee has deleted the language of the bill as introduced which required objective criteria and evaluation procedures by which to assure that the short term instructional goals were met."

Thus, the district court's major holding, that proof of an educational benefit is a prerequisite before a handicapped child is entitled to a public education, is specifically belied, not only by the statutory language, but by the legislative history as well. We have not found in the Act's voluminous legislative history, nor has the school district directed our attention to, a single affirmative averment to support a benefit/eligibility requirement. But there is explicit evidence of a contrary congressional intent, that no guarantee of any particular educational outcome is required for a child to be eligible for public education. . . .

In the 14 years since passage of the Act, it has been amended four times. Congress thus has had ample opportunity to clarify any language originally used, or to make any modifications that it chose. Congress has not only repeatedly reaffirmed the original intent of the Act, to educate all handicapped children regardless of the severity of their handicap, and to give priority attention to the most severely handicapped, it has in fact expanded the provisions covering the most severely handicapped children. Most significantly, Congress has never intimated that a benefit/eligibility requirement was to be instituted. . . .

The courts have also made it clear that education for the severely handicapped under the Act is to be broadly defined. In *Battle,* the court stated that under the Act, the concept of education is necessarily broad with respect to severely and profoundly handicapped children, and "where basic self help and social skills such as toilet training, dressing, feeding and communication are lacking, formal education begins at that point." . . .

In the instant case, the district court's conclusion that education must be measured by the acquirement of traditional "cognitive skills" has no basis whatsoever in the 14 years of case law since the passage of the Act. All other courts have consistently held that education under the Act encompasses a wide spectrum of training, and that for the severely handicapped it may include the most elemental of life skills.

The district court relied heavily on *Board of Education of Hendrick Hudson Central School District v. Rowley* in concluding that as a matter of law a child is not entitled to a public education unless he or she can benefit from it. The district court, however, has misconstrued *Rowley.* In that case, the Supreme Court held that a deaf child, who was an above average student and was advancing from grade to grade in a regular public school classroom, and who was already receiving substantial specialized instruction and related services, was not entitled, in addition, to a full time sign-language interpreter, because she was already benefiting from the special education and services she was receiving. The Court held that the school district was not required to maximize her educational achievement. It stated, "if personalized instruction is being provided with sufficient supportive services to permit the child to benefit from the instruction, . . . the child is receiving a 'free appropriate public education'" and that "certainly the language of the statute contains no requirement . . . that States maximize the potential of handicapped children."

Rowley focused on the level of services and the quality of programs that a state must provide, not the criteria for access to those programs. The Court's use of "benefit" in *Rowley* was a substantive limitation placed on the state's choice of an educational program; it was not a license for the state to exclude certain handicapped children. In ruling that a state was not required to provide the maximum benefit possible, the Court was not saying that there must be proof that a child will benefit before the state is obligated to provide any education at all. Indeed, the Court in *Rowley* explicitly acknowledged Congress' intent to ensure public education to all handicapped children without regard to the level of achievement that they might attain. . . .

Rowley simply does not lend support to the district court's finding of a benefit/eligibility standard in the Act. As the Court explained, while the Act does not require a school to maximize a child's potential for learning, it does provide a "basic floor of opportunity" for the handicapped, consisting of "access to specialized instruction and related services." Nowhere does the Court imply that such a "floor" contains a trap door for the severely handicapped. Indeed, *Rowley* explicitly states: "the Act requires special educational services for children 'regardless of the severity of their handicap,'" and "the Act requires participating States to educate a wide spectrum of handicapped children, from the marginally hearing-impaired to the profoundly retarded and palsied." This is a far cry from a requirement of proof that educational benefit will definitely result, before a child is entitled to receive that education. . . .

The statutory language of the Act, its legislative history, and the case law construing it, mandate that all handicapped children, regardless of the severity of their handicap, are entitled to a public education. The district court erred in requiring a benefit/eligibility test as a prerequisite to implicating the Act. School districts cannot avoid the provisions of the Act by returning to the practices that were widespread prior to the Act's passage, and which indeed were the impetus for the Act's passage, of unilaterally excluding certain handicapped children from a public education on the ground that they are uneducable.

The law explicitly recognizes that education for the severely handicapped is to be broadly defined, to include not only traditional academic skills, but also basic functional life skills, and that educational methodologies in these areas are not static, but are constantly evolving and improving. It is the school district's responsibility to avail itself of these new approaches in providing an education program geared to each child's individual needs. The only question for the school district to determine, in conjunction with the child's parents, is what constitutes an appropriate individualized education program (IEP) for the handicapped child. We emphasize that the phrase "appropriate individualized education program" cannot be interpreted, as the school district has done, to mean "no educational program." . . .

The judgment of the district court is reversed, judgment shall issue for Timothy W. The case is remanded to the district court which shall retain jurisdiction until a suitable individualized education program (IEP) for Timothy W. is effectuated by the school district. Timothy W. is entitled to an interim special educational placement until a final IEP is developed and agreed upon by the parties. The district court shall also determine the question of damages.

Costs are assessed against the school district.

The *Timothy W.* case illustrates that a child with disabilities may not be excluded from receiving a free appropriate public education. The basic premise of IDEA is that all children can be educated, even if the education teaches basic life skills. Unfortunately, as illustrated in *Timothy W.*, before the federal statute and clarification by the courts, some institutions evaluated students as unable to benefit from education. In response, the courts established a "zero reject" policy by which all students must be given the opportunity to a free appropriate education, regardless of the severity of their disabilities.

INDIVIDUALIZED EDUCATIONAL PROGRAM

AFTER a student is identified as having a disability, an individualized education program (IEP) must be prepared. An IEP is "the written statement which sets out an educational program to meet the particularized needs of a child with disabilities."[3] The IEP is prepared by members of the school with participants including the student's parents or guardians and at least one of the student's current teachers. The intent is to provide the student with

---

[3]*Tennessee Department of Mental Health and Mental Retardation v. Paul B.*, 88 F.3d 1466, 1471 (1996)

the opportunity for meaningful, not merely trivial, advancement within the free public educational system.[4] The current IDEA requires an IEP to contain the following:

> *(i) a statement of the child's present levels of educational performance, . . .*
>
> *(ii) a statement of measurable annual goals, including benchmarks or short-term objectives, . . .*
>
> *(iii) a statement of the special education and related services and supplementary aids and services to be provided to the child, or on behalf of the child, and a statement of the program modifications or supports for school personnel that will be provided for the child, . . .*
>
> *(iv) an explanation of the extent, if any, to which the child will not participate with nondisabled children in the regular class, . . .*
>
> *(vi) the projected date for the beginning of the services and modifications described in clause (iii), and the anticipated frequency, location, and duration of those services and modifications; . . .*
>
> *(viii) a statement of —(I) how the child's progress toward the annual goals described in clause (ii) will be measured; and (II) how the child's parents will be regularly informed . . . of . . . [their child's progress].*[5]

The IEP document must include "statements of the child's present levels of educational performance; annual goals, including short-term instructional objectives; the specific special education and related services to be provided to the child and the extent that the child will be able to participate in regular educational programs; dates for the presentation of services; and appropriate evaluation criteria and procedures for ascertaining the program's success."[6]

The act also mandates numerous procedural safeguards to ensure that students receive the required free appropriate public education. One of these safeguards requires that each IEP be reviewed on an annual basis in the parents' language, even if they do not speak English. Additionally, parents must receive proper notice if there are any proposed initiations or changes on the student's IEP. If parents are dissatisfied with the adequacy of their child's IEP or any changes, they have the right to request an impartial due process hearing conducted by the local educational agency. If the parents are still dissatisfied, they have the right to appeal to the state educational system and then to the courts.

In some cases, parents who have been dissatisfied with their child's IEP have alternatively placed the student in a private facility. If parents place the child there through their own actions, all financial responsibilities lie with the parents. Additionally, if parents place their child in a private institution while awaiting the outcome of a hearing, they may also be financially responsible, unless they can prove that the public school was "unable to provide [their] child with an appropriate education."[7]

---

[4]*Walczak v. Florida Union Free School District*, 142 F.3d 119, 132 (1998)

[5]20 U.S.C.A. § 1414(d)(1)(A)

[6]20 C.F.R. § 300.346

[7]*Gillette v. Fairland Board of Education*, 932 F.2d 551, at 554 (1991)

> **Best Practices**
>
> - Train staff on how to create an IEP.
> - Do not make changes to an IEP without parental consent.
> - Document all efforts to reach parents concerning a child's IEP. Such documentation can include a call log of attempted phone contacts, certified mail, and a return-receipt requirement.

LEAST RESTRICTIVE ENVIRONMENT

The act also contains what is known as a mainstreaming preference, mandating that states educate disabled children alongside nondisabled children "to the maximum extent appropriate."[8] The philosophy behind mainstreaming, or placing students within the "least restrictive environment," is twofold. One benefit is to normalize the education process for students with disabilities. The second is to teach nondisabled students the concept of diversity and acceptance of others. But while the benefits of mainstreaming are undisputable, the issue of whether or not a placement is the least restrictive environment is often decided in the courts.

Daniel R.R. v. State Board of Education
U.S. Court of Appeals for the Fifth Circuit, 1989
874 F.2d 1036

Opinion by Circuit Judge Gee.

Plaintiffs in this action, a handicapped boy and his parents, urge that a local school district failed to comply with the Education of the Handicapped Act. Specifically, they maintain that a school district's refusal to place the child in a class with nonhandicapped students violates the Act. The district court disagreed and, after a careful review of the record, we affirm the district court.

I. Background

A. General

In 1975, on a finding that almost half of the handicapped children in the United States were receiving an inadequate education or none at all, Congress passed the Education of the Handicapped Act (EHA or Act). . . . Educating a handicapped child in a regular education

---

[8]20 U.S.C. § 1412(5)

classroom with nonhandicapped children is familiarly known as "mainstreaming," and the mainstreaming requirement is the source of the controversy between the parties before us today.

B. Particular

Daniel R. is a six year old boy who was enrolled, at the time this case arose, in the El Paso Independent School District (EPISD). A victim of Downs Syndrome, Daniel is mentally retarded and speech impaired. By September 1987, Daniel's developmental age was between two and three years and his communication skills were slightly less than those of a two year old.

In 1985, Daniel's parents, Mr. and Mrs. R., enrolled him in EPISD's Early Childhood Program, a half-day program devoted entirely to special education. Daniel completed one academic year in the Early Childhood Program. Before the 1986–87 school year began, Mrs. R. requested a new placement that would provide association with nonhandicapped children. Mrs. R. wanted EPISD to place Daniel in Pre-kindergarten—a half-day, regular education class. Mrs. R. conferred with Joan Norton, the Pre-kindergarten instructor, proposing that Daniel attend the half-day Pre-kindergarten class in addition to the half-day Early Childhood class. As a result, EPISD's Admission, Review and Dismissal (ARD) Committee met and designated the combined regular and special education program as Daniel's placement.

This soon proved unwise, and not long into the school year Mrs. Norton began to have reservations about Daniel's presence in her class. Daniel did not participate without constant, individual attention from the teacher or her aide, and failed to master any of the skills Mrs. Norton was trying to teach her students. Modifying the Pre-kindergarten curriculum and her teaching methods sufficiently to reach Daniel would have required Mrs. Norton to modify the curriculum almost beyond recognition. In November 1986, the ARD Committee met again, concluded that Pre-kindergarten was inappropriate for Daniel, and decided to change Daniel's placement. Under the new placement, Daniel would attend only the special education, Early Childhood class; would eat lunch in the school cafeteria, with nonhandicapped children, three days a week if his mother was present to supervise him; and would have contact with nonhandicapped students during recess. Believing that the ARD had improperly shut the door to regular education for Daniel, Mr. and Mrs. R. exercised their right to a review of the ARD Committee's decision.

As the EHA requires, Mr. and Mrs. R. appealed to a hearing officer who upheld the ARD Committee's decision. After a hearing which consumed five days of testimony and produced over 2500 pages of transcript, the hearing officer concluded that Daniel could not participate in the Pre-kindergarten class without constant attention from the instructor because the curriculum was beyond his abilities. In addition, the hearing officer found, Daniel was receiving little educational benefit from Pre-kindergarten and was disrupting the class—not in the ordinary sense of the term, but in the sense that his needs absorbed most of the teacher's time and diverted too much of her attention away from the rest of the class. Finally, the instructor would have to downgrade 90 to 100 percent of the Pre-kindergarten curriculum to bring it to a level that Daniel could master. Thus, the hearing officer concluded, the regular education, Pre-kindergarten class was not the appropriate placement for Daniel.

Dissatisfied with the hearing officer's decision, Mr. and Mrs. R. proceeded to the next level of review by filing this action in the district court. Although the EHA permits the parties to supplement the administrative record, Daniel's representatives declined to do so; and the court conducted its de novo review on the basis of the administrative record alone. The district court decided the case on cross motions for summary judgment. Relying primarily on Daniel's inability to receive an educational benefit in regular education, the district court affirmed the hearing officer's decision. . . .

IV. Substantive Violations

A. Mainstreaming Under the EHA

The cornerstone of the EHA is the "free appropriate public education." As a condition of receiving federal funds, states must have "in effect a policy that assures all handicapped children the right to a free appropriate public education." The Act defines a free appropriate public education in broad, general terms without dictating substantive educational policy or mandating specific educational methods. In *Rowley,* the Supreme Court fleshed out the Act's skeletal definition of its principal term: "a 'free appropriate public education' consists of educational instruction specially designed to meet the unique needs of the handicapped child, supported by such services as are necessary to permit the child 'to benefit' from the instruction." The Court's interpretation of the Act's language does not, however, add substance to the Act's vague terms; instruction specially designed to meet each student's unique needs is as imprecise a directive as the language actually found in the Act.

In contrast to the EHA's vague mandate for a free appropriate public education lies one very specific directive prescribing the educational environment for handicapped children. Each state must establish procedures to assure that, to the maximum extent appropriate, handicapped children . . . are educated with children who are not handicapped, and that special education, separate schooling or other removal of handicapped children from the regular educational environment occurs only when the nature or severity of the handicap is such that education in regular classes with the use of supplementary aids and services cannot be achieved satisfactorily.

With this provision, Congress created a strong preference in favor of mainstreaming.

By creating a statutory preference for mainstreaming, Congress also created a tension between two provisions of the Act. School districts must both seek to mainstream handicapped children and, at the same time, must tailor each child's educational placement and program to his special needs. Regular classes, however, will not provide an education that accounts for each child's particular needs in every case. The nature or severity of some children's handicaps is such that only special education can address their needs. For these children, mainstreaming does not provide an education designed to meet their unique needs and, thus, does not provide a free appropriate public education. As a result, we cannot evaluate in the abstract whether a challenged placement meets the EHA's mainstreaming requirement. "Rather, that laudable policy objective must be weighed in tandem with the Act's principal goal of ensuring that the public schools provide handicapped children with a free appropriate public education."

Although Congress preferred education in the regular education environment, it also recognized that regular education is not a suitable setting for educating many handicapped children. Thus, the EHA allows school officials to remove a handicapped child from regular education or to provide special education if they cannot educate the child satisfactorily in the regular classroom. Even when school officials can mainstream the child, they need not provide for an exclusively mainstreamed environment; the Act requires school officials to mainstream each child only to the maximum extent appropriate. In short, the Act's mandate for a free appropriate public education qualifies and limits its mandate for education in the regular classroom. Schools must provide a free appropriate public education and must do so, to the maximum extent appropriate, in regular education classrooms. But when education in a regular classroom cannot meet the handicapped child's unique needs, the presumption in favor of mainstreaming is overcome and the school need not place the child in regular education. The Act does not, however, provide any substantive standards for striking the proper balance between its requirement for mainstreaming and its mandate for a free appropriate public education.

B. Determining Compliance with the Mainstreaming Requirement

Determining the contours of the mainstreaming requirement is a question of first impression for us. In the seminal interpretation of the EHA, the Supreme Court posited a two-part test for determining whether a school has provided a free appropriate public education: "First, has the State complied with the procedures set forth in the Act. And second, is the individualized educational program developed through the Act's procedures reasonably calculated to enable the child to receive educational benefits."

Although we have not yet developed a standard for evaluating mainstreaming questions, we decline to adopt the approach that other circuits have taken. In *Roncker*, visiting the same question which we address today, the Sixth Circuit devised its own test to determine when and to what extent a handicapped child must be mainstreamed. According to the *Roncker* court,

> the proper inquiry is whether a proposed placement is appropriate under the Act. . . . In a case where the segregated facility is considered superior, the court should determine whether the services which make that placement superior could be feasibly provided in a non-segregated setting. If they can, the placement in the segregated school would be inappropriate under the Act.

We respectfully decline to follow the Sixth Circuit's analysis. Certainly, the *Roncker* test accounts for factors that are important in any mainstreaming case. We believe, however, that the test necessitates too intrusive an inquiry into the educational policy choices that Congress deliberately left to state and local school officials. Whether a particular service feasibly can be provided in a regular or special education setting is an administrative determination that state and local school officials are far better qualified and situated than are we to make. Moreover, the test makes little reference to the language of the EHA. Yet, as we shall see, we believe that the language of the Act itself provides a workable test for determining whether a state has complied with the Act's mainstreaming requirement. . . .

Ultimately, our task is to balance competing requirements of the EHA's dual mandate: a free appropriate public education that is provided, to the maximum extent appropriate, in the regular education classroom. As we begin our task we must keep in mind that Congress left the choice of educational policies and methods where it properly belongs—in the hands of state and local school officials. Our task is not to second-guess state and local policy decisions; rather, it is the narrow one of determining whether state and local school officials have complied with the Act. Adhering to the language of the EHA, we discern a two part test for determining compliance with the mainstreaming requirement. First, we ask whether education in the regular classroom, with the use of supplemental aids and services, can be achieved satisfactorily for a given child. If it cannot and the school intends to provide special education or to remove the child from regular education, we ask, second, whether the school has mainstreamed the child to the maximum extent appropriate. A variety of factors will inform each stage of our inquiry; the factors that we consider today do not constitute an exhaustive list of factors relevant to the mainstreaming issue. Moreover, no single factor is dispositive in all cases. Rather, our analysis is an individualized, fact-specific inquiry that requires us to examine carefully the nature and severity of the child's handicapping condition, his needs and abilities, and the schools' response to the child's needs.

In this case, several factors assist the first stage of our inquiry, whether EPISD can achieve education in the regular classroom satisfactorily. At the outset, we must examine whether the state has taken steps to accommodate the handicapped child in regular education. The Act requires states to provide supplementary aids and services and to modify the regular education program when they mainstream handicapped children. If the state has made no effort to take such accommodating steps, our inquiry ends, for the state is in violation of the Act's express mandate to supplement and modify regular education. If the state is providing supplementary aids and services and is modifying its regular education program, we must examine whether its efforts are sufficient. The Act does not permit states to make mere token gestures to accommodate handicapped students; its requirement for modifying and supplementing regular education is broad. Indeed, Texas expressly requires its local school districts to modify their regular education program when necessary to accommodate a handicapped child.

Although broad, the requirement is not limitless. States need not provide every conceivable supplementary aid or service to assist the child. Furthermore, the Act does not require regular education instructors to devote all or most of their time to one handicapped child or to modify the regular education program beyond recognition. If a regular education instructor must devote all of her time to one handicapped child, she will be acting as a special education teacher in a regular education classroom. Moreover, she will be focusing her attentions on one child to the detriment of her entire class, including, perhaps, other, equally deserving, handicapped children who also may require extra attention. Likewise, mainstreaming would be pointless if we forced instructors to modify the regular education curriculum to the extent that the handicapped child is not required to learn any of the skills normally taught in regular education. The child would be receiving special education instruction in the regular education classroom; the only advantage to such an arrangement would be that the child is sitting next to a nonhandicapped student.

Next, we examine whether the child will receive an educational benefit from regular education. This inquiry necessarily will focus on the student's ability to grasp the essential elements of the regular education curriculum. Thus, we must pay close attention to the nature and severity of the child's handicap as well as to the curriculum and goals of the regular education class. For example, if the goal of a particular program is enhancing the child's development, as opposed to teaching him specific subjects such as reading or mathematics, our inquiry must focus on the child's ability to benefit from the developmental lessons, not exclusively on his potential for learning to read. We reiterate, however, that academic achievement is not the only purpose of mainstreaming. Integrating a handicapped child into a nonhandicapped environment may be beneficial in and of itself. Thus, our inquiry must extend beyond the educational benefits that the child may receive in regular education.

We also must examine the child's overall educational experience in the mainstreamed environment, balancing the benefits of regular and special education for each individual child. For example, a child may be able to absorb only a minimal amount of the regular education program, but may benefit enormously from the language models that his nonhandicapped peers provide for him. In such a case, the benefit that the child receives from mainstreaming may tip the balance in favor of mainstreaming, even if the child cannot flourish academically. On the other hand, placing a child in regular education may be detrimental to the child. In such a case, mainstreaming would not provide an education that is attuned to the child's unique needs and would not be required under the Act. Indeed, mainstreaming a child who will suffer from the experience would violate the Act's mandate for a free appropriate public education.

Finally, we ask what effect the handicapped child's presence has on the regular classroom environment and, thus, on the education that the other students are receiving. A handicapped child's placement in regular education may prove troublesome for two reasons. First, the handicapped child may, as a result of his handicap, engage in disruptive behavior. "Where a handicapped child is so disruptive in a regular classroom that the education of other students is significantly impaired, the needs of the handicapped child cannot be met in that environment. Therefore regular placement would not be appropriate to his or her needs." Second, the child may require so much of the instructor's attention that the instructor will have to ignore the other student's needs in order to tend to the handicapped child. The Act and its regulations mandate that the school provide supplementary aids and services in the regular education classroom. A teaching assistant or an aide may minimize the burden on the teacher. If, however, the handicapped child requires so much of the teacher or the aide's time that the rest of the class suffers, then the balance will tip in favor of placing the child in special education.

If we determine that education in the regular classroom cannot be achieved satisfactorily, we next ask whether the child has been mainstreamed to the maximum extent appropriate. The EHA and its regulations do not contemplate an all-or-nothing educational system in which handicapped children attend either regular or special education. Rather, the Act and its regulations require schools to offer a continuum of services. Thus, the school must take intermediate steps where appropriate, such as placing the child in regular education for some academic classes and in special education for others, mainstreaming the child for nonacademic classes only, or providing interaction with nonhandicapped children during lunch and recess. The appropriate mix will vary from child to child and, it may be hoped, from school year to school year as the child develops. If the school officials have provided the maximum appropriate exposure to non-handicapped students, they have fulfilled their obligation under the EHA.

C.   EPISD's Compliance with the Mainstreaming Requirement

After a careful review of the voluminous administrative record, we must agree with the trial court that EPISD's decision to remove Daniel from regular education does not run afoul of the EHA's preference for mainstreaming. Accounting for all of the factors we have identified today, we find that EPISD cannot educate Daniel satisfactorily in the regular education classroom. Furthermore, EPISD has taken creative steps to provide Daniel as much access to nonhandicapped students as it can, while providing him an education that is tailored to his unique needs. Thus, EPISD has mainstreamed Daniel to the maximum extent appropriate.

EPISD cannot educate Daniel satisfactorily in the regular education classroom; each of the factors we identified today counsels against placing Daniel in regular education. First, EPISD took steps to modify the Pre-kindergarten program and to provide supplementary aids and services for Daniel—all of which constitute a sufficient effort. Daniel contends that EPISD took no such steps and that, as a result, we can never know whether Daniel could have been educated in a regular classroom. Daniel's assertion is not supported by the record. The Pre-kindergarten teacher made genuine and creative efforts to reach Daniel, devoting a substantial—indeed, a disproportionate—amount of her time to him and modifying the class curriculum to meet his abilities. Unfortunately, Daniel's needs commanded most of the Pre-kindergarten instructor's time and diverted much of her attention away from the rest of her students. Furthermore, the instructor's efforts to modify the Pre-kindergarten curriculum produced few benefits to Daniel. Indeed, she would have to alter 90 to 100 percent of the curriculum to tailor it to Daniel's abilities. Such an effort would modify the curriculum beyond recognition, an effort which we will not require in the name of mainstreaming.

Second, Daniel receives little, if any, educational benefit in Pre-kindergarten. Dr. Bonnie Fairall, EPISD's Director of Special Education, testified that the Pre-kindergarten curriculum is "developmental in nature; communication skills, gross motor [skills]" and the like. The curriculum in Kindergarten and other grades is an academic program; the developmental skills taught in Pre-kindergarten are essential to success in the academic classes. Daniel's handicap has slowed his development so that he is not yet ready to learn the developmental skills offered in Pre-kindergarten. Daniel does not participate in class activities; he cannot master most or all of the lessons taught in the class. Very simply, Pre-kindergarten offers Daniel nothing but an opportunity to associate with nonhandicapped students.

Third, Daniel's overall educational experience has not been entirely beneficial. As we explained, Daniel can grasp little of the Pre-kindergarten curriculum; the only value of regular education for Daniel is the interaction which he has with nonhandicapped students. Daniel asserts that the opportunity for interaction, alone, is a sufficient ground for mainstreaming him. When we balance the benefits of regular education against those of special education, we cannot agree that the opportunity for Daniel to interact with nonhandicapped students is a sufficient ground for mainstreaming him. Regular education not only offers Daniel little in the way of academic or other benefits, it also may be harming him. When Daniel was placed in Pre-kindergarten, he attended school for a full day; both Pre-kindergarten and Early Childhood were half-day classes. The experts who testified before the hearing officer indicated that the full day program is too strenuous for a child with Daniel's condition. Simply put, Daniel is exhausted and, as a result, he sometimes falls asleep at school. Moreover, the record indicates that the stress of regular education may be causing Daniel to develop a stutter. Special education, on the other hand, is an educational environment in which Daniel is making progress. Balancing the benefits of a program that is only marginally beneficial and is somewhat detrimental against the benefits of a program that is clearly beneficial, we must agree that the beneficial program provides the more appropriate placement.

Finally, we agree that Daniel's presence in regular Pre-kindergarten is unfair to the rest of the class. When Daniel is in the Pre-kindergarten classroom, the instructor must devote all or most of her time to Daniel. Yet she has a classroom filled with other, equally deserving students who need her attention. Although regular education instructors must devote extra attention to their handicapped students, we will not require them to do so at the expense of their entire class.

Alone, each of the factors that we have reviewed suggests that EPISD cannot educate Daniel satisfactorily in the regular education classroom. Together, they clearly tip the balance in favor of placing Daniel in special education. Thus, we turn to the next phase of our inquiry and conclude that EPISD has mainstreamed Daniel to the maximum extent appropriate. Finding that a placement that allocates Daniel's time equally between regular and special education is not appropriate, EPISD has taken the intermediate step of mainstreaming Daniel for lunch and recess. This opportunity for association with nonhandicapped students is not as extensive as Daniel's parents would like. It is, however, an appropriate step that may help to prepare Daniel for regular education in the future. As education in the regular classroom, with the use of supplementary aids and services cannot be achieved satisfactorily, and as EPISD has placed Daniel with nonhandicapped students to the maximum extent appropriate, we affirm the district court. . . .

We thus affirm.

RELATED SERVICES

THE DEFINITION of *related services* is broader than most educators first assume. According to IDEA,

> The term "related services" means transportation, and such developmental, corrective, and other supportive services (including speech-language pathology and audiology services, psychological services, physical and occupational therapy, recreation, including therapeutic recreation, social work services, counseling services, including rehabilitation counseling, orientation and mobility services, and medical services, except that such medical services shall be for diagnostic and evaluation purposes only)

*as may be required to assist a child with a disability to benefit from special education,
and includes the early identification and assessment of disabling conditions in
children.*[9]

In 1984, the Supreme Court decided the *Irving Independent School District v. Tatro*
case and clarified the difference between a medical service and a related service.

Irving Independent School District v. Tatro
Supreme Court of the United States, 1984
468 U.S. 883

Chief Justice Burger delivered the opinion of the Court.

We granted certiorari to determine whether the Education of the Handicapped Act or the
Rehabilitation Act of 1973 requires a school district to provide a handicapped child with
clean intermittent catheterization during school hours.

I

Amber Tatro is an 8-year-old girl born with a defect known as spinal bifida. As a result, she
suffers from orthopedic and speech impairments and a neurogenic bladder, which prevents
her from emptying her bladder voluntarily. Consequently, she must be catheterized every
three or four hours to avoid injury to her kidneys. In accordance with accepted medical
practice, clean intermittent catheterization (CIC), a procedure involving the insertion of a
catheter into the urethra to drain the bladder, has been prescribed. The procedure is a simple one that may be performed in a few minutes by a layperson with less than an hour's
training. Amber's parents, babysitter, and teenage brother are all qualified to administer
CIC, and Amber soon will be able to perform this procedure herself.

In 1979 petitioner Irving Independent School District agreed to provide special education
for Amber, who was then three and one-half years old. In consultation with her parents,
who are respondents here, petitioner developed an individualized education program for
Amber under the requirements of the Education of the Handicapped Act. The individualized education program provided that Amber would attend early childhood development
classes and receive special services such as physical and occupational therapy. That program,
however, made no provision for school personnel to administer CIC.

Respondents unsuccessfully pursued administrative remedies to secure CIC services for
Amber during school hours. In October 1979 respondents brought the present action in
District Court against petitioner, the State Board of Education, and others. . . . The [issue] is
whether the Education of the Handicapped Act requires petitioner to provide CIC services
to Amber. . . .

---

[9]20 U.S.C.S. § 1401

States receiving funds under the Act are obliged to satisfy certain conditions. A primary condition is that the state implement a policy "that assures all handicapped children the right to a free appropriate public education." Each educational agency applying to a state for funding must provide assurances in turn that its program aims to provide "a free appropriate public education to all handicapped children."

A "free appropriate public education" is explicitly defined as "special education and related services." The term "special education" means "specially designed instruction, at no cost to parents or guardians, to meet the unique needs of a handicapped child, including classroom instruction, instruction in physical education, home instruction, and instruction in hospitals and institutions."

> "Related services" are defined as transportation, and such developmental, corrective, and other supportive services (including speech pathology and audiology, psychological services, physical and occupational therapy, recreation, and medical and counseling services, except that such medical services shall be for diagnostic and evaluation purposes only) as may be required to assist a handicapped child to benefit from special education, and includes the early identification and assessment of handicapping conditions in children.

The issue in this case is whether CIC is a "related service" that petitioner is obliged to provide to Amber. We must answer two questions: first, whether CIC is a "supportive [service] . . . required to assist a handicapped child to benefit from special education"; and second, whether CIC is excluded from this definition as a "medical [service]" serving purposes other than diagnosis or evaluation.

A

The Court of Appeals was clearly correct in holding that CIC is a "supportive [service] . . . required to assist a handicapped child to benefit from special education." It is clear on this record that, without having CIC services available during the school day, Amber cannot attend school and thereby "benefit from special education." CIC services therefore fall squarely within the definition of a "supportive service."

As we have stated before, "Congress sought primarily to make public education available to handicapped children" and "to make such access meaningful." A service that enables a handicapped child to remain at school during the day is an important means of providing the child with the meaningful access to education that Congress envisioned. The Act makes specific provision for services, like transportation, for example, that do no more than enable a child to be physically present in class, and the Act specifically authorizes grants for schools to alter buildings and equipment to make them accessible to the handicapped. Services like CIC that permit a child to remain at school during the day are no less related to the effort to educate than are services that enable the child to reach, enter, or exit the school.

We hold that CIC services in this case qualify as a "supportive [service] . . . required to assist a handicapped child to benefit from special education."

B

We also agree with the Court of Appeals that provision of CIC is not a "medical [service]," which a school is required to provide only for purposes of diagnosis or evaluation. . . . The regulations define "related services" for handicapped children to include "school health services," which are defined in turn as "services provided by a qualified school nurse or other qualified person." "Medical services" are defined as "services provided by a licensed physician." Thus, the Secretary has determined that the services of a school nurse otherwise qualifying as a "related service" are not subject to exclusion as a "medical service," but that the services of a physician are excludable as such.

This definition of "medical services" is a reasonable interpretation of congressional intent. Although Congress devoted little discussion to the "medical services" exclusion, the Secretary could reasonably have concluded that it was designed to spare schools from an obligation to provide a service that might well prove unduly expensive and beyond the range of their competence. From this understanding of congressional purpose, the Secretary could reasonably have concluded that Congress intended to impose the obligation to provide school nursing services.

Congress plainly required schools to hire various specially trained personnel to help handicapped children, such as "trained occupational therapists, speech therapists, psychologists, social workers and other appropriately trained personnel." School nurses have long been a part of the educational system, and the Secretary could therefore reasonably conclude that school nursing services are not the sort of burden that Congress intended to exclude as a "medical service." By limiting the "medical services" exclusion to the services of a physician or hospital, both far more expensive, the Secretary has given a permissible construction to the provision.

Petitioner's contrary interpretation of the "medical services" exclusion is unconvincing. In petitioner's view, CIC is a "medical service," even though it may be provided by a nurse or trained layperson; that conclusion rests on its reading of Texas law that confines CIC to uses in accordance with a physician's prescription and under a physician's ultimate supervision. Aside from conflicting with the Secretary's reasonable interpretation of congressional intent, however, such a rule would be anomalous. Nurses in petitioner School District are authorized to dispense oral medications and administer emergency injections in accordance with a physician's prescription. This kind of service for nonhandicapped children is difficult to distinguish from the provision of CIC to the handicapped. It would be strange indeed if Congress, in attempting to extend special services to handicapped children, were unwilling to guarantee them services of a kind that are routinely provided to the nonhandicapped.

To keep in perspective the obligation to provide services that relate to both the health and educational needs of handicapped students, we note several limitations that should minimize the burden petitioner fears. First, to be entitled to related services, a child must be handicapped so as to require special education. In the absence of a handicap that requires special education, the need for what otherwise might qualify as a related service does not create an obligation under the Act.

Second, only those services necessary to aid a handicapped child to benefit from special education must be provided, regardless how easily a school nurse or layperson could furnish them. For example, if a particular medication or treatment may appropriately be administered to a handicapped child other than during the school day, a school is not required to provide nursing services to administer it.

Third, the regulations state that school nursing services must be provided only if they can be performed by a nurse or other qualified person, not if they must be performed by a physician. It bears mentioning that here not even the services of a nurse are required; as is conceded, a layperson with minimal training is qualified to provide CIC. Finally, we note that respondents are not asking petitioner to provide equipment that Amber needs for CIC. They seek only the services of a qualified person at the school.

We conclude that provision of CIC to Amber is not subject to exclusion as a "medical service," and we affirm the Court of Appeals' holding that CIC is a "related service" under the Education of the Handicapped Act.

Justice Brennan concurred in part and Justice Stevens in part. Justice Brennan, with whom Justice Marshall joined, filed a dissent.

According to the facts in *Tatro*, the catheterization procedure that Amber needed was relatively easy to perform. Of her family, even her teenage brother was trained to perform the procedure. When Amber began school, the district refused to perform the procedure, claiming it was a medical service, not a related service. The U.S. Supreme Court disagreed and held that the procedure was a related service under IDEA.

The line between school health services required as related services and medical services that are not required is not always clear. In *Cedar Rapids Community School District v. Garret F.*, however, the Supreme Court determined that the school district was required to pay for a licensed registered nurse to attend to a student while he was in school.[10] The student, a 16-year-old male, was paralyzed in a motorcycle accident at age 4. Garret, who had no mental impairments, operated a motorized wheelchair but needed urinary bladder catheterization once a day and suctioning of his tracheotomy tube as needed, usually after lunch. The school district argued that such care fell under "medical services" and additionally argued that the nurse, who cost approximately $40,000 per year, would create a financial hardship for the institution. The Court in its analysis stated:

> The District may have legitimate financial concerns, but our role in this dispute is to interpret existing law. Defining "related services" in a manner that accommodates the cost concerns Congress may have had is altogether different from using cost itself as the definition. Given that § 1401(a)(17) does not employ cost in its definition of "related services" or excluded "medical services," accepting the District's cost-based standard as the sole test for determining the scope of the provision would require us to engage in judicial lawmaking without any guidance from Congress. It would also create some tension with the purposes of the IDEA. The statute may not require public schools to maximize the potential of disabled students commensurate with the

---

[10]*Cedar Rapids County School District v. Garret F.*, 526 U.S. 66, at 77 (1999)

opportunities provided to other children, and the potential financial burdens imposed on participating States may be relevant to arriving at a sensible construction of the IDEA. But Congress intended "to open the door of public education" to all qualified children and "required participating States to educate handicapped children with nonhandicapped children whenever possible."[11]

Nevertheless, as students are being mainstreamed into the regular classrooms, school personnel are required to perform related services such as catheterization. While required by IDEA, an issue sometimes overlooked is the importance of performing the related services in a safe and reasonable manner.

Best Practices

To avoid a negligence lawsuit, train teachers and staff who perform related services and ensure they meet a reasonable standard of care. If teachers are uncomfortable about performing related services that require certain medical procedures, the school nurse (if possible) should perform the procedures.

The definition of related services is explained in *Tatro*, but it does not mean that a school must offer the best services. The Supreme Court decision in *Rowley* held that schools are not required to maximize a child's potential in the classroom. Rather, schools are required only to offer tools that ensure that students receive an appropriate education and give them the services necessary for equivalence among other students.

Board of Education v. Rowley
Supreme Court of the United States, 1982
458 U.S. 176

Justice Rehnquist delivered the opinion of the Court.

This case presents a question of statutory interpretation. Petitioners contend that the Court of Appeals and the District Court misconstrued the requirements imposed by Congress upon States which receive federal funds under the Education of the Handicapped Act. We agree and reverse the judgment of the Court of Appeals. . . .

This case arose in connection with the education of Amy Rowley, a deaf student at the Furnace Woods School in the Hendrick Hudson Central School District, Peekskill, N.Y. Amy has minimal residual hearing and is an excellent lipreader. During the year before she began

---

[11]Ibid., at 77

attending Furnace Woods, a meeting between her parents and school administrators resulted in a decision to place her in a regular kindergarten class in order to determine what supplemental services would be necessary to her education. Several members of the school administration prepared for Amy's arrival by attending a course in sign-language interpretation, and a teletype machine was installed in the principal's office to facilitate communication with her parents who are also deaf. At the end of the trial period it was determined that Amy should remain in the kindergarten class, but that she should be provided with an FM hearing aid which would amplify words spoken into a wireless receiver by the teacher or fellow students during certain classroom activities. Amy successfully completed her kindergarten year.

As required by the Act, an IEP was prepared for Amy during the fall of her first-grade year. The IEP provided that Amy should be educated in a regular classroom at Furnace Woods, should continue to use the FM hearing aid, and should receive instruction from a tutor for the deaf for one hour each day and from a speech therapist for three hours each week. The Rowleys agreed with parts of the IEP but insisted that Amy also be provided a qualified sign-language interpreter in all her academic classes in lieu of the assistance proposed in other parts of the IEP. Such an interpreter had been placed in Amy's kindergarten class for a 2-week experimental period, but the interpreter had reported that Amy did not need his services at that time. The school administrators likewise concluded that Amy did not need such an interpreter in her first-grade classroom. They reached this conclusion after consulting the school district's Committee on the Handicapped, which had received expert evidence from Amy's parents on the importance of a sign-language interpreter, received testimony from Amy's teacher and other persons familiar with her academic and social progress, and visited a class for the deaf.

When their request for an interpreter was denied, the Rowleys demanded and received a hearing before an independent examiner. After receiving evidence from both sides, the examiner agreed with the administrators' determination that an interpreter was not necessary because "Amy was achieving educationally, academically, and socially" without such assistance. The examiner's decision was affirmed on appeal by the New York Commissioner of Education on the basis of substantial evidence in the record. Pursuant to the Act's provision for judicial review, the Rowleys then brought an action in the United States District Court for the Southern District of New York, claiming that the administrators' denial of the sign-language interpreter constituted a denial of the "free appropriate public education" guaranteed by the Act.

The District Court found that Amy "is a remarkably well-adjusted child" who interacts and communicates well with her classmates and has "developed an extraordinary rapport" with her teachers. It also found that "she performs better than the average child in her class and is advancing easily from grade to grade," but "that she understands considerably less of what goes on in class than she could if she were not deaf" and thus "is not learning as much, or performing as well academically, as she would without her handicap." This disparity between Amy's achievement and her potential led the court to decide that she was not receiving a "free appropriate public education," which the court defined as "an opportunity to achieve [her] full potential commensurate with the opportunity provided to other children." According to the District Court, such a standard "requires that the potential of the handicapped child be measured and compared to his or her performance, and that the resulting differential or 'shortfall' be compared to the shortfall experienced by nonhandicapped children." The District Court's definition arose from its assumption that the responsibility for "[giving] content to the requirement of an 'appropriate education'" had "been left entirely to the [federal] courts and the hearing officers."

A divided panel of the United States Court of Appeals for the Second Circuit affirmed. The Court of Appeals "[agreed] with the [District Court's] conclusions of law," and held that its "findings of fact [were] not clearly erroneous."

We granted certiorari to review the lower courts' interpretation of the Act. Such review requires us to consider two questions: What is meant by the Act's requirement of a "free appropriate public education"? And what is the role of state and federal courts in exercising the review granted by 20 U.S.C. § 1415? We consider these questions separately. . . .

This is the first case in which this Court has been called upon to interpret any provision of the Act. As noted previously, the District Court and the Court of Appeals concluded that "[the] Act itself does not define 'appropriate education,'" but leaves "to the courts and the hearing officers" the responsibility of "[giving] content to the requirement of an 'appropriate education.'" Petitioners contend that the definition of the phrase "free appropriate public education" used by the courts below overlooks the definition of that phrase actually found in the Act. Respondents agree that the Act defines "free appropriate public education," but contend that the statutory definition is not "functional" and thus "offers judges no guidance in their consideration of controversies involving 'the identification, evaluation, or educational placement of the child or the provision of a free appropriate public education.'" The United States, appearing as amicus curiae on behalf of respondents, states that "[although] the Act includes definitions of a 'free appropriate public education' and other related terms, the statutory definitions do not adequately explain what is meant by 'appropriate.'"

We are loath to conclude that Congress failed to offer any assistance in defining the meaning of the principal substantive phrase used in the Act. It is beyond dispute that, contrary to the conclusions of the courts below, the Act does expressly define "free appropriate public education": "The term 'free appropriate public education' means special education and related services which (A) have been provided at public expense, under public supervision and direction, and without charge, (B) meet the standards of the State educational agency, (C) include an appropriate preschool, elementary, or secondary school education in the State involved, and (D) are provided in conformity with the individualized education program required under section 1414(a)(5) of this title."

"Special education," as referred to in this definition, means "specially designed instruction, at no cost to parents or guardians, to meet the unique needs of a handicapped child, including classroom instruction, instruction in physical education, home instruction, and instruction in hospitals and institutions." "Related services" are defined as "transportation, and such developmental, corrective, and other supportive services . . . as may be required to assist a handicapped child to benefit from special education." . . .

According to the definitions contained in the Act, a "free appropriate public educa-tion" consists of educational instruction specially designed to meet the unique needs of the handicapped child, supported by such services as are necessary to permit the child "to benefit" from the instruction. Almost as a checklist for adequacy under the Act, the def-inition also requires that such instruction and services be provided at public expense and under public supervision, meet the State's educational standards, approximate the grade levels used in the State's regular education, and comport with the child's IEP. Thus, if per-sonalized instruction is being provided with sufficient supportive services to permit the child to benefit from the instruction, and the other items on the definitional checklist are satisfied, the child is receiving a "free appropriate public education" as defined by the Act. . . .

Noticeably absent from the language of the statute is any substantive standard prescrib-ing the level of education to be accorded handicapped children. Certainly the language of the statute contains no requirement like the one imposed by the lower courts—that States maximize the potential of handicapped children "commensurate with the opportunity pro-vided to other children." That standard was expounded by the District Court without refer-ence to the statutory definitions or even to the legislative history of the Act. Although we find the statutory definition of "free appropriate public education" to be helpful in our in-terpretation of the Act, there remains the question of whether the legislative history indi-cates a congressional intent that such education meet some additional substantive standard. For an answer, we turn to that history. . . .

Federal support for education of the handicapped is a fairly recent development. Before passage of the Act some States had passed laws to improve the educational services af-forded handicapped children, but many of these children were excluded completely from any form of public education or were left to fend for themselves in classrooms designed for education of their nonhandicapped peers. As previously noted, the House Report begins by emphasizing this exclusion and misplacement, noting that millions of handicapped children "were either totally excluded from schools or [were] sitting idly in regular classrooms await-ing the time when they were old enough to 'drop out.'" One of the Act's two principal sponsors in the Senate urged its passage in similar terms: "While much progress has been made in the last few years, we can take no solace in that progress until all handicapped chil-dren are, in fact, receiving an education. The most recent statistics provided by the Bureau of Education for the Handicapped estimate that . . . 1.75 million handicapped children do not receive any educational services, and 2.5 million handicapped children are not receiving an appropriate education."

This concern, stressed repeatedly throughout the legislative history, confirms the im-pression conveyed by the language of the statute: By passing the Act, Congress sought primarily to make public education available to handicapped children. But in seeking to provide such access to public education, Congress did not impose upon the States any greater substantive educational standard than would be necessary to make such access meaningful. Indeed, Congress expressly "[recognized] that in many instances the process of providing special education and related services to handicapped children is not guaranteed to produce any particular outcome." Thus, the intent of the Act was more to open the door of public education to handicapped children on appropriate terms than to guarantee any particular level of education once inside. . . .

Respondents contend that "the goal of the Act is to provide each handicapped child with an equal educational opportunity." We think, however, that the requirement that a State provide specialized educational services to handicapped children generates no additional requirement that the services so provided be sufficient to maximize each child's potential "commensurate with the opportunity provided other children." Respondents and the United States correctly note that Congress sought "to provide assistance to the States in carrying out their responsibilities under . . . the Constitution of the United States to provide equal protection of the laws." But we do not think that such statements imply a congressional intent to achieve strict equality of opportunity or services.

The educational opportunities provided by our public school systems undoubtedly differ from student to student, depending upon a myriad of factors that might affect a particular student's ability to assimilate information presented in the classroom. The requirement that States provide "equal" educational opportunities would thus seem to present an entirely unworkable standard requiring impossible measurements and comparisons. Similarly, furnishing handicapped children with only such services as are available to nonhandicapped children would in all probability fall short of the statutory requirement of "free appropriate public education"; to require, on the other hand, the furnishing of every special service necessary to maximize each handicapped child's potential is, we think, further than Congress intended to go. Thus to speak in terms of "equal" services in one instance gives less than what is required by the Act and in another instance more. The theme of the Act is "free appropriate public education," a phrase which is too complex to be captured by the word "equal" whether one is speaking of opportunities or services.

The legislative conception of the requirements of equal protection was undoubtedly informed by the two District Court decisions. . . . But cases such as *Mills* and *PARC* held simply that handicapped children may not be excluded entirely from public education. In *Mills*, the District Court said: "If sufficient funds are not available to finance all of the services and programs that are needed and desirable in the system then the available funds must be expended equitably in such a manner that no child is entirely excluded from a publicly supported education consistent with his needs and ability to benefit therefrom."

The *PARC* court used similar language, saying "[it] is the commonwealth's obligation to place each mentally retarded child in a free, public program of education and training appropriate to the child's capacity. . . ." The right of access to free public education enunciated by these cases is significantly different from any notion of absolute equality of opportunity regardless of capacity. To the extent that Congress might have looked further than these cases which are mentioned in the legislative history, at the time of enactment of the Act this Court had held at least twice that the Equal Protection Clause of the Fourteenth Amendment does not require States to expend equal financial resources on the education of each child. . . .

Implicit in the congressional purpose of providing access to a "free appropriate public education" is the requirement that the education to which access is provided be sufficient to confer some educational benefit upon the handicapped child. It would do little good for Congress to spend millions of dollars in providing access to a public education only to have the handicapped child receive no benefit from that education. The statutory definition of "free appropriate public education," in addition to requiring that States provide each child with "specially designed instruction," expressly requires the provision of "such . . . supportive services . . . as may be required to assist a handicapped child to benefit from special education." We therefore conclude that the "basic floor of opportunity" provided by the Act consists of access to specialized instruction and related services which are individually designed to provide educational benefit to the handicapped child.

The determination of when handicapped children are receiving sufficient educational benefits to satisfy the requirements of the Act presents a more difficult problem. The Act requires participating States to educate a wide spectrum of handicapped children, from the marginally hearing-impaired to the profoundly retarded and palsied. It is clear that the benefits obtainable by children at one end of the spectrum will differ dramatically from those obtainable by children at the other end, with infinite variations in between. One child may have little difficulty competing successfully in an academic setting with nonhandicapped children while another child may encounter great difficulty in acquiring even the most basic of self-maintenance skills. We do not attempt today to establish any one test for determining the adequacy of educational benefits conferred upon all children covered by the Act. Because in this case we are presented with a handicapped child who is receiving substantial specialized instruction and related services, and who is performing above average in the regular classrooms of a public school system, we confine our analysis to that situation.

The Act requires participating States to educate handicapped children with nonhandicapped children whenever possible. When that "mainstreaming" preference of the Act has been met and a child is being educated in the regular classrooms of a public school system, the system itself monitors the educational progress of the child. Regular examinations are administered, grades are awarded, and yearly advancement to higher grade levels is permitted for those children who attain an adequate knowledge of the course material. The grading and advancement system thus constitutes an important factor in determining educational benefit. Children who graduate from our public school systems are considered by our society to have been "educated" at least to the grade level they have completed, and access to an "education" for handicapped children is precisely what Congress sought to provide in the Act. . . .

When the language of the Act and its legislative history are considered together, the requirements imposed by Congress become tolerably clear. Insofar as a State is required to provide a handicapped child with a "free appropriate public education," we hold that it satisfies this requirement by providing personalized instruction with sufficient support services to permit the child to benefit educationally from that instruction. Such instruction and services must be provided at public expense, must meet the State's educational standards, must approximate the grade levels used in the State's regular education, and must comport with the child's IEP. In addition, the IEP, and therefore the personalized instruction, should be formulated in accordance with the requirements of the Act and, if the child is being educated in the regular classrooms of the public education system, should be reasonably calculated to enable the child to achieve passing marks and advance from grade to grade. . . .

Applying these principles to the facts of this case, we conclude that the Court of Appeals erred in affirming the decision of the District Court. Neither the District Court nor the Court of Appeals found that petitioners had failed to comply with the procedures of the Act, and the findings of neither court would support a conclusion that Amy's educational program failed to comply with the substantive requirements of the Act. On the contrary, the District Court found that the "evidence firmly establishes that Amy is receiving an 'adequate' education, since she performs better than the average child in her class and is advancing easily from grade to grade." In light of this finding, and of the fact that Amy was receiving personalized instruction and related services calculated by the Furnace Woods school administrators to meet her educational needs, the lower courts should not have concluded that the Act requires the provision of a sign-language interpreter. Accordingly, the decision of the Court of Appeals is reversed, and the case is remanded for further proceedings consistent with this opinion.

Justice Blackmun filed a concurring opinion. Justice White filed a dissenting opinion, joined by Brennan and Marshall.

Cost Issues

IN *BOARD of Education of Montgomery County v. Hunter*, the public school was unable to provide adequate related services to a child with epilepsy.[12] Due to the severity of the child's disability, he was unable to be mainstreamed in the regular classroom; and the school was unable to develop an individual student plan based on the child's IEP. Based on the theory that all children will receive a free appropriate education, the court held that the student should be placed in a private institution and that the public school was required to pay for such placement. Because the public school could not accommodate the student, such a transfer was the school's financial responsibility and was extremely expensive.

It is important to recognize that if the parents of a disabled child independently decide to place that child in a private institution, they may do so. But "if a handicapped child has available a free appropriate public education and the parents choose to place the child in a private school or facility, the public agency is not required by this part to pay for the child's education at the private school or facility."[13] Nevertheless, parents will be reimbursed for the cost of private school if they can prove that the school has misplaced the child or if the district can not provide adequate services to support the child's needs.

---

[12]84 F.Supp.2d 702 (2000)

[13]*School Committee of the Town of Burlington, Massachusetts, v. Department of Education of Massachusetts*, 471 U.S. 359, at 373, (1985)

SUMMARY

Prior to the passage of legislation protecting students with disabilities, millions of students were not educated within the public school system and never given the opportunity to learn. Today the law requires that federally funded schools provide a free appropriate public education to all students, regardless of their disability. Additionally, as laid out within the Individuals with Disabilities Education Act (IDEA), students must be given related services, have an annual Individualized Educational Plan with involvement by the parent or guardian, and mainstreamed into the classroom with non-disabled students to the extent possible. Such requirements are both time consuming and expensive, but required by federal law.

Ensuring students with disabilities gain an appropriate education is an area of education law which has changed dramatically over the years and has set forth mandatory requirements on the public schools. The most recent change occurred in 1997, hence, another example of why it is critical that administrators understand the new law, as well as keep abreast of any changes within this area.

DISCUSSION QUESTIONS

1. Before the 1970s, how were students with disabilities educated in the United States? Discuss the typical education of a child with a disability before the passage of IDEA.
2. It has been estimated that some schools spend at least 20 percent of their budgets on providing appropriate educational services to students with disabilities. Although this education is indisputably expensive, what is the cost of failing to educate children with disabilities?
3. How are children identified under the child-find provision of IDEA (see the appendix)? What can school districts do if parents will not consent to the identification procedures?
4. Define both related services and medical services under IDEA and then compare and contrast them using examples from case law.
5. The court in *Tatro* stated that educational institutions must provide related services. But since most educators are not medically trained, they must be extra careful to avoid negligence when performing the related services. Discuss this paradox using real-life examples.
6. Define *free appropriate public education.*
7. Discuss the intention behind the theory of mainstreaming and least restrictive environment.
8. The students in the *Rowley* and *Tatro* cases both needed special educational assistance. Why did the courts find different results? Discuss the courts' rationales.
9. What procedural safeguards are in place if parents are not satisfied with their child's placement or IEP?

10. Parents of nondisabled students have no legal standing under IDEA to challenge the placement or services of their children. Should they? Is this an area for potential litigation?

DEEPENING YOUR UNDERSTANDING

1. Using the resources in the appendix, define *disability*.
2. Using the resources in the appendix, research and discuss the remedies set forth for parents who believe a school has violated IDEA.

STUDENTS' RIGHTS

INTRODUCTION

The right to free speech has long been protected under the First Amendment of the U.S. Constitution. The amendment reads: "Congress shall make no law respecting an establishment of religion, or prohibiting the free exercise thereof; or abridging the freedom of speech, or of the press; or the right of the people peaceably to assemble, and to petition the Government for a redress of grievances." Concerning freedom of speech, the First Amendment is interpreted to mean that the government, which includes public schools, will not interfere with or restrict one's right to expression.

"The Fourteenth Amendment, as now applied to the States, protects the citizen against the State itself and all of its creatures, Boards of Education not excepted."[1] Especially within an educational institution, the learning experience is enhanced by the sharing of ideas and opinions. Knowledge would be stagnated if the marketplace of ideas could not be explored. Due to their importance, the rights protected by the First Amendment are closely guarded by the courts.

FREEDOM OF EXPRESSION

EARLY in educational history, students' speech had little protection under the Constitution, especially once children entered school. In 1969, however, the U.S. Supreme Court determined that students did have constitutional rights and that rights were not lost once they entered the public school system. In the landmark case *Tinker v. Des*

---

[1] *West Virginia State Board of Education v. Barnette,* 319 U.S. 624, at 637 (1943)

Moines Independent Community School District, the Court balanced the interest of the school in its quest to provide a safe learning environment order against the rights of students to express their opinions.[2] This balancing test is commonly referred to as the *Tinker* test.

Tinker v. Des Moines Independent Community School District
Supreme Court of the United States, 1969
393 U.S. 503

Mr. Justice Fortas delivered the opinion of the Court.

Petitioner John F. Tinker, 15 years old, and petitioner Christopher Eckhardt, 16 years old, attended high schools in Des Moines, Iowa. Petitioner Mary Beth Tinker, John's sister, was a 13-year-old student in junior high school.

In December 1965, a group of adults and students in Des Moines held a meeting at the Eckhardt home. The group determined to publicize their objections to the hostilities in Vietnam and their support for a truce by wearing black armbands during the holiday season and by fasting on December 16 and New Year's Eve. Petitioners and their parents had previously engaged in similar activities, and they decided to participate in the program.

The principals of the Des Moines schools became aware of the plan to wear armbands. On December 14, 1965, they met and adopted a policy that any student wearing an armband to school would be asked to remove it, and if he refused he would be suspended until he returned without the armband. Petitioners were aware of the regulation that the school authorities adopted.

On December 16, Mary Beth and Christopher wore black armbands to their schools. John Tinker wore his armband the next day. They were all sent home and suspended from school until they would come back without their armbands. They did not return to school until after the planned period for wearing armbands had expired—that is, until after New Year's Day.

This complaint was filed in the United States District Court by petitioners, through their fathers, under § 1983 of Title 42 of the United States Code. It prayed for an injunction restraining the respondent school officials and the respondent members of the board of directors of the school district from disciplining the petitioners, and it sought nominal damages. After an evidentiary hearing the District Court dismissed the complaint. It upheld the constitutionality of the school authorities' action on the ground that it was reasonable in order to prevent disturbance of school discipline. The court referred to but expressly declined to follow the Fifth Circuit's holding in a similar case that the wearing of symbols like the armbands cannot be prohibited unless it "materially and substantially interfere[s] with the requirements of appropriate discipline in the operation of the school."

---

[2]393 U.S. 503 (1969)

On appeal, the Court of Appeals for the Eighth Circuit considered the case en banc. The court was equally divided, and the District Court's decision was accordingly affirmed, without opinion. We granted certiorari.

The District Court recognized that the wearing of an armband for the purpose of expressing certain views is the type of symbolic act that is within the Free Speech Clause of the First Amendment. As we shall discuss, the wearing of armbands in the circumstances of this case was entirely divorced from actually or potentially disruptive conduct by those participating in it. It was closely akin to "pure speech" which, we have repeatedly held, is entitled to comprehensive protection under the First Amendment.

First Amendment rights, applied in light of the special characteristics of the school environment, are available to teachers and students. It can hardly be argued that either students or teachers shed their constitutional rights to freedom of speech or expression at the schoolhouse gate. This has been the unmistakable holding of this Court for almost 50 years.

In *West Virginia v. Barnette*, this Court held that under the First Amendment, the student in public school may not be compelled to salute the flag. Speaking through Mr. Justice Jackson, the Court said: "The Fourteenth Amendment, as now applied to the States, protects the citizen against the State itself and all of its creatures—Boards of Education not excepted. These have, of course, important, delicate, and highly discretionary functions, but none that they may not perform within the limits of the Bill of Rights. That they are educating the young for citizenship is reason for scrupulous protection of Constitutional freedoms of the individual, if we are not to strangle the free mind at its source and teach youth to discount important principles of our government as mere platitudes."

On the other hand, the Court has repeatedly emphasized the need for affirming the comprehensive authority of the States and of school officials, consistent with fundamental constitutional safeguards, to prescribe and control conduct in the schools. Our problem lies in the area where students in the exercise of First Amendment rights collide with the rules of the school authorities.

The problem posed by the present case does not relate to regulation of the length of skirts or the type of clothing, to hairstyle, or deportment. It does not concern aggressive, disruptive action or even group demonstrations. Our problem involves direct, primary First Amendment rights akin to "pure speech."

The school officials banned and sought to punish petitioners for a silent, passive expression of opinion, unaccompanied by any disorder or disturbance on the part of petitioners. There is here no evidence whatever of petitioners' interference, actual or nascent, with the schools' work or of collision with the rights of other students to be secure and to be let alone. Accordingly, this case does not concern speech or action that intrudes upon the work of the schools or the rights of other students.

Only a few of the 18,000 students in the school system wore the black armbands. Only five students were suspended for wearing them. There is no indication that the work of the schools or any class was disrupted. Outside the classrooms, a few students made hostile remarks to the children wearing armbands, but there were no threats or acts of violence on school premises.

The District Court concluded that the action of the school authorities was reasonable because it was based upon their fear of a disturbance from the wearing of the armbands. But, in our system, undifferentiated fear or apprehension of disturbance is not enough to overcome the right to freedom of expression. Any departure from absolute regimentation may cause trouble. Any variation from the majority's opinion may inspire fear. Any word spoken, in class, in the lunchroom, or on the campus, that deviates from the views of another person may start an argument or cause a disturbance. But our Constitution says we must take this risk; . . . and our history says that it is this sort of hazardous freedom—this kind of openness—that is the basis of our national strength and of the independence and vigor of Americans who grow up and live in this relatively permissive, often disputatious, society.

In order for the State in the person of school officials to justify prohibition of a particular expression of opinion, it must be able to show that its action was caused by something more than a mere desire to avoid the discomfort and unpleasantness that always accompany an unpopular viewpoint. Certainly where there is no finding and no showing that engaging in the forbidden conduct would "materially and substantially interfere with the requirements of appropriate discipline in the operation of the school," the prohibition cannot be sustained.

In the present case, the District Court made no such finding, and our independent examination of the record fails to yield evidence that the school authorities had reason to anticipate that the wearing of the armbands would substantially interfere with the work of the school or impinge upon the rights of other students. Even an official memorandum prepared after the suspension that listed the reasons for the ban on wearing the armbands made no reference.

On the contrary, the action of the school authorities appears to have been based upon an urgent wish to avoid the controversy which might result from the expression, even by the silent symbol of armbands, of opposition to this Nation's part in the conflagration in Vietnam. It is revealing, in this respect, that the meeting at which the school principals decided to issue the contested regulation was called in response to a student's statement to the journalism teacher in one of the schools that he wanted to write an article on Vietnam and have it published in the school paper. (The student was dissuaded.)

It is also relevant that the school authorities did not purport to prohibit the wearing of all symbols of political or controversial significance. The record shows that students in some of the schools wore buttons relating to national political campaigns, and some even wore the Iron Cross, traditionally a symbol of Nazism. The order prohibiting the wearing of armbands did not extend to these. Instead, a particular symbol—black armbands worn to exhibit opposition to this Nation's involvement in Vietnam—was singled out for prohibition. Clearly, the prohibition of expression of one particular opinion, at least without evidence that it is necessary to avoid material and substantial interference with schoolwork or discipline, is not constitutionally permissible.

In our system, state-operated schools may not be enclaves of totalitarianism. School officials do not possess absolute authority over their students. Students in school as well as out of school are "persons" under our Constitution. They are possessed of fundamental rights which the State must respect, just as they themselves must respect their obligations to the State. In our system, students may not be regarded as closed-circuit recipients of only that which the State chooses to communicate. They may not be confined to the expression of those sentiments that are officially approved. In the absence of a specific showing of constitutionally valid reasons to regulate their speech, students are entitled to freedom of expression of their views. As Judge Gewin, speaking for the Fifth Circuit, said, school officials cannot suppress "expressions of feelings with which they do not wish to contend."

In *Meyer v. Nebraska*, Mr. Justice McReynolds expressed this Nation's repudiation of the principle that a State might so conduct its schools as to "foster a homogeneous people." He said: "In order to submerge the individual and develop ideal citizens, Sparta assembled the males at seven into barracks and entrusted their subsequent education and training to official guardians. Although such measures have been deliberately approved by men of great genius, their ideas touching the relation between individual and State were wholly different from those upon which our institutions rest; and it hardly will be affirmed that any legislature could impose such restrictions upon the people of a State without doing violence to both letter and spirit of the Constitution."

This principle has been repeated by this Court on numerous occasions during the intervening years. In *Keyishian v. Board of Regents*, 385 U.S. 589, 603, Mr. Justice Brennan, speaking for the Court, said: "The vigilant protection of constitutional freedoms is nowhere more vital than in the community of American schools. The classroom is peculiarly the 'marketplace of ideas.' The Nation's future depends upon leaders trained through wide exposure to that robust exchange of ideas which discovers truth 'out of a multitude of tongues, [rather] than through any kind of authoritative selection.'"

The principle of these cases is not confined to the supervised and ordained discussion which takes place in the classroom. The principal use to which the schools are dedicated is to accommodate students during prescribed hours for the purpose of certain types of activities. Among those activities is personal intercommunication among the students. This is not only an inevitable part of the process of attending school; it is also an important part of the educational process. A student's rights, therefore, do not embrace merely the classroom hours. When he is in the cafeteria, or on the playing field, or on the campus during the authorized hours, he may express his opinions, even on controversial subjects like the conflict in Vietnam, if he does so without "materially and substantially interfer[ing] with the requirements of appropriate discipline in the operation of the school" and without colliding with the rights of others. But conduct by the student, in class or out of it, which for any reason—whether it stems from time, place, or type of behavior—materially disrupts classwork or involves substantial disorder or invasion of the rights of others is, of course, not immunized by the constitutional guarantee of freedom of speech.

Under our Constitution, free speech is not a right that is given only to be so circumscribed that it exists in principle but not in fact. Freedom of expression would not truly exist if the right could be exercised only in an area that a benevolent government has provided as a safe haven for crackpots. The Constitution says that Congress (and the States) may not abridge the right to free speech. This provision means what it says. We properly read it to permit reasonable regulation of speech-connected activities in carefully restricted circumstances. But we do not confine the permissible exercise of First Amendment rights to a telephone booth or the four corners of a pamphlet, or to supervised and ordained discussion in a school classroom.

If a regulation were adopted by school officials forbidding discussion of the Vietnam conflict, or the expression by any student of opposition to it anywhere on school property except as part of a prescribed classroom exercise, it would be obvious that the regulation would violate the constitutional rights of students, at least if it could not be justified by showing that the students' activities would materially and substantially disrupt the work and discipline of the school. In the circumstances of the present case, the prohibition of the silent, passive "witness of the armbands," as one of the children called it, is no less offensive to the Constitution's guarantees.

As we have discussed, the record does not demonstrate any facts which might reasonably have led school authorities to forecast substantial disruption of or material interference with school activities, and no disturbances or disorders on the school premises in fact occurred. These petitioners merely went about their ordained rounds in school. Their deviation consisted only in wearing on their sleeve a band of black cloth, not more than two inches wide. They wore it to exhibit their disapproval of the Vietnam hostilities and their advocacy of a truce, to make their views known, and, by their example, to influence others to adopt them. They neither interrupted school activities nor sought to intrude in the school affairs or the lives of others. They caused discussion outside of the classrooms, but no interference with work and no disorder. In the circumstances, our Constitution does not permit officials of the State to deny their form of expression.

We express no opinion as to the form of relief which should be granted, this being a matter for the lower courts to determine. We reverse and remand for further proceedings consistent with this opinion.

Reversed and remanded.

In the early history of education in the United States, public school authorities were accustomed to restricting the expression of students under the doctrine of *in loco parentis* (Latin for "in place of the parent"). As society changed in the 1960s and 1970s, however, the idea of individualism grew, as did the focus on freedom of expression.

As students like the Tinkers became more outspoken, school officials became more concerned about the breakdown of discipline. Nevertheless, the United States was created on the basis of open expression without fear of government retribution for stating unpopular views; and according to the Supreme Court, "undifferentiated fear or apprehension of disturbance is not enough to overcome the right to freedom of expression."[3] Because students are "persons" under the Constitution, a state-operated school can only restrict a student's fundamental right if there is a substantial and material disruption of the learning environment.

Recognizing the fact that school officials have a duty to maintain order within the institution while allowing students to express their beliefs freely, the Court initiated a balancing test. This test allows school officials to prohibit student speech that "materially and substantially interfere[s] with the requirements of appropriate discipline in the operation of the school."[4] In spite of this holding, school officials cannot prohibit speech

---

[3] 393 U.S. 503, at 508
[4] Ibid.

simply because they do not agree with a particular viewpoint or fear that the speech may cause a disruption. "Any word spoken in class, in the lunchroom, or on the campus, that deviates from the views of another person may start an argument or cause a disturbance. But our Constitution says we must take this risk."[5] Additionally, "in order for . . . school officials to justify prohibition of a particular expression of opinion, [the school] must be able to show that its action was caused by something more than a mere desire to avoid the discomfort and unpleasantness that always accompany an unpopular viewpoint."[6]

While *Tinker* grants students protection under the First Amendment, that protection is not unlimited. In *Backwell v. Issaquena County Board of Education*, the school principal banned the wearing of political buttons in response to a two-day student disturbance.[7] In addition to making noise, students wearing the buttons were pinning them onto other students who did not consent to such acts. As a result, the students were suspended; and their families sued, claiming violation of their First Amendment rights. Due to the "unusual degree of commotion, boisterous conduct, a collision with the rights of others, an undermining of authority, and a lack of order, discipline and decorum", the court determined that the school's action was not a violation of the students' First Amendment rights.[8] The Fifth Circuit Court noted that "the proper operation of public school systems is one of the highest and most fundamental responsibilities of the state. The school authorities in the instant case had a legitimate and substantial interest in the orderly conduct of the school and a duty to protect such substantial interests in the school's operation."[9]

OFFENSIVE SPEECH

THE *TINKER* case granted students the right to freedom of speech. But what restrictions can be placed on offensive words or profanity? The U.S. Supreme Court clarified this question in *Bethel School District No. 403 v. Fraser*.[10] In *Fraser*, a student was suspended for giving a speech at a mandatory school assembly that included lewd, "graphic and explicit sexual metaphors" to describe another student.[11] The student argued that *Tinker* protected his First Amendment rights. Distinguishing the two cases, the Court concluded that the school acted within its authority by protecting a captive audience from such language, which materially and substantially interfered with the educational process. The expression by the student in *Fraser* was very different from the political message in *Tinker;* and "the schools, as instruments of the state, may determine that the essential lessons of civil, mature conduct cannot be conveyed in a school that tolerates lewd, indecent or offensive speech."[12] Under

---

[5]Ibid.
[6]Ibid.
[7]363 F.2d 749 (1966)
[8]Ibid., at 751
[9]Ibid.
[10]478 U.S. 675 (1986)
[11]Ibid.
[12]Ibid.

the First Amendment, adults making a political speech are not prohibited from using offensive language. Such protection does not, however, transfer to students in the public school system. "It does not follow, however, that simply because the use of an offensive form of expression may not be prohibited to adults making what the speaker considers a political point, the same latitude must be permitted to children in a public school."[13]

More recently, the Eighth Circuit upheld a seventh-grade student's expulsion after a letter he wrote to his ex-girlfriend was found and reported to school authorities. The student wrote two letters that contained "violent, misogynic, and obscenity-laden rants expressing a desire to molest, rape, and murder" the girl after she refused to date him for a second time.[14] The expelled student claimed the letter was protected under the First Amendment. The court, however, held that anyone who read the letters would perceive them as "a true threat, and the school's administrators and the school board did not violate [the student's] First Amendment rights by initiating disciplinary action based on the letter's threatening content."[15]

Best Practices

- School officials may restrict a student's speech if there is evidence of a material and substantial disruption.
- *Do not* restrict speech based on the mere desire to avoid the discomfort and unpleasantness of an unpopular view.
- Obscenities, profanity, or sexual gestures are not protected under the First Amendment.

School-Sponsored Speech

IN 1988, the U.S. Supreme Court drew a constitutional distinction between school-sponsored speech and non–school-sponsored speech and the protection that each should receive under the First Amendment. In *Hazelwood v. Kuhlmeier*, three students claimed that the school had violated their First Amendment rights by deleting two articles from the school newspaper.[16] One of the articles covered the story of a student's experiences with pregnancy, the other a student's reaction to his parents' divorce. Submitting articles to the school newspaper was incorporated into the curriculum of the students' journalism class.

In its analysis, the Court focused on the type of forum in which the expression was made. Determining that the school was not a public forum, the Court ruled that school officials had the right to reasonably restrict the speech of students.

---

[13]Ibid., at 682
[14]*Doe v. Pulaski*, 306 F.3d 616, at 619 (2002)
[15]Ibid., at 616–617
[16]484 U.S. 260 (1988)

A decision to teach leadership skills in the context of a classroom activity hardly implies a decision to relinquish school control over that activity. In sum, the evidence relied upon by the Court of Appeals fails to demonstrate the "clear intent to create a public forum," that existed in cases in which we found public forums to have been created. School officials did not evince either "by policy or by practice," any intent to open the pages of Spectrum *[the school newspaper] to "indiscriminate use," by its student reporters and editors, or by the student body generally. Instead, they "reserve[d] the forum for its intended purpos[e]," as a supervised learning experience for journalism students. Accordingly, school officials were entitled to regulate the contents of* Spectrum *in any reasonable manner.*[17]

Finding in favor of the school, the Court concluded that there was no violation of the students' First Amendment rights and that the educational institution had a right to exercise control over school-sponsored publications. The right to exercise such control, however, is not unrestricted. Rather, the school must ensure that the restriction of such speech is reasonable. The *Hazelwood* Court suggested that a school could reasonably restrict school-sponsored speech for several reasons:

Hence, a school may in its capacity as publisher of a school newspaper or producer of a school play disassociate itself, . . . not only from speech that would substantially interfere with [its] work . . . or impinge upon the rights of other students, but also from speech that is, for example, ungrammatical, poorly written, inadequately researched, biased or prejudiced, vulgar or profane, or unsuitable for immature children. A school must be able to set high standards for the student speech that is disseminated under its auspices—standards that may be higher than those demanded by some newspaper publishers or theatrical producers in the real world—and may refuse to disseminate student speech that does not meet those standards. In addition, a school must be able to take into account the emotional maturity of the intended audience in determining sensitive topics, which might range from the existence of Santa Claus in an elementary school setting to the particulars of teenage sexual activity in a high school setting. A school must also retain the authority to refuse to censor student speech that might reasonably be perceived to advocate drug or alcohol use, irresponsible sex, or conduct otherwise inconsistent with the shared values of a civilized social order.[18]

Hazelwood's five-to-three decision is vastly different from the holding in *Tinker.* Distinguishing the two issues, *Hazelwood* focused on educational authorities' restrictions on school-sponsored publications, while *Tinker* revolved around the issue of restricting a student's personal expression. Focusing on the fact that the newspaper articles were part of the curriculum and that such speech was not expressed in a public forum, the Court judged that schools do have editorial control over school-sponsored material "so long as their actions are reasonably related to legitimate pedagogical concerns."[19]

---

[17]Ibid., at 270
[18]484 U.S. 260, at 272–73 (1988)
[19]Ibid., at 272

More recently, the eighth Circuit Court determined whether or not a school violated a student's First Amendment right to free speech when it disqualified him from running for student body president after he distributed condoms along with his campaign slogan. The student argued that condom distribution was no different from giving out candy. But the court declared:

> *The distribution of condoms is qualitatively different from the handing out of candy or gum. The one can be read to signify approval or encouragement of teenage sexual activity. The other constitutes the traditional bestowing of a de minimis gratuity not associated with any social or political message. School districts have an interest in maintaining decorum and in preventing the creation of an environment in which learning might be impeded, an interest that was particularly strong in the present case because the condom distribution occurred within the context of a school-sponsored election. Henerey's distribution of the condoms carried with it the implied imprimatur of the school, for the other students would most likely have assumed that Henerey had complied with Rule KJ-R and had secured approval for the distribution. The District has a legitimate interest in divorcing its extracurricular programs from controversial and sensitive topics, such as teenage sex, an interest that would be brought to naught were the school administration not allowed to discipline those whose conduct would necessarily embroil those extracurricular activities in the very topics from which they were to remain free.[20]*

In its decision, the court makes clear the importance of educating students with a focus on the responsibilities of the state, the schools, and the parents.

Best Practices

- School officials have the right to exercise restrictive control over school-sponsored publications. Such restriction must be reasonable, however, and there must be an educational purpose for doing so.
- Before restricting school-sponsored speech, ensure that there is compelling evidence to demonstrate that the content of the speech is either disruptive or inconsistent with the educational learning environment.

DRESS AND APPEARANCE

THE RIGHT to restrict students' dress and appearance has been a litigated issue since the late 1960s and is still an issue of debate. The U.S. Supreme Court has declined to address the issue, leaving the states split over whether or not student dress and appearance

---

[20]200 F.3d 1128 (1999)

are protected liberties under the Fourth Amendment or forms of expression protected under the First Amendment.

For example the First Circuit determined that, "within the commodious concept of liberty, embracing freedoms great and small, is the right to wear one's hair as he wishes."[21] When school policies have been declared unconstitutional, they have been determined to be unrelated to a legitimate educational purpose.[22]

However, on the other side of the argument some courts have upheld the restriction and determined that the freedom of dress is not a protected liberty under the Constitution. In these states, the federal courts have focused on the school's right to implement dress-code policies to maintain discipline, prevent disruptions of the learning process, or ensure the safety and health of students. "The touchstone for sustaining such regulations is the demonstration that they are necessary to alleviate interference with the educational process."[23] Hence, the courts have determined that restrictions on student dress and hair will be upheld if they are based on an educational objective.

As school violence becomes a nationwide dilemma, more schools are implementing strict dress codes. Despite their intent to provide a safe environment, schools must prove that their codes are justified and reasonable, as illustrated in *Jeglin v. San Jacinto Unified School District*.[24]

In Riverside County, California, teachers and students were being intimidated by an increased gang presence in schools. In an attempt to reduce the violence, the San Jacinto Unified School District implemented a policy that prohibited students from wearing any clothing that identified professional or college sports teams through writing, pictures, or insignia.[25] Students and parents objected, claiming that wearing such clothing was a form of speech protected by the First Amendment. Balancing the important role of the public school system to maintain order against the rights of students to express themselves, the court wrote:

> *It is equally clear that daily administration of public education is committed to school officials and that such responsibility carries with it the inherent authority to prescribe and control conduct in the school. The interest of the state in the maintenance of its education system is a compelling one and provokes a balancing of First Amendment rights with the state's efforts to pressure and protect its educational process. It is also well established that the First Amendment does not require school officials to wait until disruption actually occurs before they may act to curtail exercise of the right of free speech but that they have a duty to prevent*

---

[21]*Richard v. Thurston*, 424 F.2d 1281 (1970)
[22]*Dawson v. Hillsborough County, Florida School Board*, 445 F.2d 308 (1971)
[23]*Giffin v. Tatum*, 425 F.2d 201 (1970)
[24]827 F.Supp. 1459 (1993)
[25]Ibid.

the occurrence of disturbances. . . . [However], the teachings of Tinker v. Des
Moines Independent Community School District *are clear that public school students have a right to freedom of speech which is not shed at the schoolhouse
gates.*[26]

The holding of this case was unique based on the fact that the district offered no evidence of gang-related problems at the elementary and middle schools. Hence, the court
found that the restrictive dress code placed upon those students was an abridgment of
free speech rights and thus unconstitutional. On the other hand, the district was able to
prove the gang presence at the high school; therefore, there was clear justification for
curtailing students' First Amendment rights by enforcing the dress code.

Public schools are responsible for creating a safe environment for students. In taking proactive steps to provide such safety, school officials do not have to wait until disruption actually occurs before curtailing the right of free speech. In placing constraints
on students' rights, the school carries the burden of proof that such restrictions were
justified.

Best Practices

- Avoid dress codes that are vague and ambiguous.
- Require dress codes to be specific and reasonable.
- Record all justifications for implementing dress code policies.
- Document all disturbances related to dress.

SEARCH AND SEIZURE

THE FOURTH Amendment of the U.S. Constitution protects, in part, "The right of
people to be secure in their persons, houses, papers, and effects, against unreasonable
searches and seizures, [which] shall not be violated, and no warrants shall issue, but upon
probable cause, supported by oath or affirmation, and particularly describing the place
to be searched, and the persons or things to be seized." In criminal cases, if the government searches and seizes an individual in violation of the Fourth Amendment, all
evidence pertaining to that search will be inadmissible under the exclusionary rule.
When police are involved in an investigation, the law requires they have probable cause
before performing the search. In most circumstances, probable cause is based on sufficient evidence and a search warrant issued by a court magistrate.

---

[26]Ibid., at 1461

Over the years, students in the public school system have claimed that educational officials should be required to have probable cause and obtain a search warrant before performing a search. In *New Jersey v. T.L.O.*, the U.S. Supreme Court determined if students within the public school system were protected under the Fourth Amendment and if probable cause were needed before a school official could perform a search.[27]

New Jersey v. T.L.O.
Supreme Court of the United States, 1985
469 U.S. 325

Justice White delivered the opinion of the Court.

We granted certiorari in this case to examine the appropriateness of the exclusionary rule as a remedy for searches carried out in violation of the Fourth Amendment by public school authorities. Our consideration of the proper application of the Fourth Amendment to the public schools, however, has led us to conclude that the search that gave rise to the case now before us did not violate the Fourth Amendment. Accordingly, we here address only the questions of the proper standard for assessing the legality of searches conducted by public school officials and the application of that standard to the facts of this case.

On March 7, 1980, a teacher at Piscataway High School in Middlesex County, N.J., discovered two girls smoking in a lavatory. One of the two girls was the respondent T.L.O., who at that time was a 14-year-old high school freshman. Because smoking in the lavatory was a violation of a school rule, the teacher took the two girls to the Principal's office, where they met with Assistant Vice Principal Theodore Choplick. In response to questioning by Mr. Choplick, T.L.O.'s companion admitted that she had violated the rule. T.L.O., however, denied that she had been smoking in the lavatory and claimed that she did not smoke at all.

Mr. Choplick asked T.L.O. to come into his private office and demanded to see her purse. Opening the purse, he found a pack of cigarettes, which he removed from the purse and held before T.L.O. as he accused her of having lied to him. As he reached into the purse for the cigarettes, Mr. Choplick also noticed a package of cigarette rolling papers. In his experience, possession of rolling papers by high school students was closely associated with the use of marihuana. Suspecting that a closer examination of the purse might yield further evidence of drug use, Mr. Choplick proceeded to search the purse thoroughly. The search revealed a small amount of marihuana, a pipe, a number of empty plastic bags, a substantial quantity of money in one-dollar bills, an index card that appeared to be a list of students who owed T.L.O. money, and two letters that implicated T.L.O. in marihuana dealing.

---

[27]469 U.S. 325 (1985)

Mr. Choplick notified T.L.O.'s mother and the police, and turned the evidence of drug dealing over to the police. At the request of the police, T.L.O.'s mother took her daughter to police headquarters, where T.L.O. confessed that she had been selling marihuana at the high school. On the basis of the confession and the evidence seized by Mr. Choplick, the State brought delinquency charges against T.L.O. in the Juvenile and Domestic Relations Court of Middlesex County. Contending that Mr. Choplick's search of her purse violated the Fourth Amendment, T.L.O. moved to suppress the evidence found in her purse as well as her confession, which, she argued, was tainted by the allegedly unlawful search. The Juvenile Court denied the motion to suppress. Although the court concluded that the Fourth Amendment did apply to searches carried out by school officials, it held that "a school official may properly conduct a search of a student's person if the official has a reasonable suspicion that a crime has been or is in the process of being committed, or reasonable cause to believe that the search is necessary to maintain school discipline or enforce school policies."

Applying this standard, the court concluded that the search conducted by Mr. Choplick was a reasonable one. The initial decision to open the purse was justified by Mr. Choplick's well-founded suspicion that T.L.O. had violated the rule forbidding smoking in the lavatory. Once the purse was open, evidence of marihuana violations was in plain view, and Mr. Choplick was entitled to conduct a thorough search to determine the nature and extent of T.L.O.'s drug-related activities. Having denied the motion to suppress, the court on March 23, 1981, found T.L.O. to be a delinquent and on January 8, 1982, sentenced her to a year's probation.

On appeal from the final judgment of the Juvenile Court, a divided Appellate Division affirmed the trial court's finding that there had been no Fourth Amendment violation, but vacated the adjudication of delinquency and remanded for a determination whether T.L.O. had knowingly and voluntarily waived her Fifth Amendment rights before confessing. T.L.O. appealed the Fourth Amendment ruling, and the Supreme Court of New Jersey reversed the judgment of the Appellate Division and ordered the suppression of the evidence found in T.L.O.'s purse.

The New Jersey Supreme Court agreed with the lower courts that the Fourth Amendment applies to searches conducted by school officials. The court also rejected the State of New Jersey's argument that the exclusionary rule should not be employed to prevent the use in juvenile proceedings of evidence unlawfully seized by school officials. Declining to consider whether applying the rule to the fruits of searches by school officials would have any deterrent value, the court held simply that the precedents of this Court establish that "if an official search violates constitutional rights, the evidence is not admissible in criminal proceedings."

With respect to the question of the legality of the search before it, the court agreed with the Juvenile Court that a warrantless search by a school official does not violate the Fourth Amendment so long as the official "has reasonable grounds to believe that a student possesses evidence of illegal activity or activity that would interfere with school discipline and order." However, the court, with two justices dissenting, sharply disagreed with the Juvenile Court's conclusion that the search of the purse was reasonable. According to the majority, the contents of T.L.O.'s purse had no bearing on the accusation against T.L.O., for possession of cigarettes (as opposed to smoking them in the lavatory) did not violate school rules, and a mere desire for evidence that would impeach T.L.O.'s claim that she did not smoke cigarettes could not justify the search. Moreover, even if a reasonable suspicion that T.L.O. had cigarettes in her purse would justify a search, Mr. Choplick had no such suspicion, as no one had furnished him with any specific information that there were cigarettes in the purse. Finally, leaving aside the question whether Mr. Choplick was justified in opening the purse, the court held that the evidence of drug use that he saw inside did not justify the extensive "rummaging" through T.L.O.'s papers and effects that followed.

We granted the State of New Jersey's petition for certiorari. Although the State had argued in the Supreme Court of New Jersey that the search of T.L.O.'s purse did not violate the Fourth Amendment, the petition for certiorari raised only the question whether the exclusionary rule should operate to bar consideration in juvenile delinquency proceedings of evidence unlawfully seized by a school official without the involvement of law enforcement officers. When this case was first argued last Term, the State conceded for the purpose of argument that the standard devised by the New Jersey Supreme Court for determining the legality of school searches was appropriate and that the court had correctly applied that standard; the State contended only that the remedial purposes of the exclusionary rule were not well served by applying it to searches conducted by public authorities not primarily engaged in law enforcement.

Although we originally granted certiorari to decide the issue of the appropriate remedy in juvenile court proceedings for unlawful school searches, our doubts regarding the wisdom of deciding that question in isolation from the broader question of what limits, if any, the Fourth Amendment places on the activities of school authorities prompted us to order reargument on that question. Having heard argument on the legality of the search of T.L.O.'s purse, we are satisfied that the search did not violate the Fourth Amendment.

In determining whether the search at issue in this case violated the Fourth Amendment, we are faced initially with the question whether that Amendment's prohibition on unreasonable searches and seizures applies to searches conducted by public school officials. We hold that it does.

It is now beyond dispute that "the Federal Constitution, by virtue of the Fourteenth Amendment, prohibits unreasonable searches and seizures by state officers." Equally indisputable is the proposition that the Fourteenth Amendment protects the rights of students against encroachment by public school officials: "The Fourteenth Amendment, as now applied to the States, protects the citizen against the State itself and all of its creatures—Boards of Education not excepted. These have, of course, important, delicate, and highly discretionary functions, but none that they may not perform within the limits of the Bill of Rights. That they are educating the young for citizenship is reason for scrupulous protection of Constitutional freedoms of the individual, if we are not to strangle the free mind at its source and teach youth to discount important principles of our government as mere platitudes."

These two propositions—that the Fourth Amendment applies to the States through the Fourteenth Amendment, and that the actions of public school officials are subject to the limits placed on state action by the Fourteenth Amendment—might appear sufficient to answer the suggestion that the Fourth Amendment does not proscribe unreasonable searches by school officials. On reargument, however, the State of New Jersey has argued that the history of the Fourth Amendment indicates that the Amendment was intended to regulate only searches and seizures carried out by law enforcement officers; accordingly, although public school officials are concededly state agents for purposes of the Fourteenth Amendment, the Fourth Amendment creates no rights enforceable against them.

It may well be true that the evil toward which the Fourth Amendment was primarily directed was the resurrection of the pre-Revolutionary practice of using general warrants or "writs of assistance" to authorize searches for contraband by officers of the Crown. But this Court has never limited the Amendment's prohibition on unreasonable searches and seizures to operations conducted by the police. Rather, the Court has long spoken of the Fourth Amendment's strictures as restraints imposed upon "governmental action"—that is, "upon the activities of sovereign authority." Accordingly, we have held the Fourth Amendment applicable to the activities of civil as well as criminal authorities: building inspectors, and even firemen entering privately owned premises to battle a fire, are all subject to the restraints imposed by the Fourth Amendment. As we observed in *Camara v. Municipal Court*, "[the] basic purpose of this Amendment, as recognized in countless decisions of this Court, is to safeguard the privacy and security of individuals against arbitrary invasions by governmental officials." Because the individual's interest in privacy and personal security "suffers whether the government's motivation is to investigate violations of criminal laws or breaches of other statutory or regulatory standards," it would be "anomalous to say that the individual and his private property are fully protected by the Fourth Amendment only when the individual is suspected of criminal behavior."

Notwithstanding the general applicability of the Fourth Amendment to the activities of civil authorities, a few courts have concluded that school officials are exempt from the dictates of the Fourth Amendment by virtue of the special nature of their authority over schoolchildren. Teachers and school administrators, it is said, act in loco parentis in their dealings with students: their authority is that of the parent, not the State, and is therefore not subject to the limits of the Fourth Amendment.

Such reasoning is in tension with contemporary reality and the teachings of this Court. We have held school officials subject to the commands of the First Amendment. If school authorities are state actors for purposes of the constitutional guarantees of freedom of expression and due process, it is difficult to understand why they should be deemed to be exercising parental rather than public authority when conducting searches of their students. More generally, the Court has recognized that "the concept of parental delegation" as a source of school authority is not entirely "consonant with compulsory education laws." Today's public school officials do not merely exercise authority voluntarily conferred on them by individual parents; rather, they act in furtherance of publicly mandated educational and disciplinary policies. . . . In carrying out searches and other disciplinary functions pursuant to such policies, school officials act as representatives of the State, not merely as surrogates for the parents, and they cannot claim the parents' immunity from the strictures of the Fourth Amendment.

To hold that the Fourth Amendment applies to searches conducted by school authorities is only to begin the inquiry into the standards governing such searches. Although the underlying command of the Fourth Amendment is always that searches and seizures be reasonable, what is reasonable depends on the context within which a search takes place. The determination of the standard of reasonableness governing any specific class of searches requires "balancing the need to search against the invasion which the search entails." On one side of the balance are arrayed the individual's legitimate expectations of privacy and personal security; on the other, the government's need for effective methods to deal with breaches of public order.

We have recognized that even a limited search of the person is a substantial invasion of privacy. We have also recognized that searches of closed items of personal luggage are intrusions on protected privacy interests, for "the Fourth Amendment provides protection to the owner of every container that conceals its contents from plain view." A search of a child's person or of a closed purse or other bag carried on her person, no less than a similar search carried out on an adult, is undoubtedly a severe violation of subjective expectations of privacy.

Of course, the Fourth Amendment does not protect subjective expectations of privacy that are unreasonable or otherwise "illegitimate." To receive the protection of the Fourth Amendment, an expectation of privacy must be one that society is "prepared to recognize as legitimate." The State of New Jersey has argued that because of the pervasive supervision to which children in the schools are necessarily subject, a child has virtually no legitimate expectation of privacy in articles of personal property "unnecessarily" carried into a school. This argument has two factual premises: (1) the fundamental incompatibility of expectations of privacy with the maintenance of a sound educational environment; and (2) the minimal interest of the child in bringing any items of personal property into the school. Both premises are severely flawed.

Although this Court may take notice of the difficulty of maintaining discipline in the public schools today, the situation is not so dire that students in the schools may claim no legitimate expectations of privacy. We have recently recognized that the need to maintain order in a prison is such that prisoners retain no legitimate expectations of privacy in their cells, but it goes almost without saying that "[the] prisoner and the schoolchild stand in wholly different circumstances, separated by the harsh facts of criminal conviction and incarceration." We are not yet ready to hold that the schools and the prisons need be equated for purposes of the Fourth Amendment.

Nor does the State's suggestion that children have no legitimate need to bring personal property into the schools seem well anchored in reality. Students at a minimum must bring to school not only the supplies needed for their studies, but also keys, money, and the necessaries of personal hygiene and grooming. In addition, students may carry on their persons or in purses or wallets such nondisruptive yet highly personal items as photographs, letters, and diaries. Finally, students may have perfectly legitimate reasons to carry with them articles of property needed in connection with extracurricular or recreational activities. In short, schoolchildren may find it necessary to carry with them a variety of legitimate, noncontraband items, and there is no reason to conclude that they have necessarily waived all rights to privacy in such items merely by bringing them onto school grounds.

Against the child's interest in privacy must be set the substantial interest of teachers and administrators in maintaining discipline in the classroom and on school grounds. Maintaining order in the classroom has never been easy, but in recent years, school disorder has often taken particularly ugly forms: drug use and violent crime in the schools have become major social problems. Even in schools that have been spared the most severe disciplinary problems, the preservation of order and a proper educational environment requires close supervision of schoolchildren, as well as the enforcement of rules against conduct that would be perfectly permissible if undertaken by an adult. "Events calling for discipline are frequent occurrences and sometimes require immediate, effective action." Accordingly, we have recognized that maintaining security and order in the schools requires a certain degree of flexibility in school disciplinary procedures, and we have respected the value of preserving the informality of the student-teacher relationship.

How, then, should we strike the balance between the schoolchild's legitimate expectations of privacy and the school's equally legitimate need to maintain an environment in which learning can take place? It is evident that the school setting requires some easing of the restrictions to which searches by public authorities are ordinarily subject. The warrant requirement, in particular, is unsuited to the school environment: requiring a teacher to obtain a warrant before searching a child suspected of an infraction of school rules (or of the criminal law) would unduly interfere with the maintenance of the swift and informal disciplinary procedures needed in the schools. Just as we have in other cases dispensed with the warrant requirement when "the burden of obtaining a warrant is likely to frustrate the governmental purpose behind the search," we hold today that school officials need not obtain a warrant before searching a student who is under their authority.

The school setting also requires some modification of the level of suspicion of illicit activity needed to justify a search. Ordinarily, a search—even one that may permissibly be carried out without a warrant—must be based upon "probable cause" to believe that a violation of the law has occurred. However, "probable cause" is not an irreducible requirement of a valid search. The fundamental command of the Fourth Amendment is that searches and seizures be reasonable, and although "both the concept of probable cause and the requirement of a warrant bear on the reasonableness of a search, . . . in certain limited circumstances neither is required." Thus, we have in a number of cases recognized the legality of searches and seizures based on suspicions that, although "reasonable," do not rise to the level of probable cause. Where a careful balancing of governmental and private interests suggests that the public interest is best served by a Fourth Amendment standard of reasonableness that stops short of probable cause, we have not hesitated to adopt such a standard.

We join the majority of courts that have examined this issue in concluding that the accommodation of the privacy interests of schoolchildren with the substantial need of teachers and administrators for freedom to maintain order in the schools does not require strict adherence to the requirement that searches be based on probable cause to believe that the subject of the search has violated or is violating the law. Rather, the legality of a search of a student should depend simply on the reasonableness, under all the circumstances, of the search. Determining the reasonableness of any search involves a twofold inquiry: first, one must consider "whether the . . . action was justified at its inception," second, one must determine whether the search as actually conducted "was reasonably related in scope to the circumstances which justified the interference in the first place." Under ordinary circumstances, a search of a student by a teacher or other school official will be "justified at its inception" when there are reasonable grounds for suspecting that the search will turn up evidence that the student has violated or is violating either the law or the rules of the school. Such a search will be permissible in its scope when the measures adopted are reasonably related to the objectives of the search and not excessively intrusive in light of the age and sex of the student and the nature of the infraction.

This standard will, we trust, neither unduly burden the efforts of school authorities to maintain order in their schools nor authorize unrestrained intrusions upon the privacy of schoolchildren. By focusing attention on the question of reasonableness, the standard will spare teachers and school administrators the necessity of schooling themselves in the niceties of probable cause and permit them to regulate their conduct according to the dictates of reason and common sense. At the same time, the reasonableness standard should ensure that the interests of students will be invaded no more than is necessary to achieve the legitimate end of preserving order in the schools.

There remains the question of the legality of the search in this case. We recognize that the "reasonable grounds" standard applied by the New Jersey Supreme Court in its consideration of this question is not substantially different from the standard that we have adopted today. Nonetheless, we believe that the New Jersey court's application of that standard to strike down the search of T.L.O.'s purse reflects a somewhat crabbed notion of reasonableness. Our review of the facts surrounding the search leads us to conclude that the search was in no sense unreasonable for Fourth Amendment purposes.

The incident that gave rise to this case actually involved two separate searches, with the first—the search for cigarettes—providing the suspicion that gave rise to the second—the search for marihuana. Although it is the fruits of the second search that are at issue here, the validity of the search for marihuana must depend on the reasonableness of the initial search for cigarettes, as there would have been no reason to suspect that T.L.O. possessed marihuana had the first search not taken place. Accordingly, it is to the search for cigarettes that we first turn our attention.

The New Jersey Supreme Court pointed to two grounds for its holding that the search for cigarettes was unreasonable. First, the court observed that possession of cigarettes was not in itself illegal or a violation of school rules. Because the contents of T.L.O.'s purse would therefore have "no direct bearing on the infraction" of which she was accused (smoking in a lavatory where smoking was prohibited), there was no reason to search her purse. Second, even assuming that a search of T.L.O.'s purse might under some circumstances be reasonable in light of the accusation made against T.L.O., the New Jersey court concluded that Mr. Choplick in this particular case had no reasonable grounds to suspect that T.L.O. had cigarettes in her purse. At best, according to the court, Mr. Choplick had "a good hunch."

Both these conclusions are implausible. T.L.O. had been accused of smoking, and had denied the accusation in the strongest possible terms when she stated that she did not smoke at all. Surely it cannot be said that under these circumstances, T.L.O.'s possession of cigarettes would be irrelevant to the charges against her or to her response to those charges. T.L.O.'s possession of cigarettes, once it was discovered, would both corroborate the report that she had been smoking and undermine the credibility of her defense to the charge of smoking. To be sure, the discovery of the cigarettes would not prove that T.L.O. had been smoking in the lavatory; nor would it, strictly speaking, necessarily be inconsistent with her claim that she did not smoke at all. But it is universally recognized that evidence, to be relevant to an inquiry, need not conclusively prove the ultimate fact in issue, but only have "any tendency to make the existence of any fact that is of consequence to the determination of the action more probable or less probable than it would be without the evidence." The relevance of T.L.O.'s possession of cigarettes to the question whether she had been smoking and to the credibility of her denial that she smoked supplied the necessary "nexus" between the item searched for and the infraction under investigation. Thus, if Mr. Choplick in fact had a reasonable suspicion that T.L.O. had cigarettes in her purse, the search was justified despite the fact that the cigarettes, if found, would constitute "mere evidence" of a violation.

Of course, the New Jersey Supreme Court also held that Mr. Choplick had no reasonable suspicion that the purse would contain cigarettes. This conclusion is puzzling. A teacher had reported that T.L.O. was smoking in the lavatory. Certainly this report gave Mr. Choplick reason to suspect that T.L.O. was carrying cigarettes with her; and if she did have cigarettes, her purse was the obvious place in which to find them. Mr. Choplick's suspicion that there were cigarettes in the purse was not an "inchoate and unparticularized suspicion or hunch," rather, it was the sort of "common-sense [conclusion] about human behavior" upon which "practical people"—including government officials—are entitled to rely. Of course, even if the teacher's report were true, T.L.O. might not have had a pack of cigarettes with her; she might have borrowed a cigarette from someone else or have been sharing a cigarette with another student. But the requirement of reasonable suspicion is not a requirement of absolute certainty: "sufficient probability, not certainty, is the touchstone of reasonableness under the Fourth Amendment. . . . " Because the hypothesis that T.L.O. was carrying cigarettes in her purse was not itself unreasonable, it is irrelevant that other hypotheses were also consistent with the teacher's accusation. Accordingly, it cannot be said that Mr. Choplick acted unreasonably when he examined T.L.O.'s purse to see if it contained cigarettes.

Our conclusion that Mr. Choplick's decision to open T.L.O.'s purse was reasonable brings us to the question of the further search for marihuana once the pack of cigarettes was located. The suspicion upon which the search for marihuana was founded was provided when Mr. Choplick observed a package of rolling papers in the purse as he removed the pack of cigarettes. Although T.L.O. does not dispute the reasonableness of Mr. Choplick's belief that the rolling papers indicated the presence of marihuana, she does contend that the scope of the search Mr. Choplick conducted exceeded permissible bounds when he seized and read certain letters that implicated T.L.O. in drug dealing. This argument, too, is unpersuasive. The discovery of the rolling papers concededly gave rise to a reasonable suspicion that T.L.O. was carrying marihuana as well as cigarettes in her purse. This suspicion justified further exploration of T.L.O.'s purse, which turned up more evidence of drug-related activities: a pipe, a number of plastic bags of the type commonly used to store marihuana, a small quantity of marihuana, and a fairly substantial amount of money. Under these circumstances, it was not unreasonable to extend the search to a separate zippered compartment of the purse; and when a search of that compartment revealed an index card containing a list of "people who owe me money" as well as two letters, the inference that T.L.O. was involved in marihuana trafficking was substantial enough to justify Mr. Choplick in examining the letters to determine whether they contained any further evidence. In short, we cannot conclude that the search for marihuana was unreasonable in any respect.

Because the search resulting in the discovery of the evidence of marihuana dealing by T.L.O. was reasonable, the New Jersey Supreme Court's decision to exclude that evidence from T.L.O.'s juvenile delinquency proceedings on Fourth Amendment grounds was erroneous. Accordingly, the judgment of the Supreme Court of New Jersey is reversed.

This case illustrates the point that the U.S. Supreme Court recognizes that school-children do possess legitimate expectations of privacy in the educational system. On the other hand, the Court also recognizes the need for educational institutions to maintain a safe learning environment. Thus, school officials need not obtain a warrant before searching a student who is under their authority. This balance suggests that students do have Fourth Amendment rights and that school officials do not need probable cause to perform a search, as the police do. Rather, the standard necessary to perform a search is reasonable suspicion.

According to the Court, the rational for lowering the standard and creating a "new reasonableness standard is appropriate because it will spare teachers and school administrators the necessity of schooling themselves in the niceties of probable cause and permit them to regulate their conduct according to the dictates of reason and common sense."[28]

The test for determining reasonableness is twofold. First, was the action justified at its inception? Being justified at its inception is satisfied when there "are reasonable grounds for suspecting that the search will turn up evidence that the student has violated or is violating either the law or the rules of the school."[29] Second, was the search reasonably related in scope to the circumstances that justified the interference in the first place? According to the Court, school searches will only be reasonable in scope "when the measures adopted are reasonably related to the objectives of the search and not excessively intrusive in light of the age and sex of the student and the nature of the infraction."[30]

In acknowledging that school officials stand in loco parentis, the Court determined that schools must maintain order while recognizing that the public school system acts as an agent of the state. With a focus on reasonableness, the Court hoped that teachers could continue to educate and preserve stability while protecting the rights of students.

School Lockers

The search of lockers has commonly been upheld under the theory that they are property of the school that students are privileged to use. Nevertheless, the U.S. Supreme Court has

---

[28]Ibid., at 342
[29]Ibid., at 350
[30]Ibid., at 342

not ruled on whether or not the search of student lockers is unconstitutional, leaving mixed decisions in the lower courts. The Circuit Court of New York held that school authorities have an obligation to maintain discipline and a duty to inspect lockers if they suspect illegal activity.[31] In Pennsylvania, on the other hand, the court found that the search of a student's locker was unconstitutional.[32] In a 1999 decision in the District Court of Maine, however, the court held that a search of a student and her locker was constitutional. The principal at the middle school was given a tip that one of the students was drinking alcohol in the girls' locker room. Because of that information, the principal called the student out of class and searched, in addition to her locker, her backpack and the pockets of her clothing. Although nothing was found, the court held that there had been no violation of the student's constitutional rights because the search was justified at its inception as well as reasonable within its scope, and evidence could have been found in the places searched.[33]

Best Practices

- Mandate a written policy informing both parents and students of the school's right to search lockers. (Such a policy has been a factor in holdings in favor of the school).[34]

Personal Items

The searching of a student's personal possessions tends to receive more protection than does the searching of student lockers, as illustrated in *DesRoches by DesRoches v. Caprio*, in which a school security guard looking for a pair of stolen tennis sneakers searched the backpacks of all the students in the class.[35] Of the 19 students, one objected to the search and was suspended for 10 days. The student's parents sued the school district, claiming, among other things, that their child's Fourth Amendment right to privacy had been violated.

In its analysis, the court held that the search was unreasonable and that "ascertaining who stole the shoes clearly [wa]s not as important a governmental interest as searching for drugs or for weapons. . . . [T]his case does not present an extraordinary situation in which the school's interest was sufficiently substantial or compelling; a stolen pair of tennis shoes simply does not present exigent circumstances or a future danger to other students."[36]

---

[31]*People of the State of New York v. Overton*, 229 N.E.2d 596 (1967)

[32]*In re Guy Dumas, a Minor*, 515 A.2d 984 (1986)

[33]*Greenleaf ex rel. Greenleaf v. Cote*, 77 F. Supp. 2d 168 (1999)

[34]*Commonwealth v. Cass*, 666 A.2d 313 (1995)

[35]974 F.Supp. 542 (1997)

[36]Ibid., at 549

Strip Searches

Due to the highly intrusive nature of a strip search, it should be avoided at all costs. As stated in *Doe v. Renfrow,* "It does not require a constitutional scholar to conclude that a nude search of a . . . child is an invasion of constitutional rights of some magnitude. More than that; it is a violation of any known principle of human decency."[37]

Even courts that have permitted the use of strip searches on students warn that school districts can easily be liable if such searches are administered without training, accountability, and—most of all—without reasonableness.[38] In cases that have permitted the use of strip searches, factors such as the age and sex of the student have been carefully considered.[39] In some cases, courts have held that the reasonable standard is not high enough when it concerns a strip search. Rather, as found in *M.M. v. Anker,* "when a teacher conducts a highly intrusive invasion such as the strip search, it is reasonable to require that probable cause be present."[40]

Best Practices

- Implement a policy strictly prohibiting the use of strip searches. Ensure that faculty and staff understand that strip searches are considered extremely intrusive and will more likely than not lead to litigation for invasion of privacy.

- If a strip search must occur, consult legal counsel before performing the search.

Drug Testing

The ever-increasing use of drugs in American schools is becoming a substantial problem for both parents and school officials. Due to this problem, some educational institutions are implementing policies that require students to submit to a drug test. Due to its intrusiveness, some argue that such a test is a "search" protected by the Fourth Amendment of the Constitution. In 1988, the U.S. Supreme Court dealt with this issue in *Vernonia v. Acton.*[41]

Due to a reported increase in disciplinary problems among students at Vernonia High School, the school district began taking steps to curtail the suspected drug problem, with a special focus on the athletic teams. Both teachers and administrators at the school felt that students who were involved in athletics were the leaders of the drug culture.[42] Fearing student sports-related injuries, the school mandated a drug-testing policy. The policy

---

[37]631 F.2d 91, at 92–93 (1980)

[38]*Cornfield v. Consolidated High School District No. 230,* 991 F.2d 1316 (1993)

[39]*Jenkins v. Talladega City Board of Education,* 115 F.3d 821 (1997)

[40]607 F.2d 588 (1979)

[41]115 S.Ct. 2386 (1995)

[42]Ibid.

required that all students participating in extracurricular sports were to submit to a urinalysis drug test, which would be administered on a random basis to approximately 10%
of the athletes throughout the sports season. Parents were mailed consent letters informing them of the new policy and requiring a signature before the student was permitted to participate in the sport.

The parents of a seventh grader refused to sign the consent form; and when the
school prohibited the student from playing football, the parents sued. The suit claimed
that the drug-testing policy violated their son's Fourth Amendment right. Throughout its
analysis, the Court considered the inherent danger of drug use, the increased drug use
at Vernonia High School, the possibility of harm to students who play sports while on
drugs, and the growing disciplinary problems at the school. "Taking into account all the
factors, . . . the decreased exception of privacy, the relative unobtrusiveness of the search,
and the severity of the need met by the search—we concluded Vernonia's Policy is reasonable and hence constitutional."[43]

The Seventh Circuit reviewed a similar school policy in *Schaill by Kross v. Tippeca-
noe County School Corporation.*[44] The school implemented a drug-testing policy that
required students who were trying out for the basketball team to have their parents sign
a consent form permitting random testing of the athletes. Balancing the compelling need
to protect the students against the diminished privacy rights imposed on students who
were tested, the court held that the school's drug-testing policy was constitutional. Relying on the fact that the school's drug problem had reached epidemic levels and that the
implementation of the policy was carefully prescribed, limited in scope, and only mandatory for students on the basketball team, the court approved the policy.

In reviewing the holding in *Vernonia* and *Schaill*, one may wrongfully assume that all
drug testing of students is permitted. On the contrary, the U.S. Supreme Court cau-
tioned against the use of a "suspicionless drug test."[45] In a case concerning a Colorado
school, the Supreme Court ruled that the testing of band students was unconstitutional.[46] In its conclusions, the Court held:

> *Based on our analysis of all of these factors, we conclude that the Policy is not rea-
> sonable and thus cannot stand under the United States Constitution. First, the nature
> of the privacy interest invaded was different from that of the student athletes de-
> scribed by the* Vernonia *Court. The absence in this case of both true voluntariness and
> the type of communal undressing that occurred among the student athletes in*
> Vernonia *is significant. Second, while the District established that it has a drug abuse
> problem, the means chosen to deal with that problem were too broad. The Policy's ac-
> tual scope extended vastly beyond the policy upheld in* Vernonia. *The Policy swept
> within its reach students participating in an extracurricular activity who were not*

---

[43]115 S.Ct. 2386, at 2396 (1995)

[44]864 F.2d 1309 (1988)

[45]115 S.Ct. 2386 (1995)

[46]*Trinidad School District No. 1 v. Lopez,* 963 P.2d 1095 (1998)

demonstrated to play a role in promoting drugs and for whom there was no demonstrated risk of physical injury.[47]

From the holdings in the court cases, one can infer that a school district may enforce a drug-testing policy if it has a problem with drug use and if the policy is clear and fair and ensures due process rights. The most recent case addressing the issue of drug testing is *Board of Education of Independent School District No. 92 of Pottawatomie County v. Earls.[48]*

Board of Education of Independent School District No. 92 of Pottawatomie County v. Earls
Supreme Court of the United States, 2002
536 U.S. 822

Justice Thomas delivered the opinion of the Court.

The Student Activities Drug Testing Policy implemented by the Board of Education of Independent School District No. 92 of Pottawatomie County (School District) requires all students who participate in competitive extracurricular activities to submit to drug testing. Because this Policy reasonably serves the School District's important interest in detecting and preventing drug use among its students, we hold that it is constitutional.

I.   The city of Tecumseh, Oklahoma, is a rural community located approximately 40 miles southeast of Oklahoma City. The School District administers all Tecumseh public schools. In the fall of 1998, the School District adopted the Student Activities Drug Testing Policy (Policy), which requires all middle and high school students to consent to drug testing in order to participate in any extracurricular activity. In practice, the Policy has been applied only to competitive extracurricular activities sanctioned by the Oklahoma Secondary Schools Activities Association, such as the Academic Team, Future Farmers of America, Future Homemakers of America, band, choir, pompon, cheerleading, and athletics. Under the Policy, students are required to take a drug test before participating in an extracurricular activity, must submit to random drug testing while participating in that activity, and must agree to be tested at any time upon reasonable suspicion. The urinalysis tests are designed to detect only the use of illegal drugs, including amphetamines, marijuana, cocaine, opiates, and barbiturates, not medical conditions or the presence of authorized prescription medications.

At the time of their suit, both respondents attended Tecumseh High School. Respondent Lindsay Earls was a member of the show choir, the marching band, the Academic Team, and the National Honor Society. Respondent Daniel James sought to participate in the Academic Team. Together with their parents, Earls and James brought a 42 U.S.C. § 1983 action against the School District, challenging the Policy both on its face and as applied to their

---

[47]Ibid., at 1110
[48]536 U.S. 822 (2002)

participation in extracurricular activities. They alleged that the Policy violates the Fourth Amendment as incorporated by the Fourteenth Amendment and requested injunctive and declarative relief. They also argued that the School District failed to identify a special need for testing students who participate in extracurricular activities, and that the "Drug Testing Policy neither addresses a proven problem nor promises to bring any benefit to students or the school."

Applying the principles articulated in *Vernonia School Dist. 47J v. Acton,* in which we upheld the suspicionless drug testing of school athletes, the United States District Court for the Western District of Oklahoma rejected respondents' claim that the Policy was unconstitutional and granted summary judgment to the School District. The court noted that "special needs" exist in the public school context and that, although the School District did "not show a drug problem of epidemic proportions," there was a history of drug abuse starting in 1970 that presented "legitimate cause for concern." The District Court also held that the Policy was effective because "it can scarcely be disputed that the drug problem among the student body is effectively addressed by making sure that the large number of students participating in competitive, extracurricular activities do not use drugs."

The United States Court of Appeals for the Tenth Circuit reversed, holding that the Policy violated the Fourth Amendment. The Court of Appeals agreed with the District Court that the Policy must be evaluated in the "unique environment of the school setting," but reached a different conclusion as to the Policy's constitutionality. Before imposing a suspicionless drug testing program, the Court of Appeals concluded that a school "must demonstrate that there is some identifiable drug abuse problem among a sufficient number of those subject to the testing, such that testing that group of students will actually redress its drug problem." The Court of Appeals then held that because the School District failed to demonstrate such a problem existed among Tecumseh students participating in competitive extracurricular activities, the Policy was unconstitutional. We granted certiorari, and now reverse.

II.   The Fourth Amendment to the United States Constitution protects "the right of the people to be secure in their persons, houses, papers, and effects, against unreasonable searches and seizures." Searches by public school officials, such as the collection of urine samples, implicate Fourth Amendment interests. We must therefore review the School District's Policy for "reasonableness," which is the touchstone of the constitutionality of a governmental search.

In the criminal context, reasonableness usually requires a showing of probable cause. The probable-cause standard, however, "is peculiarly related to criminal investigations" and may be unsuited to determining the reasonableness of administrative searches where the "Government seeks to *prevent* the development of hazardous conditions." The Court has also held that a warrant and finding of probable cause are unnecessary in the public school context because such requirements "would unduly interfere with the maintenance of the swift and informal disciplinary procedures [that are] needed."

Given that the School District's Policy is not in any way related to the conduct of criminal investigations, respondents do not contend that the School District requires probable cause before testing students for drug use. Respondents instead argue that drug testing must be based at least on some level of individualized suspicion. It is true that we generally determine the reasonableness of a search by balancing the nature of the intrusion on the individual's privacy against the promotion of legitimate governmental interests. But we have long held that "the Fourth Amendment imposes no irreducible requirement of [individualized] suspicion." "In certain limited circumstances, the Government's need to discover such latent or hidden conditions, or to prevent their development, is sufficiently compelling to justify the intrusion on privacy entailed by conducting such searches without any measure of individualized suspicion." Therefore, in the context of safety and administrative regulations, a search unsupported by probable cause may be reasonable "when 'special needs, beyond the normal need for law enforcement, make the warrant and probable-cause requirement impracticable.'"

Significantly, this Court has previously held that "special needs" inhere in the public school context. While schoolchildren do not shed their constitutional rights when they enter the schoolhouse, "Fourth Amendment rights . . . are different in public schools than elsewhere; the 'reasonableness' inquiry cannot disregard the schools' custodial and tutelary responsibility for children." In particular, a finding of individualized suspicion may not be necessary when a school conducts drug testing.

In *Vernonia*, this Court held that the suspicionless drug testing of athletes was constitutional. The Court, however, did not simply authorize all school drug testing, but rather conducted a fact-specific balancing of the intrusion on the children's Fourth Amendment rights against the promotion of legitimate governmental interests. Applying the principles of *Vernonia* to the somewhat different facts of this case, we conclude that Tecumseh's Policy is also constitutional.

A. We first consider the nature of the privacy interest allegedly compromised by the drug testing. The context of the public school environment serves as the backdrop for the analysis of the privacy interest at stake and the reasonableness of the drug testing policy in general.

A student's privacy interest is limited in a public school environment where the State is responsible for maintaining discipline, health, and safety. Schoolchildren are routinely required to submit to physical examinations and vaccinations against disease. Securing order in the school environment sometimes requires that students be subjected to greater controls than those appropriate for adults.

Respondents argue that because children participating in nonathletic extracurricular activities are not subject to regular physicals and communal undress, they have a stronger expectation of privacy than the athletes tested in *Vernonia*. This distinction, however, was not essential to our decision in *Vernonia*, which depended primarily upon the school's custodial responsibility and authority.

In any event, students who participate in competitive extracurricular activities voluntarily subject themselves to many of the same intrusions on their privacy as do athletes. Some of these clubs and activities require occasional off-campus travel and communal undress. All of them have their own rules and requirements for participating students that do not apply to the student body as a whole. For example, each of the competitive extracurricular activities governed by the Policy must abide by the rules of the Oklahoma Secondary Schools

Activities Association, and a faculty sponsor monitors the students for compliance with the various rules dictated by the clubs and activities. This regulation of extracurricular activities further diminishes the expectation of privacy among schoolchildren. We therefore conclude that the students affected by this Policy have a limited expectation of privacy.

B.   Next, we consider the character of the intrusion imposed by the Policy. Urination is "an excretory function traditionally shielded by great privacy." But the "degree of intrusion" on one's privacy caused by collecting a urine sample "depends upon the manner in which production of the urine sample is monitored."

Under the Policy, a faculty monitor waits outside the closed restroom stall for the student to produce a sample and must "listen for the normal sounds of urination in order to guard against tampered specimens and to insure an accurate chain of custody." The monitor then pours the sample into two bottles that are sealed and placed into a mailing pouch along with a consent form signed by the student. This procedure is virtually identical to that reviewed in *Vernonia,* except that it additionally protects privacy by allowing male students to produce their samples behind a closed stall. Given that we considered the method of collection in *Vernonia* a "negligible" intrusion, the method here is even less problematic.

In addition, the Policy clearly requires that the test results be kept in confidential files separate from a student's other educational records and released to school personnel only on a "need to know" basis. Respondents nonetheless contend that the intrusion on students' privacy is significant because the Policy fails to protect effectively against the disclosure of confidential information and, specifically, that the school "has been careless in protecting that information: for example, the Choir teacher looked at students' prescription drug lists and left them where other students could see them." But the choir teacher is someone with a "need to know," because during off-campus trips she needs to know what medications are taken by her students. Even before the Policy was enacted the choir teacher had access to this information. In any event, there is no allegation that any other student did see such information. This one example of alleged carelessness hardly increases the character of the intrusion.

Moreover, the test results are not turned over to any law enforcement authority. Nor do the test results here lead to the imposition of discipline or have any academic consequences. Rather, the only consequence of a failed drug test is to limit the student's privilege of participating in extracurricular activities. Indeed, a student may test positive for drugs twice and still be allowed to participate in extracurricular activities. After the first positive test, the school contacts the student's parent or guardian for a meeting. The student may continue to participate in the activity if within five days of the meeting the student shows proof of receiving drug counseling and submits to a second drug test in two weeks. For the second positive test, the student is suspended from participation in all extracurricular activities for 14 days, must complete four hours of substance abuse counseling, and must submit to monthly drug tests. Only after a third positive test will the student be suspended from participating in any extracurricular activity for the remainder of the school year, or 88 school days, whichever is longer.

Given the minimally intrusive nature of the sample collection and the limited uses to which the test results are put, we conclude that the invasion of students' privacy is not significant.

C.   Finally, this Court must consider the nature and immediacy of the government's concerns and the efficacy of the Policy in meeting them. This Court has already articulated in detail the importance of the governmental concern in preventing drug use by schoolchildren. The drug abuse problem among our Nation's youth has hardly abated since *Vernonia* was decided in 1995. In fact, evidence suggests that it has only grown worse. As in *Vernonia*, "the necessity for the State to act is magnified by the fact that this evil is being visited not just upon individuals at large, but upon children for whom it has undertaken a special responsibility of care and direction." The health and safety risks identified in *Vernonia* apply with equal force to Tecumseh's children. Indeed, the nationwide drug epidemic makes the war against drugs a pressing concern in every school.

Additionally, the School District in this case has presented specific evidence of drug use at Tecumseh schools. Teachers testified that they had seen students who appeared to be under the influence of drugs and that they had heard students speaking openly about using drugs. A drug dog found marijuana cigarettes near the school parking lot. Police officers once found drugs or drug paraphernalia in a car driven by a Future Farmers of America member. And the school board president reported that people in the community were calling the board to discuss the "drug situation." We decline to second-guess the finding of the District Court that "viewing the evidence as a whole, it cannot be reasonably disputed that the [School District] was faced with a 'drug problem' when it adopted the Policy."

Respondents consider the proffered evidence insufficient and argue that there is no "real and immediate interest" to justify a policy of drug testing nonathletes. We have recognized, however, that "[a] demonstrated problem of drug abuse . . . [is] not in all cases necessary to the validity of a testing regime," but that some showing does "shore up an assertion of special need for a suspicionless general search program." The School District has provided sufficient evidence to shore up the need for its drug testing program.

Furthermore, this Court has not required a particularized or pervasive drug problem before allowing the government to conduct suspicionless drug testing. For instance, in *Von Raab* the Court upheld the drug testing of customs officials on a purely preventive basis, without any documented history of drug use by such officials. In response to the lack of evidence relating to drug use, the Court noted generally that "drug abuse is one of the most serious problems confronting our society today," and that programs to prevent and detect drug use among customs officials could not be deemed unreasonable. Likewise, the need to prevent and deter the substantial harm of childhood drug use provides the necessary immediacy for a school testing policy. Indeed, it would make little sense to require a school district to wait for a substantial portion of its students to begin using drugs before it was allowed to institute a drug testing program designed to deter drug use.

Given the nationwide epidemic of drug use, and the evidence of increased drug use in Tecumseh schools, it was entirely reasonable for the School District to enact this particular drug testing policy. We reject the Court of Appeals' novel test that "any district seeking to impose a random suspicionless drug testing policy as a condition to participation in a school activity must demonstrate that there is some identifiable drug abuse problem among a sufficient number of those subject to the testing, such that testing that group of students will actually redress its drug problem." Among other problems, it would be difficult to administer such a test. As we cannot articulate a threshold level of drug use that would suffice to justify a drug testing program for schoolchildren, we refuse to fashion what would in effect be a constitutional quantum of drug use necessary to show a "drug problem."

Respondents also argue that the testing of nonathletes does not implicate any safety concerns, and that safety is a "crucial factor" in applying the special needs framework. They contend that there must be "surpassing safety interests, or "extraordinary safety and national security hazards," in order to override the usual protections of the Fourth Amendment. Respondents are correct that safety factors into the special needs analysis, but the safety interest furthered by drug testing is undoubtedly substantial for all children, athletes and nonathletes alike. We know all too well that drug use carries a variety of health risks for children, including death from overdose.

We also reject respondents' argument that drug testing must presumptively be based upon an individualized reasonable suspicion of wrongdoing because such a testing regime would be less intrusive. In this context, the Fourth Amendment does not require a finding of individualized suspicion, and we decline to impose such a requirement on schools attempting to prevent and detect drug use by students. Moreover, we question whether testing based on individualized suspicion in fact would be less intrusive. Such a regime would place an additional burden on public school teachers who are already tasked with the difficult job of maintaining order and discipline. A program of individualized suspicion might unfairly target members of unpopular groups. The fear of lawsuits resulting from such targeted searches may chill enforcement of the program, rendering it ineffective in combating drug use. In any case, this Court has repeatedly stated that reasonableness under the Fourth Amendment does not require employing the least intrusive means, because "the logic of such elaborate less-restrictive-alternative arguments could raise insuperable barriers to the exercise of virtually all search-and-seizure powers."

Finally, we find that testing students who participate in extracurricular activities is a reasonably effective means of addressing the School District's legitimate concerns in preventing, deterring, and detecting drug use. While in *Vernonia* there might have been a closer fit between the testing of athletes and the trial court's finding that the drug problem was "fueled by the 'role model' effect of athletes' drug use," such a finding was not essential to the holding. *Vernonia* did not require the school to test the group of students most likely to use drugs, but rather considered the constitutionality of the program in the context of the public school's custodial responsibilities. Evaluating the Policy in this context, we conclude that the drug testing of Tecumseh students who participate in extracurricular activities effectively serves the School District's interest in protecting the safety and health of its students.

III.   Within the limits of the Fourth Amendment, local school boards must assess the desirability of drug testing schoolchildren. In upholding the constitutionality of the Policy, we express no opinion as to its wisdom. Rather, we hold only that Tecumseh's Policy is a reasonable means of furthering the School District's important interest in preventing and deterring drug use among its schoolchildren. Accordingly, we reverse the judgment of the Court of Appeals.

It is so ordered.

Best Practices

- Before drug-testing students, seek advice from an attorney. The law in this area is rapidly changing and is different in each state.

- Ensure that your district has a clear policy about drug testing and make sure this policy is clearly communicated to parents.

- If drug testing is permitted, due process procedures must be in place for those students who test positive. Typically, this process includes some form of rehabilitation.

SUMMARY

This chapter reviews some of the most important Supreme Court cases decided within education law. The case of *Tinker v. Des Moines* was one of the first to recognize the rights of student speech while inside the public school. However, this right is not inclusive and is restricted if it is offensive, obscene, or school sponsored. Additionally, as the *Tinker* case illustrated, speech can be verbal or nonverbal, therefore, some states have initiated restriction on student dress, but such policies are constitutional only if they are reasonable and justified.

Another landmark case reviewed within this chapter is *New Jersey v. T.L.O.* Once again, the court protects the rights of students, while at the same time granting the school the opportunity to provide a safe environment for others. The rights of students under the Fourth Amendment vary from state to state and is highly debated regarding the searches of school lockers and personal items. Regardless of the state law, one area that administrators should highly avoid is that of strip searching students. Closely related is the right for schools to drug test students. The most recent case of *Board of Education v. Earls* illustrates that drug testing of students must be done only after a clear policy has been passed by the school board.

DISCUSSION QUESTIONS

1. How did the Court in *Tinker* define a "material and substantial disruption"?
2. Should the age of the student be a factor in deciding how much constitutional protection he or she receives? For example, the *Tinker* case dealt with high school students. Do elementary students have the same rights? Should they have the same rights?
3. If school districts place no restrictions on student-run publications, what liability does the educational institution carry if someone is defamed?
4. Can a school regulate student clothing? If so, when?
5. What is the difference between the probable-cause standard required by law officials and reasonable suspicion, which is granted to educational institutions? Why are there different standards?

6. What constitutes reasonable suspicion? Excluding the facts in *New Jersey v. T.L.O.*, give examples of situations in which a school official would have reasonable suspicion to search a student. What is the two-pronged test of reasonable suspicion?

7. A local high school principal saw a small group of students huddled together outside by the bleachers. He witnessed one of the students fiddling in his pockets and consequently required all students to empty the contents of their pockets. One of the students possessed a small bag of marijuana and was suspended. The student now wants the evidence of the marijuana suppressed, claiming that the search was a violation of his Fourth Amendment rights. Discuss the outcome of this case, applying the law from *New Jersey v. T.L.O.*

8. After the shooting at Columbine High School, is the holding in *New Jersey v. T.L.O.* still appropriate law? Should students have the same constitutional rights today as they did in 1985? Discuss and defend your opinion.

9. When is it appropriate for a school official to strip-search a student?

10. When is drug testing of students permitted under the Fourth Amendment? Respond using recent decisions by the Supreme Court.

DEEPENING YOUR UNDERSTANDING

1. Perform legal research and find *Backwell v. Issaquena County Board of Education*, 363 F.2d 749, and *Burnside v. Byras*, 363 F.2d 744. Compare and contrast the court decisions.

2. Create a dress code that would not violate the students' constitutional rights. Review what is and isn't acceptable at your institution. If your institution currently has a dress code, you may want to critique it to ensure that it meets constitutional requirements.

6

STUDENT DISCIPLINE

INTRODUCTION

Under the doctrine of in loco parentis, teachers and school administrators are assumed to have the authority to discipline students while they are in the school setting. In the past, students in public schools were often disciplined by means of swatting or paddling and expelled from school without the opportunity to state their side of the story. In the early 1960s, however, the courts began to examine the constitutional rights of students who were being disciplined by school authorities.

CORPORAL PUNISHMENT

AS OF this publication, 27 states and the District of Columbia have banned corporal punishment through state regulation, by every local school board in the state, or by rescinding authorization to use. The following states have banned corporal punishment: Alaska, California, Connecticut, Hawaii, Illinois, Iowa, Maine, Maryland, Massachusetts, Michigan, Minnesota, Montana, Nebraska, Nevada, New Hampshire, New Jersey, New York, North Dakota, Oregon, Rhode Island, South Dakota, Utah, Vermont, Virginia, Washington, West Virginia, and Wisconsin (see Figure 6.1).[1]

More than half of the states prohibit corporal punishment, but the debate on corporal punishment continues, with advocates insisting that such discipline is required to maintain order and opponents arguing that such action is cruel and unusual punishment.

---

[1] National Coalition to Abolish Corporal Punishment in Schools, Corporal Punishment Facts (2001)

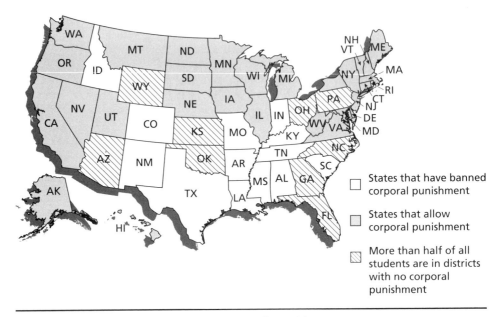

FIGURE 6.1   *U.S. states that ban corporal punishment*
Source: Reprinted with permission from National Coalition to Abolish Corporal Punishment in Schools (2001)

While the pendulum is swinging toward the abolishment of corporal punishment, just a few decades ago almost every state allowed school officials to administer corporal punishment to students. In some institutions, students were spanked, swatted, paddled, or smacked for disobeying school authority. Because of the widespread use of corporal punishment in the pubic schools, school officials commonly used force to ensure that students obeyed the rules of the institution.

In 1977, the U.S. Supreme Court addressed the issue after two students, James Ingraham and Roosevelt Andrews, were paddled for responding slowly to a teacher's request.[2] The Dade County, Florida, junior high school students were severely paddled, resulting in a hematoma on Ingraham. Roosevelt was struck in the arm, which caused him to lose the use of it for a week. Although corporal punishment was permitted in Florida when the incident occurred, the students claimed that the use of such discipline was cruel and unusual punishment, unconstitutional under the Eighth Amendment. The issue addressed by the Court was whether or not students were protected from excessive punishment by school authorities under the Eighth Amendment of the U.S. Constitution.

---

[2] *Ingraham v. Wright*, 430 U.S. 651 (1977)

Ingraham v. Wright

Supreme Court of the United States, 1977

430 U.S. 651

Mr. Justice Powell delivered the opinion of the Court.

This case presents questions concerning the use of corporal punishment in public schools: First, whether the paddling of students as a means of maintaining school discipline constitutes cruel and unusual punishment in violation of the Eighth Amendment; and, second, to the extent that paddling is constitutionally permissible, whether the Due Process Clause of the Fourteenth Amendment requires prior notice and an opportunity to be heard. . . .

Petitioners' evidence may be summarized briefly. In the 1970–1971 school year many of the 237 schools in Dade County used corporal punishment as a means of maintaining discipline pursuant to Florida legislation and a local School Board regulation. The statute then in effect authorized limited corporal punishment by negative inference, proscribing punishment which was "degrading or unduly severe" or which was inflicted without prior consultation with the principal or the teacher in charge of the school. . . . The regulation, Dade County School Board Policy 5144, contained explicit directions and limitations. The authorized punishment consisted of paddling the recalcitrant student on the buttocks with a flat wooden paddle measuring less than two feet long, three to four inches wide, and about one-half inch thick. The normal punishment was limited to one to five "licks" or blows with the paddle and resulted in no apparent physical injury to the student. School authorities viewed corporal punishment as a less drastic means of discipline than suspension or expulsion. Contrary to the procedural requirements of the statute and regulation, teachers often paddled students on their own authority without first consulting the principal.

. . . Because he was slow to respond to his teacher's instructions, Ingraham was subjected to more than 20 licks with a paddle while being held over a table in the principal's office. The paddling was so severe that he suffered a hematoma requiring medical attention and keeping him out of school for several days. Andrews was paddled several times for minor infractions. On two occasions he was struck on his arms, once depriving him of the full use of his arm for a week. . . .

The District Court made no findings on the credibility of the students' testimony. Rather, assuming their testimony to be credible, the court found no constitutional basis for relief. With respect to count three, the class action, the court concluded that the punishment authorized and practiced generally in the county schools violated no constitutional right. . . .

The court also rejected the petitioners' substantive contentions. The Eighth Amendment, in the court's view, was simply inapplicable to corporal punishment in public schools. Stressing the likelihood of civil and criminal liability in state law, if petitioners' evidence were believed, the court held that "[t]he administration of corporal punishment in public schools, whether or not excessively administered, does not come within the scope of Eighth Amendment protection." Nor was there any substantive violation of the Due Process Clause. The court noted that "[p]addling of recalcitrant children has long been an accepted method of promoting good behavior and instilling notions of responsibility and decorum into the mischievous heads of school children." The court refused to examine instances of punishment individually. . . . We granted certiorari, limited to the questions of cruel and unusual punishment and procedural due process.

The Eighth Amendment provides: "Excessive bail shall not be required, nor excessive fines imposed, nor cruel and unusual punishments inflicted." Bail, fines, and punishment traditionally have been associated with the criminal process, and by subjecting the three to parallel limitations the text of the Amendment suggests an intention to limit the power of those entrusted with the criminal-law function of government. An examination of the history of the Amendment and the decisions of this Court construing the proscription against cruel and unusual punishment confirms that it was designed to protect those convicted of crimes. We adhere to this longstanding limitation and hold that the Eighth Amendment does not apply to the paddling of children as a means of maintaining discipline in public schools. . . .

Petitioners acknowledge that the original design of the Cruel and Unusual Punishments Clause was to limit criminal punishments, but urge nonetheless that the prohibition should be extended to ban the paddling of schoolchildren. Observing that the Framers of the Eighth Amendment could not have envisioned our present system of public and compulsory education, with its opportunities for noncriminal punishments, petitioners contend that extension of the prohibition against cruel punishments is necessary lest we afford greater protection to criminals than to schoolchildren. It would be anomalous, they say, if schoolchildren could be beaten without constitutional redress, while hardened criminals suffering the same beatings at the hands of their jailers might have a valid claim under the Eighth Amendment. Whatever force this logic may have in other settings, we find it an inadequate basis for wrenching the Eighth Amendment from its historical context and extending it to traditional disciplinary practices in the public schools.

The prisoner and the schoolchild stand in wholly different circumstances, separated by the harsh facts of criminal conviction and incarceration. The prisoner's conviction entitles the State to classify him as a "criminal," and his incarceration deprives him of the freedom "to be with family and friends and to form the other enduring attachments of normal life." Prison brutality, as the Court of Appeals observed in this case, is "part of the total punishment to which the individual is being subjected for his crime and, as such, is a proper subject for Eighth Amendment scrutiny." Even so, the protection afforded by the Eighth Amendment is limited. After incarceration, only the "unnecessary and wanton infliction of pain" constitutes cruel and unusual punishment forbidden by the Eighth Amendment.

The schoolchild has little need for the protection of the Eighth Amendment. Though attendance may not always be voluntary, the public school remains an open institution. Except perhaps when very young, the child is not physically restrained from leaving school during school hours; and at the end of the school day, the child is invariably free to return home. Even while at school, the child brings with him the support of family and friends and is rarely apart from teachers and other pupils who may witness and protest any instances of mistreatment.

The openness of the public school and its supervision by the community afford significant safeguards against the kinds of abuses from which the Eighth Amendment protects the prisoner. In virtually every community where corporal punishment is permitted in the schools, these safeguards are reinforced by the legal constraints of the common law. Public school teachers and administrators are privileged at common law to inflict only such corporal punishment as is reasonably necessary for the proper education and discipline of the child; any punishment going beyond the privilege may result in both civil and criminal liability. As long as the schools are open to public scrutiny, there is no reason to believe that the common-law constraints will not effectively remedy and deter excesses such as those alleged in this case.

We conclude that when public school teachers or administrators impose disciplinary corporal punishment, the Eighth Amendment is inapplicable. The pertinent constitutional question is whether the imposition is consonant with the requirements of due process. . . .

The Fourteenth Amendment prohibits any state deprivation of life, liberty, or property without due process of law. Application of this prohibition requires the familiar two-stage analysis: We must first ask whether the asserted individual interests are encompassed within the Fourteenth Amendment's protection of "life, liberty or property"; if protected interests are implicated, we then must decide what procedures constitute "due process of law." Following that analysis here, we find that corporal punishment in public schools implicates a constitutionally protected liberty interest, but we hold that the traditional common-law remedies are fully adequate to afford due process. . . .

[The] range of interests protected by procedural due process is not infinite." We have repeatedly rejected "the notion that any grievous loss visited upon a person by the State is sufficient to invoke the procedural protections of the Due Process Clause." Due process is required only when a decision of the State implicates an interest within the protection of the Fourteenth Amendment. And "to determine whether due process requirements apply in the first place, we must look not to the 'weight' but to the nature of the interest at stake."

The Due Process Clause of the Fifth Amendment, later incorporated into the Fourteenth, was intended to give Americans at least the protection against governmental power that they had enjoyed as Englishmen against the power of the Crown. The liberty preserved from deprivation without due process included the right "generally to enjoy those privileges long recognized at common law as essential to the orderly pursuit of happiness by free men." Among the historic liberties so protected was a right to be free from, and to obtain judicial relief for, unjustified intrusions on personal security.

While the contours of this historic liberty interest in the context of our federal system of government have not been defined precisely, they always have been thought to encompass freedom from bodily restraint and punishment. It is fundamental that the state cannot hold and physically punish an individual except in accordance with due process of law.

This constitutionally protected liberty interest is at stake in this case. There is, of course, a de minimis level of imposition with which the Constitution is not concerned. But at least where school authorities, acting under color of state law, deliberately decide to punish a child for misconduct by restraining the child and inflicting appreciable physical pain, we hold that Fourteenth Amendment liberty interests are implicated. . . .

"[The] question remains what process is due." Were it not for the common-law privilege permitting teachers to inflict reasonable corporal punishment on children in their care, and the availability of the traditional remedies for abuse, the case for requiring advance procedural safeguards would be strong indeed. But here we deal with a punishment—paddling—within that tradition, and the question is whether the common-law remedies are adequate to afford due process. . . .

Whether in this case the common-law remedies for excessive corporal punishment constitute due process of law must turn on an analysis of the competing interests at stake, viewed against the background of "history, reason, [and] the past course of decisions." The analysis requires consideration of three distinct factors: "First, the private interest that will be affected . . . ; second, the risk of an erroneous deprivation of such interest . . . and the probable value, if any, of additional or substitute procedural safeguards; and finally, the [state] interest, including the function involved and the fiscal and administrative burdens that the additional or substitute procedural requirement would entail."

Because it is rooted in history, the child's liberty interest in avoiding corporal punishment while in the care of public school authorities is subject to historical limitations. Under the common law, an invasion of personal security gave rise to a right to recover damages in a subsequent judicial proceeding. But the right of recovery was qualified by the concept of justification. Thus, there could be no recovery against a teacher who gave only "moderate correction" to a child. To the extent that the force used was reasonable in light of its purpose, it was not wrongful, but rather "justifiable or lawful."

The concept that reasonable corporal punishment in school is justifiable continues to be recognized in the laws of most States. It represents "the balance struck by this country," between the child's interest in personal security and the traditional view that some limited corporal punishment may be necessary in the course of a child's education. Under that longstanding accommodation of interests, there can be no deprivation of substantive rights as long as disciplinary corporal punishment is within the limits of the common-law privilege.

This is not to say that the child's interest in procedural safeguards is insubstantial. The school disciplinary process is not "a totally accurate, unerring process, never mistaken and never unfair. . . . " In any deliberate infliction of corporal punishment on a child who is restrained for that purpose, there is some risk that the intrusion on the child's liberty will be unjustified and therefore unlawful. In these circumstances the child has a strong interest in procedural safeguards that minimize the risk of wrongful punishment and provide for the resolution of disputed questions of justification.

We turn now to a consideration of the safeguards that are available under applicable Florida law. Florida has continued to recognize, and indeed has strengthened by statute, the common-law right of a child not to be subjected to excessive corporal punishment in school. . . . If the punishment inflicted is later found to have been excessive—not reasonably believed at the time to be necessary for the child's discipline or training—the school authorities inflicting it may be held liable in damages to the child and, if malice is shown, they may be subject to criminal penalties.

Although students have testified in this case to specific instances of abuse, there is every reason to believe that such mistreatment is an aberration. The uncontradicted evidence suggests that corporal punishment in the Dade County schools was, "[w]ith the exception of a few cases, . . . unremarkable in physical severity." Moreover, because paddlings are usually inflicted in response to conduct directly observed by teachers in their presence, the risk that a child will be paddled without cause is typically insignificant. In the ordinary case, a disciplinary paddling neither threatens seriously to violate any substantive rights nor condemns the child "to suffer grievous loss of any kind."

In those cases where severe punishment is contemplated, the available civil and criminal sanctions for abuse—considered in light of the openness of the school environment—afford significant protection against unjustified corporal punishment. Teachers and school authorities are unlikely to inflict corporal punishment unnecessarily or excessively when a possible consequence of doing so is the institution of civil or criminal proceedings against them.

It still may be argued, of course, that the child's liberty interest would be better protected if the common-law remedies were supplemented by the administrative safeguards of prior notice and a hearing. We have found frequently that some kind of prior hearing is necessary to guard against arbitrary impositions on interests protected by the Fourteenth Amendment. But where the State has preserved what "has always been the law of the land," the case for administrative safeguards is significantly less compelling. . . .

But even if the need for advance procedural safeguards were clear, the question would remain whether the incremental benefit could justify the cost. Acceptance of petitioners' claims would work a transformation in the law governing corporal punishment in Florida and most other States. Given the impracticability of formulating a rule of procedural due process that varies with the severity of the particular imposition, the prior hearing petitioners seek would have to precede any paddling, however moderate or trivial.

Such a universal constitutional requirement would significantly burden the use of corporal punishment as a disciplinary measure. Hearings—even informal hearings—require time, personnel, and a diversion of attention from normal school pursuits. School authorities may well choose to abandon corporal punishment rather than incur the burdens of complying with the procedural requirements. Teachers, properly concerned with maintaining authority in the classroom, may well prefer to rely on other disciplinary measures—which they may view as less effective—rather than confront the possible disruption that prior notice and a hearing may entail. Paradoxically, such an alteration of disciplinary policy is most likely to occur in the ordinary case where the contemplated punishment is well within the common-law privilege. Elimination or curtailment of corporal punishment would be welcomed by many as a societal advance. But when such a policy choice may result from this Court's determination of an asserted right to due process, rather than from the normal processes of community debate and legislative action, the societal costs cannot be dismissed as insubstantial. We are reviewing here a legislative judgment, rooted in history and reaffirmed in the laws of many States, that corporal punishment serves important educational interests. This judgment must be viewed in light of the disciplinary problems commonplace in the schools. . . . [T]he Court has repeatedly emphasized the need for affirming the comprehensive authority of the States and of school officials, consistent with fundamental constitutional safeguards, to prescribe and control conduct in the schools.

At some point the benefit of an additional safeguard to the individual affected . . . and to society in terms of increased assurance that the action is just, may be outweighed by the cost. We think that point has been reached in this case. In view of the low incidence of abuse, the openness of our schools, and the common-law safeguards that already exist, the risk of error that may result in violation of a schoolchild's substantive rights can only be regarded as minimal. Imposing additional administrative safeguards as a constitutional requirement might reduce that risk marginally, but would also entail a significant intrusion into an area of primary educational responsibility. We conclude that the Due Process Clause does not require notice and a hearing prior to the imposition of corporal punishment in the public schools, as that practice is authorized and limited by the common law. . . . Petitioners cannot prevail on either of the theories before us in this case. The Eighth Amendment's prohibition against cruel and unusual punishment is inapplicable to school paddlings, and the Fourteenth Amendment's requirement of procedural due process is satisfied by Florida's preservation of common-law constraints and remedies. We therefore agree with the Court of Appeals that petitioners' evidence affords no basis for injunctive relief, and that petitioners cannot recover damages on the basis of any Eighth Amendment or procedural due process violation.

Affirmed.

The U.S. Supreme Court, in a five-to-four decision, held that the punishment administered to the students was both severe and unreasonable yet was not a violation of the Eighth Amendment. In its analysis, the Court reviewed the longstanding history of corporal punishment and how disciplining schoolchildren dated as far back as the colonial period but that, even today, teachers have the right to apply reasonable force when disciplining schoolchildren.[3]

The U.S. Supreme Court also completed a thorough review of the purpose of the Eighth Amendment and held that, while the Constitution does prohibit the use of cruel and unusual punishment, that prohibition does not apply to students within a school environment. Originally, the Eighth Amendment was intended to protect criminals from punishment by law enforcement officials; and the Court could not infer that such protection should be granted to schoolchildren.

The use of even excessive corporal punishment on students does not constitute cruel and unusual punishment under the Eighth Amendment. This does not mean, however, that students are not protected from unreasonable and excessive force by school officials. Accordingly, a teacher or an administrator may apply force if he or she "reasonably believe[s] it to be necessary for the child's proper control, training, or education."[4] To the extent that the force is excessive or unreasonable, any administrator or faculty member that administers punishment in an unreasonable or excessive manner will be subject to both civil and criminal liability.

In *Commonwealth v. Douglass*, the principal of a private school was convicted of simple assault and was sentenced to 12 months of probation, 150 hours of community

---

[3] Ibid.
[4] Ibid.

service and a $500 fine.[5] The principal was a 36-year-old, 6-foot-tall, 201-pound man who administered 50 to 60 swats with a paddle to John Onderdon, a seven-year-old first grader who weighed 45 pounds and was 3 feet, 10 inches in height.[6] Due to the severity of the paddling, the boy incurred bruising and swelling on his buttocks and the backs of his legs. Additionally, he received psychological counseling for depression and emotional problems, which began after the incident. According to the court, "the paddling amounted neither to reasonable discipline nor to force consistent with the welfare of the minor."[7]

In *Douglass*, the claim was for assault. *Black's Law Dictionary* defines *assault* as "any willful attempt or threat to inflict injury upon the person of another, when coupled with the apparent present ability to do so, and any intentional display of force such as would give the victim reason to fear or expect immediate bodily harm."[8] (A full discussion of assault and battery appears in Chapter 2.) Usually when punishment is administered, there are no legal repercussions. If the teacher or the administrator does not intend to injure a student while administering punishment and does so in a reasonable manner, generally he or she will not be held liable. In those states that permit corporal punishment, the act will not constitute assault and battery if the punishment is performed in a reasonable manner and in good faith.

Educational institutions can be held liable for the use of excessive corporal punishment. To avoid such liability in those states that permit corporal punishment, one should consider several important factors before administering the penalty. One factor is the evaluation of the student. Each student is different; and disciplinary history, family background, age, size, and mental capacity should be considered before punishment.

More important, the punishment should not be administered in such a manner as to be considered cruel or excessive. One step in preventing excessive punishment is to ensure that all faculty and staff members are aware of the school's corporal punishment policy and that the policy procedures are strictly followed when administering punishment to a student.

Best Practices

- Provide training to educate faculty and staff about the school's corporal punishment policy.
- Ensure that parents are aware of the policy and procedures concerning corporal punishment.
- Never punish a student out of anger.
- Insist on a cooling-off period before administering punishment.
- Avoid having the school official who may be directly involved in the conflict administer the punishment.
- Always have at least one additional school official witness the punishment, preferably a supervisor.

---

[5] 588 A.2d 53 (1991)

[6] Ibid.

[7] Ibid., at 116

[8] 6th edition, p. 114.

Procedural Due Process and Student Suspension

OTHER forms of punishment to students consist of suspension or exclusion from school. The due process clause of the Fourteenth Amendment of the U.S. Constitution reads: "the state shall not deprive any person of life, liberty, or property without due process of law." Traditionally, due process rights were only applied to individuals charged with criminal offenses. In 1975, that changed when the U.S. Supreme Court decided that students possessed a liberty and property interest in attending school and hence must receive some due process protection before having those rights taken away.[9]

Goss v. Lopez
Supreme Court of the United States, 1975
419 U.S. 565

Mr. Justice White delivered the opinion of the Court.

This appeal by various administrators of the Columbus, Ohio, Public School System (CPSS) challenges the judgment of a three-judge federal court, declaring that appellees—various high school students in the CPSS—were denied due process of law contrary to the command of the Fourteenth Amendment in that they were temporarily suspended from their high schools without a hearing either prior to suspension or within a reasonable time thereafter, and enjoining the administrators to remove all references to such suspensions from the students' records.

Ohio law, Rev. Code Ann. § 3313.64 (1972), provides for free education to all children between the ages of six and 21. Section 3313.66 of the Code empowers the principal of an Ohio public school to suspend a pupil for misconduct for up to 10 days or to expel him. In either case, he must notify the student's parents within 24 hours and state the reasons for his action. A pupil who is expelled, or his parents, may appeal the decision to the Board of Education and in connection therewith shall be permitted to be heard at the board meeting. The Board may reinstate the pupil following the hearing. No similar procedure is provided in § 3313.66 or any other provision of state law for a suspended student. Aside from a regulation tracking the statute, at the time of the imposition of the suspensions in this case the CPSS itself had not issued any written procedure applicable to suspensions. Nor, so far as the record reflects, had any of the individual high schools involved in this case. Each, however, had formally or informally described the conduct for which suspension could be imposed.

The nine named appellees, each of whom alleged that he or she had been suspended from public high school in Columbus for up to 10 days without a hearing pursuant to § 3313.66, filed an action under 42 U.S.C. § 1983 against the Columbus Board of Education and various administrators of the CPSS. The complaint sought a declaration that § 3313.66

---

[9] *Goss v. Lopez*, 419 U.S. 565 (1975)

was unconstitutional in that it permitted public school administrators to deprive plaintiffs of their rights to an education without a hearing of any kind, in violation of the procedural due process component of the Fourteenth Amendment. It also sought to enjoin the public school officials from issuing future suspensions pursuant to § 3313.66 and to require them to remove references to the past suspensions from the records of the students in question.

The proof below established that the suspensions arose out of a period of widespread student unrest in the CPSS during February and March 1971. Six of the named plaintiffs, Rudolph Sutton, Tyrone Washington, Susan Cooper, Deborah Fox, Clarence Byars, and Bruce Harris, were students at the Marion-Franklin High School and were each suspended for 10 days on account of disruptive or disobedient conduct committed in the presence of the school administrator who ordered the suspension. . . .

Two named plaintiffs, Dwight Lopez and Betty Crome, were students at the Central High School and McGuffey Junior High School, respectively. The former was suspended in connection with a disturbance in the lunchroom which involved some physical damage to school property. Lopez testified that at least 75 other students were suspended from his school on the same day. He also testified below that he was not a party to the destructive conduct but was instead an innocent bystander. Because no one from the school testified with regard to this incident, there is no evidence in the record indicating the official basis for concluding otherwise. Lopez never had a hearing.

Betty Crome was present at a demonstration at a high school other than the one she was attending. There she was arrested together with others, taken to the police station, and released without being formally charged. Before she went to school on the following day, she was notified that she had been suspended for a 10-day period. Because no one from the school testified with respect to this incident, the record does not disclose how the McGuffey Junior High School principal went about making the decision to suspend Crome, nor does it disclose on what information the decision was based. It is clear from the record that no hearing was ever held. . . .

On the basis of this evidence, the three-judge court declared that plaintiffs were denied due process of law because they were "suspended without hearing prior to suspension or within a reasonable time thereafter," and that Ohio Rev. Code Ann. § 3313.66 (1972) and regulations issued pursuant thereto were unconstitutional in permitting such suspensions. It was ordered that all references to plaintiffs' suspensions be removed from school files. . . .

The defendant school administrators have appealed the three-judge court's decision. Because the order below granted plaintiffs' request for an injunction—ordering defendants to expunge their records—this Court has jurisdiction of the appeal pursuant to 28 U.S.C. § 1253. We affirm.

Here, on the basis of state law, appellees plainly had legitimate claims of entitlement to a public education. Ohio Rev. Code Ann. §§ 3313.48 and 3313.64 direct local authorities to provide a free education to all residents between five and 21 years of age, and a compulsory-attendance law requires attendance for a school year of not less than 32 weeks. It is true that § 3313.66 of the Code permits school principals to suspend students for up to 10 days; but suspensions may not be imposed without any grounds whatsoever. All of the schools had their own rules specifying the grounds for expulsion or suspension. Having chosen to extend the right to an education to people of appellees' class generally, Ohio may not withdraw that right on grounds of misconduct, absent fundamentally fair procedures to determine whether the misconduct has occurred. . . .

The authority possessed by the State to prescribe and enforce standards of conduct in its schools although concededly very broad, must be exercised consistently with constitutional safeguards. Among other things, the State is constrained to recognize a student's legitimate entitlement to a public education as a property interest which is protected by the Due Process Clause and which may not be taken away for misconduct without adherence to the minimum procedures required by that Clause.

The Due Process Clause also forbids arbitrary deprivations of liberty. "Where a person's good name, reputation, honor, or integrity is at stake because of what the government is doing to him," the minimal requirements of the Clause must be satisfied. School authorities here suspended appellees from school for periods of up to 10 days based on charges of misconduct. If sustained and recorded, those charges could seriously damage the students' standing with their fellow pupils and their teachers as well as interfere with later opportunities for higher education and employment. It is apparent that the claimed right of the State to determine unilaterally and without process whether that misconduct has occurred immediately collides with the requirements of the Constitution.

Appellants proceed to argue that even if there is a right to a public education protected by the Due Process Clause generally, the Clause comes into play only when the State subjects a student to a "severe detriment or grievous loss." The loss of 10 days, it is said, is neither severe nor grievous and the Due Process Clause is therefore of no relevance. Appellants' argument is again refuted by our prior decisions; for in determining "whether due process requirements apply in the first place, we must look not to the 'weight' but to the nature of the interest at stake." Appellees were excluded from school only temporarily, it is true, but the length and consequent severity of a deprivation, while another factor to weigh in determining the appropriate form of hearing, "is not decisive of the basic right" to a hearing of some kind. The Court's view has been that as long as a property deprivation is not de minimis, its gravity is irrelevant to the question whether account must be taken of the Due Process Clause. A 10-day suspension from school is not de minimis in our view and may not be imposed in complete disregard of the Due Process Clause.

A short suspension is, of course, a far milder deprivation than expulsion. But, "education is perhaps the most important function of state and local governments," and the total exclusion from the educational process for more than a trivial period, and certainly if the suspension is for 10 days, is a serious event in the life of the suspended child. Neither the property interest in educational benefits temporarily denied nor the liberty interest in reputation, which is also implicated, is so insubstantial that suspensions may constitutionally be imposed by any procedure the school chooses, no matter how arbitrary. . . .

"Once it is determined that due process applies, the question remains what process is due." . . .

At the very minimum, therefore, students facing suspension and the consequent interference with a protected property interest must be given some kind of notice and afforded some kind of hearing. "Parties whose rights are to be affected are entitled to be heard; and in order that they may enjoy that right they must first be notified."

It also appears from our cases that the timing and content of the notice and the nature of the hearing will depend on appropriate accommodation of the competing interests involved. The student's interest is to avoid unfair or mistaken exclusion from the educational process, with all of its unfortunate consequences. The Due Process Clause will not shield him from suspensions properly imposed, but it disserves both his interest and the interest of the State if his suspension is in fact unwarranted. The concern would be mostly academic if the disciplinary process were a totally accurate, unerring process, never mistaken and never unfair. Unfortunately, that is not the case, and no one suggests that it is. Disciplinarians, although proceeding in utmost good faith, frequently act on the reports and advice of others; and the controlling facts and the nature of the conduct under challenge are often disputed. The risk of error is not at all trivial, and it should be guarded against if that may be done without prohibitive cost or interference with the educational process.

The difficulty is that our schools are vast and complex. Some modicum of discipline and order is essential if the educational function is to be performed. Events calling for discipline are frequent occurrences and sometimes require immediate, effective action. Suspension is considered not only to be a necessary tool to maintain order but a valuable educational device. The prospect of imposing elaborate hearing requirements in every suspension case is viewed with great concern, and many school authorities may well prefer the untrammeled power to act unilaterally, unhampered by rules about notice and hearing. But it would be a strange disciplinary system in an educational institution if no communication was sought by the disciplinarian with the student in an effort to inform him of his dereliction and to let him tell his side of the story in order to make sure that an injustice is not done.

We do not believe that school authorities must be totally free from notice and hearing requirements if their schools are to operate with acceptable efficiency. Students facing temporary suspension have interests qualifying for protection of the Due Process Clause, and due process requires, in connection with a suspension of 10 days or less, that the student be given oral or written notice of the charges against him and, if he denies them, an explanation of the evidence the authorities have and an opportunity to present his side of the story. The Clause requires at least these rudimentary precautions against unfair or mistaken findings of misconduct and arbitrary exclusion from school.

There need be no delay between the time "notice" is given and the time of the hearing. In the great majority of cases the disciplinarian may informally discuss the alleged misconduct with the student minutes after it has occurred. We hold only that, in being given an opportunity to explain his version of the facts at this discussion, the student first be told what he is accused of doing and what the basis of the accusation is. Lower courts which have addressed the question of the nature of the procedures required in short suspension cases have reached the same conclusion. Since the hearing may occur almost immediately following the misconduct, it follows that as a general rule notice and hearing should precede removal of the student from school. We agree with the District Court, however, that there are recurring situations in which prior notice and hearing cannot be insisted upon. Students whose presence poses a continuing danger to persons or property or an ongoing threat of disrupting the academic process may be immediately removed from school. In such cases, the necessary notice and rudimentary hearing should follow as soon as practicable, as the District Court indicated.

In holding as we do, we do not believe that we have imposed procedures on school dis-ciplinarians which are inappropriate in a classroom setting. Instead we have imposed re-quirements which are, if anything, less than a fair-minded school principal would impose upon himself in order to avoid unfair suspensions. . . .

We stop short of construing the Due Process Clause to require, countrywide, that hear-ings in connection with short suspensions must afford the student the opportunity to secure counsel, to confront and cross-examine witnesses supporting the charge, or to call his own witnesses to verify his version of the incident. Brief disciplinary suspensions are almost countless. To impose in each such case even truncated trial-type procedures might well over-whelm administrative facilities in many places and, by diverting resources, cost more than it would save in educational effectiveness. Moreover, further formalizing the suspension process and escalating its formality and adversary nature may not only make it too costly as a regular disciplinary tool but also destroy its effectiveness as part of the teaching process.

On the other hand, requiring effective notice and informal hearing permitting the stu-dent to give his version of the events will provide a meaningful hedge against erroneous ac-tion. At least the disciplinarian will be alerted to the existence of disputes about facts and arguments about cause and effect. He may then determine himself to summon the accuser, permit cross-examination, and allow the student to present his own witnesses. In more dif-ficult cases, he may permit counsel. In any event, his discretion will be more informed and we think the risk of error substantially reduced.

Requiring that there be at least an informal give-and-take between student and discipli-narian, preferably prior to the suspension, will add little to the factfinding function where the disciplinarian himself has witnessed the conduct forming the basis for the charge. But things are not always as they seem to be, and the student will at least have the opportunity to characterize his conduct and put it in what he deems the proper context.

We should also make it clear that we have addressed ourselves solely to the short sus-pension, not exceeding 10 days. Longer suspensions or expulsions for the remainder of the school term, or permanently, may require more formal procedures. Nor do we put aside the possibility that in unusual situations, although involving only a short suspension, something more than the rudimentary procedures will be required.

The District Court found each of the suspensions involved here to have occurred without a hearing, either before or after the suspension, and that each suspension was therefore in-valid and the statute unconstitutional insofar as it permits such suspensions without notice or hearing. Accordingly, the judgment is affirmed.

According to the Court in *Goss*, education is one of the most important functions of state and local governments; and all students have the right to receive a free public education. The right to obtain such an education is a property right that may not be taken away for mis-conduct without adherence to the minimum procedures required by the due process clause.

How much due process must students receive? This depends on the punishment sought by the school. According to the U.S. Supreme Court, "exclusion from the educa-tional process for more than a trivial period, and certainly if the suspension is for 10 days, is a serious event in the life of the suspended child."[10] Due to the seriousness of depriving a student of the right to learn, when a student is facing suspension of up to 10 days, at the minimum he or she should receive notice of the charges and the possible penalties, an opportunity to be present and heard at the hearing, and a hearing before an impartial person. The *Goss* Court indicates that the more serious the penalty, the more important it is that due process protection procedures should be followed.

EXPULSION

DUE TO the seriousness of expelling a student from school, due process procedures must include many steps that protect the student's rights. For example, according to the *Gonzales v. McEuen* court, one key requirement is notice. For "Notice to be adequate [it] must communicate to the recipient the nature of the proceeding. In an expulsion hearing, the notice given to the student must include a statement not only of the specific charge, but also the basic rights to be afforded the student: to be represented by counsel, to present evidence, and to confront and cross-examine adverse witnesses." In some states, this requirement also includes "notice to the student and the parent of the specific charge, of the right to be represented by counsel, and of the right to present evidence. Federal due process requires no less."[11]

The *Goss* Court did not address how much due process is required for minor infractions. The issue has been reviewed by lower courts, and they have continually held that penalties such as in-school suspensions do not receive the same due process protections as a temporary suspension does.[12] Additionally, a transfer to an alternative school is not an expulsion and hence does not require the heightened amount of due process required in *Goss*.

SUBSTANTIVE DUE PROCESS

IN ADDITION to violating procedural due process, excessive corporal punishment has sometimes been found to violate a student's substantive due process rights. In *Jefferson v. the Ysleta Independent School District*, an eight-year-old student in El Paso, Texas, was tied to a chair for two consecutive days by her second-grade teacher.[13] The first day the student was tied to the chair for the entire day, excluding lunch. On the second day, she was tied the chair only for periods of the day but while tied was denied access to the bathroom.[14] In its holding, the court stated that "to tie a second grade student to a chair

---

[10] Ibid., at 579
[11] 435 F.Supp. 460 at 467 (1977)
[12] *Dickens v. Johnson County Board of Education*, 661 F.Supp. 155 (1987)
[13] 817 F.2d 303 (1987)
[14] Ibid.

for an entire school day and for a substantial portion of a second day, as an educational exercise, with no suggested justification, such as punishment or discipline, was constitutionally impermissible."[15]

DANGEROUS STUDENTS

IN SOME instances, students' behavior can represent a threat to themselves or others. In such a case, a student may be removed immediately from the institution, as long as the due process requirements are satisfied as soon as possible after the incident.

Best Practices

- Ensure that educational policy requires due process for all students, regardless of how minor the offense.
- Increase due process procedures as possible consequences for the student increases.

DISCIPLINE OF STUDENTS WITH DISABILITIES

ALL STUDENTS receive due process protection under the Fourteenth Amendment. Depending on the penalty or length of suspension, due process protections consist of notice and a hearing with an impartial tribunal before encroaching upon a student's liberty or property rights. Students with disabilities are granted even more protection due to the implementation of the Individuals with Disabilities Education Act (IDEA). IDEA provides a stay-put provision that prohibits school officials from removing students from their current placement without proper due process. The U.S. Supreme Court addressed the issue of the constitutionality of the stay-put provision and the removal of students with disabilities in the 1988 landmark case, *Honig v. Doe*.

Honig v. Doe
Supreme Court of the United States, 1988
484 U.S. 305

Justice Brennan delivered the opinion of the Court.

As a condition of federal financial assistance, the Education of the Handicapped Act requires States to ensure a "free appropriate public education" for all disabled children within their jurisdictions. In aid of this goal, the Act establishes a comprehensive system of

---

[15] Ibid.

procedural safeguards designed to ensure parental participation in decisions concerning the education of their disabled children and to provide administrative and judicial review of any decisions with which those parents disagree. Among these safeguards is the so-called "stay-put" provision, which directs that a disabled child "shall remain in [his or her] then current educational placement" pending completion of any review proceedings, unless the parents and state or local educational agencies otherwise agree, 20 U.S.C. § 1415(e)(3). Today we must decide whether, in the face of this statutory proscription, state or local school authorities may nevertheless unilaterally exclude disabled children from the classroom for dangerous or disruptive conduct growing out of their disabilities. . . .

The present dispute grows out of the efforts of certain officials of the San Francisco Unified School District (SFUSD) to expel two emotionally disturbed children from school indefinitely for violent and disruptive conduct related to their disabilities. In November 1980, respondent John Doe assaulted another student at the Louise Lombard School, a developmental center for disabled children. Doe's April 1980 IEP identified him as a socially and physically awkward 17-year-old who experienced considerable difficulty controlling his impulses and anger. Among the goals set out in his IEP was "improvement in [his] ability to relate to [his] peers [and to] cope with frustrating situations without resorting to aggressive acts." Frustrating situations, however, were an unfortunately prominent feature of Doe's school career: physical abnormalities, speech difficulties, and poor grooming habits had made him the target of teasing and ridicule as early as the first grade, his 1980 IEP reflected his continuing difficulties with peers, noting that his social skills had deteriorated and that he could tolerate only minor frustration before exploding.

On November 6, 1980, Doe responded to the taunts of a fellow student in precisely the explosive manner anticipated by his IEP: he choked the student with sufficient force to leave abrasions on the child's neck, and kicked out a school window while being escorted to the principal's office afterwards. Doe admitted his misconduct and the school subsequently suspended him for five days. Thereafter, his principal referred the matter to the SFUSD Student Placement Committee (SPC or Committee) with the recommendation that Doe be expelled. On the day the suspension was to end, the SPC notified Doe's mother that it was proposing to exclude her child permanently from SFUSD and was therefore extending his suspension until such time as the expulsion proceedings were completed. The Committee further advised her that she was entitled to attend the November 25 hearing at which it planned to discuss the proposed expulsion.

After unsuccessfully protesting these actions by letter, Doe brought this suit against a host of local school officials and the State Superintendent of Public Instruction. Alleging that the suspension and proposed expulsion violated the EHA, he sought a temporary restraining order canceling the SPC hearing and requiring school officials to convene an IEP meeting. The District Judge granted the requested injunctive relief and further ordered defendants to provide home tutoring for Doe on an interim basis; shortly thereafter, she issued a preliminary injunction directing defendants to return Doe to his then current educational placement at Louise Lombard School pending completion of the IEP review process. Doe reentered school on December 15, 5½ weeks, and 24 schooldays, after his initial suspension.

Respondent Jack Smith was identified as an emotionally disturbed child by the time he entered the second grade in 1976. School records prepared that year indicated that he was unable "to control verbal or physical outburst[s]" and exhibited a "[s]evere disturbance in relationships with peers and adults." Further evaluations subsequently revealed that he had been physically and emotionally abused as an infant and young child and that, despite above average intelligence, he experienced academic and social difficulties as a result of extreme hyperactivity and low self-esteem. Of particular concern was Smith's propensity for verbal hostility; one evaluator noted that the child reacted to stress by "attempt[ing] to cover his feelings of low self worth through aggressive behavior[,] . . . primarily verbal provocations."

Based on these evaluations, SFUSD placed Smith in a learning center for emotionally disturbed children. His grandparents, however, believed that his needs would be better served in the public school setting and, in September 1979, the school district acceded to their requests and enrolled him at A. P. Giannini Middle School. His February 1980 IEP recommended placement in a Learning Disability Group, stressing the need for close supervision and a highly structured environment. Like earlier evaluations, the February 1980 IEP noted that Smith was easily distracted, impulsive, and anxious; it therefore proposed a half-day schedule and suggested that the placement be undertaken on a trial basis.

At the beginning of the next school year, Smith was assigned to a full-day program; almost immediately thereafter he began misbehaving. School officials met twice with his grandparents in October 1980 to discuss returning him to a half-day program; although the grandparents agreed to the reduction, they apparently were never apprised of their right to challenge the decision through EHA procedures. The school officials also warned them that if the child continued his disruptive behavior—which included stealing, extorting money from fellow students, and making sexual comments to female classmates—they would seek to expel him. On November 14, they made good on this threat, suspending Smith for five days after he made further lewd comments. His principal referred the matter to the SPC, which recommended exclusion from SFUSD. As it did in John Doe's case, the Committee scheduled a hearing and extended the suspension indefinitely pending a final disposition in the matter. On November 28, Smith's counsel protested these actions on grounds essentially identical to those raised by Doe, and the SPC agreed to cancel the hearing and to return Smith to a half-day program at A. P. Giannini or to provide home tutoring. Smith's grandparents chose the latter option and the school began home instruction on December 10; on January 6, 1981, an IEP team convened to discuss alternative placements.

After learning of Doe's action, Smith sought and obtained leave to intervene in the suit. The District Court subsequently entered summary judgment in favor of respondents on their EHA claims and issued a permanent injunction. In a series of decisions, the District Judge found that the proposed expulsions and indefinite suspensions of respondents for conduct attributable to their disabilities deprived them of their congressionally mandated right to a free appropriate public education, as well as their right to have that education provided in accordance with the procedures set out in the EHA. The District Judge therefore permanently enjoined the school district from taking any disciplinary action other than a 2- or 5-day suspension against any disabled child for disability-related misconduct, or from effecting any other change in the educational placement of any such child without parental consent pending completion of any EHA proceedings. In addition, the judge barred the State from authorizing unilateral placement changes and directed it to establish an EHA compliance-monitoring system or, alternatively, to enact guidelines governing local school responses to disability-related misconduct. Finally, the judge ordered the State to provide services directly to disabled children when, in any individual case, the State determined that the local educational agency was unable or unwilling to do so.

On appeal, the Court of Appeals for the Ninth Circuit affirmed the orders with slight modifications. Agreeing with the District Court that an indefinite suspension in aid of expulsion constitutes a prohibited "change in placement" under § 1415(e)(3), the Court of Appeals held that the stay-put provision admitted of no "dangerousness" exception and that the statute therefore rendered invalid those provisions of the California Education Code permitting the indefinite suspension or expulsion of disabled children for misconduct arising out of their disabilities. The court concluded, however, that fixed suspensions of up to 30 schooldays did not fall within the reach of § 1415(e)(3), and therefore upheld recent amendments to the state Education Code authorizing such suspensions. Lastly, the court affirmed that portion of the injunction requiring the State to provide services directly to a disabled child when the local educational agency fails to do so.

Petitioner Bill Honig, California Superintendent of Public Instruction, sought review in this Court, claiming that the Court of Appeals' construction of the stay-put provision conflicted with that of several other Courts of Appeals which had recognized a dangerousness exception . . . and that the direct services ruling placed an intolerable burden on the State. We granted certiorari to resolve these questions, and now affirm.

At the outset, we address the suggestion, raised for the first time during oral argument, that this case is moot. Under Article III of the Constitution this Court may only adjudicate actual, ongoing controversies. That the dispute between the parties was very much alive when suit was filed, or at the time the Court of Appeals rendered its judgment, cannot substitute for the actual case or controversy that an exercise of this Court's jurisdiction requires. In the present case, we have jurisdiction if there is a reasonable likelihood that respondents will again suffer the deprivation of EHA-mandated rights that gave rise to this suit. We believe that, at least with respect to respondent Smith, such a possibility does in fact exist and that the case therefore remains justiciable.

Respondent John Doe is now 24 years old and, accordingly, is no longer entitled to the protections and benefits of the EHA, which limits eligibility to disabled children between the ages of 3 and 21. It is clear, therefore, that whatever rights to state educational services he may yet have as a ward of the State, the Act would not govern the State's provision of those services, and thus the case is moot as to him. Respondent Jack Smith, however, is currently 20 and has not yet completed high school. Although at present he is not faced with any proposed expulsion or suspension proceedings, and indeed no longer even resides within the SFUSD, he remains a resident of California and is entitled to a "free appropriate public education" within that State. His claims under the EHA, therefore, are not moot if the conduct he originally complained of is "capable of repetition, yet evading review." Given Smith's continued eligibility for educational services under the EHA, the nature of his disability, and petitioner's insistence that all local school districts retain residual authority to exclude disabled children for dangerous conduct, we have little difficulty concluding that there is a "reasonable expectation" that Smith would once again be subjected to a unilateral "change in placement" for conduct growing out of his disabilities were it not for the statewide injunctive relief issued below.

Our cases reveal that, for purposes of assessing the likelihood that state authorities will reinflict a given injury, we generally have been unwilling to assume that the party seeking relief will repeat the type of misconduct that would once again place him or her at risk of that injury. No such reluctance, however, is warranted here. It is respondent Smith's very inability to conform his conduct to socially acceptable norms that renders him "handicapped" within the meaning of the EHA. As noted above, the record is replete with evidence that Smith is unable to govern his aggressive, impulsive behavior—indeed, his notice of suspension acknowledged that "Jack's actions seem beyond his control." In the absence of any suggestion that respondent has overcome his earlier difficulties, it is certainly reasonable to expect, based on his prior history of behavioral problems, that he will again engage in classroom misconduct. Nor is it reasonable to suppose that Smith's future educational placement will so perfectly suit his emotional and academic needs that further disruptions on his part are improbable. Although Justice Scalia suggests in his dissent, post, that school officials are unlikely to place Smith in a setting where they cannot control his misbehavior, any efforts to ensure such total control must be tempered by the school system's statutory obligations to provide respondent with a free appropriate public education in "the least restrictive environment," to educate him, "to the maximum extent appropriate," with children who are not disabled, and to consult with his parents or guardians, and presumably with respondent himself, before choosing a placement. Indeed, it is only by ignoring these mandates, as well as Congress' unquestioned desire to wrest from school officials their former unilateral authority to determine the placement of emotionally disturbed children, that the dissent can so readily assume that respondent's future placement will satisfactorily prevent any further dangerous conduct on his part. Overarching these statutory obligations, moreover, is the inescapable fact that the preparation of an IEP, like any other effort at predicting human behavior, is an inexact science at best. Given the unique circumstances and context of this case, therefore, we think it reasonable to expect that respondent will again engage in the type of misconduct that precipitated this suit.

We think it equally probable that, should he do so, respondent will again be subjected to the same unilateral school action for which he initially sought relief. In this regard, it matters not that Smith no longer resides within the SFUSD. While the actions of SFUSD officials first gave rise to this litigation, the District Judge expressly found that the lack of a state policy governing local school responses to disability-related misconduct had led to, and would continue to result in, EHA violations, and she therefore enjoined the state defendant from authorizing, among other things, unilateral placement changes. She of course also issued injunctions directed at the local defendants, but they did not seek review of those orders in this Court. Only petitioner, the State superintendent of Public Instruction, has invoked our jurisdiction, and he now urges us to hold that local school districts retain unilateral authority under the EHA to suspend or otherwise remove disabled children for dangerous conduct.

Given these representations, we have every reason to believe that were it not for the injunction barring petitioner from authorizing such unilateral action, respondent would be faced with a real and substantial threat of such action in any California school district in which he enrolled. Respondent lacked standing to seek injunctive relief because he could not plausibly allege that police officers choked all persons whom they stopped, or that the city "authorized police officers to act in such manner." Certainly, if the SFUSD's past practice of unilateral exclusions was at odds with state policy and the practice of local school districts generally, petitioner would not now stand before us seeking to defend the right of all local school districts to engage in such aberrant behavior.

We have previously noted that administrative and judicial review under the EHA is often "ponderous," *Burlington School Committee v. Massachusetts Dept. of Education,* and this case, which has taken seven years to reach us, amply confirms that observation. For obvious reasons, the misconduct of an emotionally disturbed or otherwise disabled child who has not yet reached adolescence typically will not pose such a serious threat to the well-being of other students that school officials can only ensure classroom safety by excluding the child. Yet, the adolescent student improperly disciplined for misconduct that does pose such a threat will often be finished with school or otherwise ineligible for EHA protections by the time review can be had in this Court. Because we believe that respondent Smith has demonstrated both "a sufficient likelihood that he will again be wronged in a similar way," and that any resulting claim he may have for relief will surely evade our review, we turn to the merits of his case.

The language of § 1415(e)(3) is unequivocal. It states plainly that during the pendency of any proceedings initiated under the Act, unless the state or local educational agency and the parents or guardian of a disabled child otherwise agree, "the child shall remain in the then current educational placement." Faced with this clear directive, petitioner asks us to read a "dangerousness" exception into the stay-put provision on the basis of either of two essentially inconsistent assumptions: first, that Congress thought the residual authority of school officials to exclude dangerous students from the classroom too obvious for comment; or second, that Congress inadvertently failed to provide such authority and this Court must therefore remedy the oversight. Because we cannot accept either premise, we decline petitioner's invitation to rewrite the statute.

Petitioner's arguments proceed, he suggests, from a simple, commonsense proposition: Congress could not have intended the stay-put provision to be read literally, for such a construction leads to the clearly unintended, and untenable, result that school districts must return violent or dangerous students to school while the often lengthy EHA proceedings run their course. We think it clear, however, that Congress very much meant to strip schools of the unilateral authority they had traditionally employed to exclude disabled students, particularly emotionally disturbed students, from school. In so doing, Congress did not leave school administrators powerless to deal with dangerous students; it did, however, deny school officials their former right to "self-help," and directed that in the future the removal of disabled students could be accomplished only with the permission of the parents or, as a last resort, the courts.

As noted above, Congress passed the EHA after finding that school systems across the country had excluded one out of every eight disabled children from classes. In drafting the law, Congress was largely guided by the recent decisions in *Mills v. Board of Education of District of Columbia,* both of which involved the exclusion of hard-to-handle disabled students. *Mills* in particular demonstrated the extent to which schools used disciplinary measures to bar children from the classroom. There, school officials had labeled four of the seven minor plaintiffs "behavioral problems," and had excluded them from classes without providing any alternative education to them or any notice to their parents. After finding that this practice was not limited to the named plaintiffs but affected in one way or another an estimated class of 12,000 to 18,000 disabled students, the District Court enjoined future exclusions, suspensions, or expulsions "on grounds of discipline."

Congress attacked such exclusionary practices in a variety of ways. It required participating States to educate all disabled children, regardless of the severity of their disabilities, and included within the definition of "handicapped" those children with serious emotional disturbances. It further provided for meaningful parental participation in all aspects of a child's educational placement, and barred schools, through the stay-put provision, from changing that placement over the parent's objection until all review proceedings were completed. Recognizing that those proceedings might prove long and tedious, . . . they therefore allowed for interim placements where parents and school officials are able to agree on one. Conspicuously absent from § 1415(e)(3), however, is any emergency exception for dangerous students. This absence is all the more telling in light of the injunctive decree issued in *PARC,* which permitted school officials unilaterally to remove students in "extraordinary circumstances." Given the lack of any similar exception in *Mills,* and the close attention Congress devoted to these "landmark" decisions, we can only conclude that the omission was intentional; we are therefore not at liberty to engraft onto the statute an exception Congress chose not to create.

Our conclusion that § 1415(e)(3) means what it says does not leave educators hamstrung. The Department of Education has observed that, "[w]hile the [child's] placement may not be changed [during any complaint proceeding], this does not preclude the agency from using its normal procedures for dealing with children who are endangering themselves or others." Such procedures may include the use of study carrels, timeouts, detention, or the restriction of privileges. More drastically, where a student poses an immediate threat to the safety of others, officials may temporarily suspend him or her for up to 10 schooldays. This authority, which respondent in no way disputes, not only ensures that school administrators can protect the safety of others by promptly removing the most dangerous of students, it also provides a "cooling down" period during which officials can initiate IEP review and seek to persuade the child's parents to agree to an interim placement. And in those cases in which the parents of a truly dangerous child adamantly refuse to permit any change in placement, the 10-day respite gives school officials an opportunity to invoke the aid of the courts under § 1415(e)(2), which empowers courts to grant any appropriate relief.

Petitioner contends, however, that the availability of judicial relief is more illusory than real, because a party seeking review under § 1415(e)(2) must exhaust time-consuming administrative remedies, and because under the Court of Appeals' construction of § 1415(e)(3), courts are as bound by the stay-put provision's "automatic injunction," as are schools. It is true that judicial review is normally not available under § 1415(e)(2) until all administrative proceedings are completed, but as we have previously noted, parents may bypass the administrative process where exhaustion would be futile or inadequate. While many of the EHA's procedural safeguards protect the rights of parents and children, schools can and do seek redress through the administrative review process, and we have no reason to believe that Congress meant to require schools alone to exhaust in all cases, no matter how exigent the circumstances. The burden in such cases, of course, rests with the school to demonstrate the futility or inadequacy of administrative review, but nothing in § 1415(e)(2) suggests that schools are completely barred from attempting to make such a showing. Nor do we think that § 1415(e)(3) operates to limit the equitable powers of district courts such that they cannot, in appropriate cases, temporarily enjoin a dangerous disabled child from attending school. As the EHA's legislative history makes clear, one of the evils Congress sought to remedy was the unilateral exclusion of disabled children by schools, not courts, and one of the purposes of § 1415(e)(3), therefore, was "to prevent school officials from removing a child from the regular public school classroom over the parents' objection pending completion of the review proceedings." The stay-put provision in no way purports to limit or pre-empt the authority conferred on courts by § 1415(e)(2), indeed, it says nothing whatever about judicial power.

In short, then, we believe that school officials are entitled to seek injunctive relief under § 1415(e)(2) in appropriate cases. In any such action, § 1415(e)(3) effectively creates a presumption in favor of the child's current educational placement which school officials can overcome only by showing that maintaining the child in his or her current placement is substantially likely to result in injury either to himself or herself, or to others. In the present case, we are satisfied that the District Court, in enjoining the state and local defendants from indefinitely suspending respondent or otherwise unilaterally altering his then current placement, properly balanced respondent's interest in receiving a free appropriate public education in accordance with the procedures and requirements of the EHA against the interests of the state and local school officials in maintaining a safe learning environment for all their students.

We believe the courts below properly construed and applied § 1415(e)(3), except insofar as the Court of Appeals held that a suspension in excess of 10 schooldays does not constitute a "change in placement." We therefore affirm the Court of Appeals' judgment on this issue as modified herein. Because we are equally divided on the question whether a court may order a State to provide services directly to a disabled child where the local agency has failed to do so, we affirm the Court of Appeals' judgment on this issue as well.

Affirmed.

The stay-put provision of IDEA was created to ensure that school officials could not unilaterally remove students with disabilities without proper due process of law. The history of the exclusion of disabled students was longstanding and discussed in both *Pennsylvania Association for Retarded Children (PARC) v. the Pennsylvania Commonwealth* and *Mills v. Board of Education*.[16] Both cases reviewed the many instances in which educational institutions excluded disabled students, especially those with mental disabilities.

---

[16] 334 F. Supp. 1257 (1971); 348 F. Supp. 866 (1972)

While the stay-put provision does restrict school authorities from changing a student's educational placement, it does not leave schools without options when dealing with the suspension of special-needs students. As the *Honig* Court stated, the IDEA provision gives school officials the opportunity to cool down, review the student's IEP, and come to a mutual agreement with the parents about placing the student in the proper educational learning environment.[17]

As it did for nondisabled students, the U.S. Supreme Court recognized the danger and risk involved in not removing students who were posing a threat to themselves and others. In an effort to protect all those involved, the Court found that immediately removing a disabled student from his or her current placement did not violate the stay-put provision of IDEA. But such removal for an indefinite period of time did violate the provision.

In 1997 IDEA went through a major transition and numerous amendments. One change was the placement of students in an alternative educational setting if they had brought a firearm to school or knowingly possessed illegal drugs. The amendment reads:

> *(1) Authority of school personnel.*
> *(A) School personnel under this section may order a change in the placement of a child with a disability—*
> *(i) to an appropriate interim alternative educational setting, another setting, or suspension, for not more than 10 school days (to the extent such alternatives would be applied to children without disabilities); and*
> *(ii) to an appropriate interim alternative educational setting for the same amount of time that a child without a disability would be subject to discipline, but for not more than 45 days if—*
> *(I) the child carries or possesses a weapon to or at school, on school premises, or to or at a school function under the jurisdiction of a State or a local educational agency; or*
> *(II) the child knowingly possesses or uses illegal drugs or sells or solicits the sale of a controlled substance while at school or a school function under the jurisdiction of a State or local educational agency.*[18]

In response to growing concern about violence in schools, the amended IDEA of 1997 gave school authorities the ability to change a disabled student's placement to an alternate educational setting for up to 45 days. This standard allows schools to make appropriate changes for a student who is dangerous without being confined to the previous 10-day rule and the due process procedures attached to the provision.

Corporal punishment cannot be administered to a student with a disability, if the misbehavior is a manifestation of a disability.[19] If student misconduct is not caused by

[17] 484 U.S. 305 (1988)
[18] 20 U.S.C. S1415(k)(1997)
[19] *Gonzales v. Haher,* 793 F.2d 1470 (1986)

disability, an educational institution may use the common disciplinary action used for nondisabled students. According to the U.S. Supreme Court in *Honig v. Doe,* "such procedures may include the use of study carrels, timeouts, detention, or the restriction of privileges."[20] The Court has held that minimal punishment does not change the placement of the student because it allows the student to continue to earn a free public education as set forth in the Educational Handicapped Act.[21]

SUMMARY

Although the *in loco parentis* theory still applies, the number of states which prohibit the use of corporal punishment within public schools has gone from zero to twenty-seven. The debate as to whether corporal punishment is a proper means of reprimanding students is continual. However, since the states are practically split on this issue, administrators need to know the laws within their specific state, as well as within their district. For example, there are some states which still allow corporal punishment, but the district within the state has banned such punishment. Therefore, it is critical that not only administrators, but all faculty are aware of the laws or policies on this topic. Especially in the states that still permit corporal punishment, strict policy should be followed in administering such punishment. It is easy for a faculty or staff member to discipline in the heat of the moment, which consequently can lead to other issues, including litigation for battery.

Even if corporal punishment is prohibited, any type of student discipline requires a certain amount of procedural due process. Typically, the less severe the punishment, the less due process is required. Of course, if the punishment is expulsion, a high level of procedural due process is required. Within this mix of due process, are the added procedures that attach when the discipline is being administered to a student with a disability.

DISCUSSION QUESTIONS

1. *Ingraham v. Wright* was a five-to-four decision. Is the majority opinion persuasive in concluding that cruel and unusual punishment under the Eighth Amendment should not be applied to schoolchildren? Justify your response.
2. What is the definition of due process as it pertains to the rights of children in a school setting? List the requirements set forth under due process.
3. What does the U.S. Supreme Court state is the minimal due process required for a student who is being suspended for less than 10 days?
4. Should students be permitted to bring an attorney to represent them during a disciplinary hearing? Defend your response.

---

[20] 484 U.S. 305 (1988)
[21] Ibid.

5. Can administrators and school boards be impartial tribunals at a student disciplinary hearing? Justify your response.
6. Can corporal punishment be so excessive that it violates a student's substantive due process rights? Give examples using case law.
7. The *Douglass* and *Ingraham* cases have similar facts but different outcomes. Why?
8. Are different disciplinary policies for special education and regular education students justified? Discuss the differences and your response.
9. Can schools adequately maintain order and still stay within the guidelines of IDEA when disciplining students with disabilities? Explain your response while addressing the issue of the stay-put provision.
10. Regular education students and their parents have no legal standing under IDEA to challenge the placement of disruptive or potentially dangerous students in their classroom. Should they?

Deepening Your Understanding

1. What does the legislation in your state say concerning corporal punishment? Research the legislation for your specific state.
2. Over the past decade, the use of corporal punishment has become highly controversial. Some suggest it is required to maintain order, while others feel it is a form of child abuse. In small groups, discuss both sides and the law pertaining to corporal punishment in your state.

TEACHERS' RIGHTS

INTRODUCTION

Before the 1960s, the rights of schoolteachers were strictly limited, especially their freedom of speech and freedom to associate. As public employees, teachers were traditionally held to a high moral standard; and the school board had wide authority to judge that standard. The basic belief was that teaching was a privilege; consequently, teachers worked as directed with little protection from the law. But as the nation moved toward civil rights, many teachers challenged the schools and the courts about issues concerning their constitutional rights. Various Supreme Court decisions over the past few decades have clarified that teachers do have rights, and they do not forfeit their rights by accepting public employment.

FREEDOM OF EXPRESSION

THE FIRST Amendment reads: "Congress shall make no law . . . abridging the freedom of speech." While the amendment clearly sets forth a person's right to freedom of expression, teachers working before the 1960s were commonly dismissed or disciplined for expressing their opinions. *Pickering v. Board of Education* was a landmark case that recognized public schoolteachers' right to free speech.[1] The *Pickering* case sets forth the rights and limits of public employees and creates a distinction between matters of private and public concern.

---

[1] 391 U.S. 563 (1968)

Pickering v. Board of Education
Supreme Court of the United States, 1968
391 U.S. 563

Mr. Justice Marshall delivered the opinion of the Court.

Appellant Marvin L. Pickering, a teacher in Township High School District 205, Will County, Illinois, was dismissed from his position by the appellee Board of Education for sending a letter to a local newspaper in connection with a recently proposed tax increase that was critical of the way in which the Board and the district superintendent of schools had handled past proposals to raise new revenue for the schools. Appellant's dismissal resulted from a determination by the Board, after a full hearing, that the publication of the letter was "detrimental to the efficient operation and administration of the schools of the district" and hence, under the relevant Illinois statute, that "interests of the school require[d] [his dismissal]."

Appellant's claim that his writing of the letter was protected by the First and Fourteenth Amendments was rejected. Appellant then sought review of the Board's action in the Circuit Court of Will County, which affirmed his dismissal on the ground that the determination that appellant's letter was detrimental to the interests of the school system was supported by substantial evidence and that the interests of the schools overrode appellant's First Amendment rights. On appeal, the Supreme Court of Illinois, two Justices dissenting, affirmed the judgment of the Circuit Court. . . . For the reasons detailed below we agree that appellant's rights to freedom of speech were violated and we reverse.

I.   In February of 1961 the appellee Board of Education asked the voters of the school district to approve a bond issue to raise $4,875,000 to erect two new schools. The proposal was defeated. Then, in December of 1961, the Board submitted another bond proposal to the voters which called for the raising of $ 5,500,000 to build two new schools. This second proposal passed and the schools were built with the money raised by the bond sales. In May of 1964 a proposed increase in the tax rate to be used for educational purposes was submitted to the voters by the Board and was defeated. Finally, on September 19, 1964, a second proposal to increase the tax rate was submitted by the Board and was likewise defeated. It was in connection with this last proposal of the School Board that appellant wrote the letter to the editor (which we reproduce in an Appendix to this opinion) that resulted in his dismissal.

Prior to the vote on the second tax increase proposal a variety of articles attributed to the District 205 Teachers' Organization appeared in the local paper. These articles urged passage of the tax increase and stated that failure to pass the increase would result in a decline in the quality of education afforded children in the district's schools. A letter from the superintendent of schools making the same point was published in the paper two days before the election and submitted to the voters in mimeographed form the following day. It was in response to the foregoing material, together with the failure of the tax increase to pass, that appellant submitted the letter in question to the editor of the local paper.

The letter constituted, basically, an attack on the School Board's handling of the 1961 bond issue proposals and its subsequent allocation of financial resources between the schools' educational and athletic programs. It also charged the superintendent of schools with attempting to prevent teachers in the district from opposing or criticizing the proposed bond issue.

The Board dismissed Pickering for writing and publishing the letter. Pursuant to Illinois law, the Board was then required to hold a hearing on the dismissal. At the hearing the Board charged that numerous statements in the letter were false and that the publication of the statements unjustifiably impugned the "motives, honesty, integrity, truthfulness, responsibility and competence" of both the Board and the school administration. The Board also charged that the false statements damaged the professional reputations of its members and of the school administrators, would be disruptive of faculty discipline, and would tend to foment "controversy, conflict and dissension" among teachers, administrators, the Board of Education, and the residents of the district. Testimony was introduced from a variety of witnesses on the truth or falsity of the particular statements in the letter with which the Board took issue. The Board found the statements to be false as charged. No evidence was introduced at any point in the proceedings as to the effect of the publication of the letter on the community as a whole or on the administration of the school system in particular, and no specific findings along these lines were made.

The Illinois courts reviewed the proceedings solely to determine whether the Board's findings were supported by substantial evidence and whether, on the facts as found, the Board could reasonably conclude that appellant's publication of the letter was "detrimental to the best interests of the schools." Pickering's claim that his letter was protected by the First Amendment was rejected on the ground that his acceptance of a teaching position in the public schools obliged him to refrain from making statements about the operation of the schools "which in the absence of such position he would have an undoubted right to engage in." It is not altogether clear whether the Illinois Supreme Court held that the First Amendment had no applicability to appellant's dismissal for writing the letter in question or whether it determined that the particular statements made in the letter were not entitled to First Amendment protection. In any event, it clearly rejected Pickering's claim that, on the facts of this case, he could not constitutionally be dismissed from his teaching position.

II.   To the extent that the Illinois Supreme Court's opinion may be read to suggest that teachers may constitutionally be compelled to relinquish the First Amendment rights they would otherwise enjoy as citizens to comment on matters of public interest in connection with the operation of the public schools in which they work, it proceeds on a premise that has been unequivocally rejected in numerous prior decisions of this Court. . . . At the same time it cannot be gainsaid that the State has interests as an employer in regulating the speech of its employees that differ significantly from those it possesses in connection with regulation of the speech of the citizenry in general. The problem in any case is to arrive at a balance between the interests of the teacher, as a citizen, in commenting upon matters of public concern and the interest of the State, as an employer, in promoting the efficiency of the public services it performs through its employees.

III.   The Board contends that "the teacher by virtue of his public employment has a duty of loyalty to support his superiors in attaining the generally accepted goals of education and that, if he must speak out publicly, he should do so factually and accurately, commensurate with his education and experience." Appellant, on the other hand, argues that the test applicable to defamatory statements directed against public officials by persons having no occupational relationship with them, namely, that statements to be legally actionable must be made "with knowledge that [they were] . . . false or with reckless disregard of whether [they were] . . . false or not," should also be applied to public statements made by teachers. Because of the enormous variety of fact situations in which critical statements by teachers and other public employees may be thought by their superiors, against whom the statements are directed, to furnish grounds for dismissal, we do not deem it either appropriate or feasible to attempt to lay down a general standard against which all such statements may be judged. However, in the course of evaluating the conflicting claims of First Amendment protection and the need for orderly school administration in the context of this case, we shall indicate some of the general lines along which an analysis of the controlling interests should run.

An examination of the statements in appellant's letter objected to by the Board reveals that they, like the letter as a whole, consist essentially of criticism of the Board's allocation of school funds between educational and athletic programs, and of both the Board's and the superintendent's methods of informing, or preventing the informing of, the district's taxpayers of the real reasons why additional tax revenues were being sought for the schools. The statements are in no way directed towards any person with whom appellant would normally be in contact in the course of his daily work as a teacher. Thus no question of maintaining either discipline by immediate superiors or harmony among coworkers is presented here. Appellant's employment relationships with the Board and, to a somewhat lesser extent, with the superintendent are not the kind of close working relationships for which it can persuasively be claimed that personal loyalty and confidence are necessary to their proper functioning. Accordingly, to the extent that the Board's position here can be taken to suggest that even comments on matters of public concern that are substantially correct, such as statements of appellant's letter . . . may furnish grounds for dismissal if they are sufficiently critical in tone, we unequivocally reject it.

We next consider the statements in appellant's letter which we agree to be false. The Board's original charges included allegations that the publication of the letter damaged the professional reputations of the Board and the superintendent and would foment controversy and conflict among the Board, teachers, administrators, and the residents of the district. However, no evidence to support these allegations was introduced at the hearing. So far as the record reveals, Pickering's letter was greeted by everyone but its main target, the Board, with massive apathy and total disbelief. The Board must, therefore, have decided, perhaps by analogy with the law of libel, that the statements were per se harmful to the operation of the schools.

However, the only way in which the Board could conclude, absent any evidence of the actual effect of the letter, that the statements contained therein were per se detrimental to the interest of the schools was to equate the Board members' own interests with that of the schools. Certainly an accusation that too much money is being spent on athletics by the administrators of the school system (which is precisely the import of that portion of appellant's letter containing the statements that we have found to be false) cannot reasonably be regarded as per se detrimental to the district's schools. Such an accusation reflects rather a difference of opinion between Pickering and the Board as to the preferable manner of operating the school system, a difference of opinion that clearly concerns an issue of general public interest.

In addition, the fact that particular illustrations of the Board's claimed undesirable emphasis on athletic programs are false would not normally have any necessary impact on the actual operation of the schools, beyond its tendency to anger the Board. For example, Pickering's letter was written after the defeat at the polls of the second proposed tax increase. It could, therefore, have had no effect on the ability of the school district to raise necessary revenue, since there was no showing that there was any proposal to increase taxes pending when the letter was written.

More importantly, the question whether a school system requires additional funds is a matter of legitimate public concern on which the judgment of the school administration, including the School Board, cannot, in a society that leaves such questions to popular vote, be taken as conclusive. On such a question free and open debate is vital to informed decision-making by the electorate. Teachers are, as a class, the members of a community most likely to have informed and definite opinions as to how funds allotted to the operation of the schools should be spent. Accordingly, it is essential that they be able to speak out freely on such questions without fear of retaliatory dismissal.

In addition, the amounts expended on athletics which Pickering reported erroneously were matters of public record on which his position as a teacher in the district did not qualify him to speak with any greater authority than any other taxpayer. The Board could easily have rebutted appellant's errors by publishing the accurate figures itself, either via a letter to the same newspaper or otherwise. We are thus not presented with a situation in which a teacher has carelessly made false statements about matters so closely related to the day-to-day operations of the schools that any harmful impact on the public would be difficult to counter because of the teacher's presumed greater access to the real facts. Accordingly, we have no occasion to consider at this time whether under such circumstances a school board could reasonably require that a teacher make substantial efforts to verify the accuracy of his charges before publishing them.

What we do have before us is a case in which a teacher has made erroneous public statements upon issues then currently the subject of public attention, which are critical of his ultimate employer but which are neither shown nor can be presumed to have in any way either impeded the teacher's proper performance of his daily duties in the classroom or to have interfered with the regular operation of the schools generally. In these circumstances we conclude that the interest of the school administration in limiting teachers' opportunities to contribute to public debate is not significantly greater than its interest in limiting a similar contribution by any member of the general public.

IV. The public interest in having free and unhindered debate on matters of public importance—the core value of the Free Speech Clause of the First Amendment—is so great that it has been held that a State cannot authorize the recovery of damages by a public official for defamatory statements directed at him except when such statements are shown to have been made either with knowledge of their falsity or with reckless disregard for their truth or falsity. . . . The same test has been applied to suits for invasion of privacy based on false statements where a "matter of public interest" is involved. It is therefore perfectly clear that, were appellant a member of the general public, the State's power to afford the appellee Board of Education or its members any legal right to sue him for writing the letter at issue here would be limited by the requirement that the letter be judged by the standard laid down in *New York Times*.

This Court has also indicated, in more general terms, that statements by public officials on matters of public concern must be accorded First Amendment protection despite the fact that the statements are directed at their nominal superiors. In *Garrison*, the *New York Times* test was specifically applied to a case involving a criminal defamation conviction stemming from statements made by a district attorney about the judges before whom he regularly appeared.

While criminal sanctions and damage awards have a somewhat different impact on the exercise of the right to freedom of speech from dismissal from employment, it is apparent that the threat of dismissal from public employment is nonetheless a potent means of inhibiting speech. We have already noted our disinclination to make an across-the-board equation of dismissal from public employment for remarks critical of superiors with awarding damages in a libel suit by a public official for similar criticism. However, in a case such as the present one, in which the fact of employment is only tangentially and insubstantially involved in the subject matter of the public communication made by a teacher, we conclude that it is necessary to regard the teacher as the member of the general public he seeks to be.

In sum, we hold that, in a case such as this, absent proof of false statements knowingly or recklessly made by him, a teacher's exercise of his right to speak on issues of public importance may not furnish the basis for his dismissal from public employment. Since no such showing has been made in this case regarding appellant's letter, his dismissal for writing it cannot be upheld and the judgment of the Illinois Supreme Court must, accordingly, be reversed and the case remanded for further proceedings not inconsistent with this opinion.

It is so ordered. Mr. Justice Douglas, with whom Mr. Justice Black joins, concurs in the judgment of the Court and Justice White dissented in part.

The *Pickering* case indicates that public schoolteachers have a right to freedom of speech when the issue is of public concern. One year later, the Supreme Court confirmed that teachers do not leave their constitutional rights at the schoolhouse gates.[2] Such constitutional rights, however, are not always protected. In a Second Circuit Court case, an assistant to the superintendent for curriculum and instruction claimed violation of his First Amendment rights after being dismissed for making comments of public concern at various school district meetings. In applying the *Pickering* balancing test, the court suggested that a governmental defendant may escape liability by showing that

---

[2] *Tinker v. Des Moines Independent School District*, 393 U.S. 503 (1969)

otherwise protected speech "would potentially interfere with or disrupt the government's activities" and that "the potential disruptiveness . . . outweigh[s] the First Amendment value of that speech."[3]

In deciding such a case, the "court must weigh the employee's interest, as a citizen, in commenting upon matters of public concern against the interest of the State, as an employer, in promoting the efficiency of the public services it performs through its employees. Factors important to the *Pickering* balancing test include: the time, place, and manner of the speech, the content of the speech and the extent to which it touches on matters of significant public concern, and, the nature of the disciplined employee's responsibilities."[4]

Hence, the court concluded:

> *In this regard, the facts of the present case differ markedly from those of* Pickering. *Plaintiff held a high-level policy position, and it would make little sense to treat his remarks as if they had been made by a member of the general public. As the Supreme Court indicated in* Rankin v. McPherson, *"some attention must be paid to the responsibilities of the employee within the agency. The burden of caution employees bear with respect to the words they speak will vary with the extent of authority and public accountability the employee's role entails." Plaintiff was hired as the Assistant Superintendent of Curriculum and Instruction for the School District; only the School District Superintendent occupied a superior administrative position. Plaintiff's duties included: "development and improvement of the district-wide educational programs throughout the organization, administration, supervision and coordination and evaluation of the programs;" "provided appropriate supervision of administrative and supervisory personnel of the district schools to ensure effective operation"; and "served as a member of the Superintendent's Cabinet and Administrative Staff Council." Plaintiff was also required to "provide staff leadership to ensure understanding of and promote the educational objectives of the district." It is thus beyond doubt that Plaintiff worked as a high-level administrator with a policy-making role and responsibility for implementing the objectives articulated at the highest levels of the School District's administration. Such high-level employees are "unlikely" to prevail under the* Pickering *balancing test when they have engaged in speech that is critical of their employer. In "most cases" of this type, the likelihood of disruption will outweigh the employees' right to speak.*

Numerous courts cases following *Pickering* have implemented a two-step process that focuses on the speech as a matter of public concern. Then the interest of the employee must be balanced against "the interest of the State, as an employer, in promoting the efficiency of the public services it performs through its employees."

---

[3] *McCullough v. Wyandanch Union Free School District*, 132 F.Supp. 2d 87, at 88 (2001)
[4] Ibid., at 89

This "Pickering balance," as it has come to be known, looks to the following factors: (1) the need for harmony in the office or work place; (2) whether the government's responsibilities require a close working relationship to exist between the plaintiff and coworkers when the speech in question has caused or could cause the relationship to deteriorate; (3) the time, manner, and place of the speech; (4) the context in which the dispute arose; (5) the degree of public interest in the speech; and (6) whether the speech impeded the employee's ability to perform his or her duties.[5]

Although the Supreme Court clearly indicated that teachers are protected under the First Amendment, not all speech is protected, as illustrated in *Schul v. Sherard*.[6] In *Schul*, a high school track coach recommended that long-distance runners drink soda to increase their heart rate. The coach's exact statement to one student athlete was to "consume a cola, because the caffeine would help his body to function properly during an upcoming race."[7] The coach also told one of his runners that the drink would make his "body awake and mind [feel] awake" and improve how he felt during the race; "that it [was] a legal substance, that there [was] no rule against it in the Olympic games, [and] no rule against it in [the] NCAA or in [the] high school federation."[8]

Schul argued that his discussion with the students was protected under the First Amendment. But in reviewing this argument, the court said that such speech was not of public concern and therefore was not protected. In the words of the court:

The form and context of Schul's speech both support this conclusion. Schul orally suggested the use of caffeine to Starks [a student] at the coach's home prior to a track meet. He later discussed the positive effects of caffeine after practice, while critiquing Starks' poor performance in the meet. The Court cannot envision members of the public being concerned about whether Starks' consumption of caffeine, in some form, would have helped him not to feel "loggy," thereby improving his performance at the Roosevelt Relays. The Court also notes that Schul spoke not as a citizen advocating the use of caffeine generally, but as a high school coach discussing a matter of personal concern to himself and Starks. Under such circumstances, the Court concludes that Schul's speech did not address a matter of public concern.[9]

The First Amendment clearly protects speech, both symbolic and verbal.[10] Not all speech is protected, however, especially when it includes vulgar language or threats or if it endangers others. This point is illustrated in *Amburgey v. Cassady*, where a teacher was dismissed after she insulted another teacher and then threatened an administrative

---

[5] *Roberts v. Van Buren Public Schools*, 773 F.2d 949, at 954 (1985)
[6] 102 F.Supp. 2d 877 (2000)
[7] Ibid., at 880
[8] Ibid., at 881
[9] Ibid., at 886
[10] *Tinker v. Des Moines Independent School District*, 393 U.S. 503 (1969)

official. Although the teacher claimed that her First Amendment right had been violated, the Sixth Circuit Court held that a government employee was not protected when using personal attacks and abusive language.[11]

Best Practices

- Teachers do not lose their constitutional right to freedom of speech when they accept public employment.

- Understand the *Pickering* balancing test, which stresses the importance of the speech as a matter of public concern versus an employer's right to maintain harmony in the workplace, relationships with co-workers, and whether or not the speech impedes employees' ability to perform their jobs.

In 1983, the Supreme Court reviewed *Connick v. Myers*.[12] The case was brought by Sheila Myers, who was employed as an assistant district attorney in New Orleans before being transferred to another section of the court. Upset about the transfer, Myers spoke with her supervisor, Connick. Unsatisfied with his response, she created a questionnaire, asking other staff members about their opinions of office policies. Shortly after distributing the surveys, Myers was told to stop distributing them because she was creating a "mini-insurrection" in the office. Within a day, Myers was informed that she was being terminated for insubordination. She then filed suit, claiming she was "wrongfully terminated because she had exercised her constitutionally protected right of free speech."

The Supreme Court disagreed, holding that this was an issue of private, not public, concern:

> We hold only that when a public employee speaks not as a citizen upon matters of public concern, but instead as an employee upon matters only of personal interest, absent the most unusual circumstances, a federal court is not the appropriate forum in which to review the wisdom of a personnel decision taken by a public agency allegedly in reaction to the employee's behavior. Our responsibility is to ensure that citizens are not deprived of fundamental rights by virtue of working for the government; this does not require a grant of immunity for employee grievances not afforded by the First Amendment to those who do not work for the State.
>
> Whether an employee's speech addresses a matter of public concern must be determined by the content, form, and context of a given statement, as revealed by the whole record. In this case, with but one exception, the questions posed by Myers to her co-workers do not fall under the rubric of matters of "public concern." We view the questions pertaining to the confidence and trust that Myers' co-workers possess in

---

[11] *Amburgey v. Cassady*, 507 F.2d 728 (1974)
[12] 461 U.S. 138 (1983)

various supervisors, the level of office morale, and the need for a grievance committee as mere extensions of Myers' dispute over her transfer to another section of the criminal court. Unlike the dissent, we do not believe these questions are of public import in evaluating the performance of the District Attorney as an elected official. Myers did not seek to inform the public that the District Attorney's Office was not discharging its governmental responsibilities in the investigation and prosecution of criminal cases. Nor did Myers seek to bring to light actual or potential wrongdoing or breach of public trust on the part of Connick and others. Indeed, the questionnaire, if released to the public, would convey no information at all other than the fact that a single employee is upset with the status quo. While discipline and morale in the workplace are related to an agency's efficient performance of its duties, the focus of Myers' questions is not to evaluate the performance of the office but rather to gather ammunition for another round of controversy with her superiors. These questions reflect one employee's dissatisfaction with a transfer and an attempt to turn that displeasure into a cause celebre.

To presume that all matters which transpire within a government office are of public concern would mean that virtually every remark—and certainly every criticism directed at a public official—would plant the seed of a constitutional case. While as a matter of good judgment, public officials should be receptive to constructive criticism offered by their employees, the First Amendment does not require a public office to be run as a roundtable for employee complaints over internal office affairs.

The Supreme Court clearly distinguished between *Connick* and *Pickering*. In performing the balancing test, the Court noted the importance of an efficient work environment and believed that Myers's distribution of the questionnaire interfered with the relationships among the employees in the office. "When employee speech concerning office policy arises from an employment dispute concerning the very application of that policy to the speaker, additional weight must be given to the supervisor's view that the employee has threatened the authority of the employer to run the office." Also noted was the issue of time, place, and manner of the questionnaires, which the Court believed were inappropriate in a governmental office.

It is also important to note that the decision in *Connick* should not be interpreted to mean that private speech has no First Amendment protection. In 1979, Bessie Givhan was dismissed from her teaching position after she had numerous discussions with her principal. According to the school district, there were a series of private encounters between Givhan and the school principal in which Givhan made "petty and unreasonable demands" in a manner variously described by the principal as "insulting," "hostile," "loud," and "arrogant."[13] After being dismissed, Givhan claimed she was fired because she had argued that the school district's policies were discriminatory in nature.

At trial, the court found in favor of Givhan, claiming that such dismissal was in violation of the First Amendment. On appeal, the court reversed the decision, holding that

---

[13] 439 U.S. 410, at 412

Pickering did not apply because the conversations were private and hence were not protected by the Constitution. But the U.S. Supreme Court reversed the court of appeals' finding, stating that "the First Amendment forbids abridgment of the freedom of speech. Neither the Amendment itself nor our decisions indicate that this freedom is lost to the public employee who arranges to communicate privately with his employer rather than to spread his views before the public."[14]

DRESS AND GROOMING

ALL THE educational issues that the Supreme Court has addressed have avoided the question of teachers' rights to dress as they please while performing their teaching duties. As with other civil rights issues, this discussion began seriously in the late 1960s and early 1970s. One of the first cases dealing with the question of whether or not a teacher could be dismissed for refusing to wear a tie was *East Hartford Education Association v. Board of Education of Town of East Hartford.*[15]

East Hartford Education Association v. Board of Education of the Town of East Hartford
United States Court of Appeals for the Second Circuit, 1977
562 F.2d 838

Opinion by Circuit Judge Meskill.

Although this case may at first appear too trivial to command the attention of a busy court, it raises important issues concerning the proper scope of judicial oversight of local affairs. The appellant here, Richard Brimley, is a public school teacher reprimanded for failing to wear a necktie while teaching his English class. Joined by the teachers union, he sued the East Hartford Board of Education, claiming that the reprimand for violating the dress code deprived him of his rights of free speech and privacy. Chief Judge Clarie granted summary judgment for the defendants. At the request of a member of the Court, a poll of the judges in regular active service was taken to determine if the case should be reheard *en banc*. A majority voted for rehearing. We now vacate the judgment of the panel majority and affirm the judgment of the district court.

The facts are not in dispute. In February, 1972, the East Hartford Board of Education adopted "Regulations For Teacher Dress." At that time, Mr. Brimley, a teacher of high school English and filmmaking, customarily wore a jacket and sportshirt, without a tie. His failure to wear a tie constituted a violation of the regulations, and he was reprimanded for his delict. Mr. Brimley appealed to the school principal and was told that he was to wear a tie

---

[14] Ibid., at 416
[15] 562 F.2d 838 (1977)

while teaching English, but that his informal attire was proper during filmmaking classes. He then appealed to the superintendent and the board without success, after which he began formal arbitration proceedings, which ended in a decision that the dispute was not arbitrable. This lawsuit followed. Although Mr. Brimley initially complied with the code while pursuing his remedies, he has apparently returned to his former mode of dress. The record does not disclose any disciplinary action against him other than the original reprimand.

In the vast majority of communities, the control of public schools is vested in locally-elected bodies. This commitment to local political bodies requires significant public control over what is said and done in school. It is not the federal courts, but local democratic processes, that are primarily responsible for the many routine decisions that are made in public school systems. Accordingly, it is settled that "courts do not and cannot intervene in the resolution of conflicts which arise in the daily operation of school systems and which do not directly and sharply implicate basic constitutional values." . . .

Because the appellant's clash with his employer has failed to "directly and sharply implicate basic constitutional values," we refuse to upset the policies established by the school board.

Mr. Brimley claims that by refusing to wear a necktie he makes a statement on current affairs which assists him in his teaching. In his brief, he argues that the following benefits flow from his tielessness:

> *(a) He wishes to present himself to his students as a person who is not tied to "establishment conformity."*
> *(b) He wishes to symbolically indicate to his students his association with the ideas of the generation to which those students belong, including the rejection of many of the customs and values, and of the social outlook, of the older generation.*
> *(c) He feels that dress of this type enables him to achieve closer rapport with his students, and thus enhances his ability to teach.*

Appellant's claim, therefore, is that his refusal to wear a tie is "symbolic speech," and, as such, is protected against governmental interference by the First Amendment.

We are required here to balance the alleged interest in free expression against the goals of the school board in requiring its teachers to dress somewhat more formally than they might like. When this test is applied, the school board's position must prevail.

Obviously, a great range of conduct has the symbolic, "speech-like" aspect claimed by Mr. Brimley. To state that activity is "symbolic" is only the beginning, and not the end, of constitutional inquiry. Even though intended as expression, symbolic speech remains conduct, subject to regulation by the state. . . .

As conduct becomes less and less like "pure speech" the showing of governmental interest required for its regulation is progressively lessened. In those cases where governmental regulation of expressive conduct has been struck down, the communicative intent of the actor was clear and "closely akin to pure speech." Thus, the First Amendment has been held to protect wearing a black armband to protest the Vietnam War, *Tinker v. Des Moines School District,* burning an American Flag to highlight a speech denouncing the government's failure to protect a civil rights leader.

In contrast, the claims of symbolic speech made here are vague and unfocused. Through the simple refusal to wear a tie, Mr. Brimley claims that he communicates a comprehensive view of life and society. It may well be, in an age increasingly conscious of fashion, that a significant portion of the population seeks to make a statement of some kind through its clothes. However, Mr. Brimley's message is sufficiently vague to place it close to the "conduct" end of the "speech-conduct" continuum described above. While the regulation of the school board must still pass constitutional muster, the showing required to uphold it is significantly less than if Mr. Brimley had been punished, for example, for publicly speaking out on an issue concerning school administration.

At the outset, Mr. Brimley had other, more effective means of communicating his social views to his students. He could, for example, simply have told them his views on contemporary America; if he had done this in a temperate way, without interfering with his teaching duties, we would be confronted with a very different First Amendment case. The existence of alternative, effective means of communication, while not conclusive, is a factor to be considered in assessing the validity of a regulation of expressive conduct.

Balanced against appellant's claim of free expression is the school board's interest in promoting respect for authority and traditional values, as well as discipline in the classroom, by requiring teachers to dress in a professional manner. A dress code is a rational means of promoting these goals. As to the legitimacy of the goals themselves, there can be no doubt.

. . . This balancing test is primarily a matter for the school board. Were we local officials, and not appellate judges, we might find Mr. Brimley's arguments persuasive. However, our role is not to choose the better educational policy. We may intervene in the decisions of school authorities only when it has been shown that they have strayed outside the area committed to their discretion. If Mr. Brimley's argument were to prevail, this policy would be completely eroded. Because teaching is by definition an expressive activity, virtually every decision made by school authorities would raise First Amendment issues calling for federal court intervention.

The very notion of public education implies substantial public control. Educational decisions must be made by someone; there is no reason to create a constitutional preference for the views of individual teachers over those of their employers. . . .

[T]he First Amendment claim made here is so insubstantial as to border on the frivolous. We are unwilling to expand First Amendment protection to include a teacher's sartorial choice.

Mr. Brimley also claims that the "liberty" interest grounded in the due process clause of the Fourteenth Amendment protects his choice of attire. This claim will not withstand analysis. . . .

The rights of privacy and liberty in which appellant seeks refuge are important and evolving constitutional doctrines. To date, however, the Supreme Court has extended their protection only to the most basic personal decisions. Nor has the Supreme Court been quick to expand these rights to new fields. As with any other constitutional provision, we are not given a "roving commission" to right wrongs and impose our notions of sound policy upon society. There is substantial danger in expanding the reach of due process to cover cases such as this. By bringing trivial activities under the constitutional umbrella, we trivialize the constitutional provision itself. If we are to maintain the vitality of this new doctrine, we must be careful not to "cry wolf" at every minor restraint on a citizen's liberty.

The two other Courts of Appeals which have considered this issue have reached similar conclusions. In *Miller v. School District,* the Seventh Circuit upheld a grooming regulation for teachers. . . . The First Circuit reached the same result in *Tardif v. Quinn,* where a school teacher was dismissed for wearing short skirts.

Both *Miller* and *Tardif* are stronger cases for the plaintiff's position than the instant case. Both involved dismissals rather than, as here, a reprimand. Moreover, *Miller* involved a regulation of hair and beards, as well as dress. Thus, Miller was forced to appear as his employers wished both on and off the job. In contrast, Mr. Brimley can remove his tie as soon as the school day ends. If the plaintiffs in *Miller* and *Tardif* could not prevail, neither can Mr. Brimley.

Each claim of substantive liberty must be judged in the light of that case's special circumstances. In view of the uniquely influential role of the public school teacher in the classroom, the board is justified in imposing this regulation. As public servants in a special position of trust, teachers may properly be subjected to many restrictions in their professional lives which would be invalid if generally applied. We join the sound views of the First and Seventh Circuits, and follow *Kelley* by holding that a school board may, if it wishes, impose reasonable regulations governing the appearance of the teachers it employs. There being no material factual issue to be decided, the grant of summary judgment is affirmed.

Cases concerning personal appearance are many, with issues such as length of hair or facial hair receiving more constitutional protection than clothing. Overall, school officials have the right to restrict teachers' appearance, especially if it may cause disruption in the classroom. Other factors considered by courts are safety, health, and community norms. What may be acceptable in a large city school may be prohibited in a small rural town. Public schools, however, must have a legitimate educational purpose for restrictions on both dress and appearance. Courts will not uphold policies that are arbitrary and captious.

FREEDOM OF RELIGION

OF ALL the legal issues that school officials must address, freedom of religion is one of the most controversial. According to the U.S. Constitution, the government shall not prohibit or enhance any religion. As arms of the state, public schools must ensure they do not discriminate against individuals because of their religious beliefs yet must remain neutral and guard the wall between church and state.

There is little doubt that teachers, like all individuals, have the inherent right to freedom of religion. It is illegal for schools to discriminate against a teacher based on religious preference. But teachers are considered role models in the community and work with impressionable children who are required to be in the classroom. Consequently, teachers are limited in their ability to express their religious beliefs openly while performing their teaching duties.

In *Cooper v. Eugene School District No. 41,* a special education teacher was dismissed and her teaching certificate revoked for repeatedly wearing a white turban while teaching.[16] In upholding the school's decision to dismiss her, the court did not hold that teachers were restricted from wearing religious items in school. Rather, the issue analyzed the restriction of teachers' dress when it was "a constant and inescapable visual reminder of their religious commitment . . . [and] it contributes to the child's right to the free exercise and enjoyment of its religious opinions or heritage, untroubled by being out of step with those of the teacher."[17] Additionally, the court recognized that, while the statutes did constitute a burden on the teacher's "free exercise rights, when properly construed the statutes were narrowly tailored to the compelling state interest in preserving the appearance of religious neutrality in public schools."[18]

To avoid any suggestion that the public school district is promoting or enhancing a certain religion, teachers are restricted in their right to wear religious dress or symbols in the classroom. Teachers are role models there and in the community. Hence, as argued in *Cooper,* "the teacher's appearance in religious garb may leave a conscious or unconscious impression among young people and their parents that the school endorses the particular religious commitment of the person whom it has assigned the public role of teacher."[19] Once a teacher is off duty, he or she may express religious beliefs in any manner the teacher sees fit. In the balancing of rights, the scale tips toward protecting the impressionable student who cannot escape the school environment versus the First Amendment rights of the teacher.

Right to Privacy

TEACHERS receive the same constitutional protection as non-teachers do. Nevertheless, a strong argument could be made that teachers are required to set examples for the students they teach. The Supreme Court has not specifically responded to the issue of how much privacy teachers are granted. Due to various decisions in different courts, community norms in different locations have played a role in how much privacy is granted. Chapter 10 offers a more extensive discussion of teachers' employment and tenure rights. But here it is important to state that teachers do have a right to privacy, although how much is based on court interpretation.

For example, a highly published and debated case occurred in 1999, when a constitutional law teacher was dismissed for failing to submit to a drug test. While the issue crosses the line of constitutional rights, it also concerns the teacher's right to privacy outside of the classroom.

---

[16] 723 P.2d. 298 (1987)

[17] Ibid.

[18] Ibid.

[19] Ibid.

Hearn v. the Board of Public Education
U.S. Court of Appeals for the Eleventh Circuit, 1999
191 F.3d 1329

Opinion written by Senior Circuit Judge Hill.

Sherry Hearn was terminated from her position as a high school teacher for refusing to take a drug test after marijuana was allegedly found in her car in the school's parking lot. She sued defendants alleging, among other things, denial of her substantive and procedural due process rights, intentional breach of contract, violations of the Fourth and Fifth Amendments. She sought damages as well as reinstatement. The district court granted summary judgment for defendants on all claims and Hearn brought this appeal. For the following reasons, we affirm.

I. Sherry Hearn was a teacher in Savannah for many years. She was employed under a contract which required that she abide by the policies of the Board of Education of Chatham County (Board).

In 1992, the county enacted its "Safe School Plan" which called for "zero-tolerance" of drugs, alcohol and weapons. In 1993, the Board promulgated a "Drug-Free Workplace Policy" (DFWP) governing its employees. The policy is intended to "deter users and abusers of alcohol, drugs and other controlled substances." It provides for drug testing of any employee when "supervisor observations or other objective circumstances reasonably support a suspicion that an employee may have violated the Board drug and alcohol policy." The policy further requires that such testing be conducted within two hours of the incident which generates the "reasonable suspicion." An employee's refusal to consent to the drug test, or to a search of her personal property located at the school is cause for termination. Finally, "any employee who tests positive . . . [for] alcohol, drugs or other controlled substances will be terminated."

In April of 1996, campus and Chatham County, Georgia police conducted a "drug lockdown" and random drug search at Hearn's high school in Savannah. Hearn's car was in the school's rear parking lot, unlocked and with its passenger side window down.

The Chatham County deputy's drug-sniffing dog alerted at Hearn's vehicle. The deputy let the dog enter the car through the passenger window. The dog alerted on the vehicle's closed ashtray. A campus officer opened it and found a partially burned, hand-rolled cigarette. He testified that he field-tested it for marijuana, and it tested positive. The officers noticed the faculty parking permit on the dash and took it with them.

The officers went to the school's principal, Linda Herman, and informed her of these events. She summoned Hearn, who denied knowledge or possession of any marijuana. One of the County's officers "Mirandized" Hearn, telling her that she probably would be charged with criminal possession of marijuana.

Herman informed Hearn that, under the DFWP, she must take a urinalysis drug test within two hours. Hearn refused. Herman gave Hearn a warning letter which directed her to take the drug test. The letter stated: "In the course of a drug search, a substance [found to have tested positive for cannabinoid] was found in your personal vehicle. . . . Based on this finding, in compliance with BOE Policy 766—Drug Free Workplace, you are hereby directed to submit to a drug test for reasonable suspicion within [the two-hour limit]. Your failure to comply may result in disciplinary action." Hearn, however, continued to refuse to take the drug test.

Later, the Superintendent of Schools for Chatham County suspended her. He recommended that she be terminated for "insubordination" and "other good and sufficient cause" as the result of her failure to consent to take the drug test within the prescribed two hour period.

The Board provided Hearn with a hearing. She appeared with counsel and testified. At the end of the hearing, the Board made no findings of fact, but voted to accept the superintendent's recommendation and terminated Hearn. Hearn appealed to the State Board of Education, which issued a written opinion upholding the Board.

II.   Hearn's termination was for insubordination—her refusal to take the drug test within the prescribed two hour period. She argues that she cannot be terminated for her refusal because she was under no obligation to take the drug test. She was not obliged to take the test because there was no "reasonable suspicion" as required by the Board's policy prior to directing an employee to take the test. There was no reasonable suspicion because the search of her car was illegal under both the Board's own policy which requires an employee's consent or a search warrant in order to search an employee's personal property at school, and under the Fourth Amendment. We find no merit in either of these contentions.

First, the Board's policy regarding searches of employee property is legally irrelevant to the search of Hearn's car. The Board's policy applies only to *intra*-school events, i.e., those involving only school officials and school employees. It provides what will happen when reasonable suspicion arises in an exclusively intra-school setting, as when school officials discover circumstances generating reasonable suspicion that an employee is using drugs.

That was not the case here. Reasonable suspicion arose in the context of a drug sweep of a parking lot by local law enforcement officers whose dog alerted at Hearn's car—a *law enforcement* event. Neither the Board's policy nor Hearn's contract of employment trumps the legal authority of law enforcement officers to perform such a sweep or the subsequent search. The officers' authority is limited only by the Constitution.

Hearn implicitly recognizes this distinction. She makes much of the fact that both the Superintendent and Herman testified that the "reasonable suspicion" which required Hearn's consent to a drug test was based on the campus police officer's finding of marijuana in her car, an *intra*-school event, not on the dog sniff and alert, a county law enforcement event. Her argument is that since a campus police officer actually found the marijuana, the Board's policy governed his search and it should not have been conducted without her consent. Because the search was without her consent, no reasonable suspicion could arise from it and she was not required to consent to the drug test.

We find no basis in the law or in the real world to distinguish two legally distinct events in the one sweep and search. Merely because a campus police officer was present during the sweep and happened to be the one to find the marijuana does not change the fact that this was a law enforcement event, not bound by any school policy or employment contract. Even if, as Hearn argues, the Board's policy gave employees a heightened expectation of privacy with regard to their personal property at school, that expectation does not bind local law enforcement. They are not parties to the contract. Whatever expectation of privacy Hearn had in her vehicle during a law enforcement event must be located in constitutional law, not local school board policies.

Second, the Constitution does not provide Hearn with any expectation of privacy in the odors emanating from her car. A dog sniff of a person's property located in a public place is not a search within the meaning of the Fourth Amendment.

Furthermore, the alerting of a drug-sniffing dog to a person's property supplies not only reasonable suspicion, but probable cause to search that property.

When the property alerted to is in a vehicle, the Constitution permits a search of the vehicle immediately, without resort to a warrant.

The search of Hearn's car, therefore, did not violate the Fourth Amendment. It was based upon the probable cause generated by the dog sniff, and justified by the automobile exception to the general requirement for a warrant.

Thus, there was a reasonable suspicion generated by these circumstances regarding Hearn's possible drug use. At this point, the Board's policy was triggered. Hearn's refusal to give her consent to Board's request for a drug test gave rise to the possibility of her termination under that policy. Her subsequent termination, therefore, did not violate either her contract of employment nor the Board's policy, and she is not due to be reinstated for these reasons.

Hearn's next argument is that she was wrongfully terminated for exercising her rights under the Fifth Amendment when she relied upon the exercise of her constitutional right to remain silent. She contends that because the officer *Mirandized* her, she cannot be terminated for exercising her right to remain silent. This argument is without merit. The production of body fluids is non-testimonial. Hearn has not offered any authority that the production of urine does not fall within this rule, nor do we know of any. Hearn was not forced to testify against herself in violation of the Fifth Amendment.

III.   Hearn's contract with the Board does not vitiate the authority of the law enforcement officers to search her car under the circumstances of this case. Nor were any of Hearn's constitutional rights violated. Accordingly, the judgment of the district court is affirmed.

Dissent written by Judge Ferguson:

I respectfully dissent.

Legally, the plaintiff's position is unassailable. But there are relevant factors beyond principles of contract law which have chilling ramifications. The plaintiff had been very critical of the School Board's policy of campus lock down searches for drugs which she likened to police state tactics. Because of her classroom criticism of the practice as unconstitutional, she was not in favor with the employer. Expectations of privacy guaranteed by the policy were ignored and the penalty imposed was the professional equivalent of the death penalty. The twenty-seven (27) year stellar career of a 1994 "Teacher of the Year" is shattered with only three (3) years remaining to retirement with benefits.

By the holding here the majority has recognized, implicitly, an illegal drugs exception to the law that the court will not rewrite private contracts between parties who are on equal footing. It is widely recognized that in the nation's zealous war on drugs, rights secured by the Fourth Amendment have shrunk. This may be the first case to hold that courts will not enforce private contract rights between an employer and employee, hammered out after negotiations to govern conduct of the parties in areas of privacy, where the employer has a suspicion, no matter how insubstantial, that the employee violated a drug policy. Not only is an outstanding high school teacher a casualty in this episode; so, incidentally, are basic contract principles.

Unquestionably the plaintiff's termination from employment as a teacher for not submitting to a drug test was an "intra school event." On the collateral point, whether the search for and seizure of contraband from the interior of the plaintiff's vehicle by a school board officer was a "law enforcement event", presents at least an issue of fact.

In my view this fact-driven case should go to a jury.

ACADEMIC FREEDOM

TRADITIONALLY, academic freedom has trickled down from higher education into elementary and secondary institutions. The idea behind academic freedom is to allow the instructor to teach students in the manner in which he or she sees fit. Such freedom, however, is limited in the public school system. The majority of lawsuits dealing with academic freedom are initiated by parents or community members who are unhappy with certain viewpoints or material being taught by teachers. A recent case challenging such academic freedom was *Fowler v. Board of Education of Lincoln County.*[20]

In *Fowler*, a tenured teacher was dismissed from her teaching position for allowing her high schools students to watch the movie *Pink Floyd—The Wall.* The students had asked to watch the movie on the last day of the semester, which was a noninstructional day that teachers used for completing grade cards. Unfamiliar with the movie, Fowler allowed the students to watch the movie while she completed her end-of-the-year grading. Before the viewing, Fowler asked the students about the movie's content. One student who had seen the movie stated that there was "one bad place in it." Fowler then instructed the student to edit any of the unsuitable parts by covering the 25-inch screen with an $8\frac{1}{2}$-by-11-inch file folder.

During an administrative hearing with the school board, Fowler testified that she believed the movie "had significant value" and that she was protected under the First Amendment because a motion picture is a form of expression. At trial, the court found in favor of Fowler, holding that her conduct was protected by the First Amendment. On appeal, the Sixth Circuit vacated the judgment and dismissed the case.

In its rational, the U.S. Court of Appeals focused on the important role that teachers play in our society. "The single most important element of this inculcative process is the teacher. Consciously or otherwise, teachers . . . demonstrate the appropriate form of civil

---

[20] 819 F.2d 657 (1987)

discourse and political expression by their conduct and deportment in and out of class. Inescapably, like parents, they are role models."[21] In addition, the court stated:

> *Moreover, the surrounding circumstances in the present case indicate that there was little likelihood "that the message would be understood by those who viewed it." As we have noted, the "R" rated movie was shown on a noninstructional day to students in Fowler's classes in grades nine through eleven who were of ages ranging from fourteen through seventeen. Furthermore, Fowler never at any time made an attempt to explain any message that the students might derive from viewing the movie.*
>
> *. . . The cases just discussed demonstrate that conduct is protected by the First Amendment only when it is expressive or communicative in nature. In the present case, because plaintiff's conduct in having the movie shown cannot be considered expressive or communicative, under the circumstances presented, the protection of the First Amendment is not implicated.[22]*

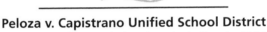

Peloza v. Capistrano Unified School District
U.S. Court of Appeals for the Ninth Circuit, 1994
37 F.3d 517

The Allegations of the Complaint

The following summarizes the allegations of Peloza's complaint: Peloza is a biology teacher in a public high school, and is employed by the Capistrano Unified School District. He is being forced by the defendants (the school district, its trustees and individual teachers and others) to proselytize his students to a belief in "evolutionism" "under the guise of [its being] a valid scientific theory." Evolutionism is an historical, philosophical and religious belief system, but not a valid scientific theory.

Evolutionism is one of "two world views on the subject of the origins of life and of the universe." The other is "creationism" which also is a "religious belief system." "The belief system of evolutionism is based on the assumption that life and the universe evolved randomly and by chance and with no Creator involved in the process. The world view and belief system of creationism is based on the assumption that a Creator created all life and the entire universe." Peloza does not wish "to promote either philosophy or belief system in teaching his biology class." "The general acceptance of . . . evolutionism in academic circles does not qualify it or validate it as a scientific theory." Peloza believes that the defendants seek to dismiss him due to his refusal to teach evolutionism. His First Amendment rights have been abridged by interference with his right "to teach his students to differentiate between a philosophical, religious belief system on the one hand and a true scientific theory on the other."

---

[21] Ibid., at 651
[22] Ibid., at 663–664

Peloza further alleges he has been forbidden to discuss religious matters with students the entire time that he is on the school campus even if a conversation is initiated by a student and the discussion is outside of class time. . . .

Discussion

I. The Section 1983 Claim

A. The Establishment Clause   To withstand an Establishment Clause challenge, a state statute, policy or action (1) must have a secular purpose; (2) must, as its primary effect, neither advance nor inhibit religion; and (3) must not foster an excessive government entanglement with religions.

Peloza's complaint alleges that the school district has violated the Establishment Clause "by pressuring and requiring him to teach evolutionism, a religious belief system, as a valid scientific theory." Complaint at 19–20. Evolutionism, according to Peloza, "postulates that the 'higher' life forms . . . evolved from the 'lower' life forms . . . and that life itself 'evolved' from non-living matter." It is therefore "based on the assumption that life and the universe evolved randomly and by chance and with no Creator involved in the process." Peloza claims that evolutionism is not a valid scientific theory because it is based on events which "occurred in the non-observable and non-recreatable past and hence are not subject to scientific observation." Finally, in his appellate brief he alleges that the school district is requiring him to teach evolutionism not just as a theory, but rather as a fact.

Peloza's complaint is not entirely consistent. In some places he seems to advance the patently frivolous claim that it is unconstitutional for the school district to require him to teach, as a valid scientific theory, that higher life forms evolved from lower ones. At other times he claims the district is forcing him to teach evolution as fact. Although possibly dogmatic or even wrong, such a requirement would not transgress the Establishment Clause if "evolution" simply means that higher life forms evolved from lower ones.

Peloza uses the words "evolution" and "evolutionism" interchangeably in the complaint. This is not wrong or imprecise for, indeed, they are synonyms. Adding "ism" does not change the meaning nor magically metamorphose "evolution" into a religion. *"Evolution"* and *"evolutionism"* define a biological concept: higher life forms evolve from lower ones. The concept has nothing to do with *how* the universe was created; it has nothing to do with whether or not there is a divine Creator.

On a motion to dismiss we are required to read the complaint charitably, to take all well-pleaded facts as true, and to assume that all general allegations embrace whatever specific facts might be necessary to support them.

Charitably read, Peloza's complaint at most makes this claim: the school district's actions establish a state-supported religion of evolutionism, or more generally of "secular humanism." According to Peloza's complaint, all persons must adhere to one of two religious belief systems concerning "the origins of life and of the universe": evolutionism, or creationism. Thus, the school district, in teaching evolutionism, is establishing a state-supported "religion."

We reject this claim because neither the Supreme Court, nor this circuit, has ever held that evolutionism or secular humanism are "religions" for Establishment Clause purposes. Indeed, both the dictionary definition of religion and the clear weight of the caselaw are to the contrary. The Supreme Court has held unequivocally that while the belief in a divine creator of the universe is a religious belief, the scientific theory that higher forms of life evolved from lower forms is not.

Peloza would have us accept his definition of "evolution" and "evolutionism" and impose his definition on the school district as its *own,* a definition that cannot be found in the dictionary, in the Supreme Court cases, or anywhere in the common understanding of the words. Only if we define "evolution" and "evolutionism" as does Peloza as a concept that embraces the belief that the universe came into existence without a Creator might he make out a claim. This we need not do. To say red is green or black is white does not make it so. Nor need we for the purposes of a 12(b)(6) motion accept a made-up definition of "evolution." Nowhere does Peloza point to anything that conceivably suggests that the school district accepts anything other than the common definition of "evolution" and "evolutionism." It simply required him as a biology teacher in the public schools of California to teach "evolution." Peloza nowhere says it required more.

The district court dismissed his claim, stating: Since the evolutionist theory is not a religion, to require an instructor to teach this theory is not a violation of the Establishment Clause. . . . Evolution is a scientific theory based on the gathering and studying of data, and modification of new data. It is an established scientific theory which is used as the basis for many areas of science. As scientific methods advance and become more accurate, the scientific community will revise the accepted theory to a more accurate explanation of life's origins. Plaintiff's assertions that the teaching of evolution would be a violation of the Establishment Clause is unfounded.

We agree.

B.   Free Speech   Peloza alleges the school district ordered him to refrain from discussing his religious beliefs with students during "instructional time," and to tell any students who attempted to initiate such conversations with him to consult their parents or clergy. He claims the school district, in the following official reprimand, defined "instructional time" as any time the students are on campus, including lunch break and the time before, between, and after classes: You are hereby directed to refrain from any attempt to convert students to Christianity or initiating conversations about your religious beliefs during instructional time, which the District believes includes any time students are required to be on campus as well as the time students immediately arrive for the purposes of attending school for instruction, lunch time, and the time immediately prior to students' departure after the instructional day.

Peloza seeks a declaration that this definition of instructional time is too broad, and that he should be allowed to participate in student-initiated discussions of religious matters when he is not actually teaching class.

The school district's restriction on Peloza's ability to talk with students about religion during the school day is a restriction on his right of free speech. Nevertheless, "the Court has repeatedly emphasized the need for affirming the comprehensive authority of the States and of school officials, consistent with fundamental constitutional safeguards, to prescribe and control conduct in the schools." "The interest of the State in avoiding an Establishment Clause violation 'may be [a] compelling' one justifying an abridgement of free speech otherwise protected by the First Amendment. . . . " This principle applies in this case. The school district's interest in avoiding an Establishment Clause violation trumps Peloza's right to free speech.

While at the high school, whether he is in the classroom or outside of it during contract time, Peloza is not just any ordinary citizen. He is a teacher. He is one of those especially respected persons chosen to teach in the high school's classroom. He is clothed with the mantle of one who imparts knowledge and wisdom. His expressions of opinion are all the more believable because he is a teacher. The likelihood of high school students equating his views with those of the school is substantial. To permit him to discuss his religious beliefs with students during school time on school grounds would violate the Establishment Clause of the First Amendment. Such speech would not have a secular purpose, would have the primary effect of advancing religion, and would entangle the school with religion. In sum, it would flunk all three parts of the test articulated in *Lemon v. Kurtzman.*

. . . We affirm the dismissal of the complaint. We reverse the district court's award of attorney fees to the defendants.

The parties shall bear their own costs on appeal.

In the case law that revolves around the issue of academic freedom, the rights of public elementary and secondary teachers are limited to approved curriculum and texts. While the educational forum is a place to express the "marketplace of ideas," teachers must follow the school district's guidelines on subject matter and content discussion.

FREEDOM OF ASSOCIATION

IN ADDITION to granting individuals freedom of speech, the First Amendment also grants people the right to assemble peacefully. This right is extended to public school teachers, who may join organizations regardless of their political, religious, or social-status affiliation. But this was not always the situation, especially during the cold war. A landmark case discussing the issue of teachers' right to freedom of association is *Keyishian v. Board of Regents.*[23]

In this 1967 Supreme Court case, the University of Buffalo required all faculty members to sign a statement under oath that stated they were not associating with "subversive" persons. Appellant Starbuck was a nonfaculty library employee and part-time lecturer in English. Personnel of that classification were not required to sign a certificate but were required to answer in writing, under oath, this question: "Have you ever advised or taught or were you ever a member of any society or group of persons which taught or advocated the doctrine that the Government of the United States or of any political subdivisions thereof should be overthrown or overturned by force, violence or any unlawful means?" Anyone who did not answer the question was not rehired or was dismissed from his or her position. In its conclusion, the Court held that public education employees have a right to freedom of association, even with members of the Communist party, as long as they have no specific intention of performing illegal acts recommended by such a group.

---

[23] 385 U.S. 589 (1967)

Freedom of association is an implied right according to the First Amendment of the U.S. Constitution. Hence, teachers cannot be fired for mere association with subversive organizations. Nevertheless, teachers should not bring their personal political, religious, or social philosophies into the classroom. While the Supreme Court sets forth the rights of teachers, courts must also consider the rights of young students, who are easily influenced by individuals whom they look up to and admire.

In the past few decades, the rights of teachers have dramatically increased and are highly protected. Today teachers have the right to express themselves verbally, through the organizations they join, through acts outside of the classroom, as well as within the classroom. These rights, however, do have some limitations.

PREGNANCY

AT ONE time, it was regular practice among public schools to set policies that required pregnant teachers to take a leave of absence before giving birth as well as set dates for returning to work once the child was born. The mandatory leave policies were based on numerous beliefs, including the idea that teachers were role models and should not be in a classroom if they looked pregnant. Some school districts had even stricter policies, requiring, for example, unwed mothers to be permanently dismissed from their teaching positions.[24] All of these policies were challenged in the early 1970s, with the claim that the rules violated teachers' constitutional rights.

Cleveland Board of Education v. LaFleur
Supreme Court of the United States, 1974
414 U.S. 632

Mr. Justice Steward delivered the opinion of the Court.

The respondents in No. 72-777 and the petitioner in No. 72-1129 are female public school teachers. During the 1970–1971 school year, each informed her local school board that she was pregnant; each was compelled by a mandatory maternity leave rule to quit her job without pay several months before the expected birth of her child. These cases call upon us to decide the constitutionality of the school boards' rules.

I.   Jo Carol LaFleur and Ann Elizabeth Nelson, the respondents in No. 72-777, are junior high school teachers employed by the Board of Education of Cleveland, Ohio. Pursuant to a rule first adopted in 1952, the school board requires every pregnant school teacher to take maternity leave without pay, beginning five months before the expected birth of her child. Application for such leave must be made no later than two weeks prior to the date of departure. A teacher on maternity leave is not allowed to return to work until the beginning

---

[24] *Andrews v. Drew Municipal Separate School District*, 504 F.2d 611 (1975)

of the next regular school semester which follows the date when her child attains the age of three months. A doctor's certificate attesting to the health of the teacher is a prerequisite to return; an additional physical examination may be required. The teacher on maternity leave is not promised re-employment after the birth of the child; she is merely given priority in re-assignment to a position for which she is qualified. Failure to comply with the mandatory maternity leave provisions is ground for dismissal.

Neither Mrs. LaFleur nor Mrs. Nelson wished to take an unpaid maternity leave; each wanted to continue teaching until the end of the school year. Because of the mandatory maternity leave rule, however, each was required to leave her job in March 1971. The two women then filed separate suits in the United States District Court for the Northern District of Ohio under 42 U.S.C. § 1983, challenging the constitutionality of the maternity leave rule. The District Court tried the cases together, and rejected the plaintiffs' arguments. A divided panel of the United States Court of Appeals for the Sixth Circuit reversed, finding the Cleveland rule in violation of the Equal Protection Clause of the Fourteenth Amendment.

The petitioner in No. 72-1129, Susan Cohen, was employed by the School Board of Chesterfield County, Virginia. That school board's maternity leave regulation requires that a pregnant teacher leave work at least four months prior to the expected birth of her child. Notice in writing must be given to the school board at least six months prior to the expected birth date. A teacher on maternity leave is declared re-eligible for employment when she submits written notice from a physician that she is physically fit for re-employment, and when she can give assurance that care of the child will cause only minimal interference with her job responsibilities. The teacher is guaranteed re-employment no later than the first day of the school year following the date upon which she is declared re-eligible.

Mrs. Cohen informed the Chesterfield County School Board in November 1970, that she was pregnant and expected the birth of her child about April 28, 1971. She initially requested that she be permitted to continue teaching until April 1, 1971. The school board rejected the request, as it did Mrs. Cohen's subsequent suggestion that she be allowed to teach until January 21, 1971, the end of the first school semester. Instead, she was required to leave her teaching job on December 18, 1970. She subsequently filed this suit under 42 U.S.C. § 1983 in the United States District Court for the Eastern District of Virginia. The District Court held that the school board regulation violates the Equal Protection Clause, and granted appropriate relief. A divided panel of the Fourth Circuit affirmed, but, on rehearing en banc, the Court of Appeals upheld the constitutionality of the challenged regulation in a 4–3 decision.

This Court has long recognized that freedom of personal choice in matters of marriage and family life is one of the liberties protected by the Due Process Clause of the Fourteenth Amendment. As we noted in *Eisenstadt v. Baird*, there is a right "to be free from unwarranted governmental intrusion into matters so fundamentally affecting a person as the decision whether to bear or beget a child."

By acting to penalize the pregnant teacher for deciding to bear a child, overly restrictive maternity leave regulations can constitute a heavy burden on the exercise of these protected freedoms. Because public school maternity leave rules directly affect "one of the basic civil rights of man," the Due Process Clause of the Fourteenth Amendment requires that such rules must not needlessly, arbitrarily, or capriciously impinge upon this vital area of a teacher's constitutional liberty. The question before us in these cases is whether the interests advanced in support of the rules of the Cleveland and Chesterfield County School Boards can justify the particular procedures they have adopted.

The school boards in these cases have offered two essentially overlapping explanations for their mandatory maternity leave rules. First, they contend that the firm cutoff dates are necessary to maintain continuity of classroom instruction, since advance knowledge of when a pregnant teacher must leave facilitates the finding and hiring of a qualified substitute. Secondly, the school boards seek to justify their maternity rules by arguing that at least some teachers become physically incapable of adequately performing certain of their duties during the latter part of pregnancy. By keeping the pregnant teacher out of the classroom during these final months, the maternity leave rules are said to protect the health of the teacher and her unborn child, while at the same time assuring that students have a physically capable instructor in the classroom at all times.

It cannot be denied that continuity of instruction is a significant and legitimate educational goal. Regulations requiring pregnant teachers to provide early notice of their condition to school authorities undoubtedly facilitate administrative planning toward the important objective of continuity. But, as the Court of Appeals for the Second Circuit noted in *Green v. Waterford Board of Education:* "Where a pregnant teacher provides the Board with a date certain for commencement of leave . . . that value [continuity] is preserved; an arbitrary leave date set at the end of the fifth month is no more calculated to facilitate a planned and orderly transition between the teacher and a substitute than is a date fixed closer to confinement. Indeed, the latter . . . would afford the Board more, not less, time to procure a satisfactory long-term substitute."

Thus, while the advance-notice provisions in the Cleveland and Chesterfield County rules are wholly rational and may well be necessary to serve the objective of continuity of instruction, the absolute requirements of termination at the end of the fourth or fifth month of pregnancy are not. Were continuity the only goal, cut-off dates much later during pregnancy would serve as well as or better than the challenged rules, providing that ample advance notice requirements were retained. Indeed, continuity would seem just as well attained if the teacher herself were allowed to choose the date upon which to commence her leave, at least so long as the decision were required to be made and notice given of it well in advance of the date selected.

In fact, since the fifth or sixth month of pregnancy will obviously begin at different times in the school year for different teachers, the present Cleveland and Chesterfield County rules may serve to hinder attainment of the very continuity objectives that they are purportedly designed to promote. For example, the beginning of the fifth month of pregnancy for both Mrs. LaFleur and Mrs. Nelson occurred during March of 1971. Both were thus required to leave work with only a few months left in the school year, even though both were fully willing to serve through the end of the term. Similarly, if continuity were the only goal, it seems ironic that the Chesterfield County rule forced Mrs. Cohen to leave work in mid-December 1970 rather than at the end of the semester in January, as she requested.

We thus conclude that the arbitrary cutoff dates embodied in the mandatory leave rules before us have no rational relationship to the valid state interest of preserving continuity of instruction. As long as the teachers are required to give substantial advance notice of their condition, the choice of firm dates later in pregnancy would serve the boards' objectives just

as well, while imposing a far lesser burden on the women's exercise of constitutionally protected freedom.

The question remains as to whether the cutoff dates at the beginning of the fifth and
sixth months can be justified on the other ground advanced by the school boards—the necessity of keeping physically unfit teachers out of the classroom. There can be no doubt that
such an objective is perfectly legitimate, both on educational and safety grounds. And, despite the plethora of conflicting medical testimony in these cases, we can assume, that at
least some teachers become physically disabled from effectively performing their duties
during the latter stages of pregnancy.

The mandatory termination provisions of the Cleveland and Chesterfield County rules
surely operate to insulate the classroom from the presence of potentially incapacitated pregnant teachers. But the question is whether the rules sweep too broadly. That question must be
answered in the affirmative, for the provisions amount to a conclusive presumption that every
pregnant teacher who reaches the fifth or sixth month of pregnancy is physically incapable of
continuing. There is no individualized determination by the teacher's doctor—or the school
board's—as to any particular teacher's ability to continue at her job. The rules contain an irrebuttable presumption of physical incompetency, and that presumption applies even when the
medical evidence as to an individual woman's physical status might be wholly to the contrary.

As the Court noted last Term in *Vlandis v. Kline,* "permanent irrebuttable presumptions
have long been disfavored under the Due Process Clauses of the Fifth and Fourteenth
Amendments." In *Vlandis,* the Court declared unconstitutional, under the Due Process
Clause of the Fourteenth Amendment, a Connecticut statute mandating an irrebuttable
presumption of nonresidency for the purposes of qualifying for reduced tuition rates at a
state university. We said in that case: "It is forbidden by the Due Process Clause to deny an
individual the resident rates on the basis of a permanent and irrebuttable presumption of
nonresidence, when that presumption is not necessarily or universally true in fact, and when
the State has reasonable alternative means of making the crucial determination."

Similarly, in *Stanley v. Illinois,* the Court held that an Illinois statute containing an irrebuttable presumption that unmarried fathers are incompetent to raise their children violated
the Due Process Clause. Because of the statutory presumption, the State took custody of all
illegitimate children upon the death of the mother, without allowing the father to attempt
to prove his parental fitness. As the Court put the matter: "It may be, as the State insists, that
most unmarried fathers are unsuitable and neglectful parents. It may also be that Stanley is
such a parent and that his children should be placed in other hands. But all unmarried fathers
are not in this category; some are wholly suited to have custody of their children."

Hence, we held that the State could not conclusively presume that any particular unmarried father was unfit to raise his child; the Due Process Clause required a more individualized determination.

These principles control our decision in the cases before us. While the medical experts in
these cases differed on many points, they unanimously agreed on one—the ability of any
particular pregnant woman to continue at work past any fixed time in her pregnancy is very
much an individual matter. Even assuming that there are some women who would be physically unable to work past the particular cutoff dates embodied in the challenged rules, it is
evident that there are large numbers of teachers who are fully capable of continuing work

for longer than the Cleveland and Chesterfield County regulations will allow. Thus, the conclusive presumption embodied in these rules, like that in *Vlandis,* is neither "necessarily [nor] universally true," and is violative of the Due Process Clause.

The school boards have argued that the mandatory termination dates serve the interest of administrative convenience, since there are many instances of teacher pregnancy, and the rules obviate the necessity for case-by-case determinations. Certainly, the boards have an interest in devising prompt and efficient procedures to achieve their legitimate objectives in this area. But, as the Court stated in *Stanley v. Illinois:* "The Constitution recognizes higher values than speed and efficiency. Indeed, one might fairly say of the Bill of Rights in general, and the Due Process Clause in particular, that they were designed to protect the fragile values of a vulnerable citizenry from the overbearing concern for efficiency and efficacy that may characterize praiseworthy government officials no less, and perhaps more, than mediocre ones."

While it might be easier for the school boards to conclusively presume that all pregnant women are unfit to teach past the fourth or fifth month or even the first month, of pregnancy, administrative convenience alone is insufficient to make valid what otherwise is a violation of due process of law. The Fourteenth Amendment requires the school boards to employ alternative administrative means, which do not so broadly infringe upon basic constitutional liberty, in support of their legitimate goals.

We conclude, therefore, that neither the necessity for continuity of instruction nor the state interest in keeping physically unfit teachers out of the classroom can justify the sweeping mandatory leave regulations that the Cleveland and Chesterfield County School Boards have adopted. While the regulations no doubt represent a good-faith attempt to achieve a laudable goal, they cannot pass muster under the Due Process Clause of the Fourteenth Amendment, because they employ irrebuttable presumptions that unduly penalize a female teacher for deciding to bear a child.

In addition to the mandatory termination provisions, both the Cleveland and Chesterfield County rules contain limitations upon a teacher's eligibility to return to work after giving birth. Again, the school boards offer two justifications for the return rules—continuity of instruction and the desire to be certain that the teacher is physically competent when she returns to work. As is the case with the leave provisions, the question is not whether the school board's goals are legitimate, but rather whether the particular means chosen to achieve those objectives unduly infringe upon the teacher's constitutional liberty.

Under the Cleveland rule, the teacher is not eligible to return to work until the beginning of the next regular school semester following the time when her child attains the age of three months. A doctor's certificate attesting to the teacher's health is required before return; an additional physical examination may be required at the option of the school board.

The respondents in No. 72-777 do not seriously challenge either the medical requirements of the Cleveland rule or the policy of limiting eligibility to return to the next semester following birth. The provisions concerning a medical certificate or supplemental physical examination are narrowly drawn methods of protecting the school board's interest in teacher fitness; these requirements allow an individualized decision as to the teacher's condition, and thus avoid the pitfalls of the presumptions inherent in the leave rules. Similarly, the provision limiting eligibility to return to the semester following delivery is a precisely drawn means of serving the school board's interest in avoiding unnecessary changes in classroom personnel during any one school term.

The Cleveland rule, however, does not simply contain these reasonable medical and next-semester eligibility provisions. In addition, the school board requires the mother to wait until her child reaches the age of three months before the return rules begin to operate. The school board has offered no reasonable justification for this supplemental limitation, and we can perceive none. To the extent that the three-month provision reflects the school board's thinking that no mother is fit to return until that point in time, it suffers from the same constitutional deficiencies that plague the irrebuttable presumption in the termination rules. The presumption, moreover, is patently unnecessary, since the requirement of a physician's certificate or a medical examination fully protects the school's interests in this regard. And finally, the three-month provision simply has nothing to do with continuity of instruction, since the precise point at which the child will reach the relevant age will obviously occur at a different point throughout the school year for each teacher.

Thus, we conclude that the Cleveland return rule, insofar as it embodies the three-month age provision, is wholly arbitrary and irrational, and hence violates the Due Process Clause of the Fourteenth Amendment. The age limitation serves no legitimate state interest, and unnecessarily penalizes the female teacher for asserting her right to bear children.

We perceive no such constitutional infirmities in the Chesterfield County rule. In that school system, the teacher becomes eligible for re-employment upon submission of a medical certificate from her physician; return to work is guaranteed no later than the beginning of the next school year following the eligibility determination. The medical certificate is both a reasonable and narrow method of protecting the school board's interest in teacher fitness, while the possible deferring of return until the next school year serves the goal of preserving continuity of instruction. In short, the Chesterfield County rule manages to serve the legitimate state interests here without employing unnecessary presumptions that broadly burden the exercise of protected constitutional liberty.

For the reasons stated, we hold that the mandatory termination provisions of the Cleveland and Chesterfield County maternity regulations violate the Due Process Clause of the Fourteenth Amendment, because of their use of unwarranted conclusive presumptions that seriously burden the exercise of protected constitutional liberty. For similar reasons, we hold the three-month provision of the Cleveland return rule unconstitutional.

Accordingly, the judgment in No. 72-777 is affirmed; the judgment in No. 72-1129 is reversed, and the case is remanded to the Court of Appeals for the Fourth Circuit for further proceedings consistent with this opinion.

It is so ordered.

REASONABLE ACCOMMODATIONS

THE AMERICANS with Disabilities Act (ADA) of 1990 provides that an employer must provide reasonable accommodations for an employee that has a disability. The courts, however, interpret this definition in many ways. For example, in *Toyota Motor*

Manufacturing, Kentucky, v. Williams, the Supreme Court held in favor of the employer after an employee claimed that her work did not provide the required reasonable accommodations set forth by the ADA.[25]

> *Under the Americans with Disabilities Act of 1990, a physical impairment that "substantially limits one or more . . . major life activities" is a "disability." Respondent, claiming to be disabled because of her carpal tunnel syndrome and other related impairments, sued petitioner, her former employer, for failing to provide her with a reasonable accommodation as required by the ADA. The District Court granted summary judgment to petitioner, finding that respondent's impairments did not substantially limit any of her major life activities.*[26]

The Supreme Court determined that, in defining a disability, "merely having an impairment does not make one disabled for purposes of the ADA. Claimants also need to demonstrate that the impairment limits a major life activity."[27] While the ADA has not changed since 1990, the important point to note is the courts' narrowing interpretation of the law.

Best Practices

- If the school sets forth a dress code for teachers, ensure that the policy is reasonable.
- Teachers have a right to practice their religion, but it cannot interfere with their duties.
- Do not dismiss a teacher based on his or her political, religious, or social affiliation with an organization.
- Teachers have a right to a private life. Clearly understand the laws that allow a public school to dismiss a teacher for acts outside of the classroom.

SUMMARY

Teachers, like students, have numerous Constitutional rights. However, this was not always the case. Traditionally, school teachers were considered role models and could be dismissed for almost any reason. Today, the laws are much broader granting teachers within the public school system rights including freedom of expression, freedom of religion, right to privacy, freedom of association, as well as protection under many federal statutes such as the Americans with Disabilities Act and the Equal Pay Act.

---

[25] 122 S.Ct. 681 (2002)

[26] Ibid., at 686

[27] Ibid., at 690

Of course, such rights are not inclusive, and, as the cases within the chapter illustrate, are in some situations limited. Regardless of the limitations, teachers, like students, do not leave their constitutional rights at the schoolhouse gates and have much more protection than they did in years past. Because of this, it is essential that administrators understand these rights and make decisions based within the boundaries of the law, and not on personal biases.

Discussion Questions

1. Discuss the idea of academic freedom and how it is interpreted in the public school system.
2. Is a teacher's dress a form of expression protected under the First Amendment? If so, is clothing as protected as length of hair is? Why?
3. Do community norms affect the way in which a teacher may dress? Do they affect the amount of academic freedom a teacher may have? Use examples to justify your responses.
4. Define public speech. Is it the only type of speech protected? Justify your response with case law.
5. Discuss, using examples, the *Pickering* balancing test.
6. Discuss the burden of proof in a case involving a teacher who is being dismissed or disciplined due to his or her speech?
7. Based on the decision in *East Hartford Education Association*, decide when a school district can restrict a teacher's dress and appearance. Use examples.
8. After reading *Hearn v. the Board of Public Education*, do you agree with the majority or the dissent? Justify your answer.
9. At what point during a pregnancy must a woman be required to take leave? What are the policy reasons for such decisions?
10. What is considered a reasonable accommodation according to the Americans with Disabilities Act?

Deepening Your Understanding

1. Using the resources in the appendix, define *reasonable accommodations* under the ADA. Using a method of legal research, look up a recent case that exemplifies a reasonable accommodation and an unreasonable one. (Note that some of the cases may not directly deal with education but are still pertinent to school law and the decisions that administrators may face when dealing with employees with disabilities.)
2. Using the resources in the appendix, learn what other federal regulations protect employees from employment discrimination.

8

Parents' Rights

Introduction

Parents have a constitutional right to raise and educate their children, but states have the right to ensure that children receive an education and can set policies and procedures concerning compulsory education and home schooling. Parents, however, have the right to choose to educate their child in public, charter, or private schools or at home.

In addition to remembering parents' legal rights, educators must remember that parents are highly concerned about their children. Hence, one of the easiest ways to practice preventive law is to keep the lines of communication open with parents: return phone calls, keep track of all contacts, and, most important, keep parents informed.

Family Educational Rights and Privacy Act

THE FAMILY Educational Rights and Privacy Act (FERPA), also known as the Buckley Amendment, was enacted by Congress in 1974 after pressure from groups that believed that students were being inaccurately categorized and stigmatized.[1] Information in students' records was not available to parents but was being distributed to outside agencies such as creditors, possible employers, and law enforcement agencies. FERPA was created in an attempt to keep students' records confidential and to protect students' right to privacy.

---

[1] *Merriken v. Cressman*, 364 F.Supp. 913 (1973)

The act ensures that parents, legal guardians, or students themselves (if over age 18 or enrolled in a postsecondary educational institution) shall have the right to inspect and review a student's records. Procedurally, each educational agency must establish appropriate procedures for granting a parent's request for access to education records. The act states that the school district must allow access within a reasonable period of time but wait no longer than 45 days from the time of the request.

In addition to complying with the due process procedures set forth within the act, educators, should take prompt action once parents request access to their child's records. Typically, an appointment is made; and parents, along with an administrator, go through the records together. Parents should not be left alone with the records, nor should they be required to interpret the content without proper communication and guidance. If the parent is dissatisfied with the information in the record, the school must make a hearing available in which parents can challenge the record's content to ensure that it is not inaccurate, misleading, or otherwise in violation of the student's privacy rights and provide an opportunity for the school to correct or delete any inappropriate data and insert a written explanation from the parents respecting its content.[2]

FERPA makes it clear that, other than directory information, students' records must be protected and held as confidential. This applies to individuals within the school system as well. According to the act, only those individuals who have a *legitimate educational interest* should have access to students' records. Individuals with such an interest would include the student's teachers or guidance counselors. To keep track of which individuals are viewing the student's record, the act mandates that educational institutions keep a log of everyone who receives access to such records. The log, which should be attached to the student's file, must indicate the party's name as well as his or her reason for viewing the file. The burden of proof is on the school to prove that the individual had a legitimate educational interest in obtaining the information. Such a high standard makes record keeping a priority in student records. They should be kept in a safe place where only a small number of individuals have access to them. Finally, all access must be used only for the purposes of ensuring the best possible education for the student.

Not all information is confidential. According to FERPA, a school district may release directory information, which includes the student's name, address, telephone listing, date and place of birth, major field of study, participation in officially recognized activities and sports, weight and height if the student is a member of an athletic team, dates of attendance, degrees and awards received, and the most recent previous educational agency or institution attended by the student. The school must publish a list of all directory information it plans to make public and then give adequate time for parents to object to the release of such information. According to the act, "No funds shall be made available under any applicable program to any educational agency or institution unless such agency or institution effectively informs the parents of students, or the students, if they are eighteen years of age or older, or are attending an institution of postsecondary

---

[2] 20 U.S.C.A. § 1232g

education, of the rights accorded them by this section."[3] Such notice can be given to parents in various ways. The most common method is through the student handbook, which is typically mailed to parents at the beginning of each school year. If the parents do not speak English, the information must be sent to them in their native language.

Best Practices

- Ensure that faculty and staff are trained to understand the laws of FERPA.

- Keep a log of all individuals who request access to student records and an explanation of their legitimate educational interest. Many institutions attach this log to the inside cover of a student's file.

- Limit access to student records. They should be kept in an administrative office to which only a small number of people have access.

- Ensure that annual notification is written in the parents' native language and explains their rights under FERPA.

- Insist that teachers do not deviate from their area of expertise when writing notes in students' files. For example, English teachers should not be writing notes about a student's mental capacity. Leave the medical analysis to the experts.

- Adhere to the truth but do not attempt to diagnose mental or physical disabilities without instructions from administration and the school psychologist.

GRADING

MANY teachers commonly allow students to grade each other's work and then read out the score to the class. The Owasso Independent School District in Oklahoma was recently confronted with this issue when a mother of three middle school students claimed that such an act violated FERPA. In 2002, the U.S. Supreme Court clarified the issue.

Owasso Independent School Dist. No. 1-011 v. Falvo
Supreme Court of the United States, 2002
534 U.S. 426

Justice Kennedy delivered the opinion of the Court.

Teachers sometimes ask students to score each other's tests, papers, and assignments as the teacher explains the correct answers to the entire class. Respondent contends this practice,

---

[3] 20 U.S.C. 1232g

which the parties refer to as peer grading, violates the Family Educational Rights and Privacy Act of 1974 (FERPA or Act). We took this case to resolve the issue.

I. Under FERPA, schools and educational agencies receiving federal financial assistance must comply with certain conditions. One condition specified in the Act is that sensitive information about students may not be released without parental consent. The Act states that federal funds are to be withheld from school districts that have "a policy or practice of permitting the release of education records (or personally identifiable information contained therein . . .) of students without the written consent of their parents." The phrase "education records" is defined, under the Act, as "records, files, documents, and other materials" containing information directly related to a student, which "are maintained by an educational agency or institution or by a person acting for such agency or institution." The definition of education records contains an exception for "records of instructional, supervisory, and administrative personnel . . . which are in the sole possession of the maker thereof and which are not accessible or revealed to any other person except a substitute." The precise question for us is whether peer-graded classroom work and assignments are education records.

Three of respondent Kristja J. Falvo's children are enrolled in Owasso Independent School District No. I-011, in a suburb of Tulsa, Oklahoma. The children's teachers, like many teachers in this country, use peer grading. In a typical case, the students exchange papers with each other and score them according to the teacher's instructions, then return the work to the student who prepared it. The teacher may ask the students to report their own scores. In this case it appears the student could either call out the score or walk to the teacher's desk and reveal it in confidence, though by that stage, of course, the score was known at least to the one other student who did the grading. Both the grading and the system of calling out the scores are in contention here.

Respondent claimed the peer grading embarrassed her children. She asked the school district to adopt a uniform policy banning peer grading and requiring teachers either to grade assignments themselves or at least to forbid students from grading papers other than their own. The school district declined to do so, and respondent brought a class action pursuant to Rev. Stat. § 1979, 42 U.S.C. § 1983, against the school district, Superintendent Dale Johnson, Assistant Superintendent Lynn Johnson, and Principal Rick Thomas (petitioners). Respondent alleged the school district's grading policy violated FERPA and other laws not relevant here. The United States District Court for the Northern District of Oklahoma granted summary judgment in favor of the school district's position. The court held that grades put on papers by another student are not, at that stage, records "maintained by an educational agency or institution or by a person acting for such agency or institution," and thus do not constitute "education records" under the Act. On this reasoning it ruled that peer grading does not violate FERPA.

The Court of Appeals for the Tenth Circuit reversed. FERPA is directed to the conditions schools must meet to receive federal funds, and as an initial matter the court considered whether the Act confers a private right of action upon students and parents if the conditions are not met. Despite the absence of an explicit authorization in the Act conferring a cause of action on private parties, the court held respondent could sue to enforce FERPA's terms under 42 U.S.C. § 1983. Turning to the merits, the Court of Appeals held that peer grading violates the Act. The grades marked by students on each other's work, it held, are education records protected by the statute, so the very act of grading was an impermissible release of the information to the student grader.

We granted certiorari to decide whether peer grading violates FERPA. Finding no violation of the Act, we reverse.

II.   At the outset, we note it is an open question whether FERPA provides private parties, like respondent, with a cause of action enforceable under § 1983. We have granted certiorari on this issue in another case. The parties, furthermore, did not contest the § 1983 issue before the Court of Appeals. That court raised the issue *sua sponte,* and petitioners did not seek certiorari on the question. We need not resolve the question here as it is our practice "to decide cases on the grounds raised and considered in the Court of Appeals and included in the question on which we granted certiorari." In these circumstances we assume, but without so deciding or expressing an opinion on the question, that private parties may sue an educational agency under § 1983 to enforce the provisions of FERPA here at issue. Though we leave open the § 1983 question, the Court has subject-matter jurisdiction because respondent's federal claim is not so "completely devoid of merit as not to involve a federal controversy." With these preliminary observations concluded, we turn to the merits.

The parties appear to agree that if an assignment becomes an education record the moment a peer grades it, then the grading, or at least the practice of asking students to call out their grades in class, would be an impermissible release of the records under § 1232g(b)(1). Without deciding the point, we assume for the purposes of our analysis that they are correct. The parties disagree, however, whether peer-graded assignments constitute education records at all. The papers do contain information directly related to a student, but they are records under the Act only when and if they "are maintained by an educational agency or institution or by a person acting for such agency or institution."

Petitioners, supported by the United States as *amicus curiae,* contend the definition covers only institutional records—namely, those materials retained in a permanent file as a matter of course. They argue that records "maintained by an educational agency or institution" generally would include final course grades, student grade point averages, standardized test scores, attendance records, counseling records, and records of disciplinary actions—but not student homework or classroom work.

Respondent, adopting the reasoning of the Court of Appeals, contends student-graded assignments fall within the definition of education records. That definition contains an exception for "records of instructional, supervisory, and administrative personnel . . . which are in the sole possession of the maker thereof and which are not accessible or revealed to any other person except a substitute." The Court of Appeals reasoned that if grade books are not education records, then it would have been unnecessary for Congress to enact the exception. Grade books and the grades within, the court concluded, are "maintained" by a teacher and so are covered by FERPA. The court recognized that teachers do not maintain the grades on individual student assignments until they have recorded the result in the grade books. It reasoned, however, that if Congress forbids teachers to disclose students' grades once written in a grade book, it makes no sense to permit the disclosure immediately beforehand. The court thus held that student graders maintain the grades until they are reported to the teacher.

The Court of Appeals' logic does not withstand scrutiny. Its interpretation, furthermore, would effect a drastic alteration of the existing allocation of responsibilities between States and the National Government in the operation of the Nation's schools. We would hesitate before interpreting the statute to effect such a substantial change in the balance of federalism unless that is the manifest purpose of the legislation. This principle guides our decision.

Two statutory indicators tell us that the Court of Appeals erred in concluding that an assignment satisfies the definition of education records as soon as it is graded by another student. First, the student papers are not, at that stage, "maintained" within the meaning of § 1232g(a)(4)(A). The ordinary meaning of the word "maintain" is "to keep in existence or continuance; preserve; retain." Even assuming the teacher's grade book is an education record—a point the parties contest and one we do not decide here—the score on a student-graded assignment is not "contained therein," § 1232g(b)(1), until the teacher records it. The teacher does not maintain the grade while students correct their peers' assignments or call out their own marks. Nor do the student graders maintain the grades within the meaning of § 1232g(a)(4)(A). The word "maintain" suggests FERPA records will be kept in a filing cabinet in a records room at the school or on a permanent secure database, perhaps even after the student is no longer enrolled. The student graders only handle assignments for a few moments as the teacher calls out the answers. It is fanciful to say they maintain the papers in the same way the registrar maintains a student's folder in a permanent file.

The Court of Appeals was further mistaken in concluding that each student grader is "a person acting for" an educational institution for purposes of § 1232g(a)(4)(A). The phrase "acting for" connotes agents of the school, such as teachers, administrators, and other school employees. Just as it does not accord with our usual understanding to say students are "acting for" an educational institution when they follow their teacher's direction to take a quiz, it is equally awkward to say students are "acting for" an educational institution when they follow their teacher's direction to score it. Correcting a classmate's work can be as much a part of the assignment as taking the test itself. It is a way to teach material again in a new context, and it helps show students how to assist and respect fellow pupils. By explaining the answers to the class as the students correct the papers, the teacher not only reinforces the lesson but also discovers whether the students have understood the material and are ready to move on. We do not think FERPA prohibits these educational techniques. We also must not lose sight of the fact that the phrase "by a person acting for [an educational] institution" modifies "maintain." Even if one were to agree students are acting for the teacher when they correct the assignment, that is different from saying they are acting for the educational institution in maintaining it.

Other sections of the statute support our interpretation. FERPA, for example, requires educational institutions to "maintain a record, kept with the education records of each student." This record must list those who have requested access to a student's education records and their reasons for doing so. The record of access "shall be available only to parents, [and] to the school official and his assistants who are responsible for the custody of such records."

Under the Court of Appeals' broad interpretation of education records, every teacher would have an obligation to keep a separate record of access for each student's assignments. Indeed, by that court's logic, even students who grade their own papers would bear the burden of maintaining records of access until they turned in the assignments. We doubt Congress would have imposed such a weighty administrative burden on every teacher, and certainly it would not have extended the mandate to students.

Also FERPA requires "a record" of access for each pupil. This single record must be kept "with the education records." This suggests Congress contemplated that education records would be kept in one place with a single record of access. By describing a "school official" and "his assistants" as the personnel responsible for the custody of the records, FERPA implies that education records are institutional records kept by a single central custodian, such as a registrar, not individual assignments handled by many student graders in their separate classrooms.

FERPA also requires recipients of federal funds to provide parents with a hearing at which they may contest the accuracy of their child's education records. The hearings must be conducted "in accordance with regulations of the Secretary," which in turn require adjudication by a disinterested official and the opportunity for parents to be represented by an attorney. It is doubtful Congress would have provided parents with this elaborate procedural machinery to challenge the accuracy of the grade on every spelling test and art project the child completes.

Respondent's construction of the term "education records" to cover student homework or classroom work would impose substantial burdens on teachers across the country. It would force all instructors to take time, which otherwise could be spent teaching and in preparation, to correct an assortment of daily student assignments. Respondent's view would make it much more difficult for teachers to give students immediate guidance. The interpretation respondent urges would force teachers to abandon other customary practices, such as group grading of team assignments. Indeed, the logical consequences of respondent's view are all but unbounded. At argument, counsel for respondent seemed to agree that if a teacher in any of the thousands of covered classrooms in the Nation puts a happy face, a gold star, or a disapproving remark on a classroom assignment, federal law does not allow other students to see it.

We doubt Congress meant to intervene in this drastic fashion with traditional state functions. Under the Court of Appeals' interpretation of FERPA, the federal power would exercise minute control over specific teaching methods and instructional dynamics in classrooms throughout the country. The Congress is not likely to have mandated this result, and we do not interpret the statute to require it.

For these reasons, even assuming a teacher's grade book is an education record, the Court of Appeals erred, for in all events the grades on students' papers would not be covered under FERPA at least until the teacher has collected them and recorded them in his or her grade book. We limit our holding to this narrow point, and do not decide the broader question whether the grades on individual student assignments, once they are turned in to teachers, are protected by the Act.

The judgment of the Court of Appeals is reversed, and the case is remanded for further proceedings consistent with this opinion.

It is so ordered. Concur by Justice Scalia.

The 9-to-0 decision held that peer grading does not violate FERPA. Recognizing teachers' time constraints, the Court determined that the grading of assignments were not protected. The holding is very narrow, however, and does not permit teachers to hang grades on their door or allow students the right to know other students' class grades. Such information is still protected under FERPA.

Best Practices

- Teachers are permitted to ask children to grade each other's assignments, but class grades are still protected under FERPA and should be kept confidential.

- Do not permit test scores or overall grades to be posted on doors or walls, even if you are using Social Security numbers. Such information is private and should not be made public.

ALTERNATIVE SCHOOLING

TODAY, parents have choices about how to educate their children. The public school system is available, but there are also alternatives: charter schools, private schools, and home schooling. According to the Tenth Amendment, public schools are run by the states and are considered arms of the state. Hence, they must abide by both the U.S. Constitution and all federal laws. Because charter schools are a fairly new type of institution, there have been few cases that set forth the laws these schools must follow. Private schools that do not receive federal funding must still abide by the law but are not considered an arm of the state so need not abide by the Constitution. The laws pertaining to home-schooled students vary depending on the state. Some states have very strict requirements, while others have lenient ones.

Pierce v. Society of Sisters allowed parents the right to choose which type of school they want their children to attend.[4] In its decision, the Court confirmed the idea of compulsory education, the rights of parents to choose, and the rights of the state to ensure that all students receive an appropriate education, regardless of the type of school a student attends.

Pierce v. Society of Sisters
Supreme Court of the United States, 1925
268 U.S. 510

Mr. Justice McReynolds delivered the opinion of the Court.

These appeals are from decrees, based upon undenied allegations, which granted preliminary orders restraining appellants from threatening or attempting to enforce the Compulsory

---

[4] 268 U.S. 510 (1925)

Education Act adopted November 7, 1922, under the initiative provision of her Constitution by the voters of Oregon. They present the same points of law; there are no controverted questions of fact. Rights said to be guaranteed by the federal Constitution were specially set up, and appropriate prayers asked for their protection.

The challenged Act, effective September 1, 1926, requires every parent, guardian or other person having control or charge or custody of a child between eight and sixteen years to send him "to a public school for the period of time a public school shall be held during the current year" in the district where the child resides; and failure so to do is declared a misdemeanor. There are exemptions—not specially important here—for children who are not normal, or who have completed the eighth grade, or who reside at considerable distances from any public school, or whose parents or guardians hold special permits from the County Superintendent. The manifest purpose is to compel general attendance at public schools by normal children, between eight and sixteen, who have not completed the eighth grade. And without doubt enforcement of the statute would seriously impair, perhaps destroy, the profitable features of appellees' business and greatly diminish the value of their property.

Appellee, the Society of Sisters, is an Oregon corporation, organized in 1880, with power to care for orphans, educate and instruct the youth, establish and maintain academies or schools, and acquire necessary real and personal property. It has long devoted its property and effort to the secular and religious education and care of children, and has acquired the valuable good will of many parents and guardians. It conducts interdependent primary and high schools and junior colleges, and maintains orphanages for the custody and control of children between eight and sixteen. In its primary schools many children between those ages are taught the subjects usually pursued in Oregon public schools during the first eight years. Systematic religious instruction and moral training according to the tenets of the Roman Catholic Church are also regularly provided. All courses of study, both temporal and religious, contemplate continuity of training under appellee's charge; the primary schools are essential to the system and the most profitable. It owns valuable buildings, especially constructed and equipped for school purposes. The business is remunerative—the annual income from primary schools exceeds thirty thousand dollars—and the successful conduct of this requires long time contracts with teachers and parents. The Compulsory Education Act of 1922 has already caused the withdrawal from its schools of children who would otherwise continue, and their income has steadily declined. The appellants, public officers, have proclaimed their purpose strictly to enforce the statute.

After setting out the above facts the Society's bill alleges that the enactment conflicts with the right of parents to choose schools where their children will receive appropriate mental and religious training, the right of the child to influence the parents' choice of a school, the right of schools and teachers therein to engage in a useful business or profession, and is accordingly repugnant to the Constitution and void. And, further, that unless enforcement of the measure is enjoined the corporation's business and property will suffer irreparable injury.

Appellee, Hill Military Academy, is a private corporation organized in 1908 under the laws of Oregon, engaged in owning, operating and conducting for profit an elementary, college preparatory and military training school for boys between the ages of five and twenty-one years. The average attendance is one hundred, and the annual fees received for each student amount to some eight hundred dollars. The elementary department is divided into eight grades, as in the public schools; the college preparatory department has four grades, similar to those of the public high schools; the courses of study conform to the requirements of the State Board of Education. Military instruction and training are also given, under the supervision of an Army officer. It owns considerable real and personal property, some useful only for school purposes. The business and incident good will are very valuable. In order to conduct its affairs long time contracts must be made for supplies, equipment, teachers and pupils. Appellants, law officers of the State and County, have publicly announced that the Act of November 7, 1922, is valid and have declared their intention to enforce it. By reason of the statute and threat of enforcement appellee's business is being destroyed and its property depreciated; parents and guardians are refusing to make contracts for the future instruction of their sons, and some are being withdrawn.

The Academy's bill states the foregoing facts and then alleges that the challenged Act contravenes the corporation's rights guaranteed by the Fourteenth Amendment and that unless appellants are restrained from proclaiming its validity and threatening to enforce it irreparable injury will result. The prayer is for an appropriate injunction.

No answer was interposed in either cause, and after proper notices they were heard by three judges on motions for preliminary injunctions upon the specifically alleged facts. The court ruled that the Fourteenth Amendment guaranteed appellees against the deprivation of their property without due process of law consequent upon the unlawful interference by appellants with the free choice of patrons, present and prospective. It declared the right to conduct schools was property and that parents and guardians, as a part of their liberty, might direct the education of children by selecting reputable teachers and places. Also, that these schools were not unfit or harmful to the public, and that enforcement of the challenged statute would unlawfully deprive them of patronage and thereby destroy their owners' business and property. Finally, that the threats to enforce the Act would continue to cause irreparable injury; and the suits were not premature.

No question is raised concerning the power of the State reasonably to regulate all schools, to inspect, supervise and examine them, their teachers and pupils; to require that all children of proper age attend some school, that teachers shall be of good moral character and patriotic disposition, that certain studies plainly essential to good citizenship must be taught, and that nothing be taught which is manifestly inimical to the public welfare.

The inevitable practical result of enforcing the Act under consideration would be destruction of appellees' primary schools, and perhaps all other private primary schools for normal children within the State of Oregon. These parties are engaged in a kind of undertaking not inherently harmful, but long regarded as useful and meritorious. Certainly there is nothing in the present records to indicate that they have failed to discharge their obligations to patrons, students or the State. And there are no peculiar circumstances or present emergencies which demand extraordinary measures relative to primary education.

Under the doctrine of *Meyer v. Nebraska,* we think it entirely plain that the Act of 1922 unreasonably interferes with the liberty of parents and guardians to direct the upbringing and education of children under their control. As often heretofore pointed out, rights guaranteed by the Constitution may not be abridged by legislation which has no reasonable relation to some purpose within the competency of the State. The fundamental theory of liberty upon which all governments in this Union repose excludes any general power of the State to standardize its children by forcing them to accept instruction from public teachers only. The child is not the mere creature of the State; those who nurture him and direct his destiny have the right, coupled with the high duty, to recognize and prepare him for additional obligations.

Appellees are corporations and therefore, it is said, they cannot claim for themselves the liberty which the Fourteenth Amendment guarantees. Accepted in the proper sense, this is true. But they have business and property for which they claim protection. These are threatened with destruction through the unwarranted compulsion which appellants are exercising over present and prospective patrons of their schools. And this court has gone very far to protect against loss threatened by such action. . . .

Generally it is entirely true, as urged by counsel, that no person in any business has such an interest in possible customers as to enable him to restrain exercise of proper power of the State upon the ground that he will be deprived of patronage. But the injunctions here sought are not against the exercise of any proper power. Plaintiffs asked protection against arbitrary, unreasonable and unlawful interference with their patrons and the consequent destruction of their business and property. Their interest is clear and immediate, within the rule approved in . . . many cases where injunctions have issued to protect business enterprises against interference with the freedom of patrons or customers.

The suits were not premature. The injury to appellees was present and very real, not a mere possibility in the remote future. If no relief had been possible prior to the effective date of the Act, the injury would have become irreparable. Prevention of impending injury by unlawful action is a well recognized function of courts of equity.

The decrees below are affirmed.

The 1925 decision gave private schools the right to exist and parents the right to choose where they sent their children to obtain an education. Regardless of the type of school a child attends, the government requires some form of compulsory education. Based on the doctrine of parent's partriae, the state sets the laws to protect those who cannot protect themselves—children. The laws that pertain to education commonly balance the rights of the parents to raise their children as they see fit and the state's interest in ensuring that children receive an appropriate education.

Each state has mandated compulsory education. Depending on a state's specific law, the ages covered range from 6 to 18, with some exceptions. However there is one notable exception which arose from the Supreme Court's decision in *Wisconsin v. Yoder.*

Wisconsin v. Yoder

Supreme Court of the United States, 1972

406 U.S. 205

Mr. Chief Justice Burger delivered the opinion of the Court.

On petition of the State of Wisconsin, we granted the writ of certiorari in this case to review a decision of the Wisconsin Supreme Court holding that respondents' convictions of violating the State's compulsory school-attendance law were invalid under the Free Exercise Clause of the First Amendment to the United States Constitution made applicable to the States by the Fourteenth Amendment. For the reasons hereafter stated we affirm the judgment of the Supreme Court of Wisconsin.

Respondents Jonas Yoder and Wallace Miller are members of the Old Order Amish religion, and respondent Adin Yutzy is a member of the Conservative Amish Mennonite Church. They and their families are residents of Green County, Wisconsin. Wisconsin's compulsory school-attendance law required them to cause their children to attend public or private school until reaching age 16 but the respondents declined to send their children, ages 14 and 15, to public school after they completed the eighth grade. The children were not enrolled in any private school, or within any recognized exception to the compulsory-attendance law, and they are conceded to be subject to the Wisconsin statute.

On complaint of the school district administrator for the public schools, respondents were charged, tried, and convicted of violating the compulsory-attendance law in Green County Court and were fined the sum of $5 each. Respondents defended on the ground that the application of the compulsory-attendance law violated their rights under the First and Fourteenth Amendments. The trial testimony showed that respondents believed, in accordance with the tenets of Old Order Amish communities generally, that their children's attendance at high school, public or private, was contrary to the Amish religion and way of life. They believed that by sending their children to high school, they would not only expose themselves to the danger of the censure of the church community, but, as found by the county court, also endanger their own salvation and that of their children. The State stipulated that respondents' religious beliefs were sincere.

In support of their position, respondents presented as expert witnesses scholars on religion and education whose testimony is uncontradicted. They expressed their opinions on the relationship of the Amish belief concerning school attendance to the more general tenets of their religion, and described the impact that compulsory high school attendance could have on the continued survival of Amish communities as they exist in the United States today. The history of the Amish sect was given in some detail, beginning with the Swiss Anabaptists of the 16th century who rejected institutionalized churches and sought to return to the early, simple, Christian life de-emphasizing material success, rejecting the competitive spirit, and seeking to insulate themselves from the modern world. As a result of their common heritage, Old Order Amish communities today are characterized by a fundamental belief that salvation requires life in a church community separate and apart from the world and worldly influence. This concept of life aloof from the world and its values is central to their faith.

A related feature of Old Order Amish communities is their devotion to a life in harmony with nature and the soil, as exemplified by the simple life of the early Christian era that continued in America during much of our early national life. Amish beliefs require members of the community to make their living by farming or closely related activities. Broadly speaking, the Old Order Amish religion pervades and determines the entire mode of life of its adherents. Their conduct is regulated in great detail by the Ordnung, or rules, of the church community. Adult baptism, which occurs in late adolescence, is the time at which Amish young people voluntarily undertake heavy obligations, not unlike the Bar Mitzvah of the Jews, to abide by the rules of the church community.

Amish objection to formal education beyond the eighth grade is firmly grounded in these central religious concepts. They object to the high school, and higher education generally, because the values they teach are in marked variance with Amish values and the Amish way of life; they view secondary school education as an impermissible exposure of their children to a "worldly" influence in conflict with their beliefs. The high school tends to emphasize intellectual and scientific accomplishments, self-distinction, competitiveness, worldly success, and social life with other students. Amish society emphasizes informal learning-through-doing; a life of "goodness," rather than a life of intellect; wisdom, rather than technical knowledge; community welfare, rather than competition; and separation from, rather than integration with, contemporary worldly society.

Formal high school education beyond the eighth grade is contrary to Amish beliefs, not only because it places Amish children in an environment hostile to Amish beliefs with increasing emphasis on competition in class work and sports and with pressure to conform to the styles, manners, and ways of the peer group, but also because it takes them away from their community, physically and emotionally, during the crucial and formative adolescent period of life. During this period, the children must acquire Amish attitudes favoring manual work and self-reliance and the specific skills needed to perform the adult role of an Amish farmer or housewife. They must learn to enjoy physical labor. Once a child has learned basic reading, writing, and elementary mathematics, these traits, skills, and attitudes admittedly fall within the category of those best learned through example and "doing" rather than in a classroom. And, at this time in life, the Amish child must also grow in his faith and his relationship to the Amish community if he is to be prepared to accept the heavy obligations imposed by adult baptism. In short, high school attendance with teachers who are not of the Amish faith—and may even be hostile to it—interposes a serious barrier to the integration of the Amish child into the Amish religious community. Dr. John Hostetler, one of the experts on Amish society, testified that the modern high school is not equipped, in curriculum or social environment, to impart the values promoted by Amish society.

The Amish do not object to elementary education through the first eight grades as a general proposition because they agree that their children must have basic skills in the "three R's" in order to read the Bible, to be good farmers and citizens, and to be able to deal with non-Amish people when necessary in the course of daily affairs. They view such a basic education as acceptable because it does not significantly expose their children to worldly values or interfere with their development in the Amish community during the crucial adolescent period. While Amish accept compulsory elementary education generally, wherever possible they have established their own elementary schools in many respects like the small local schools of the past. In the Amish belief higher learning tends to develop values they reject as influences that alienate man from God.

On the basis of such considerations, Dr. Hostetler testified that compulsory high school attendance could not only result in great psychological harm to Amish children, because of the conflicts it would produce, but would also, in his opinion, ultimately result in the destruction of the Old Order Amish church community as it exists in the United States today. The testimony of Dr. Donald A. Erickson, an expert witness on education, also showed that the Amish succeed in preparing their high school age children to be productive members of the Amish community. He described their system of learning through doing the skills directly relevant to their adult roles in the Amish community as "ideal" and perhaps superior to ordinary high school education. The evidence also showed that the Amish have an excellent record as law-abiding and generally self-sufficient members of society.

Although the trial court in its careful findings determined that the Wisconsin compulsory school-attendance law "does interfere with the freedom of the Defendants to act in accordance with their sincere religious belief" it also concluded that the requirement of high school attendance until age 16 was a "reasonable and constitutional" exercise of governmental power, and therefore denied the motion to dismiss the charges. The Wisconsin Circuit Court affirmed the convictions. The Wisconsin Supreme Court, however, sustained respondents' claim under the Free Exercise Clause of the First Amendment and reversed the convictions. A majority of the court was of the opinion that the State had failed to make an adequate showing that its interest in "establishing and maintaining an educational system overrides the defendants' right to the free exercise of their religion.

I

There is no doubt as to the power of a State, having a high responsibility for education of its citizens, to impose reasonable regulations for the control and duration of basic education. Providing public schools ranks at the very apex of the function of a State. Yet even this paramount responsibility was, in Pierce, made to yield to the right of parents to provide an equivalent education in a privately operated system. There the Court held that Oregon's statute compelling attendance in a public school from age eight to age 16 unreasonably interfered with the interest of parents in directing the rearing of their offspring, including their education in church-operated schools. As that case suggests, the values of parental direction of the religious upbringing and education of their children in their early and formative years have a high place in our society. Thus, a State's interest in universal education, however highly we rank it, is not totally free from a balancing process when it impinges on fundamental rights and interests, such as those specifically protected by the Free Exercise Clause of the First Amendment, and the traditional interest of parents with respect to the religious upbringing of their children so long as they, in the words of Pierce, "prepare [them] for additional obligations."

It follows that in order for Wisconsin to compel school attendance beyond the eighth grade against a claim that such attendance interferes with the practice of a legitimate religious belief, it must appear either that the State does not deny the free exercise of religious belief by its requirement, or that there is a state interest of sufficient magnitude to override the interest claiming protection under the Free Exercise Clause. Long before there was general acknowledgment of the need for universal formal education, the Religion Clauses had specifically and firmly fixed the right to free exercise of religious beliefs, and buttressing this fundamental right was an equally firm, even if less explicit, prohibition against the establishment of any religion by government. The values underlying these two provisions relating to religion have been zealously protected, sometimes even at the expense of other interests of admittedly high social importance. The invalidation of financial aid to parochial schools by government grants for a salary subsidy for teachers is but one example of the extent to which courts have gone in this regard, notwithstanding that such aid programs were legislatively determined to be in the public interest and the service of sound educational policy by States and by Congress. . . .

II

We come then to the quality of the claims of the respondents concerning the alleged encroachment of Wisconsin's compulsory school-attendance statute on their rights and the rights of their children to the free exercise of the religious beliefs they and their forebears have adhered to for almost three centuries. In evaluating those claims we must be careful to determine whether the Amish religious faith and their mode of life are, as they claim, inseparable and interdependent. A way of life, however virtuous and admirable, may not be interposed as a barrier to reasonable state regulation of education if it is based on purely secular considerations; to have the protection of the Religion Clauses, the claims must be rooted in religious belief. Although a determination of what is a "religious" belief or practice entitled to constitutional protection may present a most delicate question, the very concept of ordered liberty precludes allowing every person to make his own standards on matters of conduct in which society as a whole has important interests. Thus, if the Amish asserted their claims because of their subjective evaluation and rejection of the contemporary secular values accepted by the majority, much as Thoreau rejected the social values of his time and isolated himself at Walden Pond, their claims would not rest on a religious basis. Thoreau's choice was philosophical and personal rather than religious, and such belief does not rise to the demands of the Religion Clauses.

Giving no weight to such secular considerations, however, we see that the record in this case abundantly supports the claim that the traditional way of life of the Amish is not merely a matter of personal preference, but one of deep religious conviction, shared by an organized group, and intimately related to daily living. That the Old Order Amish daily life and religious practice stem from their faith is shown by the fact that it is in response to their literal interpretation of the Biblical injunction from the Epistle of Paul to the Romans, "be not conformed to this world. . . . " This command is fundamental to the Amish faith. Moreover, for the Old Order Amish, religion is not simply a matter of theocratic belief. As the expert witnesses explained, the Old Order Amish religion pervades and determines virtually their entire way of life, regulating it with the detail of the Talmudic diet through the strictly enforced rules of the church community.

The record shows that the respondents' religious beliefs and attitude toward life, family, and home have remained constant—perhaps some would say static—in a period of unparalleled progress in human knowledge generally and great changes in education. The respondents freely concede, and indeed assert as an article of faith, that their religious beliefs and what we would today call "life style" have not altered in fundamentals for centuries. Their way of life in a church-oriented community, separated from the outside world and "worldly" influences, their attachment to nature and the soil, is a way inherently simple and uncomplicated, albeit difficult to preserve against the pressure to conform. Their rejection of telephones, automobiles, radios, and television, their mode of dress, of speech, their habits of manual work do indeed set them apart from much of contemporary society; these customs are both symbolic and practical.

As the society around the Amish has become more populous, urban, industrialized, and complex, particularly in this century, government regulation of human affairs has correspondingly become more detailed and pervasive. The Amish mode of life has thus come into conflict increasingly with requirements of contemporary society exerting a hydraulic insistence on conformity to majoritarian standards. So long as compulsory education laws were confined to eight grades of elementary basic education imparted in a nearby rural schoolhouse, with a large proportion of students of the Amish faith, the Old Order Amish had little basis to fear that school attendance would expose their children to the worldly influence they reject. But modern compulsory secondary education in rural areas is now largely carried on in a consolidated school, often remote from the student's home and alien to his daily home life. As the record so strongly shows, the values and programs of the modern secondary school are in sharp conflict with the fundamental mode of life mandated by the Amish religion; modern laws requiring compulsory secondary education have accordingly engendered great concern and conflict. The conclusion is inescapable that secondary schooling, by exposing Amish children to worldly influences in terms of attitudes, goals, and values contrary to beliefs, and by substantially interfering with the religious development of the Amish child and his integration into the way of life of the Amish faith community at the crucial adolescent stage of development, contravenes the basic religious tenets and practice of the Amish faith, both as to the parent and the child.

The impact of the compulsory-attendance law on respondents' practice of the Amish religion is not only severe, but inescapable, for the Wisconsin law affirmatively compels them, under threat of criminal sanction, to perform acts undeniably at odds with fundamental tenets of their religious beliefs. Nor is the impact of the compulsory-attendance law confined to grave interference with important Amish religious tenets from a subjective point of view. It carries with it precisely the kind of objective danger to the free exercise of religion that the First Amendment was designed to prevent. As the record shows, compulsory school attendance to age 16 for Amish children carries with it a very real threat of undermining the Amish community and religious practice as they exist today; they must either abandon belief and be assimilated into society at large, or be forced to migrate to some other and more tolerant region.

In sum, the unchallenged testimony of acknowledged experts in education and religious history, almost 300 years of consistent practice, and strong evidence of a sustained faith pervading and regulating respondents' entire mode of life support the claim that enforcement of the State's requirement of compulsory formal education after the eighth grade would gravely endanger if not destroy the free exercise of respondents' religious beliefs.

III

Neither the findings of the trial court nor the Amish claims as to the nature of their faith are challenged in this Court by the State of Wisconsin. Its position is that the State's interest in universal compulsory formal secondary education to age 16 is so great that it is paramount to the undisputed claims of respondents that their mode of preparing their youth for Amish life, after the traditional elementary education, is an essential part of their religious belief and practice. Nor does the State undertake to meet the claim that the Amish mode of life and education is inseparable from and a part of the basic tenets of their religion—indeed, as much a part of their religious belief and practices as baptism, the confessional, or a sabbath may be for others.

Wisconsin concedes that under the Religion Clauses religious beliefs are absolutely free from the State's control, but it argues that "actions," even though religiously grounded, are outside the protection of the First Amendment. But our decisions have rejected the idea that religiously grounded conduct is always outside the protection of the Free Exercise Clause. It is true that activities of individuals, even when religiously based, are often subject to regulation by the States in the exercise of their undoubted power to promote the health, safety, and general welfare, or the Federal Government in the exercise of its delegated powers. But to agree that religiously grounded conduct must often be subject to the broad police power of the State is not to deny that there are areas of conduct protected by the Free Exercise Clause of the First Amendment and thus beyond the power of the State to control, even under regulations of general applicability. . . .

Nor can this case be disposed of on the grounds that Wisconsin's requirement for school attendance to age 16 applies uniformly to all citizens of the State and does not, on its face, discriminate against religions or a particular religion, or that it is motivated by legitimate secular concerns. A regulation neutral on its face may, in its application, nonetheless offend the constitutional requirement for governmental neutrality if it unduly burdens the free exercise of religion. . . .

We turn, then, to the State's broader contention that its interest in its system of compulsory education is so compelling that even the established religious practices of the Amish must give way. Where fundamental claims of religious freedom are at stake, however, we cannot accept such a sweeping claim; despite its admitted validity in the generality of cases, we must searchingly examine the interests that the State seeks to promote by its requirement for compulsory education to age 16, and the impediment to those objectives that would flow from recognizing the claimed Amish exemption.

The State advances two primary arguments in support of its system of compulsory education. It notes, as Thomas Jefferson pointed out early in our history, that some degree of education is necessary to prepare citizens to participate effectively and intelligently in our open political system if we are to preserve freedom and independence. Further, education prepares individuals to be self-reliant and self-sufficient participants in society. We accept these propositions.

However, the evidence adduced by the Amish in this case is persuasively to the effect that an additional one or two years of formal high school for Amish children in place of their long-established program of informal vocational education would do little to serve those interests. Respondents' experts testified at trial, without challenge, that the value of all education must be assessed in terms of its capacity to prepare the child for life. It is one thing to say that compulsory education for a year or two beyond the eighth grade may be necessary when its goal is the preparation of the child for life in modern society as the majority live, but it is quite another if the goal of education be viewed as the preparation of the child for life in the separated agrarian community that is the keystone of the Amish faith.

The State attacks respondents' position as one fostering "ignorance" from which the child must be protected by the State. No one can question the State's duty to protect children from ignorance but this argument does not square with the facts disclosed in the record. Whatever their idiosyncrasies as seen by the majority, this record strongly shows that the Amish community has been a highly successful social unit within our society, even if apart from the conventional "mainstream." Its members are productive and very law-abiding members of society; they reject public welfare in any of its usual modern forms. The Congress itself recognized their self-sufficiency by authorizing exemption of such groups as the Amish from the obligation to pay social security taxes.

It is neither fair nor correct to suggest that the Amish are opposed to education beyond the eighth grade level. What this record shows is that they are opposed to conventional formal education of the type provided by a certified high school because it comes at the child's crucial adolescent period of religious development. Dr. Donald Erickson, for example, testified that their system of learning-by-doing was an "ideal system" of education in terms of preparing Amish children for life as adults in the Amish community, and that "I would be inclined to say they do a better job in this than most of the rest of us do." As he put it, "These people aren't purporting to be learned people, and it seems to me the self-sufficiency of the community is the best evidence I can point to—whatever is being done seems to function well."

We must not forget that in the Middle Ages important values of the civilization of the Western World were preserved by members of religious orders who isolated themselves from all worldly influences against great obstacles. There can be no assumption that today's majority is "right" and the Amish and others like them are "wrong." A way of life that is odd or even erratic but interferes with no rights or interests of others is not to be condemned because it is different.

The State, however, supports its interest in providing an additional one or two years of compulsory high school education to Amish children because of the possibility that some such children will choose to leave the Amish community, and that if this occurs they will be ill-equipped for life. The State argues that if Amish children leave their church they should not be in the position of making their way in the world without the education available in the one or two additional years the State requires. However, on this record, that argument is highly speculative. There is no specific evidence of the loss of Amish adherents by attrition, nor is there any showing that upon leaving the Amish community Amish children, with their practical agricultural training and habits of industry and self-reliance, would become burdens on society because of educational short-comings. Indeed, this argument of the State appears to rest primarily on the State's mistaken assumption, already noted, that the Amish do not provide any education for their children beyond the eighth grade, but allow them to grow in "ignorance." To the contrary, not only do the Amish accept the necessity for formal schooling through the eighth grade level, but continue to provide what has been character-ized by the undisputed testimony of expert educators as an "ideal" vocational education for their children in the adolescent years.

There is nothing in this record to suggest that the Amish qualities of reliability, self-reliance, and dedication to work would fail to find ready markets in today's society. Absent some contrary evidence supporting the State's position, we are unwilling to assume that persons possessing such valuable vocational skills and habits are doomed to become bur-dens on society should they determine to leave the Amish faith, nor is there any basis in the record to warrant a finding that an additional one or two years of formal school education beyond the eighth grade would serve to eliminate any such problem that might exist.

Insofar as the State's claim rests on the view that a brief additional period of formal ed-ucation is imperative to enable the Amish to participate effectively and intelligently in our democratic process, it must fall. The Amish alternative to formal secondary school education has enabled them to function effectively in their day-to-day life under self-imposed limita-tions on relations with the world, and to survive and prosper in contemporary society as a separate, sharply identifiable and highly self-sufficient community for more than 200 years in this country. In itself this is strong evidence that they are capable of fulfilling the social and political responsibilities of citizenship without compelled attendance beyond the eighth grade at the price of jeopardizing their free exercise of religious belief. When Thomas Jefferson emphasized the need for education as a bulwark of a free people against tyranny, there is nothing to indicate he had in mind compulsory education through any fixed age beyond a basic education. Indeed, the Amish communities singularly parallel and reflect many of the virtues of Jefferson's ideal of the "sturdy yeoman" who would form the basis of what he considered as the ideal of a democratic society. Even their idiosyncratic sep-arateness exemplifies the diversity we profess to admire and encourage.

The requirement for compulsory education beyond the eighth grade is a relatively recent development in our history. Less than 60 years ago, the educational requirements of almost all of the States were satisfied by completion of the elementary grades, at least where the child was regularly and lawfully employed. The independence and successful social func-tioning of the Amish community for a period approaching almost three centuries and more than 200 years in this country are strong evidence that there is at best a speculative gain, in terms of meeting the duties of citizenship, from an additional one or two years of compul-sory formal education. Against this background it would require a more particularized showing from the State on this point to justify the severe interference with religious free-dom such additional compulsory attendance would entail.

We should also note that compulsory education and child labor laws find their historical origin in common humanitarian instincts, and that the age limits of both laws have been coordinated to achieve their related objectives. In the context of this case, such considerations, if anything, support rather than detract from respondents' position. The origins of the requirement for school attendance to age 16, an age falling after the completion of elementary school but before completion of high school, are not entirely clear. But to some extent such laws reflected the movement to prohibit most child labor under age 16 that culminated in the provisions of the Federal Fair Labor Standards Act of 1938. It is true, then, that the 16-year child labor age limit may to some degree derive from a contemporary impression that children should be in school until that age. But at the same time, it cannot be denied that, conversely, the 16-year education limit reflects, in substantial measure, the concern that children under that age not be employed under conditions hazardous to their health, or in work that should be performed by adults.

The requirement of compulsory schooling to age 16 must therefore be viewed as aimed not merely at providing educational opportunities for children, but as an alternative to the equally undesirable consequence of unhealthful child labor displacing adult workers, or, on the other hand, forced idleness. The two kinds of statutes—compulsory school attendance and child labor laws—tend to keep children of certain ages off the labor market and in school; this regimen in turn provides opportunity to prepare for a livelihood of a higher order than that which children could pursue without education and protects their health in adolescence.

In these terms, Wisconsin's interest in compelling the school attendance of Amish children to age 16 emerges as somewhat less substantial than requiring such attendance for children generally. For, while agricultural employment is not totally outside the legitimate concerns of the child labor laws, employment of children under parental guidance and on the family farm from age 14 to age 16 is an ancient tradition that lies at the periphery of the objectives of such laws. There is no intimation that the Amish employment of their children on family farms is in any way deleterious to their health or that Amish parents exploit children at tender years. Any such inference would be contrary to the record before us. Moreover, employment of Amish children on the family farm does not present the undesirable economic aspects of eliminating jobs that might otherwise be held by adults.

IV

Finally, the State, on authority of *Prince v. Massachusetts,* argues that a decision exempting Amish children from the State's requirement fails to recognize the substantive right of the Amish child to a secondary education, and fails to give due regard to the power of the State as parens patriae to extend the benefit of secondary education to children regardless of the wishes of their parents. Taken at its broadest sweep, the Court's language in *Prince* might be read to give support to the State's position. However, the Court was not confronted in *Prince* with a situation comparable to that of the Amish as revealed in this record; this is shown by the Court's severe characterization of the evils that it thought the legislature could legitimately associate with child labor, even when performed in the company of an adult. . . .

This case, of course, is not one in which any harm to the physical or mental health of the child or to the public safety, peace, order, or welfare has been demonstrated or may be properly inferred. The record is to the contrary, and any reliance on that theory would find no support in the evidence. . . .

Indeed it seems clear that if the State is empowered, as parens patriae, to "save" a child from himself or his Amish parents by requiring an additional two years of compulsory formal high school education, the State will in large measure influence, if not determine, the religious future of the child. Even more markedly than in *Prince*, therefore, this case involves the fundamental interest of parents, as contrasted with that of the State, to guide the religious future and education of their children. The history and culture of Western civilization reflect a strong tradition of parental concern for the nurture and upbringing of their children. This primary role of the parents in the upbringing of their children is now established beyond debate as an enduring American tradition. . . .

The duty to prepare the child for "additional obligations," referred to by the Court, must be read to include the inculcation of moral standards, religious beliefs, and elements of good citizenship. *Pierce*, of course, recognized that where nothing more than the general interest of the parent in the nurture and education of his children is involved, it is beyond dispute that the State acts "reasonably" and constitutionally in requiring education to age 16 in some public or private school meeting the standards prescribed by the State.

However read, the Court's holding in *Pierce* stands as a charter of the rights of parents to direct the religious upbringing of their children. And, when the interests of parenthood are combined with a free exercise claim of the nature revealed by this record, more than merely a "reasonable relation to some purpose within the competency of the State" is required to sustain the validity of the State's requirement under the First Amendment. To be sure, the power of the parent, even when linked to a free exercise claim, may be subject to limitation under *Prince* if it appears that parental decisions will jeopardize the health or safety of the child, or have a potential for significant social burdens. But in this case, the Amish have introduced persuasive evidence undermining the arguments the State has advanced to support its claims in terms of the welfare of the child and society as a whole. The record strongly indicates that accommodating the religious objections of the Amish by forgoing one, or at most two, additional years of compulsory education will not impair the physical or mental health of the child, or result in an inability to be self-supporting or to discharge the duties and responsibilities of citizenship, or in any other way materially detract from the welfare of society.

In the face of our consistent emphasis on the central values underlying the Religion Clauses in our constitutional scheme of government, we cannot accept a parens patriae claim of such all-encompassing scope and with such sweeping potential for broad and unforeseeable application as that urged by the State.

V

For the reasons stated we hold, with the Supreme Court of Wisconsin, that the First and Fourteenth Amendments prevent the State from compelling respondents to cause their children to attend formal high school to age 16. Our disposition of this case, however, in no way alters our recognition of the obvious fact that courts are not school boards or legislatures, and are ill-equipped to determine the "necessity" of discrete aspects of a State's program of compulsory education. This should suggest that courts must move with great circumspection in performing the sensitive and delicate task of weighing a State's legitimate social concern when faced with religious claims for exemption from generally applicable educational requirements. It cannot be overemphasized that we are not dealing with a way of life and mode of education by a group claiming to have recently discovered some "progressive" or more enlightened process for rearing children for modern life.

Aided by a history of three centuries as an identifiable religious sect and a long history as a successful and self-sufficient segment of American society, the Amish in this case have convincingly demonstrated the sincerity of their religious beliefs, the interrelationship of belief with their mode of life, the vital role that belief and daily conduct play in the continued survival of Old Order Amish communities and their religious organization, and the hazards presented by the State's enforcement of a statute generally valid as to others. Beyond this, they have carried the even more difficult burden of demonstrating the adequacy of their alternative mode of continuing informal vocational education in terms of precisely those overall interests that the State advances in support of its program of compulsory high school education. In light of this convincing showing, one that probably few other religious groups or sects could make, and weighing the minimal difference between what the State would require and what the Amish already accept, it was incumbent on the State to show with more particularity how its admittedly strong interest in compulsory education would be adversely affected by granting an exemption to the Amish.

Nothing we hold is intended to undermine the general applicability of the State's compulsory school-attendance statutes or to limit the power of the State to promulgate reasonable standards that, while not impairing the free exercise of religion, provide for continuing agricultural vocational education under parental and church guidance by the Old Order Amish or others similarly situated. The States have had a long history of amicable and effective relationships with church-sponsored schools, and there is no basis for assuming that, in this related context, reasonable standards cannot be established concerning the content of the continuing vocational education of Amish children under parental guidance, provided always that state regulations are not inconsistent with what we have said in this opinion.

Affirmed.

The decision in *Yoder* carved out a very narrow exception to the compulsory education laws. The Court addressed three main factors. First, the children did attend school up to the eighth grade and then entered into an informal vocational education, which taught them how to work in a self-sufficient community. Second, the Amish had successfully survived within their own community for more than 300 years. Finally, the Court considered the issue of freedom of religion and the legal entitlement to exercise that right.

Other cases have been brought forward in an attempt to use *Yoder* as precedent and have failed. In *Matter of McMillan*, a father refused to send his child to school because he was of Indian heritage and the school did not teach Indian culture.[5] In finding against the father, the court stated:

> *This case is not like the one cited by appellants,* Wisconsin v. Yoder, *which dealt with religious beliefs of the Amish. There is no showing that Shelby and Abe McMillan receive any mode of educational programs alternative to those in the public school. There is also no showing that the Indian heritage or culture of these children will be endangered or threatened in any way by their attending school.*

A similar case involved a family who were members of the Pentecostal church. According to the family's beliefs, children should not attend school because others who do not share the same religious beliefs may corrupt them. The father, who was charged with violating the North Carolina compulsory school attendance law, claimed that that such a statute violated his right to freedom of religion. The court once again distinguished the case from *Yoder:*

> *The Duros, unlike their Amish counterparts, are not members of a community which has existed for three centuries and has a long history of being a successful, self-sufficient, segment of American society. Furthermore, in* Yoder, *the Amish children attended public school through the eighth grade and then obtained informal vocational training to enable them to assimilate into the self-contained Amish community. However, in the present case, Duro refuses to enroll his children in any public or non-public school for any length of time, but still expects them to be fully integrated and live normally in the modern world upon reaching the age of 18.[6]*

Due to the importance of education within a civilized society, the courts have allowed only one exception, as illustrated in *Yoder.* In the balance between parents' First Amendment rights and children's right to attend school, the state tips the scales in favor of protecting the latter.

HOME INSTRUCTION

AS ILLUSTRATED in *Pierce v. Society of Sisters*, it is clear that parents have liberty interests protected by the Fourteenth Amendment concerning how they raise and educate their children.[7] On the other hand, "the natural and legal right of parents to the custody, companionship, control and bringing up of their children is not absolute. It may be interfered with or denied for substantial and sufficient reason, and it is subject to judicial

---

[5] 30 N.C. App. 235 (1976)
[6] *Duro v. District Attorney, Second Judicial Dist. of North Carolina*, 712 F.2d 96 (1983)
[7] 268 U.S. 510 (1925)

control when the interest and welfare of the children require it."[8] Because the government is interested in ensuring that children are educated, each state has set forth statutes and regulations pertaining to home schooling.

Some states require that the parent be a certified teacher, others implement state achievement tests, while others have no standards at all. Regardless of the policy, the courts have generally held in favor of the state and its procedures. Over the years parents have challenged some of the controls over home schooling, but few have been successful. Without such support,

> *the State would be powerless to assert its interest in the case of a child who is being otherwise instructed. There is no doubt as to the power of a State, having a high responsibility for education of its citizens, to impose reasonable regulations for the control and duration of basic education. Thus, the school committee may enforce, through the approval process, . . . certain reasonable educational requirements similar to those required for public and private schools.*[9]

OPEN COMMUNICATIONS WITH PARENTS

THE *SCHOOL Superintendent's Insider* (December 2000) suggests the following best practices for keeping lines of communications open between administrators and parents. These guidelines are some of the easiest ways to practice preventive law but are sometimes overlooked due to busy schedules and untrained staff.

> ***Use Parent Contact Record for Documenting Parents' Phone Calls.*** *Parents often call superintendents with complaints and problems. Typically, you rely on your staff to screen these calls and then pass the information on to you. Since you can't respond to every call, you need to make sure your staff gets enough information so that you can decide whether to return the call yourself or to direct a staff member to do it. If your office doesn't return a parent's call, you risk alienating the parent. And if a parent calls to tell you about a safety problem and you don't respond, you risk liability if an accident occurs.*
>
> *To ensure that you get all the information you need to appropriately respond to parent calls, have your staff use a Parent Conflict Record to document these calls. Train staff to write down information about the parents' complaints or problems, says New York superintendent Joan Thompson.*
>
> ***Benefits of Parent Contact Record.*** *Most superintendents have a trained staff to deal with parent calls, but many don't use a form to document calls. Here's a look at the benefits of using a simple form to document parent calls:*
>
> ***Lets you get full picture.*** *Using a form instead of a message slip to record calls will give you a full picture of a parent's complaint or problem. The detailed information*

---

[8] *Tucker v. Tucker*, 288 N.C. 8 (1975)
[9] *Care and Protection of Charles*, 399 Mass. 324 (1987)

will help you decide how to respond. If you have to return the call, you'll have some basic information before speaking to the parents, says Thompson. And even if your staff returns the call, the completed form will help you stay in touch with parents' complaints or concerns.

Helps ensure thorough record keeping. *Using a form will help you keep records of calls. For example, suppose a student is hurt while waiting at a bus stop. A parent may claim that she called and told you that the bus stop was unsafe and that someone would get hurt. With careful record keeping, you can go back to the form and investigate the call. The information will help you decide whether to settle the case.*

Guides staff on what to ask. *The form is particularly helpful for training new staff and for serving as a reminder for current staff on the questions they should ask when a parent calls, says Thompson.*

What form should report. *Here's the basic information your parent contact record should report to you:*

Name of person calling you. *Ask the staff member filling out the record to write down his or her name.*

Date and time. *Have your staff write down the date and time of the parent's call. This will serve as proof of when the parent alerted you to the problem. When you or your staff gets back to the parent, you'll need to know how long he or she has been waiting for a return call.*

Parent information. *Get the parent's full name and home and office phone number.*

Student information. *The form should record the student's name, the school he or she attends, and his or her grade level.*

Nature of problem. *Have your staff report a brief description of the problem. This will give you an idea of who should return the parent's call. In most cases, such as a complaint about a teacher's performance, the staff member should take down the information, report it to you, and then call the parent back and direct him or her to the school principal. In other cases, such as a complaint about the school principal, the superintendent should take the call, says Sarah Redfield, an education law professor. And if the parent is reporting on a safety issue endangering students, the staff member screening the call should immediately put the call through to the superintendent, who should return all calls regarding issues that affect the district as a whole, such as a controversial religious issue, says Redfield.*

Safety issues. *The form has a specific section directing your staff to check off whether a safety issue is involved and to explain the problem. Your staff should be on the lookout for safety issues—for example, reports of weapons or a dangerous situation. If the parent is calling to report a safety issue, your staff should immediately alert you to the situation, says Thompson. When safety is an issue, either take the call or call the parent back right away, she says. It's crucial to handle safety issues immediately, agrees Trump. A prompt response could help you prevent an injury, he says. But if your staff alerts you to a safety issue and you don't respond, you risk liability, he says.*

Prior contacts about problem. *It's particularly important for superintendents to know whom the parent has already spoken to. Specifically, have your staff check* *whether the parent has contacted the principal. Parents should almost always contact the school principal before speaking to the superintendent about a problem, says Thompson. Otherwise, a superintendent may inappropriately intervene in a problem that the principal is handling and circumvent the principal's authority.*

Your form should prompt your staff to ask the caller which other district employees he or she has spoken to about the problem and specifically ask whether the caller has spoken to the principal.

For example, a parent may report to a superintendent that someone was picking on his child in school and complain that neither the principal nor the student's teacher took any action. If you take the call and promise action, you may be intervening in a situation that the principal is investigating and jeopardize the principal's authority. The parent may then go back to the principal and report how you recommended handling the situation and completely mischaracterize your response. The principal and the student's teacher are in the best situation to interview the student and the students accused of picking on her, says Thompson.

Give approximate callback time. *Your staff should give the parent an approximate time that you or the staff member will call back. In some cases you may call back, but often the secretary can get back to the parent with the information. Sometimes it may take a few days to decide who should handle the problem. Giving the parent a callback time will let him or her know you're not ducking the issue.*

For example, if a parent calls complaining about a teacher's behavior, your secretary should take down the facts and tell the parent that she'll call back in a few days. After speaking with you, the secretary should call back on the date she set and tell the parent that she needs to contact the school principal. After speaking with the parent, the secretary should document the date and time of the callback on the form.

Insider Says: When training staff, give them other tips on how to handle calls. Tell them to listen carefully and to be empathetic to parents. Some parents simply need to have someone listen. Remind your staff that although they may have heard the problem many times, the issue is nonetheless extremely important to the parent.[10]

Best Practices

- Parents need to be informed. Whether it be through weekly newsletters, personal phone calls, or one-on-one conversations, keep the lines of communication open.

- It is recommended that all contacts be documented on a parent contact record form. This makes record keeping easier and keeps all information in one place.

- Train your staff to stay calm and not take comments personally. Most of all, train staff to document all conversations and forward information to the appropriate parties.

---

[10] Reprinted with permission from the monthly newsletter, *School Superintendent's Insider* (December 2000). Copyright 2000 by Brownstone Publishers, Inc., 149 Fifth Ave. New York, NY. 10010-6801 www.brownstone.com. Call 1-800-643-8095 for a free sample issue.

Summary

One of the newest areas of educational law that administrators must take note of is that concerning the legal rights of parents. The Family Educational Rights and Privacy Act protects the records of students, grants parents the right to review their child's file, and restricts the access to the files, both inside and outside the institution. Additionally, the 2002 U.S. Supreme Court decision in *Owasso v. Falvo*, concerning the publication and grading of student work, has changed the way school districts function on a daily basis.

Not all students attend public schools and the U.S. Supreme Court made it clear early on that parents have the right to send their children to private schools, and are not required by law to make them attend public schools. Another legal alternative for children to learn is through home schooling. However, it is important to note that every state has a different set of requirements for home schooling. Some states require that the person teaching the children has a degree and is certified, while other states are much more relaxed in their views of home schooling and allow the parents to make the decisions as to what is best for their children. Regardless of the state it is important that administrators know the law within their particular state and ensure that the proper paperwork is filed before a student leaves the public school system on a permanent basis to be home schooled.

Lastly, one of the key complaints from parents before filing a lawsuit against a public school is the lack of communication they received from administrators. As illustrated within the chapter, there are numerous ways to ensure that administrators keep the lines of communications open with the parents and keep them informed.

Discussion Questions

1. Define the legislative intent of FERPA.
2. What information should be included and excluded from a student's file? Discuss, using examples of both.
3. What should be included in the FERPA annual notice to parents? How does your school comply with this requirement?
4. Who has access to student records at your institution? What procedures ensure privacy? Is there is a log sheet indicating the date, person inspecting the file, and purpose of the review?
5. Discuss the Supreme Court's decision in *Owasso Independent School Dist. No. 1-011 v. Falvo*. Describe the Court's rational for its decision. Based on your knowledge of FERPA, was the holding surprising? Why or why not?
6. At your institution, who has access to students' grades? Who grades students' papers? Assignments? Final exams? How are scores and grades distributed to students?
7. Must all children attend school? What is the policy argument for allowing choices and exceptions?

8. After reviewing the decision in *Wisconsin v. Yoder,* discuss the Court's rationale for the narrow decision in the case. What made this case so special? Do you feel there should be other exceptions?

9. Describe your school's policy for working with parents. Describe the policy for both teachers and administrators.

10. Read the executive summary of the "No Child Left Behind Act of 2001" (in the appendix) and determine how this newly enacted legislation will directly affect education in the United States.

DEEPENING YOUR UNDERSTANDING

1. Following the suggestions made in the *School Superintendent's Insider,* create a form for your institution to use when communicating with parents.

2. In your state, what is the law pertaining to compulsory education and home schooling? Perform a legal search and determine the policies and procedures for home schooling in the state in which you work or plan to work.

9

EQUAL COVERAGE UNDER THE LAW

INTRODUCTION

Unfortunately, discrimination in education has resulted in a number of famous Supreme Court cases. Before 1954, it was common practice that students were segregated in the public school system based on race. The "separate but equal" doctrine was law for almost 60 years until the Supreme Court reversed itself in Brown v. Board of Education of Topeka.[1]

Today, discrimination in employment, including gender, age, and sex discrimination, is gaining increased attention. The Civil Rights Act of 1964 prohibits discrimination based on race, color, religion, sex, or national origin. The Equal Pay Act of 1963 prohibits discrimination based on gender. The Age Discrimination Act of 1973 protects individuals who are 40 years and older from age discrimination. In addition, educational leaders must be aware of the laws that protect individuals from sexual discrimination and sexual harassment. Recent Supreme Court cases regarding school district liability for teacher-to-student and student-to-student sexual harassment have changed how school districts handle these issues.

RACIAL DISCRIMINATION

IN 1896, the U.S. Supreme Court decided the infamous case of *Plessy v. Ferguson,* which affirmed the doctrine of separate but equal.[2] The case arose over the racial

---

[1] 347 U.S. 483 (1954)
[2] 163 U.S. 537 (1896)

segregation of passengers on the railroad. According to the case, under a Louisiana statute, "all railway companies carrying passengers in their coaches in this State, shall provide equal but separate accommodation."[3] Anyone in violation of the law, would be fined 25 dollars or imprisoned for no more than 20 days. To ensure that railroad companies abided by the law, both the individual who wrongfully occupied the coach and the employee who assigned him or her to the area could be penalized.

In its decision, the Supreme Court refuted the issue of such separation as a violation of the Fourteenth Amendment:

> *The object of the amendment was undoubtedly to enforce the absolute equality of the two races before the law, but in the nature of things it could not have been intended to abolish distinctions based upon color, or to enforce social, as distinguished from political equality, or a commingling of the two races upon terms unsatisfactory to either. Laws permitting, and even requiring, their separation in places where they are liable to be brought into contact do not necessarily imply the inferiority of either race to the other, and have been generally, if not universally, recognized as within the competency of the state legislatures in the exercise of their police power. The most common instance of this is connected with the establishment of separate schools for white and colored children, which has been held to be a valid exercise of the legislative power even by courts of States where the political rights of the colored race have been longest and most earnestly enforced.[4]*

Thus, for the next 60 years, the separate but equal doctrine was the law. *Plessy* was not unanimous, however, and Justice Harlen eloquently dissented:

> *In respect of civil rights, common to all citizens, the Constitution of the United States does not, I think, permit any public authority to know the race of these entitled to be protected in the enjoyment of such rights. Every true man has pride of race, and under appropriate circumstances, when the rights of others, his equals before the law, are not to be affected, it is his privilege to express such pride and to take such action based upon it as to him seems proper. But I deny that any legislative body or judicial tribunal may have regard to the race of citizens when the civil rights of those citizens are involved. Indeed, such legislation, as that here in question, is inconsistent not only with the equality of rights which pertains to citizenship, National and State, but with the personal liberty enjoyed by every one within the United States.[5]*

In the *Plessy* decision, the Court determined that segregation was constitutional under the Fourteenth Amendment as long as the physical facilities were equal. Throughout the country, students were attending racially segregated schools; and such practices culminated

---

[3] *Acts 1890*, no. 111, p. 152.

[4] Ibid., at 544

[5] Ibid., at 555

in numerous cases. Most outcomes favored the defendant, until 1954, in the landmark decision of *Brown v. Board of Education of Topeka*.[6]

Brown v. Board of Education of Topeka (Brown I)
Supreme Court of the United States, 1954
347 U.S. 483

Mr. Chief Justice Warren delivered the opinion of the Court.

These cases come to us from the States of Kansas, South Carolina, Virginia, and Delaware. They are premised on different facts and different local conditions, but a common legal question justifies their consideration together in this consolidated opinion.

In each of the cases, minors of the Negro race, through their legal representatives, seek the aid of the courts in obtaining admission to the public schools of their community on a nonsegregated basis. In each instance, they had been denied admission to schools attended by white children under laws requiring or permitting segregation according to race. This segregation was alleged to deprive the plaintiffs of the equal protection of the laws under the Fourteenth Amendment. In each of the cases other than the Delaware case, a three-judge federal district court denied relief to the plaintiffs on the so-called "separate but equal" doctrine announced by this Court in *Plessy v. Ferguson*. Under that doctrine, equality of treatment is accorded when the races are provided substantially equal facilities, even though these facilities be separate. In the Delaware case, the Supreme Court of Delaware adhered to that doctrine, but ordered that the plaintiffs be admitted to the white schools because of their superiority to the Negro schools.

The plaintiffs contend that segregated public schools are not "equal" and cannot be made "equal," and that hence they are deprived of the equal protection of the laws. Because of the obvious importance of the question presented, the Court took jurisdiction. Argument was heard in the 1952 Term, and reargument was heard this Term on certain questions propounded by the Court.

Reargument was largely devoted to the circumstances surrounding the adoption of the Fourteenth Amendment in 1868. It covered exhaustively consideration of the Amendment in Congress, ratification by the states, then existing practices in racial segregation, and the views of proponents and opponents of the Amendment. This discussion and our own investigation convince us that, although these sources cast some light, it is not enough to resolve the problem with which we are faced. At best, they are inconclusive. The most avid proponents of the post-War Amendments undoubtedly intended them to remove all legal distinctions among "all persons born or naturalized in the United States." Their opponents, just as certainly, were antagonistic to both the letter and the spirit of the Amendments and wished them to have the most limited effect.

---

[6] 347 U.S. 483 (1954).

What others in Congress and the state legislatures had in mind cannot be determined with any degree of certainty.

An additional reason for the inconclusive nature of the Amendment's history, with respect to segregated schools, is the status of public education at that time. In the South, the movement toward free common schools, supported by general taxation, had not yet taken hold. Education of white children was largely in the hands of private groups. Education of Negroes was almost nonexistent, and practically all of the race were illiterate. In fact, any education of Negroes was forbidden by law in some states. Today, in contrast, many Negroes have achieved outstanding success in the arts and sciences as well as in the business and professional world. It is true that public school education at the time of the Amendment had advanced further in the North, but the effect of the Amendment on Northern States was generally ignored in the congressional debates. Even in the North, the conditions of public education did not approximate those existing today. The curriculum was usually rudimentary; ungraded schools were common in rural areas; the school term was but three months a year in many states; and compulsory school attendance was virtually unknown. As a consequence, it is not surprising that there should be so little in the history of the Fourteenth Amendment relating to its intended effect on public education.

In the first cases in this Court construing the Fourteenth Amendment, decided shortly after its adoption, the Court interpreted it as proscribing all state-imposed discriminations against the Negro race. The doctrine of "separate but equal" did not make its appearance in this Court until 1896 in the case of *Plessy v. Ferguson*, involving not education but transportation. American courts have since labored with the doctrine for over half a century. In this Court, there have been six cases involving the "separate but equal" doctrine in the field of public education. In *Cumming v. County Board of Education*, and *Gong Lum v. Rice*, the validity of the doctrine itself was not challenged. In more recent cases, all on the graduate school level, inequality was found in that specific benefits enjoyed by white students were denied to Negro students of the same educational qualifications. In none of these cases was it necessary to re-examine the doctrine to grant relief to the Negro plaintiff. And in *Sweatt v. Painter*, the Court expressly reserved decision on the question whether *Plessy v. Ferguson* should be held inapplicable to public education.

In the instant cases, that question is directly presented. Here, unlike *Sweatt v. Painter*, there are findings below that the Negro and white schools involved have been equalized, or are being equalized, with respect to buildings, curricula, qualifications and salaries of teachers, and other "tangible" factors. Our decision, therefore, cannot turn on merely a comparison of these tangible factors in the Negro and white schools involved in each of the cases. We must look instead to the effect of segregation itself on public education.

In approaching this problem, we cannot turn the clock back to 1868 when the Amendment was adopted, or even to 1896 when *Plessy v. Ferguson* was written. We must consider public education in the light of its full development and its present place in American life throughout the Nation. Only in this way can it be determined if segregation in public schools deprives these plaintiffs of the equal protection of the laws.

Today, education is perhaps the most important function of state and local governments. Compulsory school attendance laws and the great expenditures for education both demonstrate our recognition of the importance of education to our democratic society. It is required in the performance of our most basic public responsibilities, even service in the armed forces. It is the very foundation of good citizenship. Today it is a principal instrument in awakening the child to cultural values, in preparing him for later professional training, and in helping him to adjust normally to his environment. In these days, it is doubtful that any child may reasonably be expected to succeed in life if he is denied the opportunity of an education. Such an opportunity, where the state has undertaken to provide it, is a right which must be made available to all on equal terms.

We come then to the question presented: Does segregation of children in public schools solely on the basis of race, even though the physical facilities and other "tangible" factors may be equal, deprive the children of the minority group of equal educational opportunities? We believe that it does.

In *Sweatt v. Painter*, in finding that a segregated law school for Negroes could not provide them equal educational opportunities, this Court relied in large part on "those qualities which are incapable of objective measurement but which make for greatness in a law school." In *McLaurin v. Oklahoma State Regents*, the Court, in requiring that a Negro admitted to a white graduate school be treated like all other students, again resorted to intangible considerations: ". . . his ability to study, to engage in discussions and exchange views with other students, and, in general, to learn his profession." Such considerations apply with added force to children in grade and high schools. To separate them from others of similar age and qualifications solely because of their race generates a feeling of inferiority as to their status in the community that may affect their hearts and minds in a way unlikely ever to be undone. The effect of this separation on their educational opportunities was well stated by a finding in the Kansas case by a court which nevertheless felt compelled to rule against the Negro plaintiffs: "Segregation of white and colored children in public schools has a detrimental effect upon the colored children. The impact is greater when it has the sanction of the law; for the policy of separating the races is usually interpreted as denoting the inferiority of the negro group. A sense of inferiority affects the motivation of a child to learn. Segregation with the sanction of law, therefore, has a tendency to [retard] the educational and mental development of negro children and to deprive them of some of the benefits they would receive in a racial[ly] integrated school system."

Whatever may have been the extent of psychological knowledge at the time of *Plessy v. Ferguson*, this finding is amply supported by modern authority. Any language in *Plessy v. Ferguson* contrary to this finding is rejected.

We conclude that in the field of public education the doctrine of "separate but equal" has no place. Separate educational facilities are inherently unequal. Therefore, we hold that the plaintiffs and others similarly situated for whom the actions have been brought are, by reason of the segregation complained of, deprived of the equal protection of the laws guaranteed by the Fourteenth Amendment. This disposition makes unnecessary any discussion whether such segregation also violates the Due Process Clause of the Fourteenth Amendment.

Because these are class actions, because of the wide applicability of this decision, and because of the great variety of local conditions, the formulation of decrees in these cases presents problems of considerable complexity. On reargument, the consideration of appropriate relief was necessarily subordinated to the primary question—the constitutionality of segregation in public education. We have now announced that such segregation is a denial of the equal protection of the laws. In order that we may have the full assistance of the parties in formulating decrees, the cases will be restored to the docket, and the parties are requested to present further argument on Questions 4 and 5 previously propounded by the Court for the reargument this Term.[7] The Attorney General of the United States is again invited to participate. The Attorneys General of the states requiring or permitting segregation in public education will also be permitted to appear as amici curiae upon request to do so by September 15, 1954, and submission of briefs by October 1, 1954.

It is so ordered.

In contrast with *Plessy*, the Supreme Court in its decision in *Brown* was unanimous in its holding that segregating public schools based on race is "inherently unequal." After more than 60 years of a dual system, de jure segregation was now unconstitutional under the Fourteenth Amendment. The next issue that challenged the Court was how to implement its decision. Segregation had a long history in many states. In an attempt to remedy the problem, one year after the original decision in *Brown I*, the Supreme Court wrote a separate opinion setting forth the standard of "all deliberate speed" in *Brown II*.[8]

---

[7] Clark, *Effect of prejudice and discrimination on personality development* (1950); Witmer & Kotinsky, *Personality in the making* (1952), chap. 6; Deutscher & Chein, "The psychological effects of enforced segregation: A survey of social science opinion," 26 *J. Psychol.* 259 (1948); Chein, "What are the psychological effects of segregation under conditions of equal facilities?" 3 *Int. J. Opinion and Attitude Res.* 229 (1949); Brameld, "Educational costs," in *Discrimination and national welfare* (MacIver, ed., 1949), 44–48; Frazier, *The Negro in the United States* (1949), 674–681. And see generally Myrdal, *An American dilemma* (1944).

4. Assuming it is decided that segregation in public schools violates the Fourteenth Amendment
    (a) would a decree necessarily follow providing that, within the limits set by normal geographic school districting, Negro children should forthwith be admitted to schools of their choice, or
    (b) may this Court, in the exercise of its equity powers, permit an effective gradual adjustment to be brought about from existing segregated systems to a system not based on color distinctions?
5. On the assumption on which questions 4 (a) and (b) are based, and assuming further that this Court will exercise its equity powers to the end described in question 4 (b),
    (a) should this Court formulate detailed decrees in these cases;
    (b) if so, what specific issues should the decrees reach;
    (c) should this Court appoint a special master to hear evidence with a view to recommending specific terms for such decrees;
    (d) should this Court remand to the courts of first instance with directions to frame decrees in these cases, and if so what general directions should the decrees of this Court include and what procedures should the courts of first instance follow in arriving at the specific terms of more detailed decrees?

[8] 349 U.S. 294 (1955)

Brown v. Board of Education of Topeka (Brown II)
Supreme Court of the United States, 1955
349 U.S. 294

Chief Justice Warren delivered the opinion of the Court.

These cases were decided on May 17, 1954. The opinions of that date, declaring the fundamental principle that racial discrimination in public education is unconstitutional, are incorporated herein by reference. All provisions of federal, state, or local law requiring or permitting such discrimination must yield to this principle. There remains for consideration the manner in which relief is to be accorded.

Because these cases arose under different local conditions and their disposition will involve a variety of local problems, we requested further argument on the question of relief. In view of the nationwide importance of the decision, we invited the Attorney General of the United States and the Attorneys General of all states requiring or permitting racial discrimination in public education to present their views on that question. The parties, the United States, and the States of Florida, North Carolina, Arkansas, Oklahoma, Maryland, and Texas filed briefs and participated in the oral argument.

These presentations were informative and helpful to the Court in its consideration of the complexities arising from the transition to a system of public education freed of racial discrimination. The presentations also demonstrated that substantial steps to eliminate racial discrimination in public schools have already been taken, not only in some of the communities in which these cases arose, but in some of the states appearing as amici curiae, and in other states as well. Substantial progress has been made in the District of Columbia and in the communities in Kansas and Delaware involved in this litigation. The defendants in the cases coming to us from South Carolina and Virginia are awaiting the decision of this Court concerning relief.

Full implementation of these constitutional principles may require solution of varied local school problems. School authorities have the primary responsibility for elucidating, assessing, and solving these problems; courts will have to consider whether the action of school authorities constitutes good faith implementation of the governing constitutional principles. Because of their proximity to local conditions and the possible need for further hearings, the courts which originally heard these cases can best perform this judicial appraisal. Accordingly, we believe it appropriate to remand the cases to those courts.

In fashioning and effectuating the decrees, the courts will be guided by equitable principles. Traditionally, equity has been characterized by a practical flexibility in shaping its remedies and by a facility for adjusting and reconciling public and private needs. These cases call for the exercise of these traditional attributes of equity power. At stake is the personal interest of the plaintiffs in admission to public schools as soon as practicable on a nondiscriminatory basis. To effectuate this interest may call for elimination of a variety of obstacles in making the transition to school systems operated in accordance with the constitutional principles set forth in our May 17, 1954, decision. Courts of equity may properly take into account the public interest in the elimination of such obstacles in a systematic and effective manner. But it should go without saying that the vitality of these constitutional principles cannot be allowed to yield simply because of disagreement with them.

While giving weight to these public and private considerations, the courts will require that the defendants make a prompt and reasonable start toward full compliance with our May 17, 1954, ruling. Once such a start has been made, the courts may find that additional time is necessary to carry out the ruling in an effective manner. The burden rests upon the defendants to establish that such time is necessary in the public interest and is consistent with good faith compliance at the earliest practicable date. To that end, the courts may consider problems related to administration, arising from the physical condition of the school plant, the school transportation system, personnel, revision of school districts and attendance areas into compact units to achieve a system of determining admission to the public schools on a nonracial basis, and revision of local laws and regulations which may be necessary in solving the foregoing problems. They will also consider the adequacy of any plans the defendants may propose to meet these problems and to effectuate a transition to a racially nondiscriminatory school system. During this period of transition, the courts will retain jurisdiction of these cases.

The judgments below, except that in the Delaware case, are accordingly reversed and the cases are remanded to the District Courts to take such proceedings and enter such orders and decrees consistent with this opinion as are necessary and proper to admit to public schools on a racially nondiscriminatory basis with all deliberate speed the parties to these cases. The judgment in the Delaware case—ordering the immediate admission of the plaintiffs to schools previously attended only by white children—is affirmed. . . .

The *Brown* case opened the door for other constitutional issues based on discrimination to come forward, such as gender, age, and pregnancy. Over the years, the courts have interpreted Title VII of the Civil Rights Act of 1964, Title IX of the Educational Amendments of 1974, the Fourteenth Amendment, the Equal Pay Act, and the Age Discrimination Act, all in an attempt to protect the constitutional rights of individuals in the United States.

AGE DISCRIMINATION

THE CONGRESSIONAL purpose of the Age Discrimination in Employment Act of 1967 states that it was created to "promote employment of older persons based on their ability rather than age; to prohibit arbitrary age discrimination in employment; to help employers and workers find ways of meeting problems arising from the impact of age on employment." The Act was created due to the wrongful termination of older employees based strictly on their age. After numerous amendments, the act today protects individuals over age 40 from being discriminated against based on age.

Many companies, both public and private, encourage aging employees to retire early through voluntary incentive programs. Such initiatives do not violate the Age Discrimination in Employment Act. The act does not state that a poor employee who is over the age of 40 cannot be dismissed. Rather, the act protects older employees from being dismissed from their positions based solely on age.

In the realm of education, such cases generally arise through termination claims of teachers. In many situations, a teacher will claim that he or she was either not hired due to age or fired because of age discrimination. In either case, the plaintiff must prove that age was a determining factor in the school district's decision. To prove such a claim, the plaintiff must have prima facie evidence.

> *A plaintiff establishes a prima facie case of intentional age discrimination when he shows: (1) that he was in the protected age group, between forty and seventy years old; (2) that he applied and was qualified for a job for which the employer was seeking applicants; (3) that, despite his qualifications, he was rejected; and (4) that after his rejection, the position remained open and the employer continued to seek applicants from persons of complainant's qualifications.*[9]

Once such evidence is present, the school must then prove that age was not a motivating factor in its decision.

In a New Jersey case, the appellate court determined that a 48-year-old teacher had presented prima facie evidence after being denied tenure. "Although what constitutes evidence of pretext varies with the factual circumstances of each case, evidence suggesting that the defendant is not 'providing the whole story,' 'prefers younger employees' or behaves inconsistently or contradictorily has been sufficient to rebut a defendant's legitimate, nondiscriminatory reason for the adverse employment action."[10] Additional evidence included the fact that, during the past three years, 13 female teachers over the age of 45 had been evaluated for tenure but refused, yet no male teachers over age 45 had ever been denied tenure in the school system.

GENDER DISCRIMINATION

SHORTLY before the Age Discrimination in Employment Act of 1967 was passed, the Equal Pay Act of 1963, which protects gender-based wage discrimination, was created. The federal Equal Pay Act requires that male and female employees receive equal pay for equal work. A plaintiff must prove that the opposite sex is receiving more money for the same work. In such a claim the court will determine if the work requires the same skill, effort, responsibility, and working conditions. This does not mean that a school system must pay male teachers the same wages as female teachers simply for gender equity. If a fair seniority or merit system is in place, different genders may receive different

---

[9] *Wooden v. Board of Education of Jefferson County,* 931 F.2d 376 (1991)

[10] *Greenbery v. Camden County Vocational and Technical Schools,* 708 A.2d 460, at 468 (1998)

amounts of pay. The problem arises when two individuals with the same skills who are performing the same work are paid differently.

In a Massachusetts case, a female cafeteria worker brought a claim under the Massachusetts Equal Pay Act, claiming she was being paid lower wages than the male custodians who worked in the same school system. In finding for the school, the court noted that, while both positions "share a number of common duties, . . . the duties required of the cafeteria worker and custodian positions are so dissimilar that an objectively reasonable person simply would not conclude that the substantive content of the jobs is comparable."[11]

Best Practices

- Develop and adopt policies to assure that neither gender nor age is a factor in hiring, firing, or promoting individuals.

- During the hiring process, ensure that all candidates are asked the same questions. To assist in this process, some organizations have their human resource offices give the members of the interview committee a standard list of questions that all candidates will be asked.

- Once interviewing is completed, outside gossip should not occur. Informing individuals on the hiring committee that the interviews are to be confidential can reduce outside discussion once the process is complete.

- Ensure that merit pay is fair and equitable and that equal pay is given for equal work. Don't play favorites.

SEXUAL HARASSMENT

OVER the past decade, the number of sexual harassment claims has dramatically increased. According to the Equal Employment Opportunity Commission, more than 15,000 sexual harassment claims were filed in 2001; and almost 14 percent of those claims were brought by males. These statistics illustrate the growing problem of sexual harassment in the workplace. Unfortunately, sexual harassment in schools is also on the rise.

Sexual harassment is categorized into two areas: quid pro quo sexual harassment and hostile environment. Quid pro quo sexual harassment, the more serious of the two, is interpreted to mean "this for that" or "something for something else." In 1996, the U.S. Supreme Court addressed this issue in *Meritor Savings Bank v. Vinson*.[12] In its analysis, the Court created a standard for employers, who would now be liable if they "knew or should have known" of the harassment.

---

[11] *Jancey v. School Community of Everett*, 695 N.E.2d 194, at 199 (1998)
[12] 106 S. Ct. 2399 (1986)

The decision in the *Meritor* case required businesses to set forth clear policies concerning sexual harassment and to ensure that such policies are clearly communicated to all employees. Additionally, the decision required that employees have a clear road to follow when reporting any sexual misconduct. In the past reporting was often difficult because the offender was also the person who was being reported to. Now alternative methods must be in place to avoid liability.

While every institution most likely has a policy stating that such actions are wrong and will not be tolerated, having a policy is not enough. All employees, especially supervisors, should have annual training pertaining to sexual harassment and be aware of their responsibilities, both morally and legally.

Teacher-to-Student Sexual Harassment

Due to the in loco parentis doctrine and the growing number of sexual harassment claims in schools, the Supreme Court has set forth two critical decisions that affect education. The first deals with teacher-to-student sexual harassment, the second with student-to-student sexual harassment.

Gebser v. Lago Vista Independent School District
Supreme Court of the United States, 1998
524 U.S. 274

Justice O'Connor delivered the opinion of the Court.

The question in this case is when a school district may be held liable in damages in an implied right of action under Title IX of the Education Amendments of 1972, 86 Stat. 373, as amended, 20 U.S.C. § 1681 et seq. (Title IX), for the sexual harassment of a student by one of the district's teachers. We conclude that damages may not be recovered in those circumstances unless an official of the school district who at a minimum has authority to institute corrective measures on the district's behalf has actual notice of, and is deliberately indifferent to, the teacher's misconduct.

I

In the spring of 1991, when petitioner Alida Star Gebser was an eighth-grade student at a middle school in respondent Lago Vista Independent School District (Lago Vista), she joined a high school book discussion group led by Frank Waldrop, a teacher at Lago Vista's high school. Lago Vista received federal funds at all pertinent times. During the book discussion sessions, Waldrop often made sexually suggestive comments to the students. Gebser entered high school in the fall and was assigned to classes taught by Waldrop in both semesters. Waldrop continued to make inappropriate remarks to the students, and he began to direct more of his suggestive comments toward Gebser, including during the substantial amount of time that the two were alone in his classroom. He initiated sexual contact with Gebser in the spring, when, while visiting her home ostensibly to give her a book, he kissed and fondled her. The two had sexual intercourse on a number of occasions during the remainder of the school year. Their relationship continued through the summer and into the following school year, and they often had intercourse during class time, although never on school property.

Gebser did not report the relationship to school officials, testifying that while she realized Waldrop's conduct was improper, she was uncertain how to react and she wanted to continue having him as a teacher. In October 1992, the parents of two other students complained to the high school principal about Waldrop's comments in class. The principal arranged a meeting, at which, according to the principal, Waldrop indicated that he did not believe he had made offensive remarks but apologized to the parents and said it would not happen again. The principal also advised Waldrop to be careful about his classroom comments and told the school guidance counselor about the meeting, but he did not report the parents' complaint to Lago Vista's superintendent, who was the district's Title IX coordinator. A couple of months later, in January 1993, a police officer discovered Waldrop and Gebser engaging in sexual intercourse and arrested Waldrop. Lago Vista terminated his employment, and subsequently, the Texas Education Agency revoked his teaching license. During this time, the district had not promulgated or distributed an official grievance procedure for lodging sexual harassment complaints; nor had it issued a formal anti-harassment policy.

Gebser and her mother filed suit against Lago Vista and Waldrop in state court in November 1993, raising claims against the school district under Title IX, Rev. Stat. § 1979, 42 U.S.C. § 1983, and state negligence law, and claims against Waldrop primarily under state law. They sought compensatory and punitive damages from both defendants. After the case was removed, the United States District Court for the Western District of Texas granted summary judgment in favor of Lago Vista on all claims, and remanded the allegations against Waldrop to state court. In rejecting the Title IX claim against the school district, the court reasoned that the statute "was enacted to counter policies of discrimination . . . in federally funded education programs," and that "only if school administrators have some type of notice of the gender discrimination and fail to respond in good faith can the discrimination be interpreted as a policy of the school district." Here, the court determined, the parents' complaint to the principal concerning Waldrop's comments in class was the only one Lago Vista had received about Waldrop, and that evidence was inadequate to raise a genuine issue on whether the school district had actual or constructive notice that Waldrop was involved in a sexual relationship with a student.

Petitioners appealed only on the Title IX claim. The Court of Appeals for the Fifth Circuit affirmed, *Doe v. Lago Vista Independent School Dist.,* relying in large part on two of its recent decisions, *Rosa H. v. San Elizario Independent School Dist.,* and *Canutillo Independent School Dist. v. Leija.* The court first declined to impose strict liability on school districts for a teacher's sexual harassment of a student, reiterating its conclusion in *Leija* that strict liability is inconsistent with "the Title IX contract." The court then determined that Lago Vista could not be liable on the basis of constructive notice, finding that there was insufficient evidence to suggest that a school official should have known about Waldrop's relationship with Gebser. Finally, the court refused to invoke the common law principle that holds an employer vicariously liable when an employee is "aided in accomplishing [a] tort by the existence of the agency relation," explaining that application of that principle would result in school district liability in essentially every case of teacher-student harassment.

The court concluded its analysis by reaffirming its holding in *Rosa H.* that, "school districts are not liable in tort for teacher-student sexual harassment under Title IX unless an employee who has been invested by the school board with supervisory power over the offending employee actually knew of the abuse, had the power to end the abuse, and failed to do so," and ruling that petitioners could not satisfy that standard. The Fifth Circuit's analysis represents one of the varying approaches adopted by the Courts of Appeals in assessing a school district's liability under Title IX for a teacher's sexual harassment of a student. . . . We granted certiorari to address the issue, and we now affirm.

II

Title IX provides in pertinent part that, "no person . . . shall, on the basis of sex, be excluded from participation in, be denied the benefits of, or be subjected to discrimination under any education program or activity receiving Federal financial assistance." The express statutory means of enforcement is administrative: The statute directs federal agencies who distribute education funding to establish requirements to effectuate the nondiscrimination mandate, and permits the agencies to enforce those requirements through "any . . . means authorized by law," including ultimately the termination of federal funding. The Court held in *Cannon v. University of Chicago,* that Title IX is also enforceable through an implied private right of action, a conclusion we do not revisit here. We subsequently established in *Franklin v. Gwinnett County Public Schools,* that monetary damages are available in the implied private action.

In *Franklin,* a high school student alleged that a teacher had sexually abused her on repeated occasions and that teachers and school administrators knew about the harassment but took no action, even to the point of dissuading her from initiating charges. The lower courts dismissed Franklin's complaint against the school district on the ground that the implied right of action under Title IX, as a categorical matter, does not encompass recovery in damages. We reversed the lower courts' blanket rule, concluding that Title IX supports a private action for damages, at least "in a case such as this, in which intentional discrimination is alleged." *Franklin* thereby establishes that a school district can be held liable in damages in cases involving a teacher's sexual harassment of a student; the decision, however, does not purport to define the contours of that liability.

We face that issue squarely in this case. Petitioners, joined by the United States as amicus curiae, would invoke standards used by the Courts of Appeals in Title VII cases involving a supervisor's sexual harassment of an employee in the workplace. In support of that approach, they point to a passage in *Franklin* in which we stated: "Unquestionably, Title IX placed on the Gwinnett County Public Schools the duty not to discriminate on the basis of sex, and 'when a supervisor sexually harasses a subordinate because of the subordinate's sex, that supervisor "discriminates" on the basis of sex.' We believe the same rule should apply when a teacher sexually harasses and abuses a student." *Meritor Savings Bank, FSB v. Vinson*, directs courts to look to common-law agency principles when assessing an employer's liability under Title VII for sexual harassment of an employee by a supervisor. Petitioners and the United States submit that, in light of *Franklin's* comparison of teacher-student harassment with supervisor-employee harassment, agency principles should likewise apply in Title IX actions.

Specifically, they advance two possible standards under which Lago Vista would be liable for Waldrop's conduct. First, relying on a 1997 "Policy Guidance" issued by the Department of Education, they would hold a school district liable in damages under Title IX where a teacher is "aided in carrying out the sexual harassment of students by his or her position of authority with the institution," irrespective of whether school district officials had any knowledge of the harassment and irrespective of their response upon becoming aware. That rule is an expression of respondeat superior liability, i.e., vicarious or imputed liability, under which recovery in damages against a school district would generally follow whenever a teacher's authority over a student facilitates the harassment. Second, petitioners and the United States submit that a school district should at a minimum be liable for damages based on a theory of constructive notice, i.e., where the district knew or "should have known" about harassment but failed to uncover and eliminate it. Both standards would allow a damages recovery in a broader range of situations than the rule adopted by the Court of Appeals, which hinges on actual knowledge by a school official with authority to end the harassment. . . .

In this case, moreover, petitioners seek not just to establish a Title IX violation but to recover damages based on theories of respondeat superior and constructive notice. It is that aspect of their action, in our view, which is most critical to resolving the case. Unlike Title IX, Title VII contains an express cause of action, § 2000e-5(f), and specifically provides for relief in the form of monetary damages, § 1981a. Congress therefore has directly addressed the subject of damages relief under Title VII and has set out the particular situations in which damages are available as well as the maximum amounts recoverable. § 1981a(b). With respect to Title IX, however, the private right of action is judicially implied, and there is thus no legislative expression of the scope of available remedies, including when it is appropriate to award monetary damages. In addition, although the general presumption that courts can award any appropriate relief in an established cause of action, coupled with Congress' abrogation of the States' Eleventh Amendment immunity under Title IX, led us to conclude in *Franklin* that Title IX recognizes a damages remedy, we did so in response to lower court decisions holding that Title IX does not support damages relief at all. We made no effort in *Franklin* to delimit the circumstances in which a damages remedy should lie.

III

. . . As a general matter, it does not appear that Congress contemplated unlimited recovery in damages against a funding recipient where the recipient is unaware of discrimination in its programs. When Title IX was enacted in 1972, the principal civil rights statutes containing an express right of action did not provide for recovery of monetary damages at all, instead allowing only injunctive and equitable relief. It was not until 1991 that Congress made damages available under Title VII, and even then, Congress carefully limited the amount recoverable in any individual case, calibrating the maximum recovery to the size of the employer. Adopting petitioners' position would amount, then, to allowing unlimited recovery of damages under Title IX where Congress has not spoken on the subject of either the right or the remedy, and in the face of evidence that when Congress expressly considered both in Title VII it restricted the amount of damages available.

Congress enacted Title IX in 1972 with two principal objectives in mind: "to avoid the use of federal resources to support discriminatory practices" and "to provide individual citizens effective protection against those practices." The statute was modeled after Title VI of the Civil Rights Act of 1964, . . . which is parallel to Title IX except that it prohibits race discrimination, not sex discrimination, and applies in all programs receiving federal funds, not only in education programs. The two statutes operate in the same manner, conditioning an offer of federal funding on a promise by the recipient not to discriminate, in what amounts essentially to a contract between the Government and the recipient of funds. . . .

That contractual framework distinguishes Title IX from Title VII, which is framed in terms not of a condition but of an outright prohibition. Title VII applies to all employers without regard to federal funding and aims broadly to "eradicate discrimination throughout the economy." Title VII, moreover, seeks to "make persons whole for injuries suffered through past discrimination." Thus, whereas Title VII aims centrally to compensate victims of discrimination, Title IX focuses more on "protecting" individuals from discriminatory practices carried out by recipients of federal funds. That might explain why, when the Court first recognized the implied right under Title IX in Cannon, the opinion referred to injunctive or equitable relief in a private action. . . .

Title IX's contractual nature has implications for our construction of the scope of available remedies. When Congress attaches conditions to the award of federal funds under its spending power, as it has in Title IX and Title VI, we examine closely the propriety of private actions holding the recipient liable in monetary damages for noncompliance with the condition. Our central concern in that regard is with ensuring "that the receiving entity of federal funds [has] notice that it will be liable for a monetary award." Justice White's opinion announcing the Court's judgment in *Guardians Assn. v. Civil Serv. Comm'n of New York City,* for instance, concluded that the relief in an action under Title VI alleging unintentional discrimination should be prospective only, because where discrimination is unintentional, "it is surely not obvious that the grantee was aware that it was administering the program in violation of the [condition]." We confront similar concerns here. If a school district's liability for a teacher's sexual harassment rests on principles of constructive notice or respondeat superior, it will likewise be the case that the recipient of funds was unaware of the discrimination. It is sensible to assume that Congress did not envision a recipient's liability in damages in that situation.

Most significantly, Title IX contains important clues that Congress did not intend to allow recovery in damages where liability rests solely on principles of vicarious liability or constructive notice. Title IX's express means of enforcement—by administrative agencies—operates on an assumption of actual notice to officials of the funding recipient. The statute entitles agencies who disburse education funding to enforce their rules implementing the non-discrimination mandate through proceedings to suspend or terminate funding or through "other means authorized by law." Significantly, however, an agency may not initiate enforcement proceedings until it "has advised the appropriate person or persons of the failure to comply with the requirement and has determined that compliance cannot be secured by voluntary means." The administrative regulations implement that obligation, requiring resolution of compliance issues "by informal means whenever possible," and prohibiting commencement of enforcement proceedings until the agency has determined that voluntary compliance is unobtainable and "the recipient . . . has been notified of its failure to comply and of the action to be taken to effect compliance."

Presumably, a central purpose of requiring notice of the violation "to the appropriate person" and an opportunity for voluntary compliance before administrative enforcement proceedings can commence is to avoid diverting education funding from beneficial uses where a recipient was unaware of discrimination in its programs and is willing to institute prompt corrective measures. The scope of private damages relief proposed by petitioners is at odds with that basic objective. When a teacher's sexual harassment is imputed to a school district or when a school district is deemed to have "constructively" known of the teacher's harassment, by assumption the district had no actual knowledge of the teacher's conduct. Nor, of course, did the district have an opportunity to take action to end the harassment or to limit further harassment.

It would be unsound, we think, for a statute's express system of enforcement to require notice to the recipient and an opportunity to come into voluntary compliance while a judicially implied system of enforcement permits substantial liability without regard to the recipient's knowledge or its corrective actions upon receiving notice. Moreover, an award of damages in a particular case might well exceed a recipient's level of federal funding. Where a statute's express enforcement scheme hinges its most severe sanction on notice and unsuccessful efforts to obtain compliance, we cannot attribute to Congress the intention to have implied an enforcement scheme that allows imposition of greater liability without comparable conditions.

IV

Because the express remedial scheme under Title IX is predicated upon notice to an "appropriate person" and an opportunity to rectify any violation, we conclude, in the absence of further direction from Congress, that the implied damages remedy should be fashioned along the same lines. An "appropriate person" under § 1682 is, at a minimum, an official of the recipient entity with authority to take corrective action to end the discrimination. Consequently, in cases like this one that do not involve official policy of the recipient entity, we hold that a damages remedy will not lie under Title IX unless an official who at a minimum has authority to address the alleged discrimination and to institute corrective measures on the recipient's behalf has actual knowledge of discrimination in the recipient's programs and fails adequately to respond.

We think, moreover, that the response must amount to deliberate indifference to discrimination. The administrative enforcement scheme presupposes that an official who is advised of a Title IX violation refuses to take action to bring the recipient into compliance. The premise, in other words, is an official decision by the recipient not to remedy the violation. That framework finds a rough parallel in the standard of deliberate indifference. Under a lower standard, there would be a risk that the recipient would be liable in damages not for its own official decision but instead for its employees' independent actions. Comparable considerations led to our adoption of a deliberate indifference standard for claims under § 1983 alleging that a municipality's actions in failing to prevent a deprivation of federal rights was the cause of the violation.

Applying the framework to this case is fairly straightforward, as petitioners do not contend they can prevail under an actual notice standard. The only official alleged to have had information about Waldrop's misconduct is the high school principal. That information, however, consisted of a complaint from parents of other students charging only that Waldrop had made inappropriate comments during class, which was plainly insufficient to alert the principal to the possibility that Waldrop was involved in a sexual relationship with a student. Lago Vista, moreover, terminated Waldrop's employment upon learning of his relationship with Gebser. Justice Stevens points out in his dissenting opinion that Waldrop of course had knowledge of his own actions. Where a school district's liability rests on actual notice principles, however, the knowledge of the wrongdoer himself is not pertinent to the analysis.

Petitioners focus primarily on Lago Vista's asserted failure to promulgate and publicize an effective policy and grievance procedure for sexual harassment claims. They point to Department of Education regulations requiring each funding recipient to "adopt and publish grievance procedures providing for prompt and equitable resolution" of discrimination complaints, and to notify students and others "that it does not discriminate on the basis of sex in the educational programs or activities which it operates." . . . Lago Vista's alleged failure to comply with the regulations, however, does not establish the requisite actual notice and deliberate indifference. And in any event, the failure to promulgate a grievance procedure does not itself constitute "discrimination" under Title IX. Of course, the Department of Education could enforce the requirement administratively: Agencies generally have authority to promulgate and enforce requirements that effectuate the statute's non-discrimination mandate, 20 U.S.C. § 1682, even if those requirements do not purport to represent a definition of discrimination under the statute. We have never held, however, that the implied private right of action under Title IX allows recovery in damages for violation of those sorts of administrative requirements.

V

The number of reported cases involving sexual harassment of students in schools confirms that harassment unfortunately is an all too common aspect of the educational experience. No one questions that a student suffers extraordinary harm when subjected to sexual harassment and abuse by a teacher, and that the teacher's conduct is reprehensible and undermines the basic purposes of the educational system. The issue in this case, however, is whether the independent misconduct of a teacher is attributable to the school district that employs him under a specific federal statute designed primarily to prevent recipients of federal financial assistance from using the funds in a discriminatory manner. Our decision does not affect any right of recovery that an individual may have against a school district as a matter of state law or against the teacher in his individual capacity under state law or under 42 U.S.C. § 1983. Until Congress speaks directly on the subject, however, we will not hold a school district liable in damages under Title IX for a teacher's sexual harassment of a student absent actual notice and deliberate indifference. We therefore affirm the judgment of the Court of Appeals.

It is so ordered.

Student-to-Student Sexual Harassment

One recent and important case that educational leaders must understand occurred in 1999. In *Davis v. Monroe County Board of Education*, a mother filed suit after the school district was unresponsive to her claim that her daughter was being sexually harassed by other students.[13] The facts suggest that the student was repeatedly harassed; and though the parents made numerous requests for the school to take action, nothing was done to stop the abuse. The U.S. Supreme Court reviewed the case and, after a bitterly divided five-to-four decision, determined that a school district could be held liable under Title IX if the district had knowledge of the harassment and was "deliberately indifferent" to it.

Davis v. Monroe County Board of Education
Supreme Court of the United States, 1999
526 U.S. 629

Justice O'Connor delivered the opinion of the Court.

Petitioner brought suit against the Monroe County Board of Education and other defendants, alleging that her fifth-grade daughter had been the victim of sexual harassment by another student in her class. Among petitioner's claims was a claim for monetary and injunctive relief under Title IX of the Education Amendments of 1972. The District Court dismissed petitioner's Title IX claim on the ground that "student-on-student," or peer, harassment provides no ground for a private cause of action under the statute. The Court of Appeals for the Eleventh Circuit, sitting en banc, affirmed. We consider here whether a private damages action may lie against the school board in cases of student-on-student harassment. We conclude that it may, but only where the funding recipient acts with deliberate indifference to known acts of harassment in its programs or activities. Moreover, we conclude that such an action will lie only for harassment that is so severe, pervasive, and objectively offensive that it effectively bars the victim's access to an educational opportunity or benefit.

---

[13] 526 U.S. 629 (1999)

I.   Petitioner's Title IX claim was dismissed under Federal Rule of Civil Procedure 12(b)(6) for failure to state a claim upon which relief could be granted. Accordingly, in reviewing the legal sufficiency of petitioner's cause of action, "we must assume the truth of the material facts as alleged in the complaint."

A.   Petitioner's minor daughter, LaShonda, was allegedly the victim of a prolonged pattern of sexual harassment by one of her fifth-grade classmates at Hubbard Elementary School, a public school in Monroe County, Georgia. According to petitioner's complaint, the harassment began in December 1992, when the classmate, G. F., attempted to touch LaShonda's breasts and genital area and made vulgar statements such as "I want to get in bed with you" and "I want to feel your boobs." Similar conduct allegedly occurred on or about January 4 and January 20, 1993. LaShonda reported each of these incidents to her mother and to her classroom teacher, Diane Fort. Petitioner, in turn, also contacted Fort, who allegedly assured petitioner that the school principal, Bill Querry, had been informed of the incidents. Petitioner contends that, notwithstanding these reports, no disciplinary action was taken against G. F.

G. F.'s conduct allegedly continued for many months. In early February, G. F. purportedly placed a door stop in his pants and proceeded to act in a sexually suggestive manner toward LaShonda during physical education class. LaShonda reported G. F.'s behavior to her physical education teacher, Whit Maples. Approximately one week later, G. F. again allegedly engaged in harassing behavior, this time while under the supervision of another classroom teacher, Joyce Pippin. Again, LaShonda allegedly reported the incident to the teacher, and again petitioner contacted the teacher to follow up.

Petitioner alleges that G. F. once more directed sexually harassing conduct toward LaShonda in physical education class in early March, and that LaShonda reported the incident to both Maples and Pippen. In mid-April 1993, G. F. allegedly rubbed his body against LaShonda in the school hallway in what LaShonda considered a sexually suggestive manner, and LaShonda again reported the matter to Fort.

The string of incidents finally ended in mid-May, when G. F. was charged with, and pleaded guilty to, sexual battery for his misconduct. The complaint alleges that LaShonda had suffered during the months of harassment, however; specifically, her previously high grades allegedly dropped as she became unable to concentrate on her studies, and, in April 1993, her father discovered that she had written a suicide note. The complaint further alleges that, at one point, LaShonda told petitioner that she "didn't know how much longer she could keep [G. F.] off her."

Nor was LaShonda G. F.'s only victim; it is alleged that other girls in the class fell prey to G. F.'s conduct. At one point, in fact, a group composed of LaShonda and other female students tried to speak with Principal Querry about G. F.'s behavior. According to the complaint, however, a teacher denied the students' request with the statement, "If [Querry] wants you, he'll call you."

Petitioner alleges that no disciplinary action was taken in response to G. F.'s behavior toward LaShonda. In addition to her conversations with Fort and Pippen, petitioner alleges that she spoke with Principal Querry in mid-May 1993. When petitioner inquired as to what action the school intended to take against G. F., Querry simply stated, "I guess I'll have to threaten him a little bit harder." Yet, petitioner alleges, at no point during the many months of his reported misconduct was G. F. disciplined for harassment. Indeed, Querry allegedly asked petitioner why LaShonda "was the only one complaining."

Nor, according to the complaint, was any effort made to separate G. F. and LaShonda. On the contrary, notwithstanding LaShonda's frequent complaints, only after more than three months of reported harassment was she even permitted to change her classroom seat so that she was no longer seated next to G. F. Moreover, petitioner alleges that, at the time of the events in question, the Monroe County Board of Education (Board) had not instructed its personnel on how to respond to peer sexual harassment and had not established a policy on the issue.

B.   On May 4, 1994, petitioner filed suit in the United States District Court for the Middle District of Georgia against the Board, Charles Dumas, the school district's superintendent, and Principal Querry. The complaint alleged that the Board is a recipient of federal funding for purposes of Title IX, that "the persistent sexual advances and harassment by the student G. F. upon [LaShonda] interfered with her ability to attend school and perform her studies and activities," and that "the deliberate indifference by Defendants to the unwelcome sexual advances of a student upon LaShonda created an intimidating, hostile, offensive and abusive school environment in violation of Title IX." The complaint sought compensatory and punitive damages, attorney's fees, and injunctive relief. . . .

We granted certiorari. . . .

Congress authorized an administrative enforcement scheme for Title IX. Federal departments or agencies with the authority to provide financial assistance are entrusted to promulgate rules, regulations, and orders to enforce the objectives of § 1681, and these departments or agencies may rely on "any . . . means authorized by law," including the termination of funding, to give effect to the statute's restrictions.

There is no dispute here that the Board is a recipient of federal education funding for Title IX purposes. Nor do respondents support an argument that student-on-student harassment cannot rise to the level of "discrimination" for purposes of Title IX. Rather, at issue here is the question whether a recipient of federal education funding may be liable for damages under Title IX under any circumstances for discrimination in the form of student-on-student sexual harassment. . . .

Invoking *Pennhurst,* respondents urge that Title IX provides no notice that recipients of federal educational funds could be liable in damages for harm arising from student-on-student harassment. Respondents contend, specifically, that the statute only proscribes misconduct by grant recipients, not third parties. Respondents argue, moreover, that it would be contrary to the very purpose of Spending Clause legislation to impose liability on a funding recipient for the misconduct of third parties, over whom recipients exercise little control.

We agree with respondents that a recipient of federal funds may be liable in damages under Title IX only for its own misconduct. The recipient itself must "exclude [persons] from participation in, . . . deny [persons] the benefits of, or . . . subject [persons] to discrimination under" its "programs or activities" in order to be liable under Title IX. The Government's enforcement power may only be exercised against the funding recipient, and we have not extended damages liability under Title IX to parties outside the scope of this power.

We disagree with respondents' assertion, however, that petitioner seeks to hold the Board liable for G. F.'s actions instead of its own. Here, petitioner attempts to hold the Board liable for its *own* decision to remain idle in the face of known student-on-student harassment in its schools. In *Gebser*, we concluded that a recipient of federal education funds may be liable in damages under Title IX where it is deliberately indifferent to known acts of sexual harassment by a teacher. In that case, a teacher had entered into a sexual relationship with an eighth grade student, and the student sought damages under Title IX for the teacher's misconduct. We recognized that the scope of liability in private damages actions under Title IX is circumscribed by *Pennhurst's* requirement that funding recipients have notice of their potential liability. Invoking *Pennhurst*, *Guardians Assn.*, and *Franklin*, in *Gebser* we once again required " that 'the receiving entity of federal funds [have] notice that it will be liable for a monetary award'" before subjecting it to damages liability. We also recognized, however, that this limitation on private damages actions is not a bar to liability where a funding recipient intentionally violates the statute. In particular, we concluded that *Pennhurst* does not bar a private damages action under Title IX where the funding recipient engages in intentional conduct that violates the clear terms of the statute.

Accordingly, we rejected the use of agency principles to impute liability to the district for the misconduct of its teachers. Likewise, we declined the invitation to impose liability under what amounted to a negligence standard—holding the district liable for its failure to react to teacher-student harassment of which it knew or *should have* known. Rather, we concluded that the district could be liable for damages only where the district itself intentionally acted in clear violation of Title IX by remaining deliberately indifferent to acts of teacher-student harassment of which it had actual knowledge. Contrary to the dissent's suggestion, the misconduct of the teacher in *Gebser* was not "treated as the grant recipient's actions." Liability arose, rather, from "an official decision by the recipient not to remedy the violation." By employing the "deliberate indifference" theory already used to establish municipal liability under Rev. Stat. § 1979, 42 U.S.C. § 1983, we concluded in *Gebser* that recipients could be liable in damages only where their own deliberate indifference effectively "caused" the discrimination. The high standard imposed in *Gebser* sought to eliminate any "risk that the recipient would be liable in damages not for its own official decision but instead for its employees' independent actions."

Gebser thus established that a recipient intentionally violates Title IX, and is subject to a private damages action, where the recipient is deliberately indifferent to known acts of teacher-student discrimination. Indeed, whether viewed as "discrimination" or "subjecting" students to discrimination, Title IX "unquestionably . . . placed on [the Board] the duty not" to permit teacher-student harassment in its schools, and recipients violate Title IX's plain terms when they remain deliberately indifferent to this form of misconduct.

We consider here whether the misconduct identified in *Gebser*—deliberate indifference to known acts of harassment—amounts to an intentional violation of Title IX, capable of supporting a private damages action, when the harasser is a student rather than a teacher. We conclude that, in certain limited circumstances, it does. As an initial matter, in *Gebser* we expressly rejected the use of agency principles in the Title IX context, noting the textual differences between Title IX and Title VII. Additionally, the regulatory scheme surrounding

Title IX has long provided funding recipients with notice that they may be liable for their failure to respond to the discriminatory acts of certain non-agents. The Department of Education requires recipients to monitor third parties for discrimination in specified circumstances and to refrain from particular forms of interaction with outside entities that are known to discriminate.

The common law, too, has put schools on notice that they may be held responsible under state law for their failure to protect students from the tortious acts of third parties. In fact, state courts routinely uphold claims alleging that schools have been negligent in failing to protect their students from the torts of their peers.

This is not to say that the identity of the harasser is irrelevant. On the contrary, both the "deliberate indifference" standard and the language of Title IX narrowly circumscribe the set of parties whose known acts of sexual harassment can trigger some duty to respond on the part of funding recipients. Deliberate indifference makes sense as a theory of direct liability under Title IX only where the funding recipient has some control over the alleged harassment. A recipient cannot be directly liable for its indifference where it lacks the authority to take remedial action.

The language of Title IX itself—particularly when viewed in conjunction with the requirement that the recipient have notice of Title IX's prohibitions to be liable for damages—also cabins the range of misconduct that the statute proscribes. The statute's plain language confines the scope of prohibited conduct based on the recipient's degree of control over the harasser and the environment in which the harassment occurs. If a funding recipient does not engage in harassment directly, it may not be liable for damages unless its deliberate indifference "subjects" its students to harassment. That is, the deliberate indifference must, at a minimum, "cause [students] to undergo" harassment or "make them liable or vulnerable" to it.

These factors combine to limit a recipient's damages liability to circumstances wherein the recipient exercises substantial control over both the harasser and the context in which the known harassment occurs. Only then can the recipient be said to "expose" its students to harassment or "cause" them to undergo it "under" the recipient's programs. We agree with the dissent that these conditions are satisfied most easily and most obviously when the offender is an agent of the recipient. We rejected the use of agency analysis in *Gebser*, however, and we disagree that the term "under" somehow imports an agency requirement into Title IX. As noted above, the theory in *Gebser* was that the recipient was *directly* liable for its deliberate indifference to discrimination. Liability in that case did not arise because the "teacher's actions [were] treated" as those of the funding recipient, the district was directly liable for its *own* failure to act. The terms "subject" and "under" impose limits, but nothing about these terms requires the use of agency principles.

Where, as here, the misconduct occurs during school hours and on school grounds—the bulk of G. F.'s misconduct, in fact, took place in the classroom—the misconduct is taking place "under" an "operation" of the funding recipient. In these circumstances, the recipient retains substantial control over the context in which the harassment occurs. More importantly, however, in this setting the Board exercises significant control over the harasser. We have observed, for example, "that the nature of [the State's] power [over public schoolchildren] is custodial and tutelary, permitting a degree of supervision and control that could not be exercised over free adults." On more than one occasion, this Court has recognized the importance of school officials' "comprehensive authority, . . . consistent with fundamental constitutional safeguards, to prescribe and control conduct in the schools." The common law, too, recognizes the school's disciplinary authority. We thus conclude that recipients of federal funding may be liable for "subjecting" their students to discrimination where the recipient is deliberately indifferent to known acts of student-on-student sexual harassment and the harasser is under the school's disciplinary authority. . . .

We stress that our conclusion here—that recipients may be liable for their deliberate indifference to known acts of peer sexual harassment—does not mean that recipients can avoid liability only by purging their schools of actionable peer harassment or that administrators must engage in particular disciplinary action. We thus disagree with respondents' contention that, if Title IX provides a cause of action for student-on-student harassment, "nothing short of expulsion of every student accused of misconduct involving sexual overtones would protect school systems from liability or damages." Likewise, the dissent erroneously imagines that victims of peer harassment now have a Title IX right to make particular remedial demands. In fact, as we have previously noted, courts should refrain from second guessing the disciplinary decisions made by school administrators.

School administrators will continue to enjoy the flexibility they require so long as funding recipients are deemed "deliberately indifferent" to acts of student-on-student harassment only where the recipient's response to the harassment or lack thereof is clearly unreasonable in light of the known circumstances. . . .

[W]e acknowledge that school administrators shoulder substantial burdens as a result of legal constraints on their disciplinary authority. To the extent that these restrictions arise from federal statutes, Congress can review these burdens with attention to the difficult position in which such legislation may place our Nation's schools. We believe, however, that the standard set out here is sufficiently flexible to account both for the level of disciplinary authority available to the school and for the potential liability arising from certain forms of disciplinary action. A university might not, for example, be expected to exercise the same degree of control over its students that a grade school would enjoy, and it would be entirely reasonable for a school to refrain from a form of disciplinary action that would expose it to constitutional or statutory claims.

While it remains to be seen whether petitioner can show that the Board's response to reports of G. F.'s misconduct was clearly unreasonable in light of the known circumstances, petitioner may be able to show that the Board "subjected" LaShonda to discrimination by failing to respond in any way over a period of five months to complaints of G. F.'s in-school misconduct from LaShonda and other female students.

B.   The requirement that recipients receive adequate notice of Title IX's proscriptions also bears on the proper definition of "discrimination" in the context of a private damages action. We have elsewhere concluded that sexual harassment is a form of discrimination for Title IX purposes and that Title IX proscribes harassment with sufficient clarity to satisfy *Pennhurst*'s notice requirement and serve as a basis for a damages action. Having previously determined that "sexual harassment" is "discrimination" in the school context under Title IX, we are constrained to conclude that student-on-student sexual harassment, if sufficiently severe, can likewise rise to the level of discrimination actionable under the statute. The statute's other prohibitions, moreover, help give content to the term "discrimination" in this context. Students are not only protected from discrimination, but also specifically shielded from being "excluded from participation in" or "denied the benefits of" any "education program or activity receiving Federal financial assistance." The statute makes clear that, whatever else it prohibits, students must not be denied access to educational benefits and opportunities on the basis of gender. We thus conclude that funding recipients are properly held liable in damages only where they are deliberately indifferent to sexual harassment, of which they have actual knowledge, that is so severe, pervasive, and objectively offensive that it can be said to deprive the victims of access to the educational opportunities or benefits provided by the school.

The most obvious example of student-on-student sexual harassment capable of triggering a damages claim would thus involve the overt, physical deprivation of access to school resources. Consider, for example, a case in which male students physically threaten their female peers every day, successfully preventing the female students from using a particular school resource—an athletic field or a computer lab, for instance. District administrators are well aware of the daily ritual, yet they deliberately ignore requests for aid from the female students wishing to use the resource. The district's knowing refusal to take any action in response to such behavior would fly in the face of Title IX's core principles, and such deliberate indifference may appropriately be subject to claims for monetary damages. It is not necessary, however, to show physical exclusion to demonstrate that students have been deprived by the actions of another student or students of an educational opportunity on the basis of sex. Rather, a plaintiff must establish sexual harassment of students that is so severe, pervasive, and objectively offensive, and that so undermines and detracts from the victims' educational experience, that the victim-students are effectively denied equal access to an institution's resources and opportunities.

Whether gender-oriented conduct rises to the level of actionable "harassment" thus "depends on a constellation of surrounding circumstances, expectations, and relationships," including, but not limited to, the ages of the harasser and the victim and the number of individuals involved. Courts, moreover, must bear in mind that schools are unlike the adult workplace and that children may regularly interact in a manner that would be unacceptable among adults. Indeed, at least early on, students are still learning how to interact appropriately with their peers. It is thus understandable that, in the school setting, students often engage in insults, banter, teasing, shoving, pushing, and gender-specific conduct that is upsetting to the students subjected to it. Damages are not available for simple acts of teasing and name-calling among school children, however, even where these comments target differences in gender. Rather, in the context of student-on-student harassment, damages are available only where the behavior is so severe, pervasive, and objectively offensive that it denies its victims the equal access to education that Title IX is designed to protect.

The dissent fails to appreciate these very real limitations on a funding recipient's liability under Title IX. It is not enough to show, as the dissent would read this opinion to provide, that a student has been "teased," or "called . . . offensive names." Comparisons to an "overweight child who skips gym class because the other children tease her about her size," the student "who refuses to wear glasses to avoid the taunts of 'four-eyes,'" and "the child who refuses to go to school because the school bully calls him a 'scaredy-cat' at recess," are inapposite and misleading. Nor do we contemplate, much less hold, that a mere "decline in grades is enough to survive" a motion to dismiss. The drop-off in LaShonda's grades provides necessary evidence of a potential link between her education and G. F.'s misconduct, but petitioner's ability to state a cognizable claim here depends equally on the alleged persistence and severity of G. F.'s actions, not to mention the Board's alleged knowledge and deliberate indifference. We trust that the dissent's characterization of our opinion will not mislead courts to impose more sweeping liability than we read Title IX to require.

Moreover, the provision that the discrimination occur "under any education program or activity" suggests that the behavior be serious enough to have the systemic effect of denying the victim equal access to an educational program or activity. Although, in theory, a single instance of sufficiently severe one-on-one peer harassment could be said to have such an effect, we think it unlikely that Congress would have thought such behavior sufficient to rise to this level in light of the inevitability of student misconduct and the amount of litigation that would be invited by entertaining claims of official indifference to a single instance of one-on-one peer harassment. By limiting private damages actions to cases having a systemic effect on educational programs or activities, we reconcile the general principle that Title IX prohibits official indifference to known peer sexual harassment with the practical realities of responding to student behavior, realities that Congress could not have meant to be ignored. Even the dissent suggests that Title IX liability may arise when a funding recipient remains indifferent to severe, gender-based mistreatment played out on a "widespread level" among students.

The fact that it was a teacher who engaged in harassment in *Franklin* and *Gebser* is relevant. The relationship between the harasser and the victim necessarily affects the extent to which the misconduct can be said to breach Title IX's guarantee of equal access to educational benefits and to have a systemic effect on a program or activity. Peer harassment, in particular, is less likely to satisfy these requirements than is teacher-student harassment.

C.   Applying this standard to the facts at issue here, we conclude that the Eleventh Circuit erred in dismissing petitioner's complaint. Petitioner alleges that her daughter was the victim of repeated acts of sexual harassment by G. F. over a 5-month period, and there are allegations in support of the conclusion that G. F.'s misconduct was severe, pervasive, and objectively offensive. The harassment was not only verbal; it included numerous acts of objectively offensive touching, and, indeed, G. F. ultimately pleaded guilty to criminal sexual misconduct. Moreover, the complaint alleges that there were multiple victims who were sufficiently disturbed by G. F.'s misconduct to seek an audience with the school principal. Further, petitioner contends that the harassment had a concrete, negative effect on her daughter's ability to receive an education. The complaint also suggests that petitioner may be able to show both actual knowledge and deliberate indifference on the part of the Board, which made no effort whatsoever either to investigate or to put an end to the harassment.

On this complaint, we cannot say "beyond doubt that [petitioner] can prove no set of facts in support of [her] claim which would entitle [her] to relief." Accordingly, the judgment of the United States Court of Appeals for the Eleventh Circuit is reversed, and the case is remanded for further proceedings consistent with this opinion.

It is so ordered.

As in *Gebser*, the Supreme Court was closely divided in its decision in *Davis*. In his dissent, Justice Kennedy claimed that such a standard was too high to place on educational officials. The majority, however, determined that school districts receiving federal funding under Title IX could be held liable if a two-part test were met. First, the school had knowledge of the sexual harassment. Second, members of the school were "deliberately indifferent" to the situation, thus depriving the student access to an education or the benefits provided by the school.

Shortly after the *Davis* decision, the 10th Circuit Court applied the test and mirrored the result. In *Murrell v. School District No.1, Denver Colorado*, the parents of a physically and mentally challenged female student sued the school district after the principal refused to investigate allegations of repeated sexual assault by a classmate.[14] According to the facts, the parents of both students had met with the principal to discuss the problem. During the meeting the principal suggested that the acts were consensual. As a result, the court determined that both teachers and administrators had knowledge of the harassment and were deliberately indifferent, thus creating a hostile environment for the child.

Best Practices

- Based on the new cases concerning sexual harassment in education, schools *must* have zero tolerance policies concerning such conduct.

- Train, train, train. Make sure all employees are trained in the area of sexual harassment. It is recommended that some form of mandatory training on these laws occur at least once a year. Such training illustrates that the school was attempting to prohibit such issues and may help if a claim is brought in the future.

- Recommend that all employees keep doors open while with students. Additionally, be aware when dealing with students that innocent actions may be wrongly interpreted.

SUMMARY

This chapter covers many of the laws which ensure that there is equal protection under the law, especially for those inside the public school system. Included in the Appendix of the text is a section titled *Resources for Administrators*. This section includes excerpts from the U.S. Constitution, as well as the Civil Rights Act, Title VII, Title IX, the Americans

---

[14] 186 F.3d 1238 (1999)

with Disabilities Act, the Age Discrimination Act and the Pregnancy Discrimination Act—all of which are important for educational administrators to be familiar with and understand.

DISCUSSION QUESTIONS

1. Discuss the various federal statutes that protect individuals from discrimination.
2. Compare and contrast *Plessy v. Ferguson* and *Brown v. Board of Education.*
3. Discuss your opinion about why the Supreme Court remedy in *Brown II* set forth the standard for segregation in schools with "all deliberate speed."
4. Are all schools desegregated? Is segregation illegal? Discuss the law concerning this issue.
5. Discuss the law concerning age discrimination. Should all people be protected from age discrimination? For example, a recent age discrimination claim was brought by an eight-year-old. Does he have a valid claim? Should he win? Defend your response.
6. Is it a violation of the Equal Pay Act to pay the female coach of the girl's basketball team less than the male coach of the boy's basketball team? What about at the college level? Discuss and defend your response.
7. Define quid pro quo sexual harassment and hostile environment. Discuss the differences using examples.
8. What is the standard in proving a sexual harassment claim outside of education? What is the standard within education? Do the different standards protect students more or less?
9. Using the cases in the chapter, define *deliberately indifferent* and give examples.
10. Should school districts be responsible for student-to-student sexual harassment? What is your school's policy on such harassment?

DEEPENING YOUR UNDERSTANDING

1. In small groups, create a sexual harassment training program for your school district. Many schools may have a program in place, but it may need to be updated based on the most recent Supreme Court decisions.
2. Find the webpage for the Office of Civil Rights (www.ed.gov) and research the publication *Sexual Harassment Guidance: Harassment of Students by School Employees, Other Students, or Third Parties.* Review the liability of a public school for sexual harassment occurring during instructional hours. What is the reporting procedure?

10

Employment and Tenure

Introduction

Unlike people in most professions, tenured teachers have a property right that is protected under the Fourteenth Amendment. Tenure, however, is commonly misinterpreted and misunderstood. It does not mean one cannot be dismissed. Rather, it means that the individual has a right to due process. Because of the numerous state statutes concerning teacher certification requirements, the laws concerning hiring and firing are broad. Regardless, those who have acquired a property right in their positions are granted due process rights.

The distinction of when due process is granted has been reviewed in two Supreme Court decisions: Board of Regents of State Colleges v. Roth *and* Perry v. Sindermann. *As discussed later in the chapter, a teacher can be dismissed from a tenured position for numerous reasons, including insubordination, poor classroom management, incompetence, immoral conduct, inappropriate sexual activity, criminal activity, and just cause.*

Procedural Due Process and the Fourteenth Amendment

PART of the Fourteenth Amendment reads, "No State shall make or enforce any law which shall abridge the privileges or immunities of citizens of the United States; nor shall any State deprive any person of life, liberty, or property, without due process of law; nor deny to any person within its jurisdiction the equal protection of the laws." In respect to protection, tenured teachers are granted due process procedures before dismissal. Such procedures vary slightly because each state has its own regulatory statutes pertaining to tenure. Nevertheless, each state has some form of due process protection that ensures teachers the right to a fair hearing and protection from arbitrary and capricious actions by school districts.

In general, tenured teachers hold a property right in their positions, which generally grants reemployment. The word *tenured*, however, does not indicate that an individual cannot be dismissed from his or her position. Rather, tenure status requires that the school district must give the teacher adequate notice of the charges for dismissal and an opportunity to dispute the charges at a hearing before an impartial tribunal.

The law strongly protects those individuals who acquire tenure. But what about those teaching professionals who have not yet acquired tenure? What protections do probationary or nontenured teachers receive? The U.S. Supreme Court answered this question in 1972 with their decision in *Board of Regents of State Colleges v. Roth.*[1]

Board of Regents of State College v. Roth
Supreme Court of the United States, 1972
408 U.S. 564

Mr. Justice Stewart delivered the opinion of the Court.

In 1968 the respondent, David Roth, was hired for his first teaching job as assistant professor of political science at Wisconsin State University—Oshkosh. He was hired for a fixed term of one academic year. The notice of his faculty appointment specified that his employment would begin on September 1, 1968, and would end on June 30, 1969. The respondent completed that term. But he was informed that he would not be rehired for the next academic year.

The respondent had no tenure rights to continued employment. Under Wisconsin statutory law a state university teacher can acquire tenure as a "permanent" employee only after four years of year-to-year employment. Having acquired tenure, a teacher is entitled to continued employment "during efficiency and good behavior." A relatively new teacher without tenure, however, is under Wisconsin law entitled to nothing beyond his one-year appointment. There are no statutory or administrative standards defining eligibility for reemployment. State law thus clearly leaves the decision whether to rehire a nontenured teacher for another year to the unfettered discretion of university officials.

The procedural protection afforded a Wisconsin State University teacher before he is separated from the University corresponds to his job security. As a matter of statutory law, a tenured teacher cannot be "discharged except for cause upon written charges" and pursuant to certain procedures. A nontenured teacher, similarly, is protected to some extent during his one-year term. Rules promulgated by the Board of Regents provide that a nontenured teacher "dismissed" before the end of the year may have some opportunity for review of the "dismissal." But the Rules provide no real protection for a nontenured teacher who simply is not re-employed for the next year. He must be informed by February 1

---

[1] 408 U.S. 564 (1972)

"concerning retention or nonretention for the ensuing year." But "no reason for nonreten-tion need be given. No review or appeal is provided in such case."

In conformance with these Rules, the President of Wisconsin State University—Oshkosh informed the respondent before February 1, 1969, that he would not be rehired for the 1969–1970 academic year. He gave the respondent no reason for the decision and no op-portunity to challenge it at any sort of hearing. The respondent then brought this action in Federal District Court alleging that the decision not to rehire him for the next year infringed his Fourteenth Amendment rights. He attacked the decision both in substance and proce-dure. First, he alleged that the true reason for the decision was to punish him for certain statements critical of the University administration, and that it therefore violated his right to freedom of speech. Second, he alleged that the failure of University officials to give him notice of any reason for nonretention and an opportunity for a hearing violated his right to procedural due process of law.

The District Court granted summary judgment for the respondent on the procedural is-sue, ordering the University officials to provide him with reasons and a hearing. The Court of Appeals, with one judge dissenting, affirmed this partial summary judgment. We granted certiorari. The only question presented to us at this stage in the case is whether the respon-dent had a constitutional right to a statement of reasons and a hearing on the University's decision not to rehire him for another year. We hold that he did not.

I

The requirements of procedural due process apply only to the deprivation of interests en-compassed by the Fourteenth Amendment's protection of liberty and property. When pro-tected interests are implicated, the right to some kind of prior hearing is paramount. But the range of interests protected by procedural due process is not infinite.

The District Court decided that procedural due process guarantees apply in this case by assessing and balancing the weights of the particular interests involved. It concluded that the respondent's interest in re-employment at Wisconsin State University—Oshkosh out-weighed the University's interest in denying him re-employment summarily. Undeniably, the respondent's re-employment prospects were of major concern to him—concern that we surely cannot say was insignificant. And a weighing process has long been a part of any determination of the form of hearing required in particular situations by procedural due process. But, to determine whether due process requirements apply in the first place, we must look not to the "weight" but to the nature of the interest at stake. We must look to see if the interest is within the Fourteenth Amendment's protection of liberty and property.

"Liberty" and "property" are broad and majestic terms. The Court has . . . made clear that the property interests protected by procedural due process extend well beyond actual ownership of real estate, chattels, or money. By the same token, the Court has required due process protection for deprivations of liberty beyond the sort of formal constraints imposed by the criminal process.

Yet, while the Court has eschewed rigid or formalistic limitations on the protection of procedural due process, it has at the same time observed certain boundaries. For the words "liberty" and "property" in the Due Process Clause of the Fourteenth Amendment must be given some meaning.

II

"While this Court has not attempted to define with exactness the liberty . . . guaranteed [by the Fourteenth Amendment], the term has received much consideration and some of the included things have been definitely stated. Without doubt, it denotes not merely freedom from bodily restraint but also the right of the individual to contract, to engage in any of the common occupations of life, to acquire useful knowledge, to marry, establish a home and bring up children, to worship God according to the dictates of his own conscience, and generally to enjoy those privileges long recognized . . . as essential to the orderly pursuit of happiness by free men." In a Constitution for a free people, there can be no doubt that the meaning of "liberty" must be broad indeed. There might be cases in which a State refused to reemploy a person under such circumstances that interests in liberty would be implicated. But this is not such a case.

The State, in declining to rehire the respondent, did not make any charge against him that might seriously damage his standing and associations in his community. It did not base the nonrenewal of his contract on a charge, for example, that he had been guilty of dishonesty, or immorality. Had it done so, this would be a different case. For "where a person's good name, reputation, honor, or integrity is at stake because of what the government is doing to him, notice and an opportunity to be heard are essential." In such a case, due process would accord an opportunity to refute the charge before University officials. In the present case, however, there is no suggestion whatever that the respondent's "good name, reputation, honor, or integrity" is at stake.

Similarly, there is no suggestion that the State, in declining to re-employ the respondent, imposed on him a stigma or other disability that foreclosed his freedom to take advantage of other employment opportunities. The State, for example, did not invoke any regulations to bar the respondent from all other public employment in state universities. Had it done so, this, again, would be a different case. . . .

To be sure, the respondent has alleged that the nonrenewal of his contract was based on his exercise of his right to freedom of speech. But this allegation is not now before us. The District Court stayed proceedings on this issue, and the respondent has yet to prove that the decision not to rehire him was, in fact, based on his free speech activities.

Hence, on the record before us, all that clearly appears is that the respondent was not rehired for one year at one university. It stretches the concept too far to suggest that a person is deprived of "liberty" when he simply is not rehired in one job but remains as free as before to seek another.

III

The Fourteenth Amendment's procedural protection of property is a safeguard of the security of interests that a person has already acquired in specific benefits. These interests—property interests—may take many forms.

Thus, the Court has held that a person receiving welfare benefits under statutory and administrative standards defining eligibility for them has an interest in continued receipt of those benefits that is safeguarded by procedural due process. Similarly, in the area of public employment, the Court has held that a public college professor dismissed from an office held under tenure provisions, and college professors and staff members dismissed during the terms of their contracts, have interests in continued employment that are safeguarded by due process. Only last year, the Court held that this principle "proscribing summary dismissal from public employment without hearing or inquiry required by due process" also applied to a teacher recently hired without tenure or a formal contract, but nonetheless with a clearly implied promise of continued employment.

Certain attributes of "property" interests protected by procedural due process emerge from these decisions. To have a property interest in a benefit, a person clearly must have more than an abstract need or desire for it. He must have more than a unilateral expectation of it. He must, instead, have a legitimate claim of entitlement to it. It is a purpose of the ancient institution of property to protect those claims upon which people rely in their daily lives, reliance that must not be arbitrarily undermined. It is a purpose of the constitutional right to a hearing to provide an opportunity for a person to vindicate those claims.

Property interests, of course, are not created by the Constitution. Rather, they are created and their dimensions are defined by existing rules or understandings that stem from an independent source such as state law—rules or understandings that secure certain benefits and that support claims of entitlement to those benefits. Thus, the welfare recipients in *Goldberg v. Kelly* had a claim of entitlement to welfare payments that was grounded in the statute defining eligibility for them. The recipients had not yet shown that they were, in fact, within the statutory terms of eligibility. But we held that they had a right to a hearing at which they might attempt to do so.

Just as the welfare recipients' "property" interest in welfare payments was created and defined by statutory terms, so the respondent's "property" interest in employment at Wisconsin State University—Oshkosh was created and defined by the terms of his appointment. Those terms secured his interest in employment up to June 30, 1969. But the important fact in this case is that they specifically provided that the respondent's employment was to terminate on June 30. They did not provide for contract renewal absent "sufficient cause." Indeed, they made no provision for renewal whatsoever.

Thus, the terms of the respondent's appointment secured absolutely no interest in re-employment for the next year. They supported absolutely no possible claim of entitlement to re-employment. Nor, significantly, was there any state statute or University rule or policy that secured his interest in re-employment or that created any legitimate claim to it. In these circumstances, the respondent surely had an abstract concern in being rehired, but he did not have a property interest sufficient to require the University authorities to give him a hearing when they declined to renew his contract of employment.

IV

Our analysis of the respondent's constitutional rights in this case in no way indicates a view that an opportunity for a hearing or a statement of reasons for nonretention would, or would not, be appropriate or wise in public colleges and universities. For it is a written Constitution that we apply. Our role is confined to interpretation of that Constitution.

We must conclude that the summary judgment for the respondent should not have been granted, since the respondent has not shown that he was deprived of liberty or property protected by the Fourteenth Amendment. The judgment of the Court of Appeals, accordingly, is reversed and the case is remanded for further proceedings consistent with this opinion.

It is so ordered.

Roth was hired as a nontenured teacher for one year and was not rehired for the next year. He sued, claiming that his Fourteenth Amendment rights had been violated. The Supreme Court, however, concluded that, because Roth was a probational teacher, he had no legal interest in reemployment. Hence, there was no property interest that would entitle him to protection under the Fourteenth Amendment. While the Supreme Court clearly held that teachers are entitled to due process protection, that protection is applied only if they are considered to be tenured; nontenured teachers have no such right. In other words, a legal property right does not attach to a mere expectation of reemployment. Nontenured teachers do not have a property right in their position and therefore are not entitled to due process.

So can a teacher with tenure be fired? Of course. Due process requires only that a hearing must be held before an impartial body, that there be advanced and specific notice of charges, and that both sides have the opportunity to present evidence and confront adverse witnesses. Because each state has its own statutes pertaining to due process, what happens if a state decides to abolish tenure? On the same day it decided *Board of Regents of State Colleges v. Roth*, the Supreme Court reviewed *Perry v. Sindermann*.[2]

Perry v. Sindermann
Supreme Court of the United States, 1972
408 U.S. 593

Mr. Justice Stewart delivered the opinion of the Court.

From 1959 to 1969 the respondent, Robert Sindermann, was a teacher in the state college system of the State of Texas. After teaching for two years at the University of Texas and for four years at San Antonio Junior College, he became a professor of Government and Social Science at Odessa Junior College in 1965. He was employed at the college for four successive years, under a series of one-year contracts. He was successful enough to be appointed, for a time, the cochairman of his department.

During the 1968–1969 academic year, however, controversy arose between the respondent and the college administration. The respondent was elected president of the Texas Junior College Teachers Association. In this capacity, he left his teaching duties on several occasions to testify before committees of the Texas Legislature, and he became involved in

---

[2] 408 U.S. 593 (1972)

public disagreements with the policies of the college's Board of Regents. In particular, he aligned himself with a group advocating the elevation of the college to four-year status—a change opposed by the Regents. And, on one occasion, a newspaper advertisement appeared over his name that was highly critical of the Regents.

Finally, in May 1969, the respondent's one-year employment contract terminated and the Board of Regents voted not to offer him a new contract for the next academic year. The Regents issued a press release setting forth allegations of the respondent's insubordination. But they provided him no official statement of the reasons for the nonrenewal of his contract. And they allowed him no opportunity for a hearing to challenge the basis of the nonrenewal.

The respondent then brought this action in Federal District Court. He alleged primarily that the Regents' decision not to rehire him was based on his public criticism of the policies of the college administration and thus infringed his right to freedom of speech. He also alleged that their failure to provide him an opportunity for a hearing violated the Fourteenth Amendment's guarantee of procedural due process. The petitioners—members of the Board of Regents and the president of the college—denied that their decision was made in retaliation for the respondent's public criticism and argued that they had no obligation to provide a hearing. On the basis of these bare pleadings and three brief affidavits filed by the respondent, the District Court granted summary judgment for the petitioners. It concluded that the respondent had "no cause of action against the [petitioners] since his contract of employment terminated May 31, 1969, and Odessa Junior College has not adopted the tenure system."

The Court of Appeals reversed the judgment of the District Court. First, it held that, despite the respondent's lack of tenure, the nonrenewal of his contract would violate the Fourteenth Amendment if it in fact was based on his protected free speech. Since the actual reason for the Regents' decision was "in total dispute" in the pleadings, the court remanded the case for a full hearing on this contested issue of fact. Second, the Court of Appeals held that, despite the respondent's lack of tenure, the failure to allow him an opportunity for a hearing would violate the constitutional guarantee of procedural due process if the respondent could show that he had an "expectancy" of re-employment. It, therefore, ordered that this issue of fact also be aired upon remand. We granted a writ of certiorari, and we have considered this case along with *Board of Regents v. Roth.*

I

The first question presented is whether the respondent's lack of a contractual or tenure right to re-employment, taken alone, defeats his claim that the nonrenewal of his contract violated the First and Fourteenth Amendments. We hold that it does not.

For at least a quarter-century, this Court has made clear that even though a person has no "right" to a valuable governmental benefit and even though the government may deny him the benefit for any number of reasons, there are some reasons upon which the government may not rely. It may not deny a benefit to a person on a basis that infringes his constitutionally protected interests—especially, his interest in freedom of speech. For if the government could deny a benefit to a person because of his constitutionally protected speech or associations, his exercise of those freedoms would in effect be penalized and inhibited. This would allow the government to "produce a result which [it] could not command directly." Such interference with constitutional rights is impermissible. . . .

Thus, the respondent's lack of a contractual or tenure "right" to re-employment for the 1969–1970 academic year is immaterial to his free speech claim. Indeed, twice before, this Court has specifically held that the nonrenewal of a nontenured public school teacher's one-year contract may not be predicated on his exercise of First and Fourteenth Amendment rights. We reaffirm those holdings here.

In this case, of course, the respondent has yet to show that the decision not to renew his contract was, in fact, made in retaliation for his exercise of the constitutional right of free speech. The District Court foreclosed any opportunity to make this showing when it granted summary judgment. Hence, we cannot now hold that the Board of Regents' action was invalid.

But we agree with the Court of Appeals that there is a genuine dispute as to "whether the college refused to renew the teaching contract on an impermissible basis—as a reprisal for the exercise of constitutionally protected rights." The respondent has alleged that his nonretention was based on his testimony before legislative committees and his other public statements critical of the Regents' policies. And he has alleged that this public criticism was within the First and Fourteenth Amendments' protection of freedom of speech. Plainly, these allegations present a bona fide constitutional claim. For this Court has held that a teacher's public criticism of his superiors on matters of public concern may be constitutionally protected and may, therefore, be an impermissible basis for termination of his employment. For this reason we hold that the grant of summary judgment against the respondent, without full exploration of this issue, was improper.

II

The respondent's lack of formal contractual or tenure security in continued employment at Odessa Junior College, though irrelevant to his free speech claim, is highly relevant to his procedural due process claim. But it may not be entirely dispositive.

We have held today in *Board of Regents v. Roth*, that the Constitution does not require opportunity for a hearing before the nonrenewal of a nontenured teacher's contract, unless he can show that the decision not to rehire him somehow deprived him of an interest in "liberty" or that he had a "property" interest in continued employment, despite the lack of tenure or a formal contract. In *Roth* the teacher had not made a showing on either point to justify summary judgment in his favor.

Similarly, the respondent here has yet to show that he has been deprived of an interest that could invoke procedural due process protection. As in *Roth*, the mere showing that he was not rehired in one particular job, without more, did not amount to a showing of a loss of liberty. Nor did it amount to a showing of a loss of property.

But the respondent's allegations—which we must construe most favorably to the respondent at this stage of the litigation—do raise a genuine issue as to his interest in continued employment at Odessa Junior College. He alleged that this interest, though not secured by a formal contractual tenure provision, was secured by a no less binding understanding fostered by the college administration. In particular, the respondent alleged that the college had a de facto tenure program, and that he had tenure under that program. He claimed that he and others legitimately relied upon an unusual provision that had been in the college's official Faculty Guide for many years:

"*Teacher Tenure:* Odessa College has no tenure system. The Administration of the College wishes the faculty member to feel that he has permanent tenure as long as his teaching services are satisfactory and as long as he displays a cooperative attitude toward his co-workers and his superiors, and as long as he is happy in his work."

Moreover, the respondent claimed legitimate reliance upon guidelines promulgated by the Coordinating Board of the Texas College and University System that provided that a person, like himself, who had been employed as a teacher in the state college and university system for seven years or more has some form of job tenure. Thus, the respondent offered to prove that a teacher with his long period of service at this particular State College had no less a "property" interest in continued employment than a formally tenured teacher at other colleges, and had no less a procedural due process right to a statement of reasons and a hearing before college officials upon their decision not to retain him.

We have made clear in *Roth*, that "property" interests subject to procedural due process protection are not limited by a few rigid, technical forms. Rather, "property" denotes a broad range of interests that are secured by "existing rules or understandings." A person's interest in a benefit is a "property" interest for due process purposes if there are such rules or mutually explicit understandings that support his claim of entitlement to the benefit and that he may invoke at a hearing.

A written contract with an explicit tenure provision clearly is evidence of a formal understanding that supports a teacher's claim of entitlement to continued employment unless sufficient "cause" is shown. Yet absence of such an explicit contractual provision may not always foreclose the possibility that a teacher has a "property" interest in re-employment. For example, the law of contracts in most, if not all, jurisdictions long has employed a process by which agreements, though not formalized in writing, may be "implied." Explicit contractual provisions may be supplemented by other agreements implied from "the promisor's words and conduct in the light of the surrounding circumstances." And, "the meaning of [the promisor's] words and acts is found by relating them to the usage of the past."

A teacher, like the respondent, who has held his position for a number of years, might be able to show from the circumstances of this service—and from other relevant facts—that he has a legitimate claim of entitlement to job tenure. Just as this Court has found there to be a "common law of a particular industry or of a particular plant" that may supplement a collective-bargaining agreement, so there may be an unwritten "common law" in a particular university that certain employees shall have the equivalent of tenure. This is particularly likely in a college or university, like Odessa Junior College, that has no explicit tenure system even for senior members of its faculty, but that nonetheless may have created such a system in practice.

In this case, the respondent has alleged the existence of rules and understandings, promulgated and fostered by state officials, that may justify his legitimate claim of entitlement to continued employment absent "sufficient cause." We disagree with the Court of Appeals insofar as it held that a mere subjective "expectancy" is protected by procedural due process, but we agree that the respondent must be given an opportunity to prove the legitimacy of his claim of such entitlement in light of "the policies and practices of the institution." Proof of such a property interest would not, of course, entitle him to reinstatement. But such proof would obligate college officials to grant a hearing at his request, where he could be informed of the grounds for his nonretention and challenge their sufficiency.

Therefore, while we do not wholly agree with the opinion of the Court of Appeals, its judgment remanding this case to the District Court is affirmed.

Mr. Justice Powell took no part in the decision of this case. Concur Justice Burger.

Unlike Roth in the previous case, Sindermann was not tenured, so how could the Fourteenth Amendment attach legal protection to him? Although Odessa College has no tenure system, Sindermann claimed the school operated a de facto tenure program—*defacto* meaning "one who has a position but does not have the lawful title." This case is important because numerous states do not give tenure. State legislatures have the power to create the laws that govern whether or not teachers have tenure. According to the Supreme Court, however, the word *tenure* is not the critical fact in the case. Rather, it revolves around whether a teacher has held a position for a certain number of years and can claim job tenure without the explicit provision but through tenure-like custom. The *Sindermann* case is important, especially for states without tenure laws; but note the factual differences between *Sindermann* and *Roth*. Sindermann had worked at the same educational institution for four years, while Roth had only been employed for one year.

A tenured teacher's due process rights are highly protected. In an attempt to ensure high-quality education while maintaining fiscal restraints, schools sometimes dismiss faculty. There is no law that prevents faculty members from being fired based on budgetary constraints or reductions in force. Nevertheless, Fourteenth Amendment protections are still in place. For example, a tenured teacher of 22 years was informed that his position had been eliminated. With no other explanation, the teacher was dismissed and placed in a group of reassigned teachers but was unable to find employment. According to the facts, the teacher was never informed about the reasons for his dismissal. Even though a school district has the right to dismiss faculty based on reductions, in this case, according to the court, "the Board deprived him of his property rights without due process by terminating his teaching position."[3]

Best Practices

- The Fourteenth Amendment does not protect a teacher from being fired. Rather, it gives teachers the right to due process.
- Before dismissing any teacher, perform a due process hearing. This includes, in most cases, a hearing on the issue before an impartial tribunal, advance and specific notice, and the opportunity to present evidence and confront adverse witnesses.

---

[3] *Chandler v. Board of Education of City of Chicago*, 92 F.Supp. 2d 760 (2000)

Collective Bargaining

COLLECTIVE bargaining powers and their impact on teachers vary from state to state. The power of unions in a particular district within a particular state will determine the collective bargaining process. For example, states that are heavily unionized have representation that works with management to negotiate items such as salary, work conditions, benefits, governance, and class size. Teachers in some states have unions that represent them directly. Other states, where unions are not as powerful, still implement the idea of "meet and confer," where faculty choose a representative who deals with management to resolve issues of importance. The meet-and-confer process is generally less adversarial. Regardless of whether there is collective bargaining or meet-and-confer meetings, teacher representation has increased dramatically in the past 25 years.

The movement toward representation and collective bargaining has met some legal deterrents. As illustrated in the *Lehnert* case, states such as Michigan once used an agency shop arrangement, which created a union for public school employees. As part of the union, members were required to pay dues; but those teachers who did not want to join the union were also required to pay a fee, which was slightly less. To dispute this service fee, nonmembers brought suit, claiming that it was a constitutional violation.

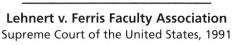

Lehnert v. Ferris Faculty Association
Supreme Court of the United States, 1991
500 U.S. 507

Opinion written by Justice Blackmun announced the judgment of the Court.

This case presents issues concerning the constitutional limitations, if any, upon the payment, required as a condition of employment, of dues by a nonmember to a union in the public sector.

Michigan's Public Employment Relations Act (Act), Mich. Comp. Laws §423.201 *et seq.* (1978), provides that a duly selected union shall serve as the exclusive collective-bargaining representative of public employees in a particular bargaining unit. The Act, which applies to faculty members of a public educational institution in Michigan, permits a union and a government employer to enter into an "agency-shop" arrangement under which employees within the bargaining unit who decline to become members of the union are compelled to pay a "service fee" to the union.

Respondent Ferris Faculty Association (FFA), an affiliate of the Michigan Education Association (MEA) and the National Education Association (NEA), serves, pursuant to this provision, as the exclusive bargaining representative of the faculty of Ferris State College in Big Rapids, Mich. Ferris is a public institution established under the Michigan Constitution and is funded by the State. Since 1975, the FFA and Ferris have entered into successive collective-bargaining agreements containing agency-shop provisions. Those agreements were the fruit of negotiations between the FFA and respondent Board of Control, the governing body of Ferris.

Subsequent to this Court's decision in *Abood v. Detroit Board of Education*, in which the Court upheld the constitutionality of the Michigan agency-shop provision and outlined permissible uses of the compelled fee by public-employee unions, Ferris proposed, and the FFA agreed to, the agency-shop arrangement at issue here. That agreement required all employees in the bargaining unit who did not belong to the FFA to pay a service fee equivalent to the amount of dues required of a union member. Of the $284 service fee for 1981–1982, the period at issue, $24.80 went to the FFA, $211.20 to the MEA, and $48 to the NEA. . . .

Following a partial settlement, petitioners took an appeal limited to the claim that the District Court erred in holding that the costs of certain disputed union activities were constitutionally chargeable to the plaintiff faculty members. Specifically, petitioners objected to the District Court's conclusion that the union constitutionally could charge them for the costs of (1) lobbying and electoral politics; (2) bargaining, litigation, and other activities on behalf of persons not in petitioners' bargaining unit; (3) public-relations efforts; (4) miscellaneous professional activities; (5) meetings and conventions of the parent unions; and (6) preparation for a strike which, had it materialized, would have violated Michigan law. . . .

It was not until the decision in *Abood* that this Court addressed the constitutionality of union-security provisions in the public-employment context. There, the Court upheld the same Michigan statute which is before us today against a facial First Amendment challenge. At the same time, it determined that the claim that a union has utilized an individual agency-shop agreement to force dissenting employees to subsidize ideological activities could establish, upon a proper showing, a First Amendment violation. In so doing, the Court set out several important propositions: First, it recognized that "to compel employees financially to support their collective-bargaining representative has an impact upon their First Amendment interests." Unions traditionally have aligned themselves with a wide range of social, political, and ideological viewpoints, any number of which might bring vigorous disapproval from individual employees. To force employees to contribute, albeit indirectly, to the promotion of such positions implicates core First Amendment concerns.

Second, the Court in *Abood* determined that, as in the private sector, compulsory affiliation with, or monetary support of, a public-employment union does not, without more, violate the First Amendment rights of public employees. Similarly, an employee's free speech rights are not unconstitutionally burdened because the employee opposes positions taken by a union in its capacity as collective-bargaining representative. "The judgment clearly made in *Hanson* and *Street* is that such interference as exists is constitutionally justified by the legislative assessment of the important contribution of the union shop to the system of labor relations established by Congress."

In this connection, the Court indicated that the considerations that justify the union shop in the private context—the desirability of labor peace and eliminating "free riders"—are equally important in the public-sector workplace. Consequently, the use of dissenters' assessments "for the purposes of collective bargaining, contract administration, and grievance adjustment," approved under the RLA, is equally permissible when authorized by a State vis-a-vis its own workers.

Third, the Court established that the constitutional principles that prevent a State from conditioning public employment upon association with a political party, or upon professed religious allegiance, similarly prohibit a public employer "from requiring [an employee] to contribute to the support of an ideological cause he may oppose as a condition of holding a job" as a public educator.

The Court in *Abood* did not attempt to draw a precise line between permissible assessments for public-sector collective-bargaining activities and prohibited assessments for ideological activities. It did note, however, that, while a similar line must be drawn in the private sector under the RLA, the distinction in the public sector may be "somewhat hazier." This is so because the "process of establishing a written collective-bargaining agreement prescribing the terms and conditions of public employment may require not merely concord at the bargaining table, but subsequent approval by other public authorities; related budgetary and appropriations decisions might be seen as an integral part of the bargaining process."

Finally, in *Ellis*, the Court considered, among other issues, a First Amendment challenge to the use of dissenters' funds for various union expenses including union conventions, publications, and social events. Recognizing that by allowing union-security arrangements at all, it has necessarily countenanced a significant burdening of First Amendment rights, it limited its inquiry to whether the expenses at issue "involved *additional* interference with the First Amendment interests of objecting employees, and, if so, whether they are nonetheless adequately supported by a governmental interest."

Applying that standard to the challenged expenses, the Court found all three to be properly supportable through mandatory assessments. The dissenting employees in *Ellis* objected to charges relating to union social functions, not because those activities were inherently expressive or ideological in nature, but purely because they were sponsored by the union. Because employees may constitutionally be compelled to affiliate with a union, the Court found that forced contribution to union social events that were open to all imposed no additional burden on their First Amendment rights. Although the challenged expenses for union publications and conventions were clearly communicative in nature, the Court found them to entail little additional encroachment upon freedom of speech, "and none that is not justified by the governmental interests behind the union shop itself."

Thus, although the Court's decisions in this area prescribe a case-by-case analysis in determining which activities a union constitutionally may charge to dissenting employees, they also set forth several guidelines to be followed in making such determinations. *Hanson* and *Street* and their progeny teach that chargeable activities must (1) be "germane" to collective-bargaining activity; (2) be justified by the government's vital policy interest in labor peace and avoiding "free riders"; and (3) not significantly add to the burdening of free speech that is inherent in the allowance of an agency or union shop. . . ."

The Court of Appeals determined that unions constitutionally may subsidize lobbying and other political activities with dissenters' fees so long as those activities are "pertinent to the duties of the union as a bargaining representative." In reaching this conclusion, the court relied upon the inherently political nature of salary and other workplace decisions in public employment. "To represent their members effectively," the court concluded, "public sector unions must necessarily concern themselves not only with negotiations at the bargaining table but also with advancing their members' interests in legislative and other 'political' arenas."

This observation is clearly correct. Public-sector unions often expend considerable resources in securing ratification of negotiated agreements by the proper state or local legislative body. Similarly, union efforts to acquire appropriations for approved collective-bargaining agreements often serve as an indispensable prerequisite to their implementation. It was in reference to these characteristics of public employment that the Court in *Abood* discussed the "somewhat hazier" line between bargaining-related and purely ideological activities in the public sector. The dual roles of government as employer and policymaker in such cases make the analogy between lobbying and collective bargaining in the public sector a close one.

This, however, is not such a case. Where, as here, the challenged lobbying activities relate not to the ratification or implementation of a dissenter's collective-bargaining agreement, but to financial support of the employee's profession or of public employees generally, the connection to the union's function as bargaining representative is too attenuated to justify compelled support by objecting employees.

We arrive at this result by looking to the governmental interests underlying our acceptance of union-security arrangements. We have found such arrangements to be justified by the government's interest in promoting labor peace and avoiding the "free-rider" problem that would otherwise accompany union recognition. Neither goal is served by charging objecting employees for lobbying, electoral, and other political activities that do not relate to their collective-bargaining agreement.

Labor peace is not especially served by allowing such charges because, unlike collective-bargaining negotiations between union and management, our national and state legislatures, the media, and the platform of public discourse are public forums open to all. Individual employees are free to petition their neighbors and government in opposition to the union which represents them in the workplace. Because worker and union cannot be said to speak with one voice, it would not further the cause of harmonious industrial relations to compel objecting employees to finance union political activities as well as their own.

Similarly, while we have endorsed the notion that nonunion workers ought not be allowed to benefit from the terms of employment secured by union efforts without paying for those services, the so-called "free-rider" concern is inapplicable where lobbying extends beyond the effectuation of a collective-bargaining agreement. The balancing of monetary and other policy choices performed by legislatures is not limited to the workplace but typically has ramifications that extend into diverse aspects of an employee's life.

Accordingly, we hold that the State constitutionally may not compel its employees to subsidize legislative lobbying or other political union activities outside the limited context of contract ratification or implementation. . . .

The essence of the affiliation relationship is the notion that the parent will bring to bear its often considerable economic, political, and informational resources when the local is in need of them. Consequently, that part of a local's affiliation fee which contributes to the pool of resources potentially available to the local is assessed for the bargaining unit's protection, even if it is not actually expended on that unit in any particular membership year. . . .

We therefore conclude that a local bargaining representative may charge objecting employees for their pro rata share of the costs associated with otherwise chargeable activities of its state and national affiliates, even if those activities were not performed for the direct benefit of the objecting employees' bargaining unit. This conclusion, however, does not serve to grant a local union *carte blanche* to expend dissenters' dollars for bargaining activities wholly unrelated to the employees in their unit. The union surely may not, for example, charge objecting employees for a direct donation or interest-free loan to an unrelated bargaining unit for the purpose of promoting employee rights or unionism generally. Further, a contribution by a local union to its parent that is not part of the local's responsibilities as an affiliate but is in the nature of a charitable donation would not be chargeable to dissenters. There must be some indication that the payment is for services that may ultimately inure to the benefit of the members of the local union by virtue of their membership in the parent organization. And, as always, the union bears the burden of proving the proportion of chargeable expenses to total expenses. We conclude merely that the union need not demonstrate a direct and tangible impact upon the dissenting employee's unit. . . .

The Court of Appeals found that the union could constitutionally charge petitioners for the costs of a Preserve Public Education (PPE) program designed to secure funds for public education in Michigan, and that portion of the MEA publication, the *Teacher's Voice*, which reported these activities. Petitioners argue that, contrary to the findings of the courts below, the PPE program went beyond lobbying activity and sought to affect the outcome of ballot issues and "millages" or local taxes for the support of public schools. Given our conclusion as to lobbying and electoral politics generally, this factual dispute is of little consequence. None of these activities was shown to be oriented toward the ratification or implementation of petitioners' collective-bargaining agreement. We hold that none may be supported through the funds of objecting employees.

Petitioners next challenge the Court of Appeals' allowance of several activities that the union did not undertake directly on behalf of persons within petitioners' bargaining unit. This objection principally concerns NEA "program expenditures" destined for States other than Michigan, and the expenses of the *Teacher's Voice* listed as "Collective Bargaining" and "Litigation." Our conclusion that unions may bill dissenting employees for their share of general collective-bargaining costs of the state or national parent union is dispositive as to the bulk of the NEA expenditures. The District Court found these costs to be germane to collective bargaining and similar support services and we decline to disturb that finding. No greater relationship is necessary in the collective-bargaining context.

This rationale does not extend, however, to the expenses of litigation that does not concern the dissenting employees' bargaining unit or, by extension, to union literature reporting on such activities. While respondents are clearly correct that precedent established through litigation on behalf of one unit may ultimately be of some use to another unit, we find extraunit litigation to be more akin to lobbying in both kind and effect. We long have recognized the important political and expressive nature of litigation. Moreover, union litigation may cover a diverse range of areas from bankruptcy proceedings to employment discrimination. When unrelated to an objecting employee's unit, such activities are not germane to the union's duties as exclusive bargaining representative. Just as the Court in *Ellis* determined that the RLA, as informed by the First Amendment, prohibits the use of dissenters' fees for extraunit litigation, we hold that the Amendment proscribes such assessments in the public sector.

The Court of Appeals determined that the union constitutionally could charge petitioners for certain public relations expenditures. In this connection, the court said: "Public relations expenditures designed to enhance the reputation of the teaching profession . . . are, in our opinion, sufficiently related to the unions' duty to represent bargaining unit employees effectively so as to be chargeable to dissenters." We disagree. Like the challenged lobbying conduct, the public relations activities at issue here entailed speech of a political nature in a public forum. More important, public speech in support of the teaching profession generally is not sufficiently related to the union's collective-bargaining functions to justify compelling dissenting employees to support it. Expression of this kind extends beyond the negotiation and grievance-resolution contexts and imposes a substantially greater burden upon First Amendment rights than do the latter activities.

The Court of Appeals ruled that the union could use the fees of objecting employees to send FFA delegates to the MEA and the NEA conventions and to participate in the 13E Coordinating Council, another union structure. Petitioners challenge that determination and argue that, unlike the national convention expenses found to be chargeable to dissenters in *Ellis*, the meetings at issue here were those of affiliated parent unions rather than the local, and therefore do not relate exclusively to petitioners' unit.

We need not determine whether petitioners could be commanded to support all the expenses of these conventions. The question before the Court is simply whether the unions may constitutionally require petitioners to subsidize the participation in these events of delegates from the local. We hold that they may. That the conventions were not solely devoted to the activities of the FFA does not prevent the unions from requiring petitioners' support. We conclude above that the First Amendment does not require so close a connection. Moreover, participation by members of the local in the formal activities of the parent is likely to be an important benefit of affiliation. This conclusion is supported by the District Court's description of the 13E Coordinating Council meeting as an event at which "bargaining strategies and representational policies are developed for the UniServ unit composed of the Ferris State College and Central Michigan University bargaining units." As was held in *Ellis*, "conventions such as those at issue here are normal events . . . and seem to us to be essential to the union's discharge of its duties as bargaining agent."

The chargeability of expenses incident to preparation for a strike which all concede would have been illegal under Michigan law, Mich. Comp. Laws §423.202 (1979), is a provocative question. At the beginning of the 1981–1982 fiscal year, the FFA and Ferris were engaged in negotiating a new collective-bargaining agreement. The union perceived these efforts to be ineffective and began to prepare a "job action" or, in more familiar terms, to go out on strike. These preparations entailed the creation by the FFA and the MEA of a "crisis center" or "strike headquarters." The District Court found that, "whatever label is attached to this facility, prior to a strike it serves as a meeting place for the local's membership, a base from which tactical activities such as informational picketing can be conducted, and serves to apply additional pressure on the employer by suggesting, whether true or not, that the local is prepared to strike if necessary." . . .

Petitioners can identify no determination by the State of Michigan that mere preparation for an illegal strike is itself illegal or against public policy, and we are aware of none. Further, we accept the rationale provided by the Court of Appeals in upholding these charges that such expenditures fall "within the range of reasonable bargaining tools available to a public sector union during contract negotiations." The District Court expressly credited trial testimony by an MEA representative that outward preparations for a potential strike serve as an effective bargaining tool and that only one out of every seven or eight "job action investigations" actually culminates in a strike. The Court of Appeals properly reviewed this finding for clear error.

In sum, these expenses are substantively indistinguishable from those appurtenant to collective-bargaining negotiations. The District Court and the Court of Appeals concluded, and we agree, that they aid in those negotiations and inure to the direct benefit of members of the dissenters' unit. Further, they impose no additional burden upon First Amendment rights. The union may properly charge petitioners for those costs.

It is so ordered.

Among other important issues concerning collective bargaining is public employees' right to strike. Historically, there have been numerous teacher strikes; and depending on the state in which the strike occurred, as well as the contract provision of the union agreement, it may or may not be held as an illegal activity. Some states prohibit strikes completely; others state in their contractual agreements that if negotiations come to an impasse after a certain amount of time, a limited strike may occur. Because this type of issue is state-specific, administrators, faculty, and their representatives should be aware of pertinent state laws.

CAUSE FOR DISMISSAL

AS DISCUSSED, the laws of tenure do not provide lifelong employment for poor-quality teachers. Teachers can be dismissed from their positions for numerous reasons. Obviously, what may have been inappropriate in 1950 may be acceptable and legally protected today. Society has become more individualized, accepting an array of lifestyles, dress, hairstyles, and beliefs. Because states and local school districts set procedures and policies pertaining to dismissal, specific reasons may vary. "County boards of education have substantial discretion in matters relating to the hiring, assignment, transfer, and promotion of school personnel. Nevertheless, this discretion must be exercised reasonably, in the best interests of the schools, and in a manner which is not arbitrary and capricious."[4] To avoid lawsuits based on wrongful discharge, most school districts have detailed dismissal policies based on insubordination, poor classroom management,

---

[4] *Dillon v. Wyoming County Board of Education*, 351 S.E.2d 58 (1986)

incompetence, immorality, sexual activity, criminal activity, and a catch-all reason known as "just cause."

Insubordination

Insubordination is generally considered to be "constant or continuing intentional refusal to obey a direct or implied order, reasonable in nature, and given by and with proper authority."[5] Other courts have defined insubordination as "the willful refusal of a teacher to obey the reasonable rules and regulations of his or her employing board of education."[6] School districts commonly dismiss teachers for acts of insubordination. In general, however, such acts must be intentional or deliberate.

Incompetence

Teachers are expected to be competent in their subject areas. But after evaluation, districts occasionally determine that a faculty member is incompetent in that position and can be legally dismissed. For example, a school district's decision to dismiss a teacher was upheld when the school determined that the teacher was not maintaining discipline in the classroom, used too many films in class instead of lecturing, lacked effective teaching techniques, and failed to improve and abide by administrative suggestions.[7]

In a similar case, a teacher's contract was not renewed due to failure to manage the classroom and keep a safe classroom environment, poor teaching evaluations, poor relations with other faculty members, as well as not following instructions after repeated meetings with administration.[8] In its decision, the court held:

> *While we cannot realistically expect a kindergarten teacher to have complete control over all of his or her students at every moment, we also cannot accept plaintiff's contention that administrative action is precluded unless the classroom is always or usually unruly or unsafe. There may be reasonable and just cause for dismissal if there is substantial evidence that the teacher's classroom is significantly more disorderly or unsafe than would be reasonably expected. In the instant case, there was more than sufficient evidence that plaintiff's classroom was lacking in control and safety more often than would be reasonably expected in any kindergarten classroom, including one utilizing plaintiff's particular pedagogical method.[9]*

Administrators may also be dismissed for incompetence. A Connecticut court upheld a school district's decision to dismiss an assistant principal based on incompetence after

---

[5] *Shockley v. Board of Education*, 149 A.2d 331, at 334 (1959)
[6] *State ex rel. Steele v. Board of Education*, 40 So.2d 689 (1988)
[7] *Board of Directors of Sioux City v. Mroz*, 295 N.W.2d 447 (1980)
[8] *Beebee v. Haslett Public Schools*, 278 N.W.2d 37 (1979)
[9] Ibid., at 41

she ordered a teacher and an aide to strip search students against school policy.[10] The incident occurred after a student reported that money had been stolen from her gym locker. School policy stated that a principal or an assistant principal be present during all searches. Against policy, the assistant principal ordered a teacher and aide to strip search 22 students in an attempt to recover the stolen money.

Immoral Conduct

As individuals working with young children, educators should be well aware of the impact they have on their students; additionally, faculty and staff are expected to act professionally. For example, a tenured elementary physical education teacher was discharged for unprofessional and immoral conduct, allegedly pinching three second-grade female students on the buttocks during class.[11] While few would argue that such conduct is immoral, the definition of immorality and unprofessional conduct is not always so clear.

Morrison v. State Board of Education
Supreme Court of California, 1969
461 P.2d 375

For a number of years prior to 1965 petitioner held a General Secondary Life Diploma and a Life Diploma to Teach Exceptional Children, issued by the State Board of Education, which qualified petitioner for employment as a teacher in the public secondary schools of California. On August 5, 1965, an accusation was filed with the State Board of Education charging that petitioner's life diplomas should be revoked for cause. On March 11, 1966, following a hearing, and pursuant to the recommendations of a hearing examiner, the board revoked petitioner's life diplomas because of immoral and unprofessional conduct and acts involving moral turpitude as authorized by section 13202 of the Education Code. This revocation rendered petitioner ineligible for employment as a teacher in any public school in the state. On February 14, 1967, petitioner sought a writ of mandate from the Superior Court of Los Angeles County to compel the board to set aside its decision and restore his life diplomas. After a hearing the superior court denied the writ, and this appeal followed.

For the reasons hereinafter set forth we conclude (a) that section 13202 authorizes disciplinary measures only for conduct indicating unfitness to teach, (b) that properly interpreted to this effect section 13202 is constitutional on its face and as here applied, and (c) that the record contains no evidence to support the conclusion that petitioner's conduct indicated his unfitness to teach. The judgment of the superior court must therefore be reversed.

---

[10] Rogers v. New Haven Board of Education, 199 Conn. Super. LEXUS 385 (1999)

[11] *Board of Education of Argo-Summit Sch. Dist. No. 104, v. State Board of Education,* 487 N.E.2d 24 (1985)

I. The Facts

For a number of years prior to 1964 petitioner worked as a teacher for the Lowell Joint School District. During this period, so far as appears from the record, no one complained about, or so much as criticized, his performance as a teacher. Moreover, with the exception of a single incident, no one suggested that his conduct outside the classroom was other than beyond reproach.

Sometime before the spring of 1963 petitioner became friends with Mr. and Mrs. Fred Schneringer. Mr. Schneringer also worked as a teacher in the public school system. To the Schneringers, who were involved in grave marital and financial difficulties at the time, petitioner gave counsel and advice. In the course of such counseling Mr. Schneringer frequently visited petitioner's apartment to discuss his problems. For a one-week period in April, during which petitioner and Mr. Schneringer experienced severe emotional stress, the two men engaged in a limited, non-criminal physical relationship which petitioner described as being of a homosexual nature. Petitioner has never been accused or convicted of any criminal activity whatever, and the record contains no evidence of any abnormal activities or desires by petitioner since the Schneringer incident some six years in the past. Petitioner and Schneringer met on numerous occasions in the spring and summer after the incident and nothing untoward occurred. When Schneringer later obtained a separation from his wife, petitioner suggested a number of women whom Schneringer might consider dating.

Approximately one year after the April 1963 incident, Schneringer reported it to the Superintendent of the Lowell Joint School District. As a result of that report petitioner resigned his teaching position on May 4, 1964.

Some 19 months after the incident became known to the superintendent, the State Board of Education conducted a hearing concerning possible revocation of petitioner's life diplomas. Petitioner there testified that he had had some undefined homosexual problem at the age of 13, but that, with the sole exception of the Schneringer incident, he had not experienced the slightest homosexual urge or inclination for more than a dozen years. Mr. Cavalier, an investigator testifying for the board, stated that the Schneringer incident "was the only time that [petitioner] ever engaged in a homosexual act with anyone." No evidence was presented that petitioner had ever committed any act of misconduct whatsoever while teaching.

The Board of Education finally revoked petitioner's life diplomas some three years after the Schneringer incident. The board concluded that that incident constituted immoral and unprofessional conduct, and an act involving moral turpitude, all of which warrant revocation of life diplomas under section 13202 of the Education Code.

II. Petitioner's actions cannot constitute immoral or unprofessional conduct or conduct involving moral turpitude within the meaning of section 13202 unless those actions indicate his unfitness to teach.

Section 13202 of the Education Code authorizes revocation of life diplomas for "immoral conduct," "unprofessional conduct," and "acts involving moral turpitude." Legislation authorizing disciplinary action against the holders of a variety of certificates, licenses and government jobs other than teaching also contain these rather general terms. This court has not attempted to formulate explicit definitions of those terms which would apply to all the statutes in which they are used. Rather, we have given those terms more precise meaning by referring in each case to the particular profession or the specific governmental position to which they were applicable.

In *Hallinan v. Committee of Bar Examiners,* for example, we considered the meaning of "acts of moral turpitude" as applied to an applicant for admission to practice law. In that case the applicant had been arrested and convicted of a number of minor offenses in connection with peace demonstrations and civil rights "sit ins"; he had likewise been involved in a number of fistfights. We held that the applicant could not be denied admission to the bar. The nature of these acts, we ruled, "does not bear a direct relationship to petitioner's fitness to practice law. Virtually all of the admission and disciplinary cases in which we have upheld decisions of the State Bar to refuse to admit applicants or to disbar, suspend, or otherwise censure members of the bar have involved acts which bear upon the individual's manifest dishonesty and thereby provide a reasonable basis for the conclusion that the applicant or attorney cannot be relied upon to fulfill the moral obligations incumbent upon members of the legal profession [citations]. . . . Although petitioner's past behavior may not be praiseworthy it does not reflect upon his honesty and veracity nor does it show him unfit for the proper discharge of the duties of an attorney."

In *Yakov v. Board of Medical Examiners,* we were also concerned with moral turpitude. In that case a doctor had been convicted of nine counts of violation of section 4227 of the Business and Professions Code (furnishing dangerous drugs without prescription), and the Board of Medical Examiners had revoked his medical certificate. The superior court reversed the board's action; we upheld that court's disposition of the matter, stating, "The purpose of an action seeking revocation of a doctor's certificate is not to punish the doctor but rather to protect the public. . . . While revocation of a certificate certainly works an unavoidable punitive effect, the board can seek to achieve a legitimate punitive purpose only through criminal prosecution. Thus, in this proceeding the inquiry must be limited to the effect of Dr. Yakov's actions upon the quality of his service to his patients."

. . . Terms such as "immoral or unprofessional conduct" or "moral turpitude" stretch over so wide a range that they embrace an unlimited area of conduct. In using them the Legislature surely did not mean to endow the employing agency with the power to dismiss any employee whose personal, private conduct incurred its disapproval. Hence the courts have consistently related the terms to the issue of whether, when applied to the performance of the employee on the job, the employee has disqualified himself.

In the instant case the terms denote immoral or unprofessional conduct or moral turpitude of the teacher which indicates unfitness to teach. Without such a reasonable interpretation the terms would be susceptible to so broad an application as possibly to subject to discipline virtually every teacher in the state. In the opinion of many people laziness, gluttony, vanity, selfishness, avarice, and cowardice constitute immoral conduct. A recent study by the State Assembly reported that educators differed among themselves as to whether "unprofessional conduct" might include "imbibing alcoholic beverages, use of tobacco, signing petitions, revealing contents of school documents to legislative committees, appealing directly to one's legislative representative, and opposing majority opinions. . . . " We cannot believe that the Legislature intended to compel disciplinary measures against teachers who committed such peccadillos if such passing conduct did not affect students or fellow teachers. Surely incidents of extramarital heterosexual conduct against a background of years of satisfactory teaching would not constitute "immoral conduct" sufficient to justify revocation of a life diploma without any showing of an adverse effect on fitness to teach.

Nor is it likely that the Legislature intended by section 13202 to establish a standard for the conduct of teachers that might vary widely with time, location, and the popular mood. One could expect a reasonably stable consensus within the teaching profession as to what conduct adversely affects students and fellow teachers. No such consensus can be presumed about "morality." "Today's morals may be tomorrow's ancient and absurd customs." And conversely, conduct socially acceptable today may be anathema tomorrow. Local boards of education, moreover, are authorized to revoke their own certificates and dismiss permanent teachers for immoral and unprofessional conduct, an overly broad interpretation of that authorization could result in disciplinary action in one county for conduct treated as permissible in another. A more constricted interpretation of "immoral," "unprofessional," and "moral turpitude" avoids these difficulties, enabling the State Board of Education to utilize its expertise in educational matters rather than having to act "as the prophet to which is revealed the state of morals of the people or the common conscience."

That the meaning of "immoral," "unprofessional," and "moral turpitude" must depend upon, and thus relate to, the occupation involved finds further confirmation in the fact that those terms are used in a wide variety of contexts. Along with public school teachers, all state college employees . . . can be disciplined for "immoral conduct." The prohibition against "acts involving moral turpitude" applies to attorneys and to technicians, bioanalysts and trainees employed in clinical laboratories, as well as to teachers. The ban on "unprofessional conduct" is particularly common, covering not only teachers, but also dentists, vocational nurses, optometrists, pharmacists, psychiatric technicians, employment agency officials, state college employees, certified shorthand reporters, and funeral directors and embalmers. Surely the Legislature did not intend that identical standards of probity should apply to more than half a million professionals and government employees in widely varying fields without regard to their differing duties, responsibilities, and degree of contact with the public.

We therefore conclude that the Board of Education cannot abstractly characterize the conduct in this case as "immoral," "unprofessional," or "involving moral turpitude" within the meaning of section 13202 of the Education Code unless that conduct indicates that the petitioner is unfit to teach. In determining whether the teacher's conduct thus indicates unfitness to teach the board may consider such matters as the likelihood that the conduct may have adversely affected students or fellow teachers, the degree of such adversity anticipated, the proximity or remoteness in time of the conduct, the type of teaching certificate held by the party involved, the extenuating or aggravating circumstances, if any, surrounding the conduct, the praiseworthiness or blameworthiness of the motives resulting in the conduct, the likelihood of the recurrence of the questioned conduct, and the extent to which disciplinary action may inflict an adverse impact or chilling effect upon the constitutional rights of the teacher involved or other teachers. These factors are relevant to the extent that they assist the board in determining whether the teacher's fitness to teach, i.e., in determining whether the teacher's future classroom performance and overall impact on his students are likely to meet the board's standards. . . .

IV. The record contains no evidence that petitioner's conduct indicated his unfitness to teach.

As we have stated above, the statutes, properly interpreted, provide that the State Board of Education can revoke a life diploma or other document of certification and thus prohibit local school officials from hiring a particular teacher only if that individual has in some manner indicated that he is unfit to teach. Thus an individual can be removed from the teaching profession only upon a showing that his retention in the profession poses a significant danger of harm to either students, school employees, or others who might be affected by his actions as a teacher. Such a showing may be based on testimony on official notice, or on both. Petitioner's conduct in this case is not disputed. Accordingly, we must inquire whether any adverse inferences can be drawn from that past conduct as to petitioner's teaching ability, or as to the possibility that publicity surrounding past conduct may in and of itself substantially impair his function as a teacher.

As to this crucial issue, the record before the board and before this court contains no evidence whatsoever. The board called no medical, psychological, or psychiatric experts to testify as to whether a man who had had a single, isolated, and limited homosexual contact would be likely to repeat such conduct in the future. The board offered no evidence that a man of petitioner's background was any more likely than the average adult male to engage in any untoward conduct with a student. The board produced no testimony from school officials or others to indicate whether a man such as petitioner might publicly advocate improper conduct. The board did not attempt to invoke the provisions of the Government Code authorizing official notice of matters within the special competence of the board.

This lack of evidence is particularly significant because the board failed to show that petitioner's conduct in any manner affected his performance as a teacher. There was not the slightest suggestion that petitioner had ever attempted, sought, or even considered any form of physical or otherwise improper relationship with any student. There was no evidence that petitioner had failed to impress upon the minds of his pupils the principles of morality as required by section 13556.5 of the Education Code. There is no reason to believe that the Schneringer incident affected petitioner's apparently satisfactory relationship with his co-workers.

The board revoked petitioner's license three years after the Schneringer incident; that incident has now receded six years into the past. Petitioner's motives at the time of the incident involved neither dishonesty nor viciousness, and the emotional pressures on both petitioner and Schneringer suggest the presence of extenuating circumstances. Finally, the record contains no evidence that the events of April 1963 have become so notorious as to impair petitioner's ability to command the respect and confidence of students and fellow teachers in schools within or without the Lowell Joint School District.

Before the board can conclude that a teacher's continued retention in the profession presents a significant danger of harm to students or fellow teachers, essential factual premises in its reasoning should be supported by evidence or official notice. In this case, despite the quantity and quality of information available about human sexual behavior, the record contains no such evidence as to the significance and implications of the Schneringer incident. Neither this court nor the superior court is authorized to rectify this failure by uninformed speculation or conjecture as to petitioner's future conduct. . . .

V. Conclusion

In deciding this case we are not unmindful of the public interest in the elimination of unfit elementary and secondary school teachers. But petitioner is entitled to a careful and reasoned inquiry into his fitness to teach by the Board of Education before he is deprived of his right to pursue his profession. "The right to practice one's profession is sufficiently precious to surround it with a panoply of legal protection" and terms such as "immoral," "unprofessional," and "moral turpitude" constitute only lingual abstractions until applied to a specific occupation and given content by reference to fitness for the performance of that vocation.

The power of the state to regulate professions and conditions of government employment must not arbitrarily impair the right of the individual to live his private life, apart from his job, as he deems fit. Moreover, since modern hiring practices purport to rest on scientific judgments of fitness for the job involved, a government decision clothed in such terms can seriously inhibit the possibility of the dismissed employee thereafter successfully seeking non-government positions. That danger becomes especially acute under circumstances such as the present case in which loss of certification will impose upon petitioner "a 'badge of infamy,' . . . fixing upon him the stigma of an official defamation of character."

Our conclusion affords no guarantee that petitioner's life diplomas cannot be revoked. If the Board of Education believes that petitioner is unfit to teach, it can reopen its inquiry into the circumstances surrounding and the implications of the 1963 incident with Mr. Schneringer. The board also has at its disposal ample means to discipline petitioner for future misconduct.

Finally, we do not, of course, hold that homosexuals must be permitted to teach in the public schools of California. As we have explained, the relevant statutes, as well as the applicable principles of constitutional law, require only that the board properly find, pursuant to the precepts set forth in this opinion, that an individual is not fit to teach. Whenever disciplinary action rests upon such grounds and has been confirmed by the judgment of a superior court following an independent review of the evidence, this court will uphold the result. ⬟

On the basis of in loco parentis and the theory that teachers must be strong role models for children, the school district fired Marc Morrison after discovering a brief homosexual relationship that he had with another male teacher at his school. In analyzing the state statutes concerning immoral conduct, the court determined that such policies were of broad interpretation and could apply to any of the 22 million federal and state workers in the country. Additionally, the court determined that the school district could not fire a teacher simply because it disapproved of his lifestyle. Rather, the court set forth various factors such as whether the teacher's conduct had an adverse affect on students and the proximity of the event. For example, was the act done in public or in the privacy of the teacher's own home. What was the nature of the conduct itself and the likelihood that such conduct would happen again? What notoriety would such conduct bring on the teacher? What impact would the act have on the teacher's ability to perform his job? Most of all, what harm would it do to the students?

Sexual Activity

There is little dispute among the courts that teachers who have sexual contact with students will be dismissed. Teachers should never have sexual contact with students. For example, a tenured teacher was dismissed for what he categorized as "good-natured horseplay" which consisted of touching and tickling the girls on various parts of their bodies and occasionally between the legs in proximity to the genital areas. There was reciprocal conduct on the part of the girls. During the course of this conduct, the dialogue between appellant and these students was occasionally vulgar, suggestive in nature, and contained many sexual innuendos."[12] Additionally, the teacher was found lying on a bed with two of the students, watching television. The teacher claimed he was just being his "natural self" and attempting to gain a rapport with the students. While all involved denied any sexual activity, the court held that there is no place for such conduct in an educational setting.

In a more recent case, a tenured teacher was fired after inviting two female students to his house, at which time both girls "drank beer and smoked pot." Offering one of the girls a ride home, the teacher had intercourse with her in his automobile. The student at the time was 15 years of age.[13]

Criminal Activity

Criminal activities can range from misdemeanors to murder. Under criminal law, a jury must conclude that a plaintiff is guilty beyond a reasonable doubt. That standard is not so strict that school districts cannot dismiss a teacher for similar acts, and numerous dismissals have been upheld when schools have determined by the preponderance of evidence that a teacher was engaged in wrongful activity. Based on the vague interpretation of immoral conduct, teachers have been dismissed for criminal activities under the immoral conduct policy. It is important to note, however, that the U.S. Supreme Court has ruled on what constitutes immoral conduct. Therefore, depending on community norms

---

[12] *Weissman v. Board of Education of Jefferson County School District No. R-1*, 547 P.2d 1267, at 1270 (1976)
[13] *Barcheski v. Board of Education of Grand Rapids.* 412 N.W.2d 296 (1987)

and school district policies, decisions vary widely and are fact-specific throughout the appellate courts.

In *Lehnert v. Ferris Faculty Association*, a tenured teacher was arrested for growing marijuana in his back yard. After he was criminally charged, the school board chose to place him on compulsory leave on the grounds that he was a convicted felon, that the crime involved moral turpitude, and that he was no longer fit for educational service. The teacher brought suit against the school, claiming that, although he was guilty of the criminal charges, they were not serious enough to warrant dismissal from his teaching position. In its holding, the court stated "that the commission of the offense here involved did not constitute moral turpitude, per se, and that a felony conviction, standing by itself, is not a ground for discipline in the absence of moral turpitude. We also hold that the findings that neither moral turpitude nor unfitness for service were established are supported by the evidence."[14]

Such a decision may have been different in a different court, but it does illustrate that a person convicted of a crime does not automatically lose his or her position as a teacher. Note also that the holding in *Board of Trustees of the Santa Maria Joint Union High School District v. Judge* case does not indicate that it is appropriate for teachers to grow marijuana, nor does it state that a teacher cannot be dismissed from a teaching position for using illegal drugs.

For example, in a California appellate court, a teacher claimed that the term *immoral conduct* was unconstitutionally vague and requested that she be reinstated to her teaching position. The case was brought after the teacher was dismissed when she, in an attempt to assist a friend who had been arrested for possession of marijuana, signed the following affidavit:

> *[U]nder penalty of perjury [she] declares: That she is a friend of Melkon Melkonian, and is aware of the charges under which he was arrested, and the conviction under which he is awaiting sentence; that she makes this affidavit in support of the motion in arrest of judgment on the grounds of the unconstitutionality of the laws making the sale, possession or use of marijuana illegal: Marijuana is not harmful to my knowledge, because I have been using it since 1949, almost daily, with only beneficial results. It has a relaxing effect when tenseness is present, my depth of perception has been increased, this carries over into times when I am not under the influence of marijuana. Teaching children is my profession. I have been a teacher for thirty years and at present am the teaching principal of a public school. During school hours I never feel the need of using cannabis sativa, however, each recess is eagerly awaited for smoking tobacco cigarettes. I do not consider marijuana a habit forming drug, but to me nicotine is. I have been smoking one or two marijuana cigarettes every evening, sometimes more if school is not in session. Then, I stay up later at night. I have known some people who have become momentarily nauseated, but neither I nor anyone I have ever known has had a*

---

[14] 50 Cal. App. 3d 920 (1975)

"hang-over" from its use. Wherefore, affiant begs this court to set aside these unconstitutional laws depicting the plant cannabis sativa as a narcotic, addictive and harmful, and setting forth harsh and cruel penalties for its possession, sale or use.[15]

Shortly after, school officials, as well as students learned of the affidavit and its contents. The school district suspended the teacher for immoral conduct. Attempting reinstatement, the teacher argued that her case was no different from *Morrison* and that signing the affidavit was a free-speech right protected under the First Amendment.

In distinguishing between the two cases, the court first analyzed the notoriety of the situation and suggested that the affidavit had received not only local attention but national coverage, even though that was not the teacher's initial intent at the time of signing. Additionally, the court asked, Was there any harm to students? While students were not directly affected, the fact that students perceive teachers as role models was reviewed. Evidence was presented that indicated that "the child is very apt to believe that which the teacher does is correct, and, therefore, establish a pattern for his own life." The same witness also testified, "I would be inclined to believe that the pupil would be thinking 'If—my teacher can gain her ends by breaking the law, then I, too, can gain my ends by breaking the law.'"[16] In the final decision, the court affirmed the school board's decision, and the teacher was not reinstated.

Just Cause

Most school districts have clauses that allow dismissal of teachers for "good cause." This catch-all phrase applies to both tenured and nontenured teachers. In a Texas case, a veteran teacher of 28 years was dismissed for good cause after failing to report to work for three months.[17] Before the dispute, the teacher had not missed a day of work in 16 years; but she had recently been transferred to a new school, which was a longer distance from her home than her previous school had been. The teacher had asked not to be transferred based on her daughter's mental instability and the need for her to be closer to home. The request was denied; and after being notified numerous times that she was obliged to return to work, the teacher was dismissed. The court upheld the school district's decision based on "good cause."

Evaluation

Evaluation of teachers is a critical part of ensuring a quality education for students. Due to administrative time constraints, however, evaluations are frequently not given the attention they deserve. In numerous cases, a nontenured teacher will not have his or her contract renewed until just before the beginning of the teacher's fourth year on the job.

---

[15] *Governing Board v. Brennan,* 18 Cal. App. 3d 396, at 400 (1971)

[16] Ibid., at 402

[17] *Miller v. Houston Independent School District,* 51 S.W.3d 676 (2001)

The teacher, in many cases, assumes that he or she is doing an adequate job and is quite surprised not to be offered a renewal contract. Hence, a lawsuit arises. Whether it wins or loses, the school district must still go through the process of defending its actions. One way to avoid such situations is to institute thorough and frequent evaluations.

Most faculty members will admit that, even though being evaluated can be slightly intimidating, they appreciate the feedback they receive and use the information to improve their teaching practices. Unfortunately, some evaluations are not always used in a positive manner, nor do they consist of clear documentation with a plan for improvement.

Best Practices

Jeff Horner's 15 Tips for Employee Documentation

The need for proper documentation of employee performance cannot be overemphasized. In today's litigious society, employers such as school districts and colleges must ensure that an effective documentation system is in place. Absent proper employee documentation, office morale will suffer, and lawsuits can be lost. This [box] will discuss . . . 15 practical tips for improving the documentation of employee performance.[18]

1. Emphasize with Your Staff the Importance of Employee Documentation   Proper documentation is a must, both from a human resources and legal perspective. Promotions can be secured or denied based on effective documentation, and lawsuits can be won or lost depending on the quality of documentation. I have handled several cases that have either been lost or had to be settled because the performance documentation did not support the well intended actions taken by school officials. Therefore all employees, particularly those in a supervisory capacity, should be given notice of the importance of proper documentation and the implementation of documentation techniques.

2. Train Your Staff on Proper Documentation   Untrained employees may unwittingly make mistakes in documentation. Training on employee documentation is essential to ensure uniform application of documentation techniques, especially for supervisory employees. Training can be secured from numerous sources, including the human resources department of your educational institution, attorneys representing your institution, and consulting companies which specialize in human resources techniques. Do not put off training; the earlier you can train your employees on documentation techniques, the better. Not only is training effective in a practical sense, it also makes for good evidentiary material in lawsuits.

3. Avoid Fighting Words   The prose of a memorandum should not read like a hot romance novel or soap opera. Remember, any documentation you produce may be used as an exhibit at a jury trial. The author of the documentation should be perceived as an even-headed, rational, and fair person. Avoid words like "outrageous," "stupid," "ridiculous," and other words that might touch the emotions of both employees and jurors. To illustrate the way words should be used, consider the following examples. First, instead of saying that an employee's action is "unbelievable," say that the action is "ill-advised." Also, instead of terming an employee's actions as "asinine," term the actions as "perplexing." These words convey the notion that something is wrong, but in an even-handed manner.

---

[18] J. Horner, Fifteen tips for better documentation of employee performance, *ELA Notes,* Fall 2001, Vol . 36, No. 4. Copyright 2001 by the Education Law Association. Reprinted with permission of the publisher.

4. Avoid the "cc" Syndrome   High circulation should not be your goal in the distribution of employee documenting. Provide copies of documentation only to those individuals with the need to know. Providing copies of potentially sensitive material throughout your educational organization may lead to liability for defamation and create office morale problems. This potential defamation liability extends not only to the person or persons who draft the documentation, but also those who circulate it.

5. Treat Everything You Write as if It Might Appear on the Front Page of the *New York Times*   Remember that spoken words are easily forgotten, but written words can last thousand of years (e.g., the Ten Commandments). While your heart may be pure in writing a memorandum, your words must be carefully chosen to avoid misinterpretation. Accordingly, draft each piece of documentation in a business-like manner, and say *only* what you mean. Flippant statements can be easily misconstrued. Also, weak attempts at humor should be avoided.

6. Remember That Sometimes What Really Counts Is What You Don't Say   Verbose, convoluted documentation, though well intended, often causes more problems than it cures. "Diarrhea of the mouth" is not a virtue when it comes to employee documentation. In documentation, say only what must be said and *stop*. Most lawyers are familiar with the adage about the lawyer who asked one too many questions and got an answer he didn't like. The same concept applies in employee documentation: writing too much verbiage can cause problems.

7. Use Documentation in Both a Positive and Negative Manner   Often, people think of documentation as being only used for negative or punitive reasons, such as reprimanding or terminating an employee. While documentation is important in these areas, it is equally important to reward superior employee performance. Memoranda or letters of commendation can go a long way toward raising morale and improving employee performance. Therefore, do not use employee documentation merely for negative reasons.

8. Come to a Conclusion   Sometimes, an investigation of alleged employee misconduct will be conducted. A through investigation and witness interviews will occur, but no conclusion is made in writing. Remember, an investigation may be an important part of a lawsuit tried in court later. Do not leave an incident hanging. Come to a conclusion on employee investigations or other matters, and reduce your conclusion to writing so the record is complete. A closeout memorandum is an effective tool in ensuring that the written record of employee performance and/or misconduct is complete.

9. Consider the Need for Documentation Prior to Reducing Your Thoughts to Writing   Sometimes, supervisors believe that every violation, no matter how minor, should be documented. As a result, a huge stack of documentation is collected against the employee, raising the inference that the supervisor is simply "out to get" the employee. Use common sense in determining whether documentation is necessary. A scathing letter of reprimand for an employee arriving at work five minutes late in most cases is not justified. Ask yourself the following question before reducing a particular event to writing: "Is this even sufficiently serious to warrant documentation?"

10. Beware of the Evils of E-mail/Internet   The information superhighway is somtimes like the German Autobahn—things move very fast, and the chance for an accident is very real. Train yourself and your employees on the downsides of e-mail and the Internet. While they are both wonderful tools at mass communication, the text of an e-mail can easily be misinterpreted in the future. An example of this phenomenon is the recent Microsoft antitrust trial, when Bill Gates was cross-examined on many of his internal e-mails to other Microsoft employees. In addition, limit the amount of e-mails received by your employees from outside sources. Often, employees will receive jokes and other miscellaneous material on the e-mail. Caution your employees to use their e-mail for business purposes only.

(continued)

11. Do Not Document in a Fit of Anger   Sometimes, employees may do things that anger you. The worst reaction is to immediately sit down and draft a letter of reprimand. Your writing may more reflect your anger than a rational analysis of the event that gave rise to the memorandum. Do not write anything out of anger. Rather, give yourself reasonable time to collect your thoughts before documenting an event. My rule of thumb is if I feel the need to document an event by an employee, give myself the night to sleep on it. I usually have a slightly different perspective on the event the following morning.

12. Use Common Vocabulary   The use of highly technical prose or big words in documentation should be avoided, to the extent possible. Draft your documentation so a layman can understand it. You should appear down-to-earth through your documentation, not like some "high-tech geek." For example, instead of using the word "reticent," use the more common word "reluctant." Also, do not write that you are taking time to "synthesize" the material. Rather, you are taking time to "think about" what you need to say.

13. Be Specific   Vague statements in documentation can be confusing and easily misconstrued. Be precise in your writing. For example, if you are referencing a prior memorandum in your documentation, reference the memo by name, author, date, and subject. The failure to be specific can cause problems in a reader's perception about what you actually mean.

14. Focus on the Present   Let past documentation speak for itself. While referencing past documentation is permissible, do not try to recreate or paraphrase past documentation in a subsequent memorandum. If reference is made to a past memorandum, simply attach a copy of it to the present memorandum, if necessary. Focus your major thoughts on the present.

15. Follow the Golden Rule   Probably the most important thing one should remember in employee documentation is to treat others as you would wish to be treated in a similar situation. Place yourself in the shoes of the person about whom you are writing. If a scathing letter of reprimand is necessary, write it. However, if something less is necessary, act as you would wish to be treated in a similar situation. While the chain of command in an employment relationship is important, showing respect for employees, especially through documentation, is equally important. Following the "Golden Rule" on the front side in employee documentation can save many problems on the backside.

CONCLUSION

WITH the use of these practical tips for better documentation, the employees of your educational institution, particularly those in a supervisory capacity, can increase office morale and minimize future legal problems. It is the author's hope that these few tips will help your institution stay out of the courthouse so it can focus on its primary mission: the education of our youth.

SUMMARY

As discussed in the chapter covering Teachers' Rights, it is known that public employees have various rights protected under the U.S. Constitution. Additionally, the U.S. Supreme Court has set forth the standard and due process protection under the Fourteenth

Amendment, in both the *Board of Regents v. Roth* and *Perry v. Sindermann* cases. Based on these decisions, once a teacher has obtained a property right in their employment, they must be given a certain amount of due process prior to being dismissed from their position.

As to how much protection a teacher may have in their employment depends on the state laws, as well as how the faculty are represented. For example, in some states faculty are represented by unions, while other states apply the meet and confer method. Depending on the location, or even the district, such protections may vary greatly.

Additionally, based on community norms, teachers may be dismissed for insubordination, being incompetent, immoral conduct, sexual activity, criminal activity, or just cause. Regardless of location or state law, one of the most important points that administrators must note concerning employment and tenure is to continually evaluate, make recommendations and document, document, document.

DISCUSSION QUESTIONS

1. Define tenure and how it protects teachers.
2. How does the general public commonly perceive tenure? Write a memo explaining the rights of teachers and the laws of due process.
3. Compare *Roth* versus *Sindermann*. Do you agree with the holdings? Why or why not?
4. What due process procedures do teachers receive in your state or school district?
5. Brief *Morrison v. State Board of Education*. What constitutes immoral conduct? Give examples. How does your district define *immorality* and *unprofessional conduct*?
6. Do community norms play any role in school district policies concerning immorality? Discuss, using case law.
7. What factors are weighed in considering the immoral conduct of a teacher? Discuss which factors carry more weight.
8. Does involvement in criminal activities always result in teacher dismissal? Discuss.
9. Define *just cause*.
10. Discuss evaluation and why it is important in preventing litigation.

DEEPENING YOUR UNDERSTANDING

1. Research and discuss the issue of collective bargaining in your state.
2. In small groups, create a standard form to evaluate faculty. The final tool should benefit your institution, be easy to use, yet be comprehensive and allow for improvement.

Appendix
Resources for Administrators

Excerpts from the U.S. Constitution That Relate to Education

WE THE people of the United States, in order to form a more perfect Union, establish justice, insure domestic Tranquility, provide for the common defense, promote the general Welfare, and secure the Blessings of Liberty to ourselves and our Posterity, do ordain and establish this Constitution for the United States of America.

Article I

Section 1

All legislative Powers herein granted shall be vested in a Congress of the United States, which shall consist of a Senate and House of Representatives.

Section 2

The House of Representatives shall be composed of Members chosen every second Year by the People of the several States, and the Electors in each State shall have the Qualifications requisite for Electors of the most numerous Branch of the State Legislature.

Section 8

The Congress shall have Power To lay and collect Taxes, Duties, Imposts and Excises, to pay the Debts and provide for the Common Defense and general Welfare of the United States; but all Duties, Imposts and Excises shall be uniform throughout the United States.

ARTICLE II

Section 1

The executive Power shall be vested in a President of the United States of America. He shall hold his Office during the Term of four Years, and, together with the Vice President, chosen for the same Term, be elected, as follows:

Section 2

The President shall be Commander in Chief of the Army and Navy of the United States, and of the Militia of the several States, when called into the actual Service of the United States; he may require the Opinion, in writing, of the principal Officer in each of the executive Departments, upon any Subject relating to the Duties of their respective Offices, and he shall have Power to grant Reprieves and Pardons for Offenses against the United States, except in Cases of Impeachment.

He shall have Power, by and with the Advice and Consent of the Senate, to make Treaties, provided two thirds of the Senators present concur; and he shall nominate, and by and with the Advice and Consent of the Senate, shall appoint Ambassadors, other public Ministers and Consuls, Judges of the Supreme Court, and all other Officers of the United States, whose Appointments are not herein otherwise provided for, and which shall be established by Law: but the Congress may by Law vest the Appointment of such inferior Officers, as they think proper, in the President alone, in the Courts of Law, or in the Heads of Departments.

The President shall have Power to fill up all Vacancies that may happen during the Recess of the Senate, by granting Commissions which shall expire at the End of their next Session.

ARTICLE III

Section 1

The judicial Power of the United States, shall be vested in one supreme Court, and in such inferior Courts as the Congress may from time to time ordain and establish. The Judges, both of the supreme and inferior Courts, shall hold their Offices during good Behavior, and shall, at stated Times, receive for their Services, a Compensation, which shall not be diminished during their Continuance in Office.

Section 2

The judicial Power shall extend to all Cases, in Law and Equity, arising under this Constitution, the Laws of the United States, and Treaties made, or which shall be made, under their Authority;—to all Cases affecting Ambassadors, other public Ministers and

Consuls;—to all Cases of admiralty and maritime Jurisdiction;—to Controversies to which the United States shall be a Party;—to Controversies between two or more States;—between a State and Citizens of another State;—between Citizens of different States,—between Citizens of the same State claiming Lands under Grants of different States, and between a State, or the Citizens thereof, and foreign States, Citizens or Subjects.

In all Cases affecting Ambassadors, other public Ministers and Consuls, and those in which a State shall be Party, the Supreme Court shall have original Jurisdiction. In all the other Cases before mentioned, the Supreme Court shall have appellate Jurisdiction, both as to Law and Fact, with such Exceptions, and under such Regulations as the Congress shall make.

AMENDMENT I [1791]

Congress shall make no law respecting an establishment of religion, or prohibiting the free exercise thereof; or abridging the freedom of speech, or of the press; or the right of the people peaceably to assemble, and to petition the Government for a redress of grievances.

AMENDMENT IV [1791]

The right of the people to be secure in their persons, houses, papers, and effects, against unreasonable searches and seizures, shall not be violated, and no Warrants shall issue, but upon probable cause, supported by Oath or affirmation, and particularly describing the place to be searched, and the persons or things to be seized.

AMENDMENT V [1791]

No person shall be held to answer for a capital, or otherwise infamous crime, unless on a presentment or indictment of a Grand Jury, except in cases arising in the land or naval forces, or in the Militia, when in actual service in time of War or public danger; nor shall any person be subject for the same offence to be twice put in jeopardy of life or limb; nor shall be compelled in any criminal case to be a witness against himself, nor be deprived of life, liberty, or property, without due process of law; nor shall private property be taken for public use, without just compensation.

AMENDMENT VI [1791]

In all criminal prosecutions, the accused shall enjoy the right to a speedy and public trial, by an impartial jury of the State and district wherein the crime shall have been committed, which district shall have been previously ascertained by law, and to be informed of the nature and cause of the accusation; to be confronted with the witnesses against him; to have compulsory process for obtaining witnesses in his favor, and to have the Assistance of Counsel for his defense.

AMENDMENT VII [1791]

In Suits at common law, where the value in controversy shall exceed twenty dollars, the right of trial by jury shall be preserved, and no fact tried by a jury shall be otherwise re-examined in any Court of the United States, than according to the rules of the common law.

AMENDMENT VIII [1791]

Excessive bail shall not be required, nor excessive fines imposed, nor cruel and unusual punishments inflicted.

AMENDMENT IX [1791]

The enumeration in the Constitution, of certain rights, shall not be construed to deny or disparage others retained by the people.

AMENDMENT X [1791]

The powers not delegated to the United States by the Constitution, nor prohibited by it to the States, are reserved to the States respectively, or to the people.

AMENDMENT XI [1798]

The Judicial power of the United States shall not be construed to extend to any suit in law or equity, commenced or prosecuted against one of the United States by Citizens of another State, or by Citizens or Subjects of any Foreign State.

AMENDMENT XIV [1868]

Section 1

All persons born or naturalized in the United States, and subject to the jurisdiction thereof, are citizens of the United States and of the State wherein they reside. No State shall make or enforce any law which shall abridge the privileges or immunities of citizens of the United States; nor shall any State deprive any person of life, liberty, or property, without due process of law; nor deny to any person within its jurisdiction the equal protection of the laws.

AMENDMENT XV

Section 1

The right of citizens of the United States to vote shall not be denied or abridged by the United States or by any State on account of race, color, or previous condition of servitude.

Section 2

The Congress shall have power to enforce this article by appropriate legislation.

AMENDMENT XVI [1913]

The Congress shall have power to lay and collect taxes on incomes, from whatever source derived, without apportionment among the several States, and without regard to any census or enumeration.

AMENDMENT XXVI [1971]

Section 1

The right of citizens of the United States, who are eighteen years of age or older, to vote shall not be denied or abridged by the United States or by any State on account of age.

Section 2

The Congress shall have power to enforce this article by appropriate legislation.

FAMILY EDUCATIONAL RIGHTS AND PRIVACY ACT (FERPA) 20 U.S.C.S. § 1232

(a)

Conditions for availability of funds to educational agencies or institutions; inspection and review of education records; specific information to be made available; procedure for access to education records; reasonableness of time for such access; hearings; written explanations by parents; definitions.

(1)

(A) No funds shall be made available under any applicable program to any educational agency or institution which has a policy of denying, or which effectively prevents, the parents of students who are or have been in attendance at a school of such agency or at such institution, as the case may be, the right to inspect and review the education records of their children. If any material or document in the education record of a student includes information on more than one student, the parents of one of such students shall have the right to inspect and review only such part of such material or document as relates to such student or to be informed of the specific information contained in such part of such material. Each educational agency or institution shall establish appropriate procedures for the granting of a request by parents for access to the education records of their children within a reasonable period of time, but in no case more than forty-five days after the request has been made.

(B) No funds under any applicable program shall be made available to any State educational agency (whether or not that agency is an educational agency or institution under this section) that has a policy of denying, or effectively prevents, the parents of students the right to inspect and review the education records maintained by the State educational agency on their children who are or have been in attendance at any school of an educational agency or institution that is subject to the provisions of this section.

(C) The first sentence of subparagraph (A) shall not operate to make available to students in institutions of postsecondary education the following materials:

   (i) financial records of the parents of the student or any information contained therein;

   (ii) confidential letters and statements of recommendation, which were placed in the education records prior to January 1, 1975, if such letters or statements are not used for purposes other than those for which they were specifically intended;

   (iii) if the student has signed a waiver of the student's right of access under this subsection in accordance with subparagraph (D), confidential recommendations—

     (I) respecting admission to any educational agency or institution,

(II) respecting an application for employment, and

(III) respecting the receipt of an honor or honorary recognition.

(D) A student or a person applying for admission may waive his right of access to confidential statements described in clause (iii) of subparagraph (C), except that such waiver shall apply to recommendations only if (i) the student is, upon request, notified of the names of all persons making confidential recommendations and (ii) such recommendations are used solely for the purpose for which they were specifically intended. Such waivers may not be required as a condition for admission to, receipt of financial aid from, or receipt of any other services or benefits from such agency or institution.

(2)

No funds shall be made available under any applicable program to any educational agency or institution unless the parents of students who are or have been in attendance at a school of such agency or at such institution are provided an opportunity for a hearing by such agency or institution, in accordance with regulations of the Secretary, to challenge the content of such student's education records, in order to insure that the records are not inaccurate, misleading, or otherwise in violation of the privacy rights of students, and to provide an opportunity for the correction or deletion of any such inaccurate, misleading, or otherwise inappropriate data contained therein and to insert into such records a written explanation of the parents respecting the content of such records.

(3)

For the purposes of this section the term "educational agency or institution" means any public or private agency or institution which is the recipient of funds under any applicable program.

(4)

(A) For the purposes of this section, the term "education records" means, except as may be provided otherwise in subparagraph (B), those records, files, documents, and other materials which—

(i) contain information directly related to a student; and

(ii) are maintained by an educational agency or institution or by a person acting for such agency or institution.

(B) The term "education records" does not include—

(i) records of instructional, supervisory, and administrative personnel and educational personnel ancillary thereto which are in the sole possession of the maker thereof and which are not accessible or revealed to any other person except a substitute;

(ii) records maintained by a law enforcement unit of the educational agency or institution that were created by that law enforcement unit for the purpose of law enforcement;

(iii) in the case of persons who are employed by an educational agency or institution but who are not in attendance at such agency or institution, records made and maintained in the normal course of business which relate exclusively to such person in that person's capacity as an employee and are not available for use for any other purpose; or

(iv) records on a student who is eighteen years of age or older, or is attending an institution of postsecondary education, which are made or maintained by a physician, psychiatrist, psychologist, or other recognized professional or paraprofessional acting in his professional or paraprofessional capacity, or assisting in that capacity, and which are made, maintained, or used only in connection with the provision of treatment to the student, and are not available to anyone other than persons providing such treatment, except that such records can be personally reviewed by a physician or other appropriate professional of the student's choice.

(5)

(A) For the purposes of this section the term "directory information" relating to a student includes the following: the student's name, address, telephone listing, date and place of birth, major field of study, participation in officially recognized activities and sports, weight and height of members of athletic teams, dates of attendance, degrees and awards received, and the most recent previous educational agency or institution attended by the student.

(B) Any educational agency or institution making public directory information shall give public notice of the categories of information which it has designated as such information with respect to each student attending the institution or agency and shall allow a reasonable period of time after such notice has been given for a parent to inform the institution or agency that any or all of the information designated should not be released without the parent's prior consent.

(6)

For the purposes of this section, the term "student" includes any person with respect to whom an educational agency or institution maintains education records or personally identifiable information, but does not include a person who has not been in attendance at such agency or institution.

(b)

Release of education records; parental consent requirement; exceptions; compliance with judicial orders and subpoenas; audit and evaluation of Federally-supported education programs; recordkeeping.

(1)

No funds shall be made available under any applicable program to any educational agency or institution which has a policy or practice of permitting the release of educational records (or personally identifiable information contained therein other than directory information, as defined in paragraph [5] of subsection [a]) of students without the written consent of their parents to any individual, agency, or organization, other than to the following—

(A) other school officials, including teachers within the educational institution or local educational agency, who have been determined by such agency or institution to have legitimate educational interests, including the educational interests of the child for whom consent would otherwise be required;

(B) officials of other schools or school systems in which the student seeks or intends to enroll, upon condition that the student's parents be notified of the transfer, receive a copy of the record if desired, and have an opportunity for a hearing to challenge the content of the record;

(C) (i) authorized representatives of (I) the Comptroller General of the United States, (II) the Secretary, or (III) State educational authorities, under the conditions set forth in paragraph (3), or (ii) authorized representatives of the Attorney General for law enforcement purposes under the same conditions as apply to the Secretary under paragraph (3);

(D) in connection with a student's application for, or receipt of, financial aid;

(E) State and local officials or authorities to whom such information is specifically allowed to be reported or disclosed pursuant to State statute adopted—

    (i) before November 19, 1974, if the allowed reporting or disclosure concerns the juvenile justice system and such system's ability to effectively serve the student whose records are released, or

    (ii) after November 19, 1974, if—

        (I) the allowed reporting or disclosure concerns the juvenile justice system and such system's ability to effectively serve, prior to adjudication, the student whose records are released; and

        (II) the officials and authorities to whom such information is disclosed certify in writing to the educational agency or institution that the information will not be disclosed to any other party except as provided under State law without the prior written consent of the parent of the student.

(F) organizations conducting studies for, or on behalf of, educational agencies or institutions for the purpose of developing, validating, or administering predictive tests, administering student aid programs, and improving instruction, if such studies are conducted in such a manner as will not permit the personal identification of students and their parents by persons other than representatives of such organizations and such information will be destroyed when no longer needed for the purpose for which it is conducted;

(G) accrediting organizations in order to carry out their accrediting functions;

(H) parents of a dependent student of such parents, as defined in section 152 of the Internal Revenue Code of 1986 [26 U.S.C.S. § 152];

(I) subject to regulations of the Secretary, in connection with an emergency, appropriate persons if the knowledge of such information is necessary to protect the health or safety of the student or other persons; and

(J)

    (i) the entity or persons designated in a Federal grand jury subpoena, in which case the court shall order, for good cause shown, the educational agency or institution (and any officer, director, employee, agent, or attorney for such agency or institution) on which the subpoena is served, to not disclose to any person the existence or contents of the subpoena or any information furnished to the grand jury in response to the subpoena; and

    (ii) the entity or persons designated in any other subpoena issued for a law enforcement purpose, in which case the court or other issuing agency may order, for good cause shown, the educational agency or institution (and any officer, director, employee, agent, or attorney for such agency or institution) on which the subpoena is served, to not disclose to any person the existence or contents of the subpoena or any information furnished in response to the subpoena.

    Nothing in clause (E) of this paragraph shall prevent a State from further limiting the number or type of State or local officials who will continue to have access thereunder.

(2)

No funds shall be made available under any applicable program to any educational agency or institution which has a policy or practice of releasing, or providing access to, any personally identifiable information in education records other than directory information, or as is permitted under paragraph (1) of this subsection unless—

(A) there is written consent from the student's parents specifying records to be released, the reasons for such release, and to whom, and with a copy of the records to be released to the student's parents and the student if desired by the parents, or

(B) except as provided in paragraph (1)(J), such information is furnished in compliance with judicial order, or pursuant to any lawfully issued subpoena, upon condition that parents and the students are notified of all such orders or subpoenas in advance of the compliance therewith by the educational institution or agency.

(3)

Nothing contained in this section shall preclude authorized representatives of (A) the Comptroller General of the United States, (B) the Secretary, or (C) State educational authorities from having access to student or other records which may be necessary in connection with the audit and evaluation of Federally-supported education programs, or in connection with the enforcement of the Federal legal requirements which relate to such programs: Provided, that except when collection of personally identifiable information is specifically authorized by Federal law, any data collected by such officials shall be protected in a manner which will not permit the personal identification of students and their parents by other than those officials, and such personally identifiable data shall be destroyed when no longer needed for such audit, evaluation, and enforcement of Federal legal requirements.

(4)

(A) Each educational agency or institution shall maintain a record, kept with the education records of each student, which will indicate all individuals (other than those specified in paragraph (1)(A) of this subsection), agencies, or organizations which have requested or obtained access to a student's education records maintained by such educational agency or institution, and which will indicate specifically the legitimate interest that each such person, agency, or organization has in obtaining this information. Such record of access shall be available only to parents, to the school official and his assistants who are responsible for the custody of such records, and to persons or organizations authorized in, and under the conditions of, clauses (A) and (C) of paragraph (1) as a means of auditing the operation of the system.

(B) With respect to this subsection, personal information shall only be transferred to a third party on the condition that such party will not permit any other party to have access to such information without the written consent of the parents of the student. If a third party outside the educational agency or institution permits access to information in violation of paragraph (2)(A), or fails to destroy information in violation of paragraph (1)(F), the educational agency or institution shall be prohibited from permitting access to information from education records to that third party for a period of not less than five years.

(5)

Nothing in this section shall be construed to prohibit State and local educational officials from having access to student or other records which may be necessary in connection with the audit and evaluation of any federally or State supported education program or in connection with the enforcement of the Federal legal requirements which relate to any such program, subject to the conditions specified in the proviso in paragraph (3).

(6)

(A) Nothing in this section shall be construed to prohibit an institution of postsecondary education from disclosing, to an alleged victim of any crime of violence (as that term is defined in section 16 of title 18, United States Code), or a nonforcible sex offense, the final results of any disciplinary proceeding conducted by such institution against the alleged perpetrator of such crime or offense with respect to such crime or offense.

(B) Nothing in this section shall be construed to prohibit an institution of postsecondary education from disclosing the final results of any disciplinary proceeding conducted by such institution against a student who is an alleged perpetrator of any crime of violence (as that term is defined in section 16 of title 18, United States Code), or a nonforcible sex offense, if the institution determines as a result of that disciplinary proceeding that the student committed a violation of the institution's rules or policies with respect to such crime or offense.

(C) For the purpose of this paragraph, the final results of any disciplinary proceeding—
   (i) shall include only the name of the student, the violation committed, and any sanction imposed by the institution on that student; and
   (ii) may include the name of any other student, such as a victim or witness, only with the written consent of that other student.

(c)

Surveys or data-gathering activities; regulations. Not later than 240 days after the date of enactment of the Improving America's Schools Act of 1994 [enacted Oct. 20, 1994], the Secretary shall adopt appropriate regulations or procedures, or identify existing regulations or procedures, which protect the rights of privacy of students and their families in connection with any surveys or data-gathering activities conducted, assisted, or authorized by the Secretary or an administrative head of an education agency. Regulations established under this subsection shall include provisions controlling the use, dissemination, and protection of such data. No survey or data-gathering activities shall be conducted by the Secretary, or an administrative head of an education agency under an applicable program, unless such activities are authorized by law.

(d)

Students' rather than parents' permission or consent. For the purposes of this section, whenever a student has attained eighteen years of age, or is attending an institution of postsecondary education, the permission or consent required of and the rights accorded to the parents of the student shall thereafter only be required of and accorded to the student.

(e)

Informing parents or students of rights under this section. No funds shall be made available under any applicable program to any educational agency or institution unless such agency or institution effectively informs the parents of students, or the students, if they are eighteen years of age or older, or are attending an institution of postsecondary education, of the rights accorded them by this section.

(f)

Enforcement; termination of assistance. The Secretary shall take appropriate actions to enforce this section and to deal with violations of this section, in accordance with this Act, except that action to terminate assistance may be taken only if the Secretary finds there has been a failure to comply with this section, and he has determined that compliance cannot be secured by voluntary means.

(g)

Office and review board; creation; functions. The Secretary shall establish or designate an office and review board within the Department for the purpose of investigating, processing, reviewing, and adjudicating violations of this section and complaints which may be filed concerning alleged violations of this section. Except for the conduct of hearings, none of the functions of the Secretary under this section shall be carried out in any of the regional offices of such Department.

(h)

Certain disciplinary action information allowable. Nothing in this section shall prohibit an educational agency or institution from—

(1) including appropriate information in the education record of any student concerning disciplinary action taken against such student for conduct that posed a significant risk to the safety or well-being of that student, other students, or other members of the school community; or

(2) disclosing such information to teachers and school officials, including teachers and school officials in other schools, who have legitimate educational interests in the behavior of the student.

(I) Drug and Alcohol Violation Disclosures

(1) In General

Nothing in this Act or the Higher Education Act of 1965 shall be construed to prohibit an institution of higher education from disclosing, to a parent or legal guardian of a student, information regarding any violation of any Federal, State, or local law, or of any rule or policy of the institution, governing the use or possession of alcohol or a controlled substance, regardless of whether that information is contained in the student's education records, if—

(A) the student is under the age of 21; and
(B) the institution determines that the student has committed a disciplinary violation with respect to such use or possession.

(2) State Law Regarding Disclosure

Nothing in paragraph (1) shall be construed to supersede any provision of State law that prohibits an institution of higher education from making the disclosure described in subsection (a).

Equal Access Act 20 U.S.C.S § 4071–74

Sec. 4071

(a) It shall be deemed unlawful for any public secondary school which receives Federal financial assistance and which has a limited open forum to deny equal access or a fair opportunity to, or discriminate against, any students who wish to conduct a meeting within that limited open forum on the basis of the religious, political, philosophical, or other content of the speech at such meetings.

(b) A public secondary school has a limited open forum whenever such school grants an offering to or opportunity for one or more non-curriculum related student groups to meet on school premises during non-instructional time.

(c) Schools shall be deemed to offer a fair opportunity to students who wish to conduct a meeting within its limited open forum if such school uniformly provides that—the meeting is voluntary and student-initiated; there is no sponsorship of the meeting by the school, government, or its agents or employees; employees of the school or government are present at the meetings only in non-participatory capacity; the meeting does not materially and substantially interfere with the orderly conduct of educational activities within the school; and non-school persons may not direct, conduct, control, or regularly attend activities of student groups.

(d) Nothing in this subchapter shall be construed to authorize the United States or any
     State or political sub-division thereof to influence the form or content of any prayer
     or other religious activity; to require any person to participate in prayer or other re-
     ligious activity; to expend public funds beyond the incidental cost of providing space
     for student-initiated meetings; to compel any school agent or employee to attend a
     school meeting if the content of the speech at the meeting is contrary to the beliefs
     of the agent or employee; to sanction meetings that are otherwise unlawful; to limit
     the rights of groups which are not of a specified numerical size, or to abridge the
     constitutional rights of any person.
(e) Not withstanding the availability of any remedy under the Constitution or the laws
     of the United States, nothing in this subchapter shall be construed to authorize the
     United States to deny or withhold Federal financial assistance to any school.
(f) Nothing in this subchapter shall be construed to limit the authority of the school, its
     agents or employees, to maintain order and discipline on school premises, to protect
     the well-being of students and faculty, and to assure that attendance of students at
     meetings is voluntary.

INDIVIDUALS WITH DISABILITIES EDUCATION ACT (IDEA) 1997 FINAL REGULATIONS

§300.1 PURPOSES

The purposes of this part are—

(a) To ensure that all children with disabilities have available to them a free appropriate
     public education that emphasizes special education and related services designed to
     meet their unique needs and prepare them for employment and independent living;
(b) To ensure that the rights of children with disabilities and their parents are protected;
(c) To assist States, localities, educational service agencies, and Federal agencies to pro-
     vide for the education of all children with disabilities; and
(d) To assess and ensure the effectiveness of efforts to educate children with disabilities.

§300.2 APPLICABILITY OF THIS PART TO STATE, LOCAL, AND PRIVATE AGENCIES

(a) States. This part applies to each State that receives payments under Part B of the Act.
(b) Public agencies within the State. The provisions of this part—
     (1) Apply to all political subdivisions of the State that are involved in the education
          of children with disabilities, including—
          (i)   The State educational agency (SEA);
          (ii) Local educational agencies (LEAs), educational service agencies (ESAs),
                and public charter schools that are not otherwise included as LEAs or ESAs
                and are not a school of an LEA or ESA;

(iii) Other State agencies and schools (such as Departments of Mental Health and Welfare and State schools for children with deafness or children with blindness);

(iv) State and local juvenile and adult correctional facilities; and

(2) Are binding on each public agency in the State that provides special education and related services to children with disabilities, regardless of whether that agency is receiving funds under Part B.

(c) Private schools and facilities. Each public agency in the State is responsible for ensuring that the rights and protections under Part B of the Act are given to children with disabilities—

(1) Referred to or placed in private schools and facilities by that public agency; or

(2) Placed in private schools by their parents under the provisions of §300.403(c). (Authority: 20 U.S.C. 1412)

§300.3   Regulations That Apply

The following regulations apply to this program:

(a) 34 CFR part 76 (State-Administered Programs) except for §§76.125–76.137 and 76.650–76.662.

(b) 34 CFR part 77 (Definitions).

(c) 34 CFR part 79 (Intergovernmental Review of Department of Education Programs and Activities).

(d) 34 CFR part 80 (Uniform Administrative Requirements for Grants and Cooperative Agreements to State and Local Governments).

(e) 34 CFR part 81 (General Education Provisions Act—Enforcement).

(f) 34 CFR part 82 (New Restrictions on Lobbying).

(g) 34 CFR part 85 (Government-wide Debarment and Suspension [Nonprocurement] and Government-wide Requirements for Drug-Free Workplace [Grants]).

(h) The regulations in this part—34 CFR part 300 (Assistance for Education of Children with Disabilities). (Authority: 20 U.S.C. 1221e-3 (a)(1))

§300.4   Act

As used in this part, Act means the Individuals with Disabilities Education Act (IDEA), as amended. (Authority: 20 U.S.C. 1400[a])

§300.5   Assistive Technology Device

As used in this part, Assistive technology device means any item, piece of equipment, or product system, whether acquired commercially off the shelf, modified, or customized, that is used to increase, maintain, or improve the functional capabilities of a child with a disability. (Authority: 20 U.S.C. 1401[1])

§300.6 Assistive Technology Service

As used in this part, Assistive technology service means any service that directly assists a child with a disability in the selection, acquisition, or use of an assistive technology device.

The term includes—

(a) The evaluation of the needs of a child with a disability, including a functional evaluation of the child in the child's customary environment;

(b) Purchasing, leasing, or otherwise providing for the acquisition of assistive technology devices by children with disabilities;

(c) Selecting, designing, fitting, customizing, adapting, applying, maintaining, repairing, or replacing assistive technology devices;

(d) Coordinating and using other therapies, interventions, or services with assistive technology devices, such as those associated with existing education and rehabilitation plans and programs;

(e) Training or technical assistance for a child with a disability or, if appropriate, that child's family; and

(f) Training or technical assistance for professionals (including individuals providing education or rehabilitation services), employers, or other individuals who provide services to, employ, or are otherwise substantially involved in the major life functions of that child. (Authority: 20 U.S.C. 1401[2])

§300.7 Child with a Disability

(a) General.

(1) As used in this part, the term child with a disability means a child evaluated in accordance with §§300.530–300.536 as having mental retardation, a hearing impairment including deafness, a speech or language impairment, a visual impairment including blindness, serious emotional disturbance (hereafter referred to as emotional disturbance), an orthopedic impairment, autism, traumatic brain injury, an other health impairment, a specific learning disability, deaf-blindness, or multiple disabilities, and who, by reason thereof, needs special education and related services.

(2)

(i) Subject to paragraph (a)(2)(ii) of this section, if it is determined, through an appropriate evaluation under §§300.530–300.536, that a child has one of the disabilities identified in paragraph (a)(1) of this section, but only needs a related service and not special education, the child is not a child with a disability under this part.

(ii) If, consistent with §300.26(a)(2), the related service required by the child is considered special education rather than a related service under State standards, the child would be determined to be a child with a disability under paragraph (a)(1) of this section.

(b) Children aged 3 through 9 experiencing developmental delays. The term child with a disability for children aged 3 through 9 may, at the discretion of the State and LEA and in accordance with §300.313, include a child—

(1) Who is experiencing developmental delays, as defined by the State and as measured by appropriate diagnostic instruments and procedures, in one or more of the following areas: physical development, cognitive development, communication development, social or emotional development, or adaptive development; and

(2) Who, by reason thereof, needs special education and related services.

(c) Definitions of disability terms. The terms used in this definition are defined as follows:

(1)

(i) Autism means a developmental disability significantly affecting verbal and nonverbal communication and social interaction, generally evident before age 3, that adversely affects a child's educational performance. Other characteristics often associated with autism are engagement in repetitive activities and stereotyped movements, resistance to environmental change or change in daily routines, and unusual responses to sensory experiences. The term does not apply if a child's educational performance is adversely affected primarily because the child has an emotional disturbance, as defined in paragraph (b)(4) of this section.

(ii) A child who manifests the characteristics of "autism" after age 3 could be diagnosed as having "autism" if the criteria in paragraph (c)(1)(i) of this section are satisfied.

(2) Deaf-blindness means concomitant hearing and visual impairments, the combination of which causes such severe communication and other developmental and educational needs that they cannot be accommodated in special education programs solely for children with deafness or children with blindness.

(3) Deafness means a hearing impairment that is so severe that the child is impaired in processing linguistic information through hearing, with or without amplification, that adversely affects a child's educational performance.

(4) Emotional disturbance is defined as follows:

(i) The term means a condition exhibiting one or more of the following characteristics over a long period of time and to a marked degree that adversely affects a child's educational performance:

(A) An inability to learn that cannot be explained by intellectual, sensory, or health factors.

    (B) An inability to build or maintain satisfactory interpersonal relationships with peers and teachers.

    (C) Inappropriate types of behavior or feelings under normal circumstances.

    (D) A general pervasive mood of unhappiness or depression.

    (E) A tendency to develop physical symptoms or fears associated with personal or school problems.

  (ii) The term includes schizophrenia. The term does not apply to children who are socially maladjusted, unless it is determined that they have an emotional disturbance.

(5) Hearing impairment means an impairment in hearing, whether permanent or fluctuating, that adversely affects a child's educational performance but that is not included under the definition of deafness in this section.

(6) Mental retardation means significantly subaverage general intellectual functioning, existing concurrently with deficits in adaptive behavior and manifested during the developmental period, that adversely affects a child's educational performance.

(7) Multiple disabilities means concomitant impairments (such as mental retardation–blindness, mental retardation–orthopedic impairment, etc.), the combination of which causes such severe educational needs that they cannot be accommodated in special education programs solely for one of the impairments. The term does not include deaf-blindness.

(8) Orthopedic impairment means a severe orthopedic impairment that adversely affects a child's educational performance. The term includes impairments caused by congenital anomaly (e.g., clubfoot, absence of some member, etc.), impairments caused by disease (e.g., poliomyelitis, bone tuberculosis, etc.), and impairments from other causes (e.g., cerebral palsy, amputations, and fractures or burns that cause contractures).

(9) Other health impairment means having limited strength, vitality or alertness, including a heightened alertness to environmental stimuli, that results in limited alertness with respect to the educational environment, that—

  (i) Is due to chronic or acute health problems such as asthma, attention deficit disorder or attention deficit hyperactivity disorder, diabetes, epilepsy, a heart condition, hemophilia, lead poisoning, leukemia, nephritis, rheumatic fever, and sickle cell anemia; and

  (ii) Adversely affects a child's educational performance.

(10) Specific learning disability is defined as follows:

  (i) General. The term means a disorder in one or more of the basic psychological processes involved in understanding or in using language, spoken or written, that may manifest itself in an imperfect ability to listen, think, speak, read, write, spell, or to do mathematical calculations, including conditions such as perceptual disabilities, brain injury, minimal brain dysfunction, dyslexia, and developmental aphasia.

(ii) Disorders not included. The term does not include learning problems that are primarily the result of visual, hearing, or motor disabilities, of mental retardation, of emotional disturbance, or of environmental, cultural, or economic disadvantage.

(11) Speech or language impairment means a communication disorder, such as stuttering, impaired articulation, a language impairment, or a voice impairment, that adversely affects a child's educational performance.

(12) Traumatic brain injury means an acquired injury to the brain caused by an external physical force, resulting in total or partial functional disability or psychosocial impairment, or both, that adversely affects a child's educational performance. The term applies to open or closed head injuries resulting in impairments in one or more areas, such as cognition; language; memory; attention; reasoning; abstract thinking; judgment; problem-solving; sensory, perceptual, and motor abilities; psychosocial behavior; physical functions; information processing; and speech. The term does not apply to brain injuries that are congenital or degenerative, or to brain injuries induced by birth trauma.

(13) Visual impairment including blindness means an impairment in vision that, even with correction, adversely affects a child's educational performance. The term includes both partial sight and blindness.

§300.8   CONSENT

As used in this part, the term consent has the meaning given that term in §300.500(b)(1).

§300.9   DAY; BUSINESS DAY; SCHOOL DAY

As used in this part, the term—

(a) Day means calendar day unless otherwise indicated as business day or school day;

(b) Business day means Monday through Friday, except for Federal and State holidays (unless holidays are specifically included in the designation of business day, as in §300.403[d][1][ii]); and

(c)

(1) School day means any day, including a partial day, that children are in attendance at school for instructional purposes.

(2) The term school day has the same meaning for all children in school, including children with and without disabilities.

§300.10 EDUCATIONAL SERVICE AGENCY

As used in this part, the term educational service agency—

(a) Means a regional public multiservice agency—
   (1) Authorized by State law to develop, manage, and provide services or programs to LEAs; and
   (2) Recognized as an administrative agency for purposes of the provision of special education and related services provided within public elementary and secondary schools of the State;
(b) Includes any other public institution or agency having administrative control and direction over a public elementary or secondary school; and
(c) Includes entities that meet the definition of intermediate educational unit in section 602(23) of IDEA as in effect prior to June 4, 1997.

§300.11 EQUIPMENT

As used in this part, the term equipment means—

(a) Machinery, utilities, and built-in equipment and any necessary enclosures or structures to house the machinery, utilities, or equipment; and
(b) All other items necessary for the functioning of a particular facility as a facility for the provision of educational services, including items such as instructional equipment and necessary furniture; printed, published and audio-visual instructional materials; telecommunications, sensory, and other technological aids and devices; and books, periodicals, documents, and other related materials.

§300.12 EVALUATION

As used in this part, the term evaluation has the meaning given that term in §300.500(b)(2).

§300.13 FREE APPROPRIATE PUBLIC EDUCATION

As used in this part, the term free appropriate public education or FAPE means special education and related services that—

(a) Are provided at public expense, under public supervision and direction, and without charge;
(b) Meet the standards of the SEA, including the requirements of this part;

(c) Include preschool, elementary school, or secondary school education in the State; and

(d) Are provided in conformity with an individualized education program (IEP) that meets the requirements of §§300.340–300.350.

§300.14   INCLUDE

As used in this part, the term include means that the items named are not all of the possible items that are covered, whether like or unlike the ones named.

§300.15   INDIVIDUALIZED EDUCATION PROGRAM

As used in this part, the term individualized education program or IEP has the meaning given the term in §300.340(a).

§300.16   INDIVIDUALIZED EDUCATION PROGRAM TEAM

As used in this part, the term individualized education program team or IEP team means a group of individuals described in §300.344 that is responsible for developing, reviewing, or revising an IEP for a child with a disability.

§300.17   INDIVIDUALIZED FAMILY SERVICE PLAN

As used in this part, the term individualized family service plan or IFSP has the meaning given the term in 34 CFR 303.340(b).

§300.18   LOCAL EDUCATIONAL AGENCY

(a) As used in this part, the term local educational agency means a public board of education or other public authority legally constituted within a State for either administrative control or direction of, or to perform a service function for, public elementary or secondary schools in a city, county, township, school district, or other political subdivision of a State, or for a combination of school districts or counties as are recognized in a State as an administrative agency for its public elementary or secondary schools.

(b) The term includes—

(1) An educational service agency, as defined in §300.10;

(2) Any other public institution or agency having administrative control and direction of a public elementary or secondary school, including a public charter school that is established as an LEA under State law; and

(3) An elementary or secondary school funded by the Bureau of Indian Affairs, and not subject to the jurisdiction of any SEA other than the Bureau of Indian Affairs, but only to the extent that the inclusion makes the school eligible for programs for which specific eligibility is not provided to the school in another provision of law and the school does not have a student population that is smaller than the student population of the LEA receiving assistance under this Act with the smallest student population.

§300.19   Native Language

(a) As used in this part, the term native language, if used with reference to an individual of limited English proficiency, means the following:
 (1) The language normally used by that individual, or, in the case of a child, the language normally used by the parents of the child, except as provided in paragraph (a)(2) of this section.
 (2) In all direct contact with a child (including evaluation of the child), the language normally used by the child in the home or learning environment.
(b) For an individual with deafness or blindness, or for an individual with no written language, the mode of communication is that normally used by the individual (such as sign language, braille, or oral communication).

§300.20   Parent

(a) General. As used in this part, the term parent means—
 (1) A natural or adoptive parent of a child;
 (2) A guardian but not the State if the child is a ward of the State;
 (3) A person acting in the place of a parent (such as a grandparent or stepparent with whom the child lives, or a person who is legally responsible for the child's welfare); or
 (4) A surrogate parent who has been appointed in accordance with §300.515.
(b) Foster parent. Unless State law prohibits a foster parent from acting as a parent, a State may allow a foster parent to act as a parent under Part B of the Act if—
 (1) The natural parents' authority to make educational decisions on the child's behalf has been extinguished under State law; and
 (2) The foster parent—
  (i) Has an ongoing, long-term parental relationship with the child;
  (ii) Is willing to make the educational decisions required of parents under the Act; and
  (iii) Has no interest that would conflict with the interests of the child.

§300.21   PERSONALLY IDENTIFIABLE

As used in this part, the term personally identifiable has the meaning given that term in §300.500(b)(3).

§300.22   PUBLIC AGENCY

As used in this part, the term public agency includes the SEA, LEAs, ESAs, public charter schools that are not otherwise included as LEAs or ESAs and are not a school of an LEA or ESA, and any other political subdivisions of the State that are responsible for providing education to children with disabilities.

§300.23   QUALIFIED PERSONNEL

As used in this part, the term qualified personnel means personnel who have met SEA-approved or SEA-recognized certification, licensing, registration, or other comparable requirements that apply to the area in which the individuals are providing special education or related services.

§300.24   RELATED SERVICES

(a) General. As used in this part, the term related services means transportation and such developmental, corrective, and other supportive services as are required to assist a child with a disability to benefit from special education, and includes speech-language pathology and audiology services, psychological services, physical and occupational therapy, recreation, including therapeutic recreation, early identification and assessment of disabilities in children, counseling services, including rehabilitation counseling, orientation and mobility services, and medical services for diagnostic or evaluation purposes. The term also includes school health services, social work services in schools, and parent counseling and training.

(b) Individual terms defined. The terms used in this definition are defined as follows:

    (1) Audiology includes—

        (i) Identification of children with hearing loss;

        (ii) Determination of the range, nature, and degree of hearing loss, including referral for medical or other professional attention for the habilitation of hearing;

        (iii) Provision of habilitative activities, such as language habilitation, auditory training, speech reading (lip-reading), hearing evaluation, and speech conservation;

    (iv) Creation and administration of programs for prevention of hearing loss;

    (v) Counseling and guidance of children, parents, and teachers regarding hearing loss; and

    (vi) Determination of children's needs for group and individual amplification, selecting and fitting an appropriate aid, and evaluating the effectiveness of amplification.

(2) Counseling services means services provided by qualified social workers, psychologists, guidance counselors, or other qualified personnel.

(3) Early identification and assessment of disabilities in children means the implementation of a formal plan for identifying a disability as early as possible in a child's life.

(4) Medical services means services provided by a licensed physician to determine a child's medically related disability that results in the child's need for special education and related services.

(5) Occupational therapy—

    (i) Means services provided by a qualified occupational therapist; and

    (ii) includes—

        (A) Improving, developing or restoring functions impaired or lost through illness, injury, or deprivation;

        (B) Improving ability to perform tasks for independent functioning if functions are impaired or lost; and

        (C) Preventing, through early intervention, initial or further impairment or loss of function.

(6) Orientation and mobility services—

    (i) Means services provided to blind or visually impaired students by qualified personnel to enable those students to attain systematic orientation to and safe movement within their environments in school, home, and community; and

    (ii) Includes teaching students the following, as appropriate:

        (A) Spatial and environmental concepts and use of information received by the senses (such as sound, temperature and vibrations) to establish, maintain, or regain orientation and line of travel (e.g., using sound at a traffic light to cross the street);

        (B) To use the long cane to supplement visual travel skills or as a tool for safely negotiating the environment for students with no available travel vision;

        (C) To understand and use remaining vision and distance low vision aids; and

        (D) Other concepts, techniques, and tools.

(7) Parent counseling and training means—

    (i) Assisting parents in understanding the special needs of their child;

    (ii) Providing parents with information about child development; and

    (iii) Helping parents to acquire the necessary skills that will allow them to support the implementation of their child's IEP or IFSP.

(8) Physical therapy means services provided by a qualified physical therapist.

(9) Psychological services includes—

    (i) Administering psychological and educational tests, and other assessment procedures;

    (ii) Interpreting assessment results;

    (iii) Obtaining, integrating, and interpreting information about child behavior and conditions relating to learning;

    (iv) Consulting with other staff members in planning school programs to meet the special needs of children as indicated by psychological tests, interviews, and behavioral evaluations;

    (v) Planning and managing a program of psychological services, including psychological counseling for children and parents; and

    (vi) Assisting in developing positive behavioral intervention strategies.

(10) Recreation includes—

    (i) Assessment of leisure function;

    (ii) Therapeutic recreation services;

    (iii) Recreation programs in schools and community agencies; and

    (iv) Leisure education.

(11) Rehabilitation counseling services means services provided by qualified personnel in individual or group sessions that focus specifically on career development, employment preparation, achieving independence, and integration in the workplace and community of a student with a disability. The term also includes vocational rehabilitation services provided to a student with disabilities by vocational rehabilitation programs funded under the Rehabilitation Act of 1973, as amended.

(12) School health services means services provided by a qualified school nurse or other qualified person.

(13) Social work services in schools includes—

    (i) Preparing a social or developmental history on a child with a disability;

    (ii) Group and individual counseling with the child and family;

    (iii) Working in partnership with parents and others on those problems in a child's living situation (home, school, and community) that affect the child's adjustment in school;

    (iv) Mobilizing school and community resources to enable the child to learn as effectively as possible in his or her educational program; and

    (v) Assisting in developing positive behavioral intervention strategies.

(14) Speech-language pathology services includes—

    (i) Identification of children with speech or language impairments;

    (ii) Diagnosis and appraisal of specific speech or language impairments;

    (iii) Referral for medical or other professional attention necessary for the habilitation of speech or language impairments;

    (iv) Provision of speech and language services for the habilitation or prevention of communicative impairments; and

    (v) Counseling and guidance of parents, children, and teachers regarding speech and language impairments.

(15) Transportation includes—

    (i) Travel to and from school and between schools;

    (ii) Travel in and around school buildings; and

    (iii) Specialized equipment (such as special or adapted buses, lifts, and ramps), if required to provide special transportation for a child with a disability.

§300.25 SECONDARY SCHOOL

As used in this part, the term secondary school means a nonprofit institutional day or residential school that provides secondary education, as determined under State law, except that it does not include any education beyond grade 12.

§300.26 SPECIAL EDUCATION

(a) General.

(1) As used in this part, the term special education means specially designed instruction, at no cost to the parents, to meet the unique needs of a child with a disability, including—

    (i) Instruction conducted in the classroom, in the home, in hospitals and institutions, and in other settings; and

    (ii) Instruction in physical education.

(2) The term includes each of the following, if it meets the requirements of paragraph (a)(1) of this section:

    (i) Speech-language pathology services, or any other related service, if the service is considered special education rather than a related service under State standards;

    (ii) Travel training; and

    (iii) Vocational education.

(b) Individual terms defined. The terms in this definition are defined as follows:

(1) At no cost means that all specially-designed instruction is provided without charge, but does not preclude incidental fees that are normally charged to nondisabled students or their parents as a part of the regular education program.

(2) Physical education—

    (i) Means the development of—

        (A) Physical and motor fitness;

        (B) Fundamental motor skills and patterns; and

        (C) Skills in aquatics, dance, and individual and group games and sports (including intramural and lifetime sports); and

    (ii) Includes special physical education, adapted physical education, movement education, and motor development.

(3) Specially-designed instruction means adapting, as appropriate to the needs of an eligible child under this part, the content, methodology, or delivery of instruction—

    (i) To address the unique needs of the child that result from the child's disability; and

    (ii) To ensure access of the child to the general curriculum, so that he or she can meet the educational standards within the jurisdiction of the public agency that apply to all children.

(4) Travel training means providing instruction, as appropriate, to children with significant cognitive disabilities, and any other children with disabilities who require this instruction, to enable them to—

    (i) Develop an awareness of the environment in which they live; and

    (ii) Learn the skills necessary to move effectively and safely from place to place within that environment (e.g., in school, in the home, at work, and in the community).

(5) Vocational education means organized educational programs that are directly related to the preparation of individuals for paid or unpaid employment, or for additional preparation for a career requiring other than a baccalaureate or advanced degree.

§300.27   STATE

As used in this part, the term State means each of the 50 States, the District of Columbia, the Commonwealth of Puerto Rico, and each of the outlying areas.

§300.28   SUPPLEMENTARY AIDS AND SERVICES

As used in this part, the term supplementary aids and services means, aids, services, and other supports that are provided in regular education classes or other education-related settings to enable children with disabilities to be educated with nondisabled children to the maximum extent appropriate in accordance with §§300.550–300.556.

§300.29   TRANSITION SERVICES

(a) As used in this part, transition services means a coordinated set of activities for a student with a disability that—

(1) Is designed within an outcome-oriented process, that promotes movement from school to post-school activities, including postsecondary education, vocational

training, integrated employment (including supported employment), continuing and adult education, adult services, independent living, or community participation;

(2) Is based on the individual student's needs, taking into account the student's preferences and interests; and

(3) Includes—
    (i) Instruction;
    (ii) Related services;
    (iii) Community experiences;
    (iv) The development of employment and other post-school adult living objectives; and
    (v) If appropriate, acquisition of daily living skills and functional vocational evaluation.

(b) Transition services for students with disabilities may be special education, if provided as specially designed instruction, or related services, if required to assist a student with a disability to benefit from special education.

NO CHILD LEFT BEHIND ACT OF 2001

Executive Summary

These reforms express my deep belief in our public schools and their mission to build the mind and character of every child, from every background, in every part of America.
President George W. Bush
January 2001

Three days after taking office in January 2001 as the 43rd President of the United States, George W. Bush announced *No Child Left Behind,* his framework for bipartisan education reform that he described as "the cornerstone of my Administration." President Bush emphasized his deep belief in our public schools, but an even greater concern that "too many of our neediest children are being left behind," despite the nearly $200 billion in Federal spending since the passage of the Elementary and Secondary Education Act of 1965 (ESEA). The President called for bipartisan solutions based on accountability, choice, and flexibility in Federal education programs.

Less than a year later, despite the unprecedented challenges of engineering an economic recovery while leading the Nation in the war on terrorism following the events of September 11, President Bush secured passage of the landmark *No Child Left Behind Act* of 2001 (NCLB Act). The new law reflects a remarkable consensus—first articulated in the President's *No Child Left Behind* framework—on how to improve the performance of America's elementary and secondary schools while at the same time ensuring that no child is trapped in a failing school.

The NCLB Act, which reauthorizes the ESEA, incorporates the principles and strategies proposed by President Bush. These include increased accountability for States, school districts, and schools; greater choice for parents and students, particularly those attending low-performing schools; more flexibility for States and local educational agencies (LEAs) in the use of Federal education dollars; and a stronger emphasis on reading, especially for our youngest children.

INCREASED ACCOUNTABILITY

The NCLB Act will strengthen Title I accountability by requiring States to implement statewide accountability systems covering all public schools and students. These systems must be based on challenging State standards in reading and mathematics, annual testing for all students in grades 3–8, and annual statewide progress objectives ensuring that all groups of students reach proficiency within 12 years. Assessment results and State progress objectives must be broken out by poverty, race, ethnicity, disability, and limited English proficiency to ensure that no group is left behind. School districts and schools that fail to make adequate yearly progress (AYP) toward statewide proficiency goals will, over time, be subject to improvement, corrective action, and restructuring measures aimed at getting them back on course to meet State standards. Schools that meet or exceed AYP objectives or close achievement gaps will be eligible for State Academic Achievement Awards.

MORE CHOICES FOR PARENTS AND STUDENTS

The NCLB Act significantly increases the choices available to the parents of students attending Title I schools that fail to meet State standards, including immediate relief—beginning with the 2002–03 school year—for students in schools that were previously identified for improvement or corrective action under the 1994 ESEA reauthorization.

LEAs must give students attending schools identified for improvement, corrective action, or restructuring the opportunity to attend a better public school, which may include a public charter school, within the school district. The district must provide transportation to the new school, and must use at least 5 percent of its Title I funds for this purpose, if needed. For students attending persistently failing schools (those that have failed to meet State standards for at least 3 of the 4 preceding years), LEAs must permit low-income students to use Title I funds to obtain supplemental educational services from the public- or private-sector provider selected by the students and their parents. Providers must meet State standards and offer services tailored to help participating students meet challenging State academic standards.

To help ensure that LEAs offer meaningful choices, the new law requires school districts to spend up to 20 percent of their Title I allocations to provide school choice and supplemental educational services to eligible students.

In addition to helping ensure that no child loses the opportunity for a quality education because he or she is trapped in a failing school, the choice and supplemental service requirements provide a substantial incentive for low-performing schools to improve. Schools that want to avoid losing students—along with the portion of their annual budgets typically associated with those students—will have to improve or, if they fail to make AYP for 5 years, run the risk of reconstitution under a restructuring plan.

GREATER FLEXIBILITY FOR STATES, SCHOOL DISTRICTS, AND SCHOOLS

One important goal of *No Child Left Behind* was to breathe new life into the "flexibility for accountability" bargain with States first struck by President George H. W. Bush during his historic 1989 education summit with the Nation's Governors at Charlottesville, Virginia. Prior flexibility efforts have focused on the waiver of program requirements; the NCLB Act moves beyond this limited approach to give States and school districts unprecedented flexibility in the use of Federal education funds in exchange for strong accountability for results.

New flexibility provisions in the NCLB Act include authority for States and LEAs to transfer up to 50 percent of the funding they receive under 4 major State grant programs to any one of the programs, or to Title I. The covered programs include Teacher Quality State Grants, Educational Technology, Innovative Programs, and Safe and Drug-Free Schools. The new law also includes a competitive State Flexibility Demonstration Program that permits up to 7 States to consolidate the State share of nearly all Federal State grant programs—including Title I, Part A Grants to Local Educational Agencies—while providing additional flexibility in their use of Title V Innovation funds. Participating States must enter into 5-year performance agreements with the Secretary covering the use of the consolidated funds, which may be used for any educational purpose authorized under the ESEA. As part of their plans, States also must enter into up to 10 local performance agreements with LEAs, which will enjoy the same level of flexibility granted under the separate Local Flexibility Demonstration Program.

The new competitive Local Flexibility Demonstration Program would allow up to 80 LEAs, in addition to the 70 LEAs under the State Flexibility Demonstration Program, to consolidate funds received under Teacher Quality State Grants, Educational Technology State Grants, Innovative Programs, and Safe and Drug-Free Schools programs. Participating LEAs would enter into performance agreements with the Secretary of Education, and would be able to use the consolidated funds for any ESEA-authorized purpose.

PUTTING READING FIRST

No Child Left Behind stated President Bush's unequivocal commitment to ensuring that every child can read by the end of third grade. To accomplish this goal, the new Reading First initiative would significantly increase the Federal investment in scientifically based reading instruction programs in the early grades. One major benefit of this approach would be reduced identification of children for special education services due to a lack of appropriate reading instruction in their early years.

The NCLB Act fully implements the President's Reading First initiative. The new Reading First State Grant program will make 6-year grants to States, which will make competitive subgrants to local communities. Local recipients will administer screening and diagnostic assessments to determine which students in grades K–3 are at risk of reading failure, and provide professional development for K–3 teachers in the essential components of reading instruction.

The new Early Reading First program will make competitive 6-year awards to LEAs to support early language, literacy, and pre-reading development of preschool-age children, particularly those from low-income families. Recipients will use instructional strategies and professional development drawn from scientifically based reading research to help young children to attain the fundamental knowledge and skills they will need for optimal reading development in kindergarten and beyond.

OTHER MAJOR PROGRAM CHANGES

The *No Child Left Behind* Act of 2001 also put the principles of accountability, choice, and flexibility to work in its reauthorization of other major ESEA programs. For example, the new law combines the Eisenhower Professional Development and Class Size Reduction programs into a new Improving Teacher Quality State Grants program that focuses on using practices grounded in scientifically based research to prepare, train, and recruit high-quality teachers. The new program gives States and LEAs flexibility to select the strategies that best meet their particular needs for improved teaching that will help them raise student achievement in the core academic subjects. In return for this flexibility, LEAs are required to demonstrate annual progress in ensuring that all teachers teaching in core academic subjects within the State are highly qualified.

The NCLB Act also simplified Federal support for English language instruction by combining categorical bilingual and immigrant education grants that benefited a small percentage of limited English proficient students in relatively few schools into a State formula program. The new formula program will facilitate the comprehensive planning by States and school districts needed to ensure implementation of programs that benefit all limited English proficient students by helping them learn English and meet the same high academic standards as other students.

Other changes will support State and local efforts to keep our schools safe and drug-free, while at the same time ensuring that students—particularly those who have been victims of violent crimes on school grounds—are not trapped in persistently dangerous schools. As proposed in *No Child Left Behind*, States must allow students who attend a persistently dangerous school, or who are victims of violent crime at school, to transfer to a safe school. States also must report school safety statistics to the public on a school-by-school basis, and LEAs must use Federal Safe and Drug-Free Schools and Communities funding to implement drug and violence prevention programs of demonstrated effectiveness.

CIVIL RIGHTS ACT OF 1964, TITLE VII

Equal Employment Opportunities 42 U.S.C.S. § 2000e-2 (2002)

§ 2000E-2   UNLAWFUL EMPLOYMENT PRACTICES

(a) Employer practices. It shall be an unlawful employment practice for an employer—

    (1) to fail or refuse to hire or to discharge any individual, or otherwise to discriminate against any individual with respect to his compensation, terms, conditions, or privileges of employment, because of such individual's race, color, religion, sex, or national origin; or

    (2) to limit, segregate, or classify his employees or applicants for employment in any way which would deprive or tend to deprive any individual of employment opportunities or otherwise adversely affect his status as an employee, because of such individual's race, color, religion, sex, or national origin.

(b) Employment agency practices. It shall be an unlawful employment practice for an employment agency to fail or refuse to refer for employment, or otherwise to discriminate against, any individual because of his race, color, religion, sex, or national origin, or to classify or refer for employment any individual on the basis of his race, color, religion, sex, or national origin.

(c) Labor organization practices. It shall be an unlawful employment practice for a labor organization—

    (1) to exclude or to expel from its membership, or otherwise to discriminate against, any individual because of his race, color, religion, sex, or national origin;

    (2) to limit, segregate, or classify its membership or applicants for membership, or to classify or fail or refuse to refer for employment any individual, in any way which would deprive or tend to deprive any individual of employment opportunities, or would limit such employment opportunities or otherwise adversely affect his status as an employee or as an applicant for employment, because of such individual's race, color, religion, sex, or national origin; or

    (3) to cause or attempt to cause an employer to discriminate against an individual in violation of this section.

(d) Training programs. It shall be an unlawful employment practice for any employer, labor organization, or joint labor-management committee controlling apprenticeship or other training or retraining, including on-the-job training programs to discriminate against any individual because of his race, color, religion, sex, or national origin in admission to, or employment in, any program established to provide apprenticeship or other training.

(e) Businesses or enterprises with personnel qualified on basis of religion, sex, or national origin; educational institutions with personnel of particular religions. Notwithstanding any other provision of this title [42 U.S.C.S. §§ 2000e et seq.], (1) it shall not be an unlawful employment practice for an employer to hire and employ employees, for an employment agency to classify, or refer for employment any individual, for a labor organization to classify its membership or to classify or refer for employment any individual, or for an employer, labor organization, or joint labor-management committee controlling apprenticeship or other training or retraining programs to admit or employ any individual in any such program, on the basis of his religion, sex, or national origin in those certain instances where religion, sex, or national origin is a bona fide occupational qualification reasonably necessary to the normal operation of that particular business or enterprise, and (2) it shall not be an unlawful employment practice for a school, college, university, or other educational institution or institution of learning to hire and employ employees of a particular religion if such school, college, university, or other educational institution or institution of learning is, in whole or in substantial part, owned, supported, controlled, or managed by a particular religion or by a particular religious corporation, association, or society, or if the curriculum of such school, college, university, or other educational institution or institution of learning is directed toward the propagation of a particular religion.

(f) Members of Communist Party or Communist-action or Communist-front organizations. As used in this title [42 U.S.C.S. §§ 2000e et seq.], the phrase "unlawful employment practice" shall not be deemed to include any action or measure taken by an employer, labor organization, joint labor-management committee, or employment agency with respect to an individual who is a member of the Communist Party of the United States or of any other organization required to register as a Communist-action or Communist-front organization by final order of the Subversive Activities Control Board pursuant to the Subversive Activities Control Act of 1950.

(g) National security. Notwithstanding any other provision of this title [42 U.S.C.S. §§ 2000e et seq.], it shall not be an unlawful employment practice for an employer to fail or refuse to hire and employ any individual for any position, for an employer to discharge any individual from any position, or for an employment agency to fail or refuse to refer any individual for employment in any position, or for a labor organization to fail or refuse to refer any individual for employment in any position, if—

(1) the occupancy of such position, or access to the premises in or upon which any part of the duties of such position is performed or is to be performed, is subject to any requirement imposed in the interest of the national security of the United States under any security program in effect pursuant to or administered under any statute of the United States or any Executive order of the President; and

(2) such individual has not fulfilled or has ceased to fulfill that requirement.

(h) Seniority or merit system; quantity or quality of production; ability tests; compensation based on sex and authorized by minimum wage provisions. Notwithstanding any other provision of this title [42 U.S.C.S. §§ 2000e et seq.], it shall not be an unlawful employment practice for an employer to apply different standards of compensation, or different terms, conditions, or privileges of employment pursuant to a bona fide seniority or merit system, or a system which measures earnings by quantity or quality of production or to employees who work in different locations, provided that such differences are not the result of an intention to discriminate because of race, color, religion, sex, or national origin, nor shall it be an unlawful employment practice for an employer to give and to act upon the results of any professionally developed ability test provided that such test, its administration or action upon the results is not designed, intended or used to discriminate because of race, color, religion, sex or national origin. It shall not be an unlawful employment practice under this title [42 U.S.C.S. §§ 2000e et seq.] for any employer to differentiate upon the basis of sex in determining the amount of the wages or compensation paid or to be paid to employees of such employer if such differentiation is authorized by the provisions of section 6(d) of the Fair Labor Standards Act of 1938, as amended (29 U.S.C. 206[d]).

(i) Businesses or enterprises extending preferential treatment to Indians. Nothing contained in this title [42 U.S.C.S. §§ 2000e et seq.] shall apply to any business or enterprise on or near an Indian reservation with respect to any publicly announced employment practice of such business or enterprise under which a preferential treatment is given to any individual because he is an Indian living on or near a reservation.

(j) Preferential treatment not to be granted on account of existing number or percentage imbalance. Nothing contained in this title [42 U.S.C.S. §§ 2000e et seq.] shall be interpreted to require any employer, employment agency, labor organization, or joint labor-management committee subject to this title [42 U.S.C.S. §§ 2000e et seq.] to grant preferential treatment to any individual or to any group because of the race, color, religion, sex, or national origin of such individual or group on account of an imbalance which may exist with respect to the total number or percentage of persons of any race, color, religion, sex, or national origin employed by an employer, referred or classified for employment by any employment agency or labor organization, admitted to membership or classified by any labor organization, or admitted to, or employed in, any apprenticeship or other training program, in comparison with the total number or percentage of persons of such race, color, religion, sex, or national origin in any community, State, section, or other area, or in the available work force in any community, State, section, or other area.

(k) Burden of proof in disparate impact cases.

(1)

(A) An unlawful employment practice based on disparate impact is established under this title only if—

(i) a complaining party demonstrates that a respondent uses a particular employment practice that causes a disparate impact on the basis of race, color, religion, sex, or national origin and the respondent fails to demonstrate that the challenged practice is job related for the position in question and consistent with business necessity; or

(ii) the complaining party makes the demonstration described in subparagraph (C) with respect to an alternative employment practice and the respondent refuses to adopt such alternative employment practice.

(B)

    (i)   With respect to demonstrating that a particular employment practice causes a disparate impact as described in subparagraph (A) (i), the complaining party shall demonstrate that each particular challenged employment practice causes a disparate impact, except that if the complaining party can demonstrate to the court that the elements of a respondent's decision making process are not capable of separation for analysis, the decision making process may be analyzed as one employment practice.

    (ii) If the respondent demonstrates that a specific employment practice does not cause the disparate impact, the respondent shall not be required to demonstrate that such practice is required by business necessity.

(C) The demonstration referred to by subparagraph (A) (ii) shall be in accordance with the law as it existed on June 4, 1989, with respect to the concept of "alternative employment practice."

(2) A demonstration that an employment practice is required by business necessity may not be used as a defense against a claim of intentional discrimination under this title.

(3) Notwithstanding any other provision of this title [42 U.S.C.S. §§ 2000e et seq.], a rule barring the employment of an individual who currently and knowingly uses or possesses a controlled substance, as defined in schedules I and II of section 102(6) of the Controlled Substances Act (21 U.S.C. 802(6)), other than the use or possession of a drug taken under the supervision of a licensed health care professional, or any other use or possession authorized by the Controlled Substances Act or any other provision of Federal law, shall be considered an unlawful employment practice under this title only if such rule is adopted or applied with an intent to discriminate because of race, color, religion, sex, or national origin.

(l) Prohibition of discriminatory use of test scores. It shall be an unlawful employment practice for a respondent, in connection with the selection or referral of applicants or candidates for employment or promotion, to adjust the scores of, use different cutoff scores for, or otherwise alter the results of, employment related tests on the basis of race, color, religion, sex, or national origin.

(m) Impermissible consideration of race, color, religion, sex, or national origin in employment practices. Except as otherwise provided in this title [42 U.S.C.S. §§ 2000e et seq.], an unlawful employment practice is established when the complaining party demonstrates that race, color, religion, sex, or national origin was a motivating factor for any employment practice, even though other factors also motivated the practice.

(n) Resolution of challenges to employment practices implementing litigated or consent judgments or orders.

(1)

    (A) Notwithstanding any other provision of law, and except as provided in paragraph (2), an employment practice that implements and is within the scope of a litigated or consent judgment or order that resolves a claim of employment discrimination under the Constitution or Federal civil rights laws may not be challenged under the circumstances described in subparagraph (B).

    (B) A practice described in subparagraph (A) may not be challenged in a claim under the Constitution or Federal civil rights laws—

        (i) by a person who, prior to the entry of the judgment or order described in subparagraph (A), had—

            (I) actual notice of the proposed judgment or order sufficient to apprise such person that such judgment or order might adversely affect the interests and legal rights of such person and that an opportunity was available to present objections to such judgment or order by a future date certain; and

            (II) a reasonable opportunity to present objections to such judgment or order; or

        (ii) by a person whose interests were adequately represented by another person who had previously challenged the judgment or order on the same legal grounds and with a similar factual situation, unless there has been an intervening change in law or fact.

(2) Nothing in this subsection shall be construed to—

    (A) alter the standards for intervention under rule 24 of the Federal Rules of Civil Procedure or apply to the rights of parties who have successfully intervened pursuant to such rule in the proceeding in which the parties intervened;

    (B) apply to the rights of parties to the action in which a litigated or consent judgment or order was entered, or of members of a class represented or sought to be represented in such action, or of members of a group on whose behalf relief was sought in such action by the Federal Government;

    (C) prevent challenges to a litigated or consent judgment or order on the ground that such judgment or order was obtained through collusion or fraud, or is transparently invalid or was entered by a court lacking subject matter jurisdiction; or

    (D) authorize or permit the denial to any person of the due process of law required by the Constitution.

(3) Any action not precluded under this subsection that challenges an employment consent judgment or order described in paragraph (1) shall be brought in the court, and if possible before the judge, that entered such judgment or order. Nothing in this subsection shall preclude a transfer of such action pursuant to section 1404 of title 28, United States Code.

Educational Amendments of 1972, Title IX

Discrimination Based on Sex, 20 U.S.C.S. § 1681

(a)

Prohibition against discrimination; exceptions. No person in the United States shall, on the basis of sex, be excluded from participation in, be denied the benefits of, or be subjected to discrimination under any education program or activity receiving Federal financial assistance, except that:

(1) Classes of educational institutions subject to prohibition. In regard to admissions to educational institutions, this section shall apply only to institutions of vocational education, professional education, and graduate higher education, and to public institutions of undergraduate higher education;

(2) Educational institutions commencing planned change in admissions. In regard to admissions to educational institutions, this section shall not apply (A) for one year from the date of enactment of this Act [enacted June 23, 1972], nor for six years after such date in the case of an educational institution which has begun the process of changing from being an institution which admits only students of one sex to being an institution which admits students of both sexes, but only if it is carrying out a plan for such a change which is approved by the Commissioner of Education or (B) for seven years from the date an educational institution begins the process of changing from being an institution which admits only students of only one sex to being an institution which admits students of both sexes, but only if it is carrying out a plan for such a change which is approved by the Commissioner of Education, whichever is the later;

(3) Educational institutions of religious organizations with contrary religious tenets. This section shall not apply to an educational institution which is controlled by a religious organization if the application of this subsection would not be consistent with the religious tenets of such organization;

(4) Educational institutions training individuals for military services or merchant marine. This section shall not apply to an educational institution whose primary purpose is the training of individuals for the military services of the United States, or the merchant marine;

(5) Public educational institutions with traditional and continuing admissions policy. In regard to admissions this section shall not apply to any public institution of undergraduate higher education which is an institution that traditionally and continually from its establishment has had a policy of admitting only students of one sex;

(6) Social fraternities or sororities; voluntary youth service organizations. This section shall not apply to membership practices—

    (A) of a social fraternity or social sorority which is exempt from taxation under section 501(a) of the Internal Revenue Code of 1954 [26 U.S.C.S. § 501(a)], the active membership of which consists primarily of students in attendance at an institution of higher education, or

(B) of the Young Men's Christian Association, Young Women's Christian Association, Girl Scouts, Boy Scouts, Camp Fire Girls, and voluntary youth service organizations which are so exempt, the membership of which has traditionally been limited to persons of one sex and principally to persons of less than nineteen years of age;

(7) Boy or Girl conferences. This section shall not apply to—

(A) any program or activity of the American Legion undertaken in connection with the organization or operation of any Boys State conference, Boys Nation conference, Girls State conference, or Girls Nation conference; or

(B) any program or activity of any secondary school or educational institution specifically for—

(i) the promotion of any Boys State conference, Boys Nation conference, Girls State conference, or Girls Nation conference; or

(ii) the selection of students to attend any such conference;

(8) Father-son or mother-daughter activities at educational institutions. This section shall not preclude father-son or mother-daughter activities at an educational institution, but if such activities are provided for students of one sex, opportunities for reasonably comparable activities shall be provided for students of the other sex; and

(9) Institution of higher education scholarship awards in "beauty" pageants. This section shall not apply with respect to any scholarship or other financial assistance awarded by an institution of higher education to any individual because such individual has received such award in any pageant in which the attainment of such award is based upon a combination of factors related to the personal appearance, poise, and talent of such individual and in which participation is limited to individuals of one sex only, so long as such pageant is in compliance with other nondiscrimination provisions of Federal law.

(b)

Preferential or disparate treatment because of imbalance in participation or receipt of Federal benefits; statistical evidence of imbalance. Nothing contained in subsection (a) of this section shall be interpreted to require any educational institution to grant preferential or disparate treatment to the members of one sex on account of an imbalance which may exist with respect to the total number or percentage of persons of that sex participating in or receiving the benefits of any federally supported program or activity, in comparison with the total number or percentage of persons of that sex in any community, State, section, or other area: Provided, that this subsection shall not be construed to prevent the consideration in any hearing or proceeding under this title of statistical evidence tending to show that such an imbalance exists with respect to the participation in, or receipt of the benefits of, any such program or activity by the members of one sex.

(c)

"Educational institution" defined. For purposes of this title an educational institution means any public or private preschool, elementary, or secondary school, or any institution of vocational, professional, or higher education, except that in the case of an educational institution composed of more than one school, college, or department which are administratively separate units, such term means each such school, college, or department.

EXCERPTS FROM THE AMERICANS WITH DISABILITIES ACT OF 1990

Public Law 101-336, 42. U.S.C. §12101

101   DEFINITIONS

As used in this title:

(1) Commission.—The term "Commission" means the Equal Employment Opportunity Commission established by section 705 of the Civil Rights Act of 1964 (42 U.S.C. 2000e-4).

(2) Covered entity.—The term "covered entity" means an employer, employment agency, labor organization, or joint labor-management committee.

(3) Direct threat.—The term "direct threat" means a significant risk to the health or safety of others that cannot be eliminated by reasonable accommodation.

(4) Employee.—The term "employee" means an individual employed by an employer.

(5) Employer.—

(A) In general.—The term "employer" means a person engaged in an industry affecting commerce who has 15 or more employees for each working day in each of 20 or more calendar weeks in the current or preceding calendar year, and any agent of such person, except that, for two years following the effective date of this title, an employer means a person engaged in an industry affecting commerce who has 25 or more employees for each working day in each of 20 or more calendar weeks in the current or preceding year, and any agent of such person.

(B) Exceptions.—The term "employer" does not include—

(i) the United States, a corporation wholly owned by the government of the United States, or an Indian tribe; or

(ii) a bona fide private membership club (other than a labor organization) that is exempt from taxation under section 501(c) of the Internal Revenue Code of 1986.

(6) Illegal use of drugs.—

(A) In general.—The term "illegal use of drugs" means the use of drugs, the possession or distribution of which is unlawful under the Controlled Substances

Act (21 U.S.C. 812). Such term does not include the use of a drug taken under supervision by a licensed health care professional, or other uses authorized by the Controlled Substances Act or other provisions of Federal law.

(B) Drugs.—The term "drug" means a controlled substance, as defined in schedules I through V of section 202 of the Controlled Substances Act.

(7) Person, etc.—The terms "person," "labor organization," "employment agency," "commerce," and "industry affecting commerce," shall have the same meaning given such terms in section 701 of the Civil Rights Act of 1964 (42 U.S.C. 2000e).

(8) Qualified individual with a disability.—The term "qualified individual with a disability" means an individual with a disability who, with or without reasonable accommodation, can perform the essential functions of the employment position that such individual holds or desires. For the purposes of this title, consideration shall be given to the employer's judgment as to what functions of a job are essential, and if an employer has prepared a written description before advertising or interviewing applicants for the job, this description shall be considered evidence of the essential functions of the job.

(9) Reasonable accommodation.—The term "reasonable accommodation" may include—

(A) making existing facilities used by employees readily accessible to and usable by individuals with disabilities; and

(B) job restructuring, part-time or modified work schedules, reassignment to a vacant position, acquisition or modification of equipment or devices, appropriate adjustment or modifications of examinations, training materials or policies, the provision of qualified readers or interpreters, and other similar accommodations for individuals with disabilities.

(10) Undue hardship.—

(A) In general.—The term "undue hardship" means an action requiring significant difficulty or expense, when considered in light of the factors set forth in subparagraph (B).

(B) Factors to be considered.–In determining whether an accommodation would impose an undue hardship on a covered entity, factors to be considered include—

(i) the nature and cost of the accommodation needed under this Act;

(ii) the overall financial resources of the facility or facilities involved in the provision of the reasonable accommodation; the number of persons employed at such facility; the effect on expenses and resources, or the impact otherwise of such accommodation upon the operation of the facility;

(iii) the overall financial resources of the covered entity; the overall size of the business of a covered entity with respect to the number of its employees; the number, type, and location of its facilities; and

(iv) the type of operation or operations of the covered entity, including the composition, structure, and functions of the workforce of such entity; the geographic separateness, administrative, or fiscal relationship of the facility or facilities in question to the covered entity.

EQUAL PAY ACT

29 U.S.C.S. § 206(d), 2002

(d)

Prohibition of sex discrimination.

(1) No employer having employees subject to any provisions of this section shall discriminate, within any establishment in which such employees are employed, between employees on the basis of sex by paying wages to employees in such establishment at a rate less than the rate at which he pays wages to employees of the opposite sex in such establishment for equal work on jobs the performance of which requires equal skill, effort, and responsibility, and which are performed under similar working conditions, except where such payment is made pursuant to (i) a seniority system; (ii) a merit system; (iii) a system which measures earnings by quantity or quality of production; or (iv) a differential based on any other factor other than sex: Provided, that an employer who is paying a wage rate differential in violation of this subsection shall not, in order to comply with the provisions of this subsection, reduce the wage rate of any employee.

(2) No labor organization, or its agents, representing employees of an employer having employees subject to any provisions of this section shall cause or attempt to cause such an employer to discriminate against an employee in violation of paragraph (1) of this subsection.

(3) For purposes of administration and enforcement, any amounts owing to any employee which have been withheld in violation of this subsection shall be deemed to be unpaid minimum wages or unpaid overtime compensation under this Act.

(4) As used in this subsection, the term "labor organization" means any organization of any kind, or any agency or employee representation committee or plan, in which employees participate and which exists for the purpose, in whole or in part, or dealing with employers concerning grievances, labor disputes, wages, rates of pay, hours of employment, or conditions of work.

PREGNANCY DISCRIMINATION ACT OF 1978

Public Law 95-555

Title VII of the Civil Rights Act of 1964 was codified as 42 U.S.C. §2000e, the statute reads as amended by the Congressional Accountability Act of 1995, effective January 23, 1996. [42 U.S.C. 2000E(K)] (k) The terms "because of sex" or "on the basis of sex" include, but are not limited to, because of or on the basis of pregnancy, childbirth or related medical conditions; and women affected by pregnancy, childbirth, or related medical conditions shall be treated the same for all employment-related purposes, including receipt of benefits under fringe benefit programs, as other persons not so affected but similar in their ability or inability to work, and nothing in section 2000e-2(h) of this title shall be interpreted to permit otherwise. This subsection shall not require an employer to pay for health insurance benefits for abortion, except where the life of the mother would be endangered if the fetus were carried to term, or except where medical complications have arisen from an abortion: Provided, that nothing herein shall preclude an employer from providing abortion benefits or otherwise affect bargaining agreements in regard to abortion.

AGE DISCRIMINATION ACT

29 U.S.C. § 621 and §623

CONGRESSIONAL STATEMENT OF FINDINGS AND PURPOSE

(a) The Congress hereby finds and declares that—
  (1) in the face of rising productivity and affluence, older workers find themselves disadvantaged in their efforts to retain employment, and especially to regain employment when displaced from jobs;
  (2) the setting of arbitrary age limits regardless of potential for job performance has become a common practice, and certain otherwise desirable practices may work to the disadvantage of older persons;
  (3) the incidence of unemployment, especially long-term unemployment with resultant deterioration of skill, morale, and employer acceptability is, relative to the younger ages, high among older workers; their numbers are great and growing; and their employment problems grave;
  (4) the existence in industries affecting commerce, of arbitrary discrimination in employment because of age, burdens commerce and the free flow of goods in commerce.
(b) It is therefore the purpose of this Act to promote employment of older persons based on their ability rather than age; to prohibit arbitrary age discrimination in employment; to help employers and workers find ways of meeting problems arising from the impact of age on employment.

PROHIBITION OF AGE DISCRIMINATION

(a) Employer practices. It shall be unlawful for an employer—
  (1) to fail or refuse to hire or to discharge any individual or otherwise discriminate against any individual with respect to his compensation, terms, conditions, or privileges of employment, because of such individual's age;

(2) to limit, segregate, or classify his employees in any way which would deprive or tend to deprive any individual of employment opportunities or otherwise adversely affect his status as an employee, because of such individual's age; or

(3) to reduce the wage rate of any employee in order to comply with this Act.

(b) Employment agency practices. It shall be unlawful for an employment agency to fail or refuse to refer for employment, or otherwise to discriminate against, any individual because of such individual's age, or to classify or refer for employment any individual on the basis of such individual's age.

(c) Labor organization practices. It shall be unlawful for a labor organization—

(1) to exclude or to expel from its membership, or otherwise to discriminate against, any individual because of his age;

(2) to limit, segregate, or classify its membership, or to classify or fail or refuse to refer for employment any individual, in any way which would deprive or tend to deprive any individual of employment opportunities, or would limit such employment opportunities or otherwise adversely affect his status as an employee or as an applicant for employment, because of such individual's age;

(3) to cause or attempt to cause an employer to discriminate against an individual in violation of this section.

(d) Opposition to unlawful practices; participation in investigations, proceedings, or litigation. It shall be unlawful for an employer to discriminate against any of his employees or applicants for employment, for an employment agency to discriminate against any individual, or for a labor organization to discriminate against any member thereof or applicant for membership, because such individual, member or applicant for membership has opposed any practice made unlawful by this section, or because such individual, member or applicant for membership has made a charge, testified, assisted, or participated in any manner in an investigation, proceeding, or litigation under this Act.

(e) Printing or publication of notice or advertisement indicating preference, limitation, etc. It shall be unlawful for an employer, labor organization, or employment agency to print or publish, or cause to be printed or published, any notice or advertisement relating to employment by such an employer or membership in or any classification or referral for employment by such a labor organization, or relating to any classification or referral for employment by such an employment agency, indicating any preference, limitation, specification, or discrimination, based on age.

(f) Lawful practices; age an occupational qualification; other reasonable factors; seniority system; employee benefit plans; discharge or discipline for good cause. It shall not be unlawful for an employer, employment agency, or labor organization—

(1) to take any action otherwise prohibited under subsections (a), (b), (c), or (e) of this section where age is a bona fide occupational qualification reasonably necessary to the normal operation of the particular business, or where the differentiation is based on reasonable factors other than age, or where such practices involve an employee in a workplace in a foreign country, and compliance with such subsections would cause such employer, or a corporation controlled by such employer, to violate the laws of the country in which such workplace is located;

(2) to take any action otherwise prohibited under subsection (a), (b),(c), or (e) of this section—

    (A) to observe the terms of a bona fide seniority system that is not intended to evade the purposes of this Act, except that no such seniority system shall require or permit the involuntary retirement of any individual specified by section 12(a) [29 U.S.C.S. § 631(a)] because of the age of such individual; or

    (B) to observe the terms of a bona fide employee benefit plan—

        (i) where, for each benefit or benefit package, the actual amount of payment made or cost incurred on behalf of an older worker is no less than that made or incurred on behalf of a younger worker, as permissible under section 1625.10, title 29, Code of Federal Regulations (as in effect on June 22, 1989); or

        (ii) that is a voluntary early retirement incentive plan consistent with the relevant purpose or purposes of this Act. Notwithstanding clause (i) or (ii) of subparagraph (B), no such employee benefit plan or voluntary early retirement incentive plan shall excuse the failure to hire any individual, and no such employee benefit plan shall require or permit the involuntary retirement of any individual specified by section 12(a) [29 U.S.C.S. § 631(a)], because of the age of such individual. An employer, employment agency, or labor organization acting under subparagraph (A), or under clause (i) or (ii) of subparagraph (B), shall have the burden of proving that such actions are lawful in any civil enforcement proceeding brought under this Act; or

(3) to discharge or otherwise discipline an individual for good cause.

Glossary

Administrative agency. An agency created by federal or state government to perform specific tasks. Agencies have the power to make laws and are given the power of enforcement.

Affidavit. Written statements which are answered by parties or witnesses of a lawsuit. The responses are made under sworn testimony.

Affirm. To agree and confirm a lower court's decision.

Alternative dispute resolution (ADR). A method used to settle conflicts outside of the courtroom. The most common forms of ADR are mediation and arbitration. Generally, ADR is less expensive and faster than going through the court.

Americans with Disabilities Act (ADA). Enacted in 1990, the law guarantees equal opportunity for individuals with disabilities in public accommodations, employment, transportation, and state and local government services.

Answer. A response by a defendant to a legal complaint filed by the plaintiff.

Appeal. To request that a higher court review a decision of law made by a lower court.

Arbitration. A form of alternative dispute resolution whereby a neutral third person, known as an arbitrator, is appointed to hear the facts from both parties and make a final decision. Arbitration may be binding or nonbinding.

Assault. Under civil law, to cause someone to be in fear of immediate harm or offensive contact.

Assumption of risk. A defense claiming that the injured party recognized the risk yet voluntarily accepted it.

Battery. Under civil law, the unprivileged intentional touching or offensive contact of another.

Beyond a reasonable doubt. In a criminal case, the standard by which the defendant must be found guilty—fully convinced, without a doubt.

Bill of Rights. The first ten amendments of the U.S. Constitution.

Breach of contract. When one or both parties fail to perform the agreed-upon obligation.

Breach of duty. Not performing an obligation either intentionally or through an omission to act.

Brief. A short summary of a case that usually includes the facts, the procedural posture, the legal issue, the court's rationale, and the holding.

Case brief.   The short summation of the case, which includes the facts, procedural posture, legal issue, reasoning, and decision.

Civil law.   The body of law that deals with noncriminal cases.

Common law.   Law made through court holdings rather than through statute or legislation.

Compensatory damages.   A monetary award granted to the successful litigant to compensate for his or her injuries. Such damages are usually only granted if those injuries were foreseeable.

Complaint.   The filing by the plaintiff, stating the facts, the parties involved, and the damages requested. It is the first official step of the lawsuit.

Concurring opinion.   A written statement by judges who agree with the majority opinion but discuss their own rationale for their decision.

Contributory negligence.   A defense used in negligence claims stating that the injured party is partially responsible since that person contributed to his or her own injuries.

Counterclaim.   When a defendant in a lawsuit files suit against the plaintiff.

Criminal law.   A body of law that deals with crimes in which the state prosecutor brings the charges; non-civil cases. In criminal law the burden of proof is beyond a reasonable doubt.

Crossclaim.   When a defendant adds another defendant to the original lawsuit. Generally, the defendant is claiming that if he or she is responsible, so is another party.

Damages.   The award given to the injured or wronged plaintiff.

Defamation.   The injury to a person's reputation through either libel or slander.

Defendant.   The party who is defending a lawsuit.

Deposition.   Testimony taken under oath by witnesses or parties to a lawsuit.

Demurrer.   A claim by a defending party that the facts are insufficient to support a legal claim.

De novo.   To start from the beginning; a clean slate, as if the case had never begun.

Discovery.   The process of gathering information that pertains to the lawsuit.

Dissenting opinion.   An opinion written by the judge who disagreed with the majority opinion and wants to clarify his or her rationale for the decision. Dissenting opinions are not law.

Duty.   A legal obligation, one of the four elements required for a negligence claim.

Education of All Handicapped Children Act (EHA).   One of the first laws to protect students with disabilities; now referred to as the Individuals with Disabilities Education Act.

Employment at will.   When one works at the will of the employer and can be terminated for any reason without due process of law.

En banc.   Where only the judge makes the decision; translates as "from the bench."

Equal Access Act (EEA).   Passed in 1984; states that it is illegal for public secondary schools that receive federal financial assistance and have a limited open forum to deny equal access or a fair opportunity to, or discriminate against, any students who wish to conduct a meeting within that limited open forum on the basis of the religious, political, philosophical, or other content of the speech at such meetings.

Equal Employment Opportunity Commission (EEOC). The agency that enforces the federal laws prohibiting job discrimination, including sexual harassment, age discrimination, civil rights, and the Americans with Disabilities Act.

Establishment clause. The Constitutional provision that states: "Congress shall make no law respecting an establishment of religion, or prohibiting the free exercise thereof."

Exclusionary rule. The rule that allows evidence to be excluded from the case if it were improperly discovered under the Fourth Amendment.

Ex parte. A proceeding for the benefit of only one party of the lawsuit.

Family Educational Rights and Privacy Act (FERPA). Also known as the Buckley Amendment. Passed in 1974 to protect students' privacy rights as pertaining to their educational records.

Free appropriate education. *Free,* meaning at no cost to the parents or guardians of the child. *Appropriate,* meaning it meets the unique educational needs of your child.

Holding. The final decision of a case.

Hostile environment. Used to describe a sexual harassment claim when the conduct of one person creates an offensive and abusive environment for another person.

Individualized educational plan (IEP). A tailor-made plan created by both the parents and the school. The IEP must be followed and updated annually to ensure that the child receives the education appropriate for his or her abilities and disabilities.

Individuals with Disabilities Education Act (IDEA). Originally called the Education of All Handicapped Children Act, this law guarantees all children a free appropriate public education.

In loco parentis. Latin for "in place of the parent."

Injunction. A court order mandating that a party should stop doing a specific act.

Least restrictive environment. An environment for a child that allows the student to learn in a regular educational program to the greatest extent possible for his or her disability.

Legal impossibility. A defense that states that the act could not be performed based on impossibility.

Libel. One of the twin torts of defamation, when one communicates a written defamatory statement about a second person to a third person.

Mainstreaming. To place a child with disabilities into a classroom with nondisabled students.

Malice. Acting with intent to harm.

Mandamus. A court order commanding that a government entity perform a certain act.

Miranda warning. A statement that police must read to any person who is under arrest. Required after the 1966 case of *Miranda v. Arizona*, it reads in part that the suspect "has the right to remain silent, the right to a lawyer, and if you cannot afford a lawyer one will be appointed to you free of charge."

Mitigation of damages. The responsibility of an injured party to minimize damages in a reasonable manner.

Moot. An issue that is no longer in dispute.

Motion.   An attorney's request that a judge make a decision about a certain action.

Negligence.   Failing to act as a reasonably prudent person might; a breach of duty, when there exists a causal connection between the breach and the injury.

Nominal damages.   A monetary award that is very small, generally amounting to one dollar.

Per curiam.   Latin for "by the court."

Peremptory challenge.   The right that a lawyer has to disqualify a potential juror without reason.

Per se.   A violation regardless of the facts.

Plaintiff.   The party who initiates the lawsuit.

Pleadings.   The formal statements by each party of a lawsuit.

Preponderance of evidence.   In a civil case, the standard that states that the evidence must more convincing than not. If the evidence in favor of a party outweighs the evidence against a party, the party will win in a civil case.

Prima facie.   The facts are presumed to be true unless proven otherwise.

Probable cause.   Enough evidence to convince a reasonably prudent person that one has committed a crime. Mere suspicion is inadequate.

Procedural law.   The laws that describe the process of enforcing the rights recognized by substantive law.

Proximate cause.   A doctrine generally used in tort law that requires that the breach be causally connected to the person's injuries.

Punitive damages.   A monetary award granted to a successful plaintiff in an effort to punish the wrongdoer. Generally awarded with the intent to make an example of one and deter others from doing the same wrong.

Quasi-contract.   Also known as "contract that is implied in law." Not a true contract but one that the courts have applied to ensure fairness and unjust enrichment by one party.

Quid pro quo.   "This for that" or "something for something." Generally used when referring to claims of sexual harassment.

Reasonable care.   The amount of care that a reasonable person in the same situation would exercise under the same circumstances.

Related services.   As defined by the IDEA, includes transportation and developmental, corrective, and other supportive services (including speech-language pathology and audiology services; psychological services; physical and occupational therapy; recreation, including therapeutic recreation; social work services; counseling services, including rehabilitation counseling; orientation and mobility services, and medical services, except that such medical services shall be for diagnostic and evaluation purposes only) that may be required to assist a child with a disability to benefit from special education. Includes the early identification and assessment of disabling conditions in children.

Remand.   A decision by a higher court to send the case back to the lower court to decide, generally with instructions to follow.

Respondeat superior.   Latin for "the master is responsible for the acts of the servant." A term used in tort liability cases imposing liability on an employer for tortious acts of their employees.

Reverse. A decision by a court to overturn a lower court's decision.

Rule of four. The U.S. Supreme Court will not grant a writ of certiorari unless at least four of the nine justices agree.

Slander. One of the twin torts of defamation; when one communicates an oral defamatory statement about a second person to a third person.

Stare decisis. The principle that courts should follow the precedents of decisions of previous courts to control and guide decisions in future cases.

Strict liability. The legal theory that holds a defendant responsible, regardless of the facts or defense.

Substantive law. A body of law that defines rights and responsibilities.

Summary judgment. A judgment entered by the court when there is no genuine factual dispute and the party is entitled to a judgment in his or her favor because only the issue of law remains.

Summons. A writ informing an individual that a lawsuit against him or her has commenced and the person must appear in court to respond to the charges.

Supremacy clause. A provision stating that when a federal law conflicts with a state law, the federal law will be supreme.

Symbolic speech. Nonverbal expression through dress or gestures.

Tort. A civil wrong that is not a breach of contract.

Writ of certiorari. The discretion by which the U.S. Supreme Court decides which cases it chooses to hear.

Index

ISBN 0-13-091550-5

9 780130 915504

90000>